MARRIAGE

Readings in Moral Theology No. 15

Previous volumes in this series

MARRIAGE

Readings in Moral Theology No. 15

Edited by
Charles E. Curran
and
Julie Hanlon Rubio

PAULIST PRESS
New York • Mahwah, NJ

Cover design by Lynn Else

Library of Congress Cataloging-in-Publication Data

Marriage / edited by Charles E. Curran and Julie Hanlon Rubio.
        p. cm.— (Readings in moral theology ; no. 15)
    Includes bibliographical references.
    ISBN 978-0-8091-4575-1 (alk. paper)
    1. Marriage—Religious aspects—Catholic Church. 2. Christian ethics—
Catholic authors. 3. Catholic Church—Doctrines. I. Curran, Charles E. II. Rubio,
Julie Hanlon.
    BX2250.M15 2009
    241´.63—dc22

                                                                    2008044045

Published by Paulist Press
997 Macarthur Boulevard
Mahwah, New Jersey 07430

www.paulistpress.com

Printed and bound in the
United States of America

Contents

PART TWO:
THEOLOGY/SPIRITUALITY OF MARRIAGE

PART THREE:
SPECIFIC ISSUES

Interchurch Marriage

Same-Sex Marriage

Cohabitation

Indissolubility and Divorce

Acknowledgments

Willard F. Jabusch, "The Myth of Cohabitation," *America* 183 (October 7, 2000): 14–16. Copyright 2000. All rights reserved: reprinted with permission of America Press. Elsie P. Radtke, "Caring for Committed Love in Good Times and Bad," *Chicago Studies* 45 (2006): 162–72, copyright Civitas Dei Foundation, reprinted with permission. Angelo Scola, "The Nuptial Mystery" published in *Communio: International Catholic Review* 25 (1998): 630–62, copyright *Communio: International Catholic Review*. Reprinted with permission. David S. Crawford, "Of Spouses, the Real World, and the 'Where' of Christian Marriage," Published in *Communio: International Catholic Review* 33 (2006): 100–116, copyright *Communio: International Catholic Review*. Reprinted with permission. "A Christian Family Vision" is reprinted by permission from *Family: A Christian Social Perspective* by Lisa Sowle Cahill, copyright 2000 by Augsburg Fortress Publishers. Kevin T. Kelly, "Cohabitation: Living in Sin or Occasion of Grace?" is reprinted by permission of *The Furrow*. Charles E. Curran, "John Paul II and Post–Vatican II U.S. Catholic Moral Theologians on Marriage" is taken from Charles E. Curran, *The Moral Theology of Pope John Paul II* (Washington, D.C.: Georgetown University Press, 2005), 160–72, and Curran, *Catholic Moral Theology: A History* (Washington, D.C.: Georgetown University Press, 2008) from the Marriage and Family section of chapter 8. Reprinted with permission. www.press. georgetown.edu. Richard M. Hogan and John M. LeVoir, "Pope John Paul II on Love, Sexuality, Marriage, and Family," from their book *Covenant of Love: John Paul II on Sexuality, Marriage, and Family in the Modern World*, 2nd ed. (San Francisco: Ignatius Press, 1992), 71–87, is reprinted by permission of Ignatius Press, copyright 1992. Robert J. Kendra, "American Annulment Mills," *Homiletic and Pastoral Review* 106 (December 2005): 14–21, copyright 2005 by Robert J. Kendra, is reprinted with permission. Susan A. Ross, "The Bride of Christ and the Body Politic: Body and Gender in Pre–Vatican II Marriage Theology,"

Journal of Religion 71 (1991): 345–61, is reprinted by permission of University of Chicago Press, copyright 1991. Luke Timothy Johnson, "The Biblical Foundations of Matrimony," *The Bible Today* 41 (2003): 113–16, copyright 2003 by Luke Timothy Johnson, is reprinted with permission. Bernard Cooke, "Historical Reflections on the Meaning of Marriage as Christian Sacrament," in *Alternative Futures for Worship*, vol. 5: *Christian Marriage*, ed. Bernard Cooke (Collegeville, Minn.: Liturgical Press, 1987), 33–46. Copyright 1987 by the Order of St. Benedict, Inc. Published by Liturgical Press, Collegeville, Minn. Reprinted with permission. William P. Roberts, "Toward a Post–Vatican II Spirituality of Marriage," in *Christian Marriage and Family: Contemporary Theological and Pastoral Perspectives,* ed. Michael G. Lawler and William P. Roberts (Collegeville, Minn.: Liturgical Press, 1996), 125–40. Copyright 1996 by the Order of St. Benedict, Inc. Published by Liturgical Press, Collegeville, Minn. Reprinted with permission. Michael G. Lawler, "Interchurch Marriages: Theological and Pastoral Reflections," in Michael G. Lawler, *Marriage and the Catholic Church: Disputed Questions* (Collegeville, Minn.: Liturgical Press, 2002), 118–39. Copyright 2002 by the Order of St. Benedict, Inc. Published by Liturgical Press, Collegeville, Minn. Reprinted with permission. International Theological Commission with Commentary by Philippe Delhaye, "Indissolubility of Marriage," in Richard Malone and John R. Connery, eds. *Contemporary Perspectives on Christian Marriage: Propositions and Papers from the International Theological Commission* (Chicago: Loyola University Press, 1984), 26–36, copyright 1984 by Richard Malone, reprinted with permission. William E. May, "On the Impossibility of Same-Sex Marriage: A Review of Catholic Teaching," originally published in the *National Catholic Bioethics Quarterly* 4.2 (Summer 2004): 303–16, copyright by the National Catholic Bioethics Center. All rights reserved. Reprinted by permission. Germain Grisez, John Finnis, and William E. May, "Indissolubility, Divorce, and Holy Communion: An Open Letter to Archbishop Saier, Bishop Lehmann, and Bishop Kasper," *New Blackfriars* 75 (1994): 321–30, copyright 1994 by Germain Grisez, reprinted with permission. Oscar Saier, Karl Lehmann, and Walter Kasper, "Pastoral Ministry: The Divorced and Remarried," *Origins* 23 (1994): 670–76, is reprinted by permission of *Origins: CNS Documentary Service*. English translation from original

German, copyright *Origins*. Used with permission. All rights reserved. John S. Grabowski, "The Theology of the Body in Pope John Paul II," taken from the foreword in Pope John Paul II, *The Theology of the Body: Human Love and the Divine Plan* (Boston: Pauline Books, 1997), 15–21, is reprinted by permission of Pauline Books and Media. Excerpts from *Contemporary Moral Theology*, vol. 2: *Marriage Questions*, by John C. Ford and Gerald Kelly. Copyright 1958 by The Missionary Society of St. Paul the Apostle in the State of New York. Paulist Press, Inc., New York/Mahwah, N.J. Reprinted by permission of Paulist Press, Inc. www.paulistpress.com. Excerpts from *Marriage in the Catholic Church: The Marital Sacrament*, by Theodore Mackin, S.J. Copyright 1989 by Theodore Mackin, S.J., Paulist Press, Inc., New York/Mahwah, N.J. Reprinted by permission of Paulist Press, Inc. www.paulistpress. com. Julie Hanlon Rubio, "The Dual Vocation of Christian Parents," *Theological Studies* 63 (2002): 786–812, and Stephen J. Pope, "The Magisterium's Arguments against 'Same-Sex Marriage': An Ethical Analysis and Critique," *Theological Studies* 65 (2004): 530–65, are reprinted by permission of *Theological Studies*. Excerpts from Florence Caffrey Bourg, *Where Two or Three are Gathered: Christian Families as Domestic Churches* (Notre Dame, Ind.: University of Notre Dame Press), 69–80, 87–96, copyright 2004 by the University of Notre Dame. Reprinted with permission. David Matzko McCarthy, "Two Households," in David Matzko McCarthy, *Sex and Love in the Home: A Theology of the Household*, 2nd ed. (London: SCM Press, 2004), 127–51, is reprinted by permission of SCM Press.

Foreword

This volume on marriage is the fifteenth volume in the series *Readings in Moral Theology* from Paulist Press. Richard A. McCormick and Charles E. Curran began editing this series in 1979, and the series has continued after McCormick's death in February 2000. Julie Hanlon Rubio of St. Louis University, a younger scholar who specializes in marriage and family, has joined Curran as a coeditor of this volume.

This series brings together previously published articles dealing with the particular theme of the volume. Very light editing has occasionally been done to adapt the articles for this volume. Three criteria ground the selection of articles. First, the volume attempts to cover all the important aspects of marriage so that the reader has a somewhat complete understanding. Second, the series has always attempted to give a fair and objective picture of what is happening in Catholic moral theology by including all pertinent perspectives: conservative and liberal, senior and younger scholars, female and male. Third, the volume attempts to include the most significant contributors to the discussion on marriage as exemplified in the monographs or important articles they have written. Such a criterion has a twofold purpose: to recognize and thereby give credit to those who have made the most significant contributions and to make the reader aware of the major figures in the field.

This volume on marriage unfolds in three parts: the historical development of the understanding of marriage in the Catholic Church, the theology and spirituality of marriage as Christians strive to integrate it into their daily lives, and specific controversial issues that have come to the fore at the present time.

The first part, on the historical development of the understanding of marriage, by definition has to be somewhat of an overview. One could dedicate an entire volume to the biblical and historical development of marriage, and even then the volume would not be able to include in detail all the aspects of this development.

Many chapters develop in detail the biblical aspects of their approach. In the first chapter, Luke Timothy Johnson, the well-known Catholic scripture scholar from Emory University, provides a clear and succinct understanding of the biblical foundations of marriage. Bernard Cooke, who is the most renowned Catholic scholar in the United States in the area of sacramentology, provides a concise and accurate overview of the historical development through the centuries.

To understand the present discussions and approaches to marriage in the Catholic Church, the reader needs to know in some detail the pre–Vatican II approaches, the changes that occurred at Vatican II, the teaching of the 1968 encyclical *Humanae vitae,* and the significant contributions of Pope John Paul II in his long tenure as bishop of Rome.

The American Jesuits, John C. Ford and Gerald Kelly, were leading Catholic moral theologians in the pre–Vatican II period and were well known because of their authorship of the "Notes on Moral Theology" in *Theological Studies.* Their chapter in this volume gives the reader the flavor of the concept of the ends of marriage that pervaded much of pre–Vatican II Catholic thinking.

Susan A. Ross of Loyola University in Chicago has written extensively on feminist approaches to the sacraments. In this volume, her chapter discusses in some detail the rise of a more personalist approach to marriage in the pre–Vatican II period that was later accepted by Vatican II and links this approach to gender equality.

No American Catholic scholar has written more on the history of marriage than the late Theodore Mackin, who taught at Santa Clara University. The chapter in this volume deals with the significant developments and the understanding of marriage proposed by Vatican II and in the encyclical *Humanae vitae* of Pope Paul VI, especially the increased focus on the spousal relationship at the core of the sacrament.

Pope John Paul II published often on marriage before he was pope, and in his long papacy he frequently issued authoritative teachings on marriage. His personalist theology is marked by a deep appreciation of the relational nature of marriage and sexuality. For some theologians and lay Catholics, this theology has been profoundly influential. From John S. Grabowski of Catholic University, a younger scholar who has published on sexual ethics, we have included a chapter that comes from his foreword to the English translation of John Paul II's *The Theology of the Body.* Richard

M. Hogan—a PhD in history—and John M. LeVoir, priests of the Archdiocese of St. Paul, have written books and articles on John Paul II and other aspects of marital ethics. Their contribution to this volume comes from their book on John Paul II's approach to marriage and sexuality.

Charles E. Curran, a coeditor of this volume and a prominent revisionist Catholic moral theologian from Southern Methodist University, takes a more critical approach to the late pope's understanding in his chapter and also provides an introduction to the second part of the volume by giving an overview of some of the late twentieth- and early twenty-first-century contributions to the theology and spirituality of marriage in the United States.

The second part of this book deals with the theology and spirituality of living out the meaning of Christian marriage. William P. Roberts, emeritus of the University of Dayton, authored and edited a number of books on marriage in the post–Vatican II period. His chapter developing a post–Vatican II spirituality of marriage deals with the areas of partnership, intimacy, and sacramentality. Angelo Scola is the cardinal patriarch of Venice and a former head of the John Paul II Institute for Studies on Marriage and Family in Rome. His contribution here, recognizing the important work of the late Swiss theologian, Hans Urs von Balthasar, as well as Pope John Paul II, is based on his two-volume Italian work on the nuptial mystery.

Three essays on married life come from younger married scholars who are seeking to develop the ethical implications of a contemporary Catholic theology of marriage. Florence Caffrey Bourg published a monograph based on her doctoral dissertation done under Lisa Sowle Cahill of Boston College. Here her chapter develops the concept of marriage as domestic church and contrasts it with a romantic understanding of love and marriage. Julie Hanlon Rubio from St. Louis University, the coeditor of this volume, in her monograph and in the chapter in this volume insists on the equal partnership of husband and wife and on the dual vocation of each to their marriage and to the world. *Sex and Love in the Home* by David Matzko McCarthy of Mount St. Mary's University in Emmitsburg, Maryland, is notable for its debt to the virtue ethics of Stanley Hauerwas, with whom McCarthy studied at Duke University. His chapter here opposes a narrow personalist understanding of marital love. In place of the closed isolated family based on affectionate and interpersonal bonds, he proposes the open family grounded in the social and economic operations of households and neighborhoods. All three scholars offer a corrective to post–Vatican II personalist views of marriage by emphasizing ecclesial and social dimensions of marriage.

Lisa Sowle Cahill, of Boston College and a member of the prestigious American Academy of Arts and Sciences, has been for decades a major contributor in many areas of Catholic moral theology including sexuality, marriage, and family. Her chapter, drawn from a book that was her contribution to the Religion, Culture, and Family project headed by Don S. Browning, proposes a program for Christian families emphasizing the role of the family as a transformative agent in the broader society. It is representative of her broader effort to connect Catholic social teaching to medical and family ethics, a charge taken up by many younger scholars influenced by her writing and teaching.

The third part of this volume deals with specific issues connected with the Catholic understanding and practice with regard to marriage. The coeditors made a conscious decision not to include a section on artificial contraception. That issue, with its many ramifications, has been discussed for fifty years in Catholic moral theology and also in some depth in previous volumes in this series. The four specific issues addressed here are interchurch marriage, same-sex marriage, cohabitation, and the theory and practice concerning the indissolubility of marriage.

Michael G. Lawler, in his chapter on interchurch marriage, traces the development in Catholic practice and offers his interpretation of the present discipline of the Catholic Church in this area. Lawler, an emeritus professor at Creighton University and the director of its Center for Marriage and Family, has published more books on marriage and family than any other Catholic theologian in this country.

With regard to same-sex marriage, Stephen Pope takes a somewhat critical view of the teaching of the hierarchical magisterium, whereas William E. May strongly supports that teaching and practice. Pope, a scholar from Boston College who has written on love, natural law, and Thomistic ethics, offers a moderately liberal natural law perspective. May, of the Pope John Paul II Institute in Washington, has been a prolific author for decades who has written in many areas of moral theology, often defending, explaining, and applying the new natural law theory developed by Germain Grisez.

Willard F. Jabusch and Kevin T. Kelly take the same moral and pastoral perspective, including paying attention to some sociological studies, but come to somewhat different conclusions concerning cohabitation. Jabusch has been a seminary professor, chaplain at the University of Chicago, and a musician who has published four books. Kelly, an English moral theologian who has tried to keep one foot in pastoral ministry and one foot in moral theology, has published extensively in moral theology, including areas of marriage and sexuality.

The discussion of the indissolubility of marriage includes a number of different aspects. The first chapter in this section comes from the International Theological Commission with a commentary by its then-secretary, the well-known Belgian moral theologian Philippe Delhaye. This chapter explains the present teaching and practice of the Catholic Church with regard to the indissolubility of marriage, including the related issues of annulments and the exclusion of divorced and remarried Catholics from full participation in the Eucharist.

The Catholic teaching on the indissolubility of marriage has significant pastoral and canonical dimensions. Elsie P. Radtke, a pastoral minister in the archdiocese of Chicago working specifically in marriage ministry, in her chapter emphasizes the importance of helping married Catholics live out their commitment to indissolubility in a society in which divorce is so prevalent. She also recognizes the role of church annulments in some cases. A quite negative judgment on the practice of church annulments comes from Robert J. Kendra, an informed layman who strongly opposes the present annulment practices in the United States. The question of annulment is primarily a canonical issue that cannot be dealt with in all its canonical depth and breadth in this volume, but we have tried to attend to its main theological and ethical dimensions.

Another disputed pastoral issue concerns the full participation of divorced and remarried Catholics in the Eucharist. Three German bishops—Oskar Saier, Karl Lehmann, and Walter Kasper—propose a more lenient pastoral policy. Lehmann and Kasper are both internationally recognized Catholic theologians and now both are cardinals in the Catholic Church. Germain Grisez, John M. Finnis, and William E. May respond to the German bishops and defend the exclusion of divorced and remarried Catholics from full Eucharistic communion. Grisez has written in great depth on many issues in moral theology, including his three-volume *Way of the Lord Jesus,* but is best known for his developing what has been called "the new natural law theory." John M. Finnis, an Australian trained at Oxford and currently teaching at Oxford and at Notre Dame Law School, is an internationally known scholar in moral, political, and legal theory who is closely associated with Grisez in developing the new natural law theory.

The final two chapters take contrasting positions on the Catholic teaching on indissolubility and divorce. David S. Crawford, a younger scholar at the Pope John Paul II Institute in Washington, supports current teaching using an approach similar to that of the late pope. Margaret A. Farley, emerita from Yale and the leading Catholic feminist moral theologian in this country who has frequently dealt with issues of marriage and sexuality, contends that given human limitation, commitments to fidelity may sometimes be broken.

In the more than forty years since Vatican II, a great deal of theological attention has centered on marriage, which the council fathers famously called "an intimate partnership of life and love." Theologians have brought to their work their experience of marriage and parenting; the call of the council to "read the signs of the times and interpret them in light of the Gospel"; the resources of natural law and virtue theory; the findings of systematic theologians, biblical scholars, and social scientists; and their conversations with one another. In this area of moral theology, the work of theologians crosses the boundaries between academic and pastoral theology. Theologians are fully aware that all of their writing about marriage has direct implications for the lives of married Catholics. Conscious of this weighty responsibility, we offer this volume as a resource for church and academy and invite further conversation.

The editors want to express their appreciation to those who helped in producing this volume. We especially thank the authors whose work we have used. Lawrence Boadt, CSP, the president of Paulist Press, has encouraged us to continue this long-running series. Paul McMahon, the managing editor of Paulist Press, has been most helpful in responding to all our queries. Annie Chen, the research associate of Julie Hanlon Rubio, helped in preparing the manuscript for publication. The volume would never have seen the light of day if it were not for the painstaking work of Carol Swartz, the administrative assistant of Charles E. Curran.

Charles E. Curran and Julie Hanlon Rubio

Part One

HISTORICAL DEVELOPMENT

1. The Biblical Foundations of Matrimony

Luke Timothy Johnson

This chapter first appeared in *The Bible Today* 41 (2003).

The Christian sacraments sanctify the moments of ordinary life and make them extraordinary through the mystery of Christ. The natural impulse to mark the transition to a new community by a ritual of initiation becomes the sacrament of baptism when joined to the death and resurrection of Jesus. The catechumen does not simply join a new group but enters into new life. The natural tendency to share food becomes the sacrament of the Eucharist through association with Jesus' final meal with his followers. Christians celebrate not simply their fellowship with each other but also their fellowship with the risen Lord Jesus Christ. The sacraments punctuate our ordinary human existence with the reminder that the simple ways in which we join ourselves to each other point also to a larger drama in which we are joined to God. The sacraments mark the moments of creation as glimpses of the new creation.

ORDER OF THE FIRST CREATION

Nothing would seem to be more natural than the joining of male and female in sexual union. That is certainly the view of Genesis, which speaks God's image as borne by male and female together (Gen 1:27) and approvingly notes how those who are "bone of bone" and "flesh of

3

flesh" seek to be bound to each other: "Therefore a man leaves his father and his mother and clings to his wife, and they become one flesh" (Gen 2:23–24). Paul refers to this same Genesis passage when speaking about human sexuality (1 Cor 6:16; Eph 5:31). In this sense, marriage is part of the order of the first creation. It is as ancient as humanity. Throughout the Old Testament, marriage is assumed to be the calling of every human being. Virginity is tragic; infertility, a curse. God's blessings are given through the process of procreation.

Because the coming together of woman and man is so natural a part of creation and declared by God with the rest of creation as "good" (Gen 1:31), the Old Testament pays relatively little attention to the sexual or affective aspects of marriage as such, focusing instead on the command given the first couple to "be fruitful and multiply and fill the earth and subdue it" (Gen 1:28). Especially after God declares to Abraham the intention of making one family (Abraham's seed) the means by which all humans would be blessed (12:1–3), the biblical story is preoccupied with issues of fertility and descent (see, for example, Gen 15:1–6; 16:1–6; 17:1–8; 21:1–14; 25:19–34; 27:18–29). The laws written for the people's observance in the land of Israel likewise concentrated on issues of descent through the male seed and the preservation of the chosen people through marriage and childbearing within the proper boundaries (Num 25:6–15; Deut 7:3). Adultery and the coveting of another's wife is forbidden (Exod 20:17; Deut 22:22), as is the marrying of foreign women. The male perspective in all of this is dominant. Thus, the man can divorce a woman who displeases him (Deut 24:1–4). And while Proverbs describes the ideal wife (Prov 31:10–31), it does not mention the ideal husband.

COVENANT PARTNER

Because the bond between woman and man was essentially a covenant, however, it could also serve to symbolize the covenant between Israel and the Lord. The analogy is clear: the Lord chose Israel as covenant partner. Obeying other gods is breaking covenant. And since the "foreign women" that Israelites might marry would also bring their "foreign gods" into Israel, it was almost inevitable that religious apostasy would be expressed in terms of adultery. The use of sexual (and specifically marriage) symbolism for the relationship between the Lord and Israel is a feature especially of the prophetic literature, although it can be detected in Wisdom writings as well (for example, Proverbs 1—9). Hosea, Jeremiah, and Isaiah all imagine the bond between Israel and God in terms of the forming and the breaking and the restoration of a marriage covenant (Hos 1:2–3:5; Jer 2:23–25; 3:1–23; Isa 50:12–2; 42:5–8). It is a powerful symbolism. When used negatively, it can also be frightening, as when Ezekiel portrays the Lord in terms that strongly evoke a violent and abusive husband (Ezekiel 16).

The Old Testament has a concern for progeny and property as well as for the powerful symbolism of covenant. Only in a few places do we spot some of the playfulness and pleasure of sexual life, some of the joy of this natural covenant between man and woman. The supreme example is the Song of Solomon, which unabashedly celebrates erotic love, without even a mention of marriage. Small wonder that commentators (both Jewish and Christian) read the Song in terms of the covenant between Israel and the Lord.

MARRIAGE IN THE NEW TESTAMENT

In the New Testament the absolute status of marriage is challenged because of the radical character of the Christian experience. First, Jesus himself lived a radical lifestyle and died violently at an early age without having married or begotten children. Second, Jesus' resurrection as "life-giving spirit" (1 Cor 15:45) made the reception of God's blessings not dependent on biological fertility but on the power of the Spirit. Third, the expectation that "the frame of this world is passing away" (1 John 2:17) made the natural order relative rather than absolute. The resurrection experience is eschatological. It inaugurates a "new creation" (2 Cor 5:17). Of this, the New Testament writings are certain. But they are less certain how this new creation affects marriage. The New Testament is ambivalent about this basic human relationship in a way that the Old Testament is not.

Thus, we see Jesus, on one side, call for a commitment in marriage (on the basis of Genesis 1!) that excludes all divorce (Mark 10:2–12;

Luke 16:18)—a command with which the early Church clearly struggled (1 Cor 7:10–16; Matt 5:31–32; 19:3–9). But on the other side, he calls his disciples to abandon their families for the sake of the kingdom of God, and he speaks of those who are "eunuchs for the Kingdom of God" (Matt 19:10–12). And he rejects the Sadducees who pin everything on marriage by declaring that those "in the resurrection of the dead neither marry nor are given in marriage" (Luke 20:32–35). Yet, Jesus also continues the image of the Scripture where he speaks of himself as the bridegroom (Luke 5:33–35). The two dimensions merge in John's account of Jesus' miracle at the wedding feast at Cana (John 2:1–11). He blesses the first creation by his presence, but he symbolizes the inauguration of the new creation by changing the water into wine.

COMPLEXITY AND AMBIGUITY

The same complex attitude toward marriage appears in the other New Testament compositions. On one side, we find the repeated approval of marriage as God's good creation (1 Tim 4:3–5) to be lived by husband and wife in fidelity and holiness (see 1 Thess 4:3–6; 1 Cor 7:1–16; Col 3:18, Eph 5:22–30; Heb 13:4). On the other side, we find that an appreciation for the new creation through Christ complicates things. Paul does not regard virginity and widowhood as the tragedies that they were in Israel. God's Holy Spirit can give life and blessing quite apart from marriage and childbearing. Indeed, Paul argues that "in the present circumstances," a single life has the advantage of enabling a commitment to the work of the Lord that is unencumbered by the (legitimate) anxiety that married people have toward spouses and children (1 Cor 7:17–40).

The same ambiguity is found in the two passages (outside the Gospels) where the marriage imagery of the prophets occurs. In Revelation 14:3–5, the 144,000 who sing a new song to the Lamb before the throne "have not defiled themselves with women, for they are virgins"; and in the final vision, the Church is "the bride, the wife of the lamb" (Rev 21:9): "the spirit and the bride say, 'Come'" (22:17). Here, the symbolism of Christ and the Church as bridegroom and bride simply displaces the human reality of marriage. But in Paul's Letter to the Ephesians, that imagery serves to strengthen the marriage between real women and men.

After addressing the attitudes of mutual submission between spouses—and the particular obligation of the husband to give his life for his spouse "just as Christ loved the church and gave himself up for her" (Eph 5:25), Paul provides the clearest basis in the New Testament for the sacramental character of the human institution of marriage. Quoting the Genesis text about the two becoming one flesh (Gen 2:24), Paul says, "This is a great mystery, and I am applying it to Christ and the church" (Eph 5:32). Placed in the overall argument of Ephesians, he means that, just as the reconciliation between Jew and Gentile in the Church symbolizes the peace that Jesus had brought about through his death and resurrection (Eph 2:1–10), so does the loving relationship between husband and wife provide a sign *to* the Church of its own truest identity.

2. Historical Reflections on the Meaning of Marriage as Christian Sacrament

Bernard Cooke

This chapter first appeared in *Alternative Futures for Worship,* vol. 5: *Christian Marriage,* ed. Bernard Cooke (Collegeville, Minn.: Liturgical, 1987).

One of the most helpful ways of understanding a reality such as Christian marriage is to examine the historical evolution that brought it to its present-day state. Such historical reflection cannot replace the more analytic approach of the social sciences, but it is a valuable complement because it permits people to compare their own situation with that of persons in other times and places. However, there is a basic problem that often makes such historical study difficult if not impossible: before one can trace the history of something, one must know what it is that one is trying to trace. This problem is very acute in the case of Christian marriage. Surprisingly it is not clear just what constitutes human marriage and even less clear just what constitutes a Christian marriage. For more than two thousand years opinions have differed as to whether a marriage was brought into existence by two persons agreeing to share their lives permanently, or by some public authority recognizing this marital intent of the couple, or by these two people giving to one another exclusive rights to sexual intercourse, or by the act of intercourse itself, or by a couple living together over a considerable period of time, or by one or other contractual agreement between the families of the two persons, or by some combination of these.

To put it quite simply, it has never been perfectly clear who is married and who is not, though there has been rather general recognition that most people in any society live with some other person (or persons) in a marriage.

So what is it whose history we wish to sketch? Without trying to add to the detailed historical studies that have recently appeared, this chapter will attempt to describe briefly three elements of the historical picture. First, what has been the Christian understanding of marriage as a human reality? Second, what has been distinctive about the way Christians became married and the nature of their married relationship? Third, what has been meant by calling Christian marriage a sacrament?

WHAT IS MARRIAGE?

Attempts to study the history of Christian marriage in the earliest periods of the Church's life are immediately stymied by the lack of evidence for anything that could be called specifically Christian. This lack, however, indicates rather clearly that apart from the fact that the two persons involved were Christian, there was nothing noticeably different about Christian marriages, about the way they originated, the way they were lived, or (in some instances) the way they were terminated.

Ideally the motivations and values that brought a Christian woman and man into a given relationship expressed their Christian faith, and the Gospel perspective deepened their loving concern for one another. But in their external forms and social identification, the marriages of Christians were not discernibly different from the other marriages in society. Christians became married according to the patterns of whatever culture they lived in. Becoming married was seen, in other words, to be a basic human undertaking that Christians did much as others did, though the nature of their relationship to one another might have been touched by their understanding of what it meant for them to be related to one another "in the Lord."

Having said this, we can trace among Christians over the centuries a varying and somewhat diverse understanding of what marriage is. Since the practical context of our understanding is that of Roman Catholic thought and practice, we can concentrate on those developments in Western Christianity that fed into what became the Catholic tradition. Some of the developments in Eastern Christianity and in Protestantism were slightly different, but that need not concern us here.

In its beginning the Christian understanding of human marriage was strongly influenced by the viewpoint of Judaism and then increasingly by the outlook of Roman law and custom. Judaism at the time of Christianity's origin had inherited a fundamentally positive attitude towards human sexuality and for that historical period a rather lofty view of marriage. Marriage was considered a responsibility intrinsic to adult life; one was expected to raise up and educate God-fearing children so that the people Israel could continue and prosper, and God be glorified.

Israel's strongly patriarchal culture still kept women in an inferior position. In marriage the woman was subordinate to her husband and expected to reverence and obey him as her lord. She did not have the rights he possessed regarding divorce, and she was bound by a stricter rule of marital fidelity than he. It was the man who took the woman in marriage, quite literally. She passed from the jurisdiction and care of her father to that of her husband. Being married for a woman was a matter of changing households and roles within the household.

Yet there was a definite tradition of marriage being a relationship of love between the spouses. The Canticle of Canticles bears witness to this tradition. Marriage arrangements were still a matter of negotiations between families, but it seems that the preferences of the young persons involved, particularly the young man, were often as not honored. Israel's key religious category, covenant, was used as a way of describing the marriage agreement, and the prophetic imagery that used marriage as metaphor of Yahweh's relation to his people gave marriage special moral and religious endorsement.

Rome's most ancient cultural traditions involved great respect for family and marriage as the key to tribal continuity. As elsewhere in the ancient world, marriages at least in the upper classes were arranged for the young couple, but the marriage itself was seen to consist essentially in the two people consenting to stable cohabitation. Marriage was a family-affair; the only involvement of the state concerned questions of property or public responsibility.

Christianity's earliest generations, then, would have regarded marriage much as did diaspora Judaism. Christians would have seen marriage as an arrangement between two people who wished to share life and establish their own household. Marital sexuality would have been taken for granted as intrinsic to this arrangement and sexual fidelity as a basic responsibility of each spouse. Christians would not have regarded their marriage as anything distinctively related to their Christian faith. They would have believed, however, that their regard for and relationship to one another in a marriage had a special character, because Christian marriage, and especially the sexual union of woman and man, was meant to mirror the love that linked Christ and his Church.

By the year 200, however, a negativity towards human sexuality infiltrated Christianity and began to limit Christians' positive esteem for marriage, so much so that "family" ceased to be a primary model for thinking about the Church. One must be careful not to judge Christians' attitude towards their own individual marriages simply by the statements of those theologians and bishops we call "Fathers of the Church," but those statements do reflect much of the current outlook. Reading those Patristic judgments on marriage, one is appalled by the shift in outlook that has occurred. Though they still pay homage to the notion that marriage is good because established by God and related to Christ's love for the Church, the Fathers see marriage as seriously "wounded" because it entails sexual intercourse.

In their view procreation of children for the next generation of Christians is the only thing that truly legitimates marital intercourse. Sexual relations without such an objective are a concession to human carnality, only somewhat legitimated by the fact that sexual activity within marriage is an outlet that keeps a man from the greater evil of extramarital promiscuity. All such considerations of marriage deal, of course, only with the man's situation, the "problems" that sexuality and women present for him, whether in or outside marriage. Implicitly, at times explicitly, the human dignity and Christian spirituality of a married woman are denigrated.

Besides, during the Patristic period (roughly 200 to 600) monasticism became a widespread phenomenon in the life of the Church. Such a way of life, which allowed a Christian to "preserve oneself" from the contamination of sexuality, came to be seen as the ideal expression of

Christian faith. Dedicated following of the Gospel could take place only if one separated oneself from the temptations and involvements of the "world" and, at least symbolically but often in reality, went to the desert. When this was combined with the growing notion that sexuality was incompatible with the sacramental ministry, it was determined that ordained clergy should, even if married, abstain from all sexual activity. Therefore married life was denied full participation in Christian faith for it was neither clerical nor monastic. Marriage was second-best; the idea of "vocation" was appropriated to those Christians who were called to a "higher way of life."

Another major element in the development of Christians' understanding of marriage came during this same period with the migrations of Teutonic peoples into southern Europe. These groups brought with them their own customs, values, and laws which, as these invaders gradually intermingled with the local population, interacted with the outlook and practices of Christians in the Mediterranean area. Among these Teutonic peoples a strong emphasis on tribal identity and continuity brought back to center stage society's role in marriage. Contrary to accepting the couple's consent as the principal agent of a marriage—which was the Roman viewpoint—the Teutonic viewpoint laid stress on marriage as a contract verified by socially conventionalized arrangements. In this northern European perspective the economic arrangements associated with marriage, the dowry and bridal gift, took on intrinsic importance as part of the contractual action. Obviously such arrangements were of concern to the families of the bride and groom, so they were not left just to the bridal couple. But the act of intercourse itself was seen as intrinsic to the enactment of a marriage, though only when linked with some agreement to marriage on the part of the two persons.

As from the ninth century onward Europe moved into the Middle Ages, there was increased involvement of society in the initiation and validation of marriage, increased emphasis on the contractual character of the couple's marital consent, and increased attention to first sexual intercourse as constitutive of the married state. It might be instructive to mention, however, that such formal understanding and practice was true of the upper classes much more than it was of the bulk of the population. For the typical peasant marriage was basically a "natural" happening that occurred quite informally and without benefit of social notice or regulation.

Educated Christians in the Middle Ages viewed marriage in the light of the inherited Patristic judgments, particularly St. Augustine's listing of the "goods" toward which marriage should be directed. Among these goods the *bonum prolis*—the "good of offspring"—enjoyed a certain primacy, for it was quite obviously the goal towards which the act of intercourse was biologically directed. It was clearly the divine intent for marriage, so it could justify a Christian experiencing the irrationality and passion, the carnal pleasure, and the sensual gratification of concupiscence that were intrinsic to sexual activity. Another good, the "good of the sacrament," was always recognized as having some superior value, but for the most part it was only vaguely understood.

What was happening as Europe began to reshape itself after the upheavals associated with the collapse of the Roman Empire and the Teutonic migrations south was an increasing emphasis on public recognition, including (as we will see) Church recognition, of the marriage contract. Married people were, then, those whose state of cohabitation conformed to these social agreements. Marriage existed not only in connection with such public, or at least publicly verifiable, acts but because of them. That particular "state in life" was caused by the couple's contractual consent and, to an extent about which there was differing opinion, by their actual sexual intercourse, but that consent had to be given in a manner that society recognized. In the midst of this increased structuring of the marriage arrangement, there continued to be a grassroots recognition of a prior power of the two people to bring their marriage into existence. Despite the lesser regard in which they were held and negative judgments made upon them by both Church and state, common-law marriages, in which a couple simply began to live together without recognition by either Church or state, remained a widespread reality. So widespread was the practice that Church and civil governments had no alternative but to give such unions a basic status as some kind of real marriage.

Since the sixteenth century and the reforms of the Council of Trent, Catholic understanding of marriage has been dominated by the teaching and practice of the Church. With the regulation that an official Church witness in the person of a duly empowered priest was needed for valid contracting of a marriage, common-law marriage lost what status it had, and the public marriage ceremony was seen to be that by which two people became married. Church law and in some instances civil law recognized "consummation" of the marriage contract by the couple's intercourse as "completing" the marriage arrangement. But in the minds of the people, Catholics included, two persons were married, if by a fundamentally free choice and not hindered by some barrier such as being already married to someone else, they had gone through the required public actions, whether they be civil or religious.

For men and women in the modern Western world, it is the legal arrangements that essentially distinguish the married from the unmarried. While the inner attitude of the spouses towards one another has been valued, two people have not been seen to be married or not because of the presence or absence of marital love and concern. There are "happy" and "unhappy" marriages, but they are all marriages, unless the latter cease to exist because of the legal arrangement of divorce.

This is not to say that there has been no reflection by Catholics on the inner reality of marriage. Just the contrary. Like others in the West, Catholics have been deeply touched by the greater emphasis on romantic love that has marked modern understanding of marriage. Linked with the more general growth in appreciation for the basic dignity and autonomy of the individual human person, regardless of social status or race or sex or talent, this shift towards the personal aspects of the married couple's life together has, in the past half-century, triggered an important reassessment of Catholic views of marriage.

Coming into the twentieth century, Catholics thought about marriage in terms of the so-called "ends (or goals) of marriage," even though the ordinary Catholic knew nothing about the technical debates about these "ends." Actually the goals being discussed by moral theologians and Church authorities and being explained to the faithful in sermons and religious instruction were the three classic "goods" stated by St. Augustine with two important differences. First, for a variety of reasons, generation of children had assumed almost unchallenged primacy as the goal of marriage with the result that ethical explanation of marital responsibility focused lopsidedly on birth control. Second, the notion of sacrament was applied to marriage almost exclusively in reference to the wedding ceremony, which was a use of the word quite different from that of St. Augustine or of most of Christian history.

Shortly before mid-century doctrinal and theological concentration on procreation as the primary goal of Catholic marriage began to be

openly challenged, and within a few years the human and Christian relation of the two people to one another achieved recognition as an equal, if
not superior, purpose of marriage. This more personalistic view, which sees
marriage as a free society of people and not primarily as an institution of
nature (with emphasis on the biological level of humans as part of nature),
received important support at the Second Vatican Council and has become
a controlling force in present-day Catholic understanding of marriage.

What Is Distinctive about Christian Marriage?

Looking at the earliest centuries of Christianity, we might be
tempted to say that there was nothing distinctive about Christian marriage, at least in the sphere of social arrangement and social identification. But that would be an oversimplification. While no specific Christian
official action, such as a marriage liturgy, was thought to be needed for a
Christian man and woman to marry, there were various forms of recognition by the Christian communities to which they belonged that gave
their marriage approval, blessing, and social impact.

As early as the letters of Ignatius at the end of the first century, there
is reference to the married couple receiving some approval and blessing
from Church leadership. While there is no indication that such blessing
was thought to be necessary to the marriage, it seems that Christians were
expected to choose marriage within the context of Christian community
life and in accord with the lifestyle of Christians. Still there was no Church
wedding or specific role of the Church in bringing the marriage into existence. The Church recognized that a couple had married, celebrated that
fact, and prayed for God's blessing on the union.

Gradually the blessing by the head of the community, bishop or
presbyter, assumed greater prominence in people's view. While not
required, the approval and blessing of the head of the community was
seen as something that devout Christians should obtain, as an indication
that they were truly marrying "in Christ."

But if the external formality of marriage among Christians in the
early centuries was basically that of their particular cultural situation so
that one finds no distinctively Christian marriage ceremony, the understanding of Christian marriage and consequently its conduct were dis-

tinctive. New Testament texts, for example the fifth chapter of Ephesians, indicate that Christians almost immediately linked the significance of their married relationship to the love between Christ and the Church. The term sacrament as we have used it in more recent centuries was not applied to marriage between two Christians, but the understanding that marriage was transformed in its meaning by the meaning of Christ's Passover—which is what we mean by saying that Christian marriage is a sacrament—goes back to the first Christian generation.

It is not clear just when and in what way the initiation of a Christian marriage was linked to a special celebration of the Eucharist. Probably the earliest form of this was simply a special reference to a couple's marriage, perhaps a special blessing, in the context of the regular community Eucharist. However, for more than a millennium there was no celebration of Eucharist that included as an early portion of the liturgy the actual marriage ceremony.

In Eastern Christianity the blessing given the marrying couple by the officiating priest or bishop came to be considered the cause of the marriage bond. This was not the case in the West. Even in the post-Tridentine discipline that requires the presence of a priest with proper authority, the priest is a witness, and his blessing just that. The two persons are themselves the effective agents of the marriage bond. Marriage is thought of as a contract, and they are the contracting parties. Still the common perception of Catholics has been that the priest's action married them, and Church authorities and Church law did not energetically contest this understanding.

The Middle Ages and early modern times saw an increasing intervention of the official Church in the initiation of a Christian marriage. This resulted in the view that a Christian marriage came into existence through the sacramental ceremony; to be a partner to a Christian marriage one had to be "married in the Church." For Catholics this view was crystallized in the decree *Tametsi* of the Council of Trent, which stated as the requirement for a valid marriage the presence of a duly empowered ordained minister in addition to two formal witnesses to the marriage contract.

Without this "proper form" no Catholic marriage came to be. With a ceremony containing the elements of this form an indissoluble bond was established. To some extent the absolute indissolubility of this bond was provisional, for Church law continued to recognize the possibility of dissolving a marriage that had been publicly formalized *(ratum)* but not yet consummated by the couple's first consequent act of sexual intercourse. Obviously for a Catholic marriage to be such, the content of the marital contract must be that proper to Christian marriage. In modern times the Catholic Church has seen the substance of this contract to be the mutual exchange of exclusive rights to sexual intercourse as directed to procreation. So clear was the emphasis on the procreational goal, the *bonum prolis*, that a marriage agreement between two people which excluded the generation of children could not be considered a true marriage contract.

In this context of emphasis on the legally established form and content of the marriage ceremony, what appeared to be distinctive of Catholic marriage was conformity in form and in the couple's intentions to the legal prescriptions. Those who had distinctively Catholic marriages were those who were "married in the Catholic Church." There was also, of course, an intrinsic difference; the bond established by a "Church marriage" enjoyed an indissolubility that did not characterize other human marriages, though other Christian marriages shared this indissolubility up to a point. Moreover both the distinctive character and indissolubility were rooted in the fact that Catholic marriages were "sacramental"; marriage was one of the seven sacraments of the Church and therefore a God-given cause of grace. This was reiterated as a regular element of Catholic teaching, but the meaning of the statement was seldom understood, which leads to our third topic.

WHAT IS MEANT BY CALLING CHRISTIAN MARRIAGE A SACRAMENT?

Some historical review of the evolution of the theology of marriage can be helpful in making it more understandable. That will be the purpose here. Two words, the Latin word *sacramentum* and the Greek word *mysterion,* stand at the beginning of Christian use of the term sacrament. It is several centuries before *sacramentum* is used, and then not with the meaning we give it when calling marriage a sacrament. On the other hand, there is a much earlier connection with the word *myste-*

rion, even though its earliest use does not directly name the sacramentality of the relation between Christian spouses.

Probably the earliest verbal evidence is found in the epistle to the Ephesians. This is the well-known passage in the fifth chapter where Christ's relation to the Church is seen as the exemplar of the relation which should exist between Christian husband and wife. *Mysterion* is used to characterize the revelation of God's saving self-giving that finds expression in Jesus' death and resurrection. Since the meaning of marriage is intertwined with this meaningful *mysterion* of Christ's death and resurrection, Christian marriages share in this mystery.

This passage in Ephesians indicates that marriage in general, and in a special way marriage between Christians, is a symbolic reality that reveals the divine saving love. Actually this early Christian view is grounded in the Israelitic prophets' use of human marriage as a metaphor to interpret the relation of Yahweh to Israel. From the time of Hosea onward, the image of Israel as the bride of Yahweh—often a wayward bride—figures prominently in the prophetic teaching, pointing both to Israel's repeated infidelity and to the unconditional faithfulness of Israel's God.

In the New Testament the Gospels and the Pauline epistles pick up this metaphor and give it a Christological focus. Jesus is himself the bridegroom of the new covenant people. In his death and resurrection he has given himself to his bride, the Church, and history will be the process of preparing this bride for the final nuptials of unending life. Though it will have an uneven history of interpretation, this imagery of Christ/Church and husband/wife will continue as an element of Christian theology of the Church and its sacramentality.

This idealistic view of marriage as revelatory of God's love manifested in Jesus, plus the biblical insistence that God had created all things good, passed on to early Christianity a very positive view of human sexuality and marriage. However, in interaction with other ancient understandings of sexuality, the Fathers of the Church, as we saw, quickly incorporated into their explanation of marriage a disastrous negativity. Faced with the texts of Genesis, the Fathers had to recognize that God had created marriage, or at least some form of marriage, good. But the original sin of Adam and Eve had introduced evil into the picture, and marriage as it now exists, vitiated by sexual lust and irrationality, was the result. Procreation of children can provide some justification for marriage. Marriage can also serve to keep sexuality within certain bounds. But it does not take much reflection to realize that the Patristic tradition leaves little possibility that marital sexuality, rooted as it is in sin, can reflect the divine saving love.

Patristic thinking on marriage finds in St. Augustine of Hippo a synthetic expression that dominates centuries of subsequent Christian thought and practice. Though St. Augustine's view was not as negative as that of many of his Patristic predecessors nor in itself as negative as is often assumed, it is clearly controlled by his understanding of original sin. Interpreting the Genesis passage about Adam and Eve as a description of an actual historical occurrence, a gravely sinful action performed a few thousand years before by two historical personages, St. Augustine believed that a "wound" from this sin passed down through all of human history. While St. Augustine did not agree with the view that this original sin was precisely the act of sexual intercourse, he taught that from the original sin there resulted in humans an imbalance in erotic attraction and passionate response that inevitably debased human sexuality, even in marriage.

According to St. Augustine sexual expression is never without grave sin outside marriage; even within marriage it is always touched by venial sin unless the couple desire only the generation of a child and do not directly seek the pleasure attached to intercourse. Thus procreation and nurture of children is for St. Augustine the first and dominant "good" that Christians should seek in their marriage. A second "good" is personal fidelity upon which each can depend, and here there are indications that St. Augustine places positive value on friendship between husband and wife, though he does not develop this element in his description of a Christian marriage. The third "good" is the unbreakable bond in a Christian marriage, and it is this permanence of their marriage commitment which St. Augustine calls the *sacramentum*. Clearly this use of the term does not point directly to the deeper symbolic dimension of Christian marriage.

Yet in the strange logic of historical use of words, the word sacrament became part of the Christian explanation of marriage and acquired a changed meaning as sacrament itself took on new theological significance. For the most part medieval theologians concentrated in their explanations of marriage on the procreative function, on the role of contractual consent in establishing a marriage, and on marriage providing a "remedy" for the unruly sexual attractions that come with concupiscence. However, at least as early as the writings of Hugh of St. Victor in the twelfth century, we find explicit teaching about the symbolic role of the married relationship and its reflection of the relation between Christ and the Church or between God and the individual Christian. Since there was agreement that somehow Christian marriage constituted a situation of grace, a natural situation of friendship and support with the possibility of overcoming sexual temptations, the ingredients for describing Christian marriage as a sacrament of the Church were now in place.

However, several centuries would elapse before the sacramentality of Christian marriage would receive much attention. The reason for this was that the procreative purpose of marriage continued to be stressed as primary. Only in the mid-twentieth century would the personal relatedness of wife and husband, that aspect of marriage which is capable of bearing metaphorical reference to the relation of God to humans, begin to receive acceptance as a primary purpose of Christian marriage. Though this new insistence on marriage as primarily a community of persons relating to one another in love and Christian faith initially received opposition, its acceptance by the Second Vatican Council has opened up a new stage in Catholic appreciation of marriage as sacrament. Today our theology locates the distinctiveness of Christian marriage in the injection of the transforming significance of Jesus' death and resurrection into the relation between the spouses. Married love and life is transformed as a human experience because of its perceived role as a revelation of God's loving presence to humans.

References

Mackin, Theodore, *What Is Marriage?* New York: Paulist Press, 1982. A thorough study of the historical development of Catholic theology and jurisprudence of marriage from New Testament times to the present. Probably the best one-volume treatment of Christian marriage available.

Martos, Joseph. *Doors to the Sacred.* Garden City, N.Y.: Doubleday,

1981. Contains a rather lengthy (pp. 397–452) review of the history of marriage in the Catholic Church with an emphasis on the question of indissolubility.

Schillebeeckx, Edward. *Marriage: Human Reality and Saving Mystery.* New York: Sheed & Ward, 1965. A pioneering study of the history and meaning of Christian marriage. Still a valuable source.

Stevenson, Kenneth. *Nuptial Blessing: A Study of Christian Marriage Rites.* Notre Dame, Ind.: Notre Dame University Press, 1983. An historical study of Christian marriage from a liturgical viewpoint, an indispensable tool for studying the history and theology of marriage.

3. The Essential Subordination of the Secondary Ends of Marriage

John C. Ford and Gerald Kelly

This chapter first appeared in John C. Ford and Gerald Kelly, *Contemporary Moral Theology*, vol. 2: *Marriage Questions* (Westminster, Md.: Newman, 1963).

We have seen that in modern Protestant thought parenthood and companionship rank equally as purposes of marriage. For Catholics, however, the subordination of the secondary ends is a point of teaching so well established in the ecclesiastical sources that when…others questioned it their theories were soon rejected by the Church.

This essential subordination of the secondary ends is expressed traditionally by the terms "primary and secondary ends." The purpose of the present chapter is to indicate what these terms do and do not mean, thereby explaining, partially at least, what this essential subordination consists in. We say partially because there are problems in this conception which invite deeper studies, philosophical and theological, not only of the purposes of marriage, but of the meaning and purposes of sexual differentiation in human nature itself.

Perhaps it will be clarifying to begin by indicating what the terms primary and secondary do not mean.

In the first place, the essential subordination of the secondary ends does not mean that they are less essential than the primary ends, if the word essential is understood as we understand it. We call essential that without which marriage cannot exist. Among the ends of marriage as a natural institution, among its intrinsic *fines operis*, one end cannot be more essential than another in this sense. Either marriage can exist without being objectively ordered to mutual help and the other secondary ends or it cannot. If it cannot, then mutual help is an essential end. There can be degrees of importance. But there can be no degrees of essentialness. Essentialness as we have defined it does not admit of degrees.[1]

In the second place, the essential subordination does not mean that the secondary ends are subordinated to procreation and rearing of children in such a way that they have value and legitimacy only when used as a means to attaining the primary ends. The secondary ends are really ends, not just means. That is why Wynen can speak of the secondary end as having "a certain independence" from the primary end.[2] Palmieri says that if a means could be used only for the purpose of achieving a given end, that end would not be the primary end; it would be the only end.[3]

It cannot be denied that this kind of subordination seems to have been part of St. Augustine's theory of marriage. But theologians nowadays, and for a long time past, in their theoretical exposition of the ends of marriage, and in their practical teachings on the morality of conjugal intimacy, have broken with the idea that the secondary ends are subordinate to the primary in the sense that they can be justified only when they are a means to the attainment of the primary ends. It is now universally recognized that the secondary ends, while remaining essentially subordinate, have a certain quasi-independence, a certain value of their own, and can be legitimately pursued even when the primary end is completely impossible of actual fulfillment, or when for sufficient reasons its fulfillment is deliberately avoided. For instance, the partners may knowingly contract and knowingly make use of a sterile marriage. Or, given proportionately serious reasons, they may avoid the realization of the primary end by systematically restricting their intercourse to sterile periods.

Pius XII authoritatively ratified this theological position in the Address to the Midwives. His teaching had been preceded by the authoritative statement of Pius XI in the encyclical *Casti Connubii*.[4]

It is clear then, that the terms primary and secondary do not mean that the secondary ends are subordinate in the sense that they have legitimate value only as means to the attainment of the primary end.

Thirdly, primary end does not mean that procreation is or should necessarily be uppermost in the minds and intentions of the contracting parties generally, or that they are under obligation to choose it as the purpose most important to them, that is, primary as far as they are concerned. They need only intend marriage as it is, and respect the obligations that go with it. Marriage "as it is" is related to all its ends essentially and objectively; and is related primarily in some sense to procreation.

In what sense? What does it mean to call procreation a primary end or purpose, and to say that the other ends are essentially subordinate to it? The primary end is called primary because it is *more important*, and *more fundamental*.

If we look at marriage as a natural and divine institution, then in the intention of God and nature procreation is seen to be an end of greater importance or greater value than mutual help, conjugal love, and the remedy for concupiscence. Perhaps it is a little rash to speculate on the comparative importance of purposes in the mind of God. Some seem to think we have no right to do so. On the other hand, it is not impossible that in a natural institution like marriage nature herself has shown her hand, and reason itself can give us a clue as to what is more important, the personal purposes, or the purposes that serve the species. Undoubtedly procreation and rearing of children are of more importance to the species. Likewise it is of more importance to human society in general, and hence to the law, both civil and canon. One must therefore, for valid philosophical reasons, call procreation primary. Since the good of the species is more important to nature than the good of individuals, procreation and rearing of children is a more important end of marriage than mutual help, conjugal love and the remedy.

But for the defense of the Catholic position it does not suffice to say merely that the primary ends are more important. "Primary and secondary are not merely synonyms for *more important* and *less important*."[5] The secondary ends presuppose, that is, depend on or are subordinate to the primary ends in a sense in which the primary ends do not presuppose or depend on the secondary ends. In a word the primary ends are more fundamental. This conception reflects basic attitudes in Catholic thought not only with regard to the purpose of marriage but with regard to the meaning and purposes of the sexual differentiation in human nature itself. Canon Leclercq expresses it thus:

> For men to be perfect and happy, they must first of all be
> men. Consequently, since the union of the sexes ensures on

the one hand the happiness of the couple, and, on the other, the continuation of the human race, the second of these effects is more important [and on this reasoning more fundamental] than the first and has to be accepted both as the primary purpose of marriage and as the very reason for sex differentiation itself.[6]

This basic Catholic position has been variously explained and defended by theologians and canonists.[7] We content ourselves with adducing one example, from a canonist, of the kind of reasoning which is used to confirm this position.

The Rota judge Monsignor Arthur Wynen, deciding a case in 1944, analyzed at length the essential subordination of mutual help to the primary end from the standpoint of canon law. His explanation is of special interest and importance because, contrary to usual custom, soon after the case was decided, it was published in the *Acta*. We have seen that in Wynen's view, although mutual help is an essential, intrinsic end *(finis operis)* of marriage, the right to this mutual help is not considered to be one of the constituting elements of the essential object of consent. The validity of his analysis, however, does not, in our opinion, depend on this part of his theory. The following excerpts are from his opinion:

> …*Concerning the relation of the secondary end of matrimony to the primary end.* Mutual help and a total sharing of life can occur between two persons of opposite sex outside marriage, also, either as a mere matter of fact, as between brother and sister living together, or in virtue of an explicit agreement to provide mutual help to one another. Therefore, inasmuch as mutual help and common life are said to be proper to matrimony and are its secondary *fines operis* they ought to be viewed in the light of some special property by which they are distinguished from any other common life involving mutual help. They are thus distinguished by their internal relation to the primary end, by which end conjugal union is set apart from every other human society.
>
> …This relation of the secondary end to the primary is found first in the origin of this end and in the origin of the

corresponding right to mutual help;—which is demonstrated as follows: the immediate and essential object of the matrimonial contract is the exclusive and perpetual right to the person of the partner with a view to acts which are *per se* apt for the generation of offspring (can. 1081, 2). There derives from this right as a natural consequence and complement, a right to all those things without which the right of generating—and consequently also of rearing—the offspring cannot be realized in a manner befitting the dignity of human nature. Now then, the right of generating and rearing offspring in the aforesaid manner cannot be realized unless to this principal right there accedes a right to mutual help, including a right to the sharing of life or a right to cohabitation, to a common bed and board, and to help in all life's needs. Be it noted, however, that the question here is not about the actual providing of the help itself, but of a right to mutual help; for just as the principal object of the matrimonial contract is not "offspring" but "the right" to generate offspring, so the secondary object is not "the mutual help" itself, but "the right" to it....

...From what has been adduced the following conclusion is to be drawn. Just as the right to the sharing of life and to total mutual help is intrinsically dependent in its origin on the principal right to generative acts, and not vice versa; and just as among the matrimonial rights there exists a definite order and a definite dependence: so also the ends of matrimony, to which those rights are ordered and for which they are granted by nature, are arranged in a certain order and connected with one another by reason of their origin. Having established the principal and primary end, the Author of nature established in marriage as an institution of nature a secondary, complementary end so that it should be and appropriately could be realized in and through the same institution which is called matrimony....

...The above described order of dependence and subordination is verified not only in the origin of the secondary right, which is destined to the attainment of the secondary end and by which the attainment is *per se* assured, but the same order is apparent also in marriage considered *"in facto esse."*

Indeed every man, simply because he is of his very nature "a social being," needs the help of others; and he finds this help both because he is a member of human society in general, and of a determinate civil and domestic society in particular. In this help which is common to all there is included also that help and completion which one sex (even prescinding from all carnal desire and activity) receives from the character of the opposite sex; for human society is made up of men and women mutually affecting one another. But this kind of common help cannot constitute a *finem operis* of matrimony; to constitute the latter it has to be further determined by some specific element, from which it may be evident why the Creator has endowed matrimony with "mutual help" as a *finis operis*. This specific element again is and must be the relation to the primary end and to the principal right. The spouses, that is, from the very nature of matrimony are linked to the primary end of this institution because they have acquired through matrimony the right and the destination of becoming "authors of new life," by procreating and rearing children, even if de facto they do not become such....[8]

A sterile marriage does create a difficulty. But perhaps it is not precisely the difficulty of showing how procreation can be its primary essential end, but rather the difficulty of showing how procreation can be an essential end of such a marriage at all. We have previously attempted to explain this point by saying that an individual marriage which is sterile remains essentially ordered to procreation as an end inasmuch as the marriage bond consists in a fundamental right to acts which are *per se* procreative. The marriage is thus fundamentally procreative by its very nature.

It is true that it may be physically impossible for the sexual acts of a given marriage to result in actual procreation. But philosophically speaking this impossibility is *per accidens*. The acts remain *per se* procreative because they are the typical acts of organs whose specific, objective purpose is procreative. They are acts which in other persons, or in these persons at other times, normally result in procreation. We say their failure as procreative is *per accidens* in much the same way that we would say the inability of a color blind person to tell certain colors is *per accidens*. His eyes are objectively and essentially destined for distinguishing these colors even if it would take a miracle to achieve this result. A similar point was made by Pius XII when he asserted that procreation remains the primary end even of a sterile marriage, declaring that the essential subordination of the secondary ends "holds true for every marriage even if it bear no fruit, just as it can be said of every eye that it is destined and constructed for seeing even if in certain abnormal cases, by reason of special conditions, either internal or external, it will never be able to attain visual perception."[9]

Once granted that procreation is an essential end even of a sterile marriage, the defense of its objective character as a primary end does not raise new or special problems. The procreative finality of sterile marriages as of fertile marriages is more fundamental to them than their other purposes. Therefore, procreation is said to be *per se* their primary end. But they are objectively ordered to procreation only in the limited, technical sense described above. And since all this seems to involve fundamental assumptions as to the meaning of human sexuality, we would welcome further investigation of this conception by Catholic theologians.

In the practical moral order the subordination of the secondary to the primary ends has its most common applications where the use of marriage is concerned. The marriage act may be used for the attainment of the secondary ends, but the partners are always bound first, to respect the physical integrity of the procreative act and faculty (that is, they must not directly deprive them of their *per se* procreative character) and, second, they are bound not to neglect the affirmative obligation to actual procreation which is *per se* a part of marriage.

But it would seem that it is not precisely the violation of a finality which is primary, but the violation of a finality which is essential and intrinsic, which makes contraception intrinsically immoral. A Protestant commentator says that even if procreation were the primary end of marriage, which it is not, contraception would not be immoral.[10] We are inclined to say, that even if procreation were not the primary end of the marriage act, which it is, contraception would still be immoral. For we consider that the secondary finality of the marriage act is essential and intrinsic to it as it is to marriage itself, and to violate such finality would also be intrinsically immoral. But since parenthood is the primary end of marriage and of the marriage act it can be concluded *a fortiori* that it is immoral to use the act for its secondary, essentially subordinate ends, while deliberately mutilating its basic character as a *per se* procreative act.

Papal documents and theological reasoning, as we shall see, have uniformly derived the immorality of contraception from the finality of the sexual act and sexual faculty. To this act and this faculty is attributed a special inviolability against human interference. To destroy directly the physical integrity of the marriage act, or to deprive directly the procreative faculty of its power of generating new life, is an attempt to exercise a dominion which we do not possess. The stewardship God has given us over our bodies does not extend that far. This would still be true even if procreation were a secondary intrinsic purpose of marriage and of the marriage act. Consequently further arguments against contraception could be based on its opposition to the secondary ends of marriage.[11] Attributing a truly essential place to the secondary ends does not deprive them of their essential subordination, nor is it a logical step in the direction of admitting contraception.

MUTUAL SANCTIFICATION THE "PRIMARY CAUSE AND REASON"

We have already alluded to the controversial passage in *Casti Connubii* which speaks of the mutual interior formation, i.e. the mutual sanctification, of the partners as being in a certain sense the primary cause and reason of marriage:

> This mutual interior formation of the partners, this earnest desire of perfecting one another, can be said in a certain very true sense, as the Roman Catechism teaches, to be the primary cause and reason of marriage—if only marriage is taken not strictly as an institution for the proper procreation and rearing of children, but in a broader sense as a sharing, a community, a union of their whole life.[12]

[Others have] used these words to bolster their rejection of procreation and rearing of children as the primary end of marriage. Certain aspects of the passage still remain obscure and probably always will, but the following may be to some extent clarifying.

This much can be said with certainty, even a priori. *Casti Connubii,* published only a dozen years after the new Code of Canon Law, would not contradict the Code. A document epitomizing the teaching of the past would certainly not break suddenly with the traditional Catholic teaching on such a well-established point. Furthermore it would be improper to interpret *Casti Connubii* in such a way as to make it contradict itself. It quotes canon 1013, 1, stating explicitly that "the primary end of marriage is the procreation and rearing of children," and in other passages speaks clearly in the traditional manner of the primary end both of marriage and of the marriage act.[13]

One of the more obscure points of the above passage is the distinction between marriage taken in the stricter sense and in the broader sense. In 1931 Vermeersch said that the broader sense here means a more "comprehensive" or extended concept of marriage, which does not exclude marriage in the strict sense but rather supposes it.[14] (He wanted to forestall any attempt to conceive as possible a marriage without its primary end.) But in 1932 he also asserted that the total community of life mentioned here is not something over and above the mutual gift of themselves which the spouses have made to one another with a view to the procreation and rearing of children "since it began and sprang from the mutual giving of self, and at the same time is its crown and glory."[15] Then in 1933, to add to the confusion, Vermeersch says, in a puzzling phrase, that this total community of life is "another natural, not secondary end" of contracting.[16]

Whatever this may mean, and whatever the reason for introducing this distinction into the text in the first place, we think that both the stricter and the broader conceptions of marriage in the Encyclical are conceptions of marriage properly so called. They both refer to essential things in marriage. For the description of marriage in the broader sense parallels very closely the classical definitions of marriage in canon law and early scholasticism, and these are essential definitions.[17] At least we do not believe that this distinction can be used to imply that a total community of life, or mutual help as a secondary end, is not essential to marriage.

Another point of obscurity is whether the "primary cause and reason" in this passage refers to a *finis operis* or a *finis operantis* of matrimony. Authors have divided on this point.[18] We favor the view that like the passage in the Catechism of the Council of Trent on which it is based, the Encyclical also is speaking both of a *finis operis* and a *finis operantis*. But this requires a word of explanation.

Obviously the mutual sanctification of the partners mentioned here is supernatural sanctification. Hitherto, in speaking of the ends of marriage, we have been mainly concerned with marriage as an institution of nature. In this passage we see the natural finality of marriage taken up and, as it were, inserted into the higher order of the supernatural.[19] Conjugal love strives for the communication of the good things proper to marriage. Even in a hypothetical natural order married partners by their very state in life would be destined to achieve "the good life" together. Conjugal love would include at least that. But since God has raised man to a supernatural destiny, the conjugal love of husband and wife has an essentially higher dimension. Their mutual love looks to the communication of supernatural perfection. They are to achieve not merely the good life, but eternal life, and are to achieve it together. Interior, supernatural perfection to be achieved in common is thus one of the good things, and in some sense the primary good thing, of marriage itself in the supernatural order.[20] Marriage is providentially directed to this as its "primary cause and reason."

The following question and answer are from Vermeersch's Catechism according to the Encyclical:

> Why does the Encyclical designate the mutual formation of the spouses, their efforts to perfect each other, as one of the primary causes and reasons for marriage?
>
> First, because the spouses can in their union make this their chief purpose.
>
> Secondly, because the community of life between the spouses—our second definition of marriage—is providentially directed by God to this last end, which, being the supreme end of man, occupies the first place in the Divine Will.[21]

This providential direction which God gives marriage in the supernatural order should be considered, we think, a *finis operis* of marriage in that order. Consequently, to the question whether the Encyclical is speaking of a *finis operis* or a *finis operantis* here, we reply: It means both, as long as marriage is understood as a total community of life in the supernatural order.[22] In other words Christian marriage is a supernatural vocation in which husband and wife are called to achieve sanctification in Christ together. Mutual sanctifaction is the primary end of this Christian vocation.

Notes

1. St. Thomas, *Suppl.,* q. 49, a. 3, corp., uses the terms "more essential" and "most essential," but with a difference of context and of terminology.

2. *Sacrae Romanae Rotae Decisiones* (Romae: Typis Polyglottis Vaticanis, 1954), vol. 36, Decisio VI, coram Arturo Wynen, 22 Jan. 1944, pp. 55–78 at p. 70 (n. 30, 4); reported also in *AAS*, 36 (1944), 179–200 at 193.

3. Dominicus Palmieri, *Tractatus de Matrimonio* (Rome: 1800), Thesis II, n. V, p. 14.

4. *AAS*, 22 (1930), 539–592 at 561.

5. Romaeus W. O'Brien, O. Carm., "The Primary End of Marriage and the Validity of Marriage," *American Ecclesiastical Review,* 135 n. 4 (1956), 272–274. Cf. Francis J. Connell, C.SS.R., "The Catholic Doctrine on the Ends of Marriage," *Proceedings of the Foundation Meeting of the Catholic Theological Society of America* (New York: 1946), 34–45 at 41: "Not only are the personal benefits inferior in importance to the social benefits, but they are subordinate to them. The blessings involved in life partnership and in the most intimate relationship possible between two human beings—mutual love and assistance, comfort and strength in the trials of life, the lawful relief of concupiscence—these, according to the plan of the Creator, are all ordained to an end outside of themselves, the welfare of the human race. In other words, the personal benefits of matrimony are intermediate ends—desirable for their own sake, but ultimately desirable as beneficial to society. This points the way to a basic principle which must be taken into account in every scientific discussion of matrimony by Catholics—that marriage is primarily a social institution, established by God for the common good of men whom He has created to His own image and likeness."

6. Jacques Leclercq, *Marriage and the Family,* trans. by Thomas B. Hanley, O.S.B. (New York: Pustet, 1941), p. 12. It is the thesis of O. A. Piper,

The Biblical View of Sex and Marriage (New York: Scribner's, 1960), p. v, that we should begin our ethical investigation of sex with the nature of sex itself, and not with the institution of marriage.

7. See, for example, Dominicus Palmieri, *Tractatus de Matrimonio* (Rome: 1880), Thesis II, n. V, p. 14, who has an unusually searching analysis of the essence of marriage and of the relation of the secondary ends to it; Francis W. Carney, *The Purposes of Christian Marriage* (Washington: Catholic University Press, 1950), pp. 59–69, citing several authors on this point; Rudolph Geis, *Principles of Catholic Sex Morality* (New York: Wagner, 1930), p. 45, who argues thus: "Procreation can be secured in no other way than by means of sexual activity, but the reenforcement of spiritual love and the allaying of concupiscence may be brought about in many other ways. Consequently, the connection of sex with procreation is closer and more essential than with the individual good of the spouses. Procreation stands out as the primary end of the sex life, whilst the other results are of a secondary and subordinate nature. The former is invariable and imbedded in the structure of nature; the latter are variable and subjectively conditioned. Childbearing is not the whole of marriage, but it is central." See also Bernard J. F. Lonergan, S.J., "Finality, Love, Marriage," *Theological Studies,* 4 (1943), 477–510, especially p. 505, n. 73, whose profound "outline" (as he calls it) of the complex interrelationships of the ends of marriage at the levels of nature, human nature and supernature, deserves further study and development.

8. *Sacrae Romanae Rotae Decisiones,* vol. 36, *decis.* 6, p. 65 f (n. 21 f.); reported also in *AAS,* 36 (1944), 188 f. This excerpt argues to the essential subordination of mutual help. The essential subordination of the remedy for concupiscence is shown by the fact that it is principally attained by means of acts which are per se procreative, and whose fundamental procreativity must never be sacrificed for the sake of the remedy; see above quoted decision, p. 64, n. 17; *AAS,* 36 (1944), p. 187, n. 18. As for the essential subordination of conjugal love, whether it is looked at as an aspect of mutual help, or of the marriage act, or of the remedy, it is distinctively matrimonial by reason of its relationship to and dependence on the primary end; cf. Michael F. McAuliffe, *Catholic Moral Teaching on the Nature and Object of Conjugal Love* (Washington: Catholic University Press, 1954), pp. 45, 46.

9. Address to the Midwives, *AAS,* 43 (1951), 835–854 at 849.

10. Richard M. Fagley, *The Population Explosion and Christian Responsibility* (New York: Oxford University Press, 1960), p. 221. Compare Joseph J. Farraher, S.J., "Notes on Moral Theology," *Theological Studies,* 21 n. 4 (Dec. 1960), 581–625 at 605: "Nor does our argument against contraception stem necessarily from placing the procreation of children as the primary purpose of sexual function and the fostering of mutual love as secondary. It is our belief

that to go directly contrary to either natural end is wrong. One need not always achieve both ends, but one may never act directly contrary to either one."

11. Dietrich von Hildebrand, "Marriage and Overpopulation," *Thought,* 36 (Spring, 1961), 81–100 at 96 f.; Stanislas de Lestapis, S.J., *Family Planning and Modern Problems* (New York: Herder and Herder, 1961), pp. 147 ff.; Paul M. Quay, S.J., "Contraception and Conjugal Love," *Theological Studies,* 23, n. 1 (March, 1961), 18–40; Joseph S. Duhamel, S.J., "The Catholic Church and Birth Control," in: *In the Eyes of Others,* edited by Robert J. Gleason, S.J. (New York: Macmillan, 1962), pp. 107–128; and also as pamphlet, *The Catholic Church and Birth Control* (New York: Paulist Press, 1963).

12. *AAS,* 22 (1930), 539–592 at 548. This passage was omitted from the English and from some other vernacular translations when they first appeared. How this accident happened nobody seems to know.

13. *Ibid.* at p. 546 and e.g. p. 561. Compare also Pius XII, Address to Midwives, *AAS,* 43 (1951), 835–854, at 848, 849: "Now the truth is that marriage, as a natural institution, by reason of the will of the Creator does not have as its primary and intimate end the personal perfection of the spouses, but the procreation and rearing of new life. The other ends, although they also are intended by nature, are not in the same rank as the first, and much less are they superior to it, but are essentially subordinate to it."

14. A. Vermeersch, S.J., "Annotationes" (on the Encyclical *Casti Connubii*) *Periodica,* 20 (1931), 42–68 at 47.

15. *What Is Marriage? A Catechism According to the Encyclical* Casti Connubii (New York: America Press, 1932), p. 24 (n. 59).

16. *Theologia Moralis* (Rome: Gregorian University Press, 1933), editio 3a of vol. IV *(De Castitate),* n. 41, margin.

17. The section of the Catechism of the Council of Trent on which this paragraph of the Encyclical is based defines marriage (and the context clearly shows that here we have an essential definition of marriage properly so called) as follows: "*Definitio.* Ita vero ex communi theologorum sententia definitur: Matrimonium est viri et mulieris maritalis conjunctio inter legitimas personas, individuam vitae consuetudinem retinens" (Pars II, De Matr. Sacr., n. 3)— Vermeersch is known to have worked on the preparation of the Encyclical. The somewhat unusual distinction it makes between marriage in a stricter and in a broader sense, is, both in language and in content, distinctly reminiscent of a passage in Vermeersch's *Theologia Moralis* Vol. IV, *De Castitate,* editio 2a, 1927, n. 35. When the next edition of this volume appeared (1933), after the publication of the Encyclical, Vermeersch expanded his remarks on the total community of life of the spouses and quoted the above passage of "the marvelous Encyclical Casti Connubii" in confirmation of them (n. 41). This leads one to speculate.

18. See, for example, Michael F. McAuliffe, *Catholic Moral Teaching on the Nature and Object of Conjugal Love* (Washington: Catholic University of America Press, 1954), p. 109 f., with authors cited there; and Bernard J. F. Lonergan, S.J., "Finality, Love, Marriage," *Theological Studies,* 4 (1943), 477–510 at 487.

19. See Lonergan, "Finality, Love, Marriage," p. 506 and *passim.*

20. See McAuliffe, *Catholic Moral Teaching,* p. 86 f., who, however, treats the mutual sanctification of the partners as the object of conjugal love, and does not consider it a *finis operis* of marriage.

21. *What Is Marriage?* (New York: America Press, 1932), p. 25 (n. 60).

22. This represents a revision of the opinion expressed by Ford, "Marriage: Its Meaning and Purposes," *Theological Studies,* 3 (1942), 333–374 at 372.

4. The Bride of Christ and the Body Politic: Body and Gender in Pre–Vatican II Marriage Theology

Susan A. Ross

This chapter first appeared in *Journal of Religion* 71 (1991).

The years preceding Vatican II were important ones for Roman Catholic theology, as developments that reached their fruition in the council were in process. The theology of marriage was no exception. During this time (approximately 1930–65), the most highly debated controversy centered on the adequacy of personalist criteria for marriage and the challenge to the prevailing scholastic definition, which saw procreation as primary.[1] Yet personalism was eventually adopted by the official theology of the church, and as Lisa Sowle Cahill in a recent article writes, "Catholic thinking about sexuality is on a trajectory toward appreciation of the interpersonal dimension [of marriage] as primary, with procreation in a secondary place."[2] This direction notwithstanding, I will argue in this chapter that an understanding of the contemporary theology of marriage is not complete without attending to the significance of the body and gender in the literature. The role of the body, I will suggest, is a key issue for the church's self-understanding in relation to the secular world and the social sciences. In addition, I will show how traditional gender roles play a crucial part in maintaining stability in marriage and within the church. Since personalist language implicitly challenges the traditional roles of the body and of gender, the movement

Cahill describes inevitably involves tension if not transformation of these roles.

The theology of marriage during this time was developed on both the scholarly and the pastoral level. On the scholarly level, the chief issue concerned the validity of personalist criteria for the theology of marriage and its distinction between marriage's "meaning" and "ends." On the pastoral level, the main concern was the challenge of living a Catholic marriage in an increasingly secularized world. But for both scholars and pastors, basic assumptions about the body, differences between male and female bodies, and gender roles were central to these discussions. This chapter will first highlight the roles that the body and gender play and, second, suggest an interpretation of this literature that places body and gender into the foreground of other debates such as the nature of the church and the role of the laity. In addition, I will show how a feminist approach illuminates otherwise hidden aspects of these issues.

CASTI CONNUBII AND ITS LEGACY

In 1930, Pope Pius XI issued the encyclical *Casti Connubii* ("Chaste Marriage"). The encyclical was in large part a response to the Anglican church's approval of the use of contraceptives in marriage. But the document also sought to define marriage's goals in the context of a world facing higher divorce rates, the movement for women's suffrage, and an increasingly secularized view of society. While Pius underscored the 1917 Code of Canon Law's ranking of the "ends" of marriage as primarily for procreation and secondarily for mutual help and remedy for concupisence,[3] he also termed marriage "an intimate life-partnership and association."[4] The predominantly "juridical and reductionistic"[5] language for marriage found in canon law and in the manuals of moral theology[6] did not rule out a somewhat more personalist approach to the sacrament in the encyclical as long as this did not challenge the basic scholastic conception of marriage. This also proved to be the case in the scholarly debates on the nature of marriage. Personalist thought, as described by Cahill, "stresses the priority of the human subject. Hence it construes sexuality's meaning in terms of a range of values, especially intersubjective ones. Although the marital relationship includes the births and education of children, the personal relationship of spouses overshadows the contributions of fertility to family and species."[7] The introduction of personalist thought potentially conflicted with the more traditional language of the hierarchy of ends in marriage. But the more "moderate" personalism used by Pius XI posed no such challenge.

In the years that followed the encyclical, a flood of literature on marriage appeared. Ranging from reprinted newspaper columns written largely by married men, reprinted sermons, and more theologically sophisticated monographs by moral theologians, these works had in common the purpose of defending the Roman Catholic institution and theology of marriage against the threats of the modern world.

While the primary purpose of defending the church's position remained uppermost in the minds of the writers, nearly all were equally concerned with presenting a positive view of the body and of sexuality.[8] In doing so, these writers moved the female body into the foreground of the discussion, defining it in such a way that female sexuality was significant only in marriage *and* that it was solely for procreative purposes. The female body took on a pivotal role in this discussion. Seemingly contradictory, it played one role before and another after marriage: first as mysterious and spiritual, second as physical vessel for reproduction. This (literally) pivotal position attempted to place Catholic thinking on the body in a positive relationship with the social sciences, especially psychology, while at the same time it preserved a traditional attitude toward women and sexuality. I will refer to this understanding of the body as the "gendered body": that is, this theology of the body was concerned solely with its male or female qualities and their social significance, and not at all with what male and female bodies had in common.

The debate on the meaning and ends of marriage took a somewhat different form. The attempt to recast the language of marriage in terms other than those of traditional scholasticism was met with spirited opposition. Interestingly, much of the response to this attempt argued that the goals of the personalist approach were met in the traditional language, if interpreted properly. But the challenge posed by personalist language also challenged the hierarchical structure of marriage and, by analogy, I believe, the hierarchical structure of the church. I will suggest that a *lack* of gender differentiation and hierarchy was crucial in the initial rejection of the personalist approach. Only later, when personalism and sexual "complementarity" were joined, could the traditional language of the "ends" of marriage incorporate personalist language.

"BODY" IN THE PASTORAL MANUALS

The pastoral manuals on marriage were largely written by clergy for engaged or newly married couples, although there were some written by married men (and a very few by married women, but none by nuns). Because of their pastoral, rather than strictly theological, orientation, their focus was on appropriate behavior. But this focus was in the wider context of developing a "healthy" and Catholic view of sexuality. Developing a positive view of sexuality in courtship and at the same time holding to traditional positions prohibiting sexual expression outside marriage posed a challenge to these writers. Their solution was to confer on marriage the power of transforming the significance of male and female bodies. Male and female constituted not only physical but metaphysical difference,[9] oriented toward different but "equal" ways of being human.

While obviously possessing a body, the woman represented the "spiritual" dimension of human life before marriage. The "obvious" physical "weakness" of the woman was assumed. Nearly every writer mentions, usually in passing, woman's "'defect' in bodily strength"[10] or the fact that "the woman...is more frail."[11] Her physical weakness is due to her more "spiritual" and "cosmic" nature, which means that she "participates in the great rhythm of creation."[12] "The proper role of woman is to be the inner environment, the soul of the home,"[13] one manual prescribes. In the woman, "passion is less carnal than in the man," although this does not mean that "she is less passionate or sensual."[14] Rather, the woman's nature is more unified and, therefore, more "extreme" than the man's.[15] Woman is "closer to nature...more attuned to the universe because of the periodic nature of her bodily function."[16] While woman's bodiliness is clearly significant here, and is key to understanding feminine nature, its significance is not sexual but spiritual. Writing to young men, Father James Kelly writes: "You should see all women in the shadow of the Virgin Mary. The young girl should be someone above you, someone in whose presence you feel unworthy."[17] Bodiliness for the woman takes on a transcendent character; female sexuality is down-played as the woman's physical nature with its reproductive capacity symbolizes a connection with "spiritual" and "cosmic" forces that men do not "naturally" possess.

These discussions of woman's bodily nature and its spiritual significance took place in a pastoral and theological context that attempted to value sexuality, especially in relation to the wider culture. These pastors acknowledged the negative connotations sexuality carried in Roman Catholicism and the need to develop a more positive view. One priest writes that his book "has as its main object the removal of a widespread prejudice against sex, and a misunderstanding of the real Catholic attitude toward such matter."[18] Another adds that Roman Catholics "are just beginning to free ourselves" from "the heresy of Jansenism" and "from the narrow and pessimistic spirit which this error created and fostered."[19] A married man writes that "it is possible to be naked and not ashamed,"[20] and the Reverend T. W. Burke deplores the "prudery and ambiguity" of most Catholic treatments of sexuality in marriage.[21] All acknowledge the prevalence of this attitude in Catholicism but maintain that it is due to a misinterpretation of the tradition.

A positive valuation of sexuality can be found in psychology, these writers note approvingly. While most regard the ideas of Sigmund Freud as reductionistic, one notes that Freud was correct in recognizing that the sexual act was "something infinitely charged with 'meaning.'"[22] Another praises Freud "for having first entered upon such a study and then advancing it to the rank of a well-organized science."[23] While critical of Freud's "complete failure to understand the spiritual structure of the personality,"[24] these writers formulate their understanding of sexuality in the context of a psychologized understanding of the person. Even the "disastrous" effects of birth control are witnessed by "all doctors, especially surgeons and psychiatrists, [who] are well acquainted with the subject."[25]

The theological anthropology of these works presents a view of human nature as both spiritual and material, with women in courtship representing the "spiritual" side of the dialectic. Young men are admonished to maintain their purity before marriage,[26] and young women are advised to break off relationships with any men who demand more than chaste kissing before marriage.[27] While little is explicitly said about male sexuality before marriage, much is assumed. The constant stress on the purity of women and the sacredness of sex suggests that materiality at this point resides in the man. His greater strength, his rootedness in the secular world, his attention to more mundane matters represent his greater physicality and thus his bodiliness (despite women's greater "closeness" to their bodies). Whenever attention is given to masturbation, it is specifically addressed to boys and young men.[28] In fact, nearly all attention on sexuality during courtship is focused on restraining male sexuality and preserving the "sacredness" of femininity. This understanding allows sexuality to be valued and praised, backed by an alleged empirical grounding in the social sciences, while it maintains both the traditional differentiation between men and women and the prohibition of any sexual activity before marriage.

In marriage, however, an important change takes place. Sexuality is still praised, but the spiritual dimension moves from the female to the male. In marriage, sexuality is for procreation alone, and women's nature is channeled strictly into reproduction. Women's greater emotional capacity, which was seen before marriage as attesting to her greater spirituality, is now seen to limit her effectiveness as a parent and to require direction and leadership from the man. Woman is "totally for reproduction" writes one;[29] women are less "reasonable" than men due to their "biological instincts and procreative function"[30] and need the firmer direction of men in marriage and in parenthood, due both to their "natural" docility and to their dependence. Recall here the contrast between marriage and courtship; in courtship it is the woman's (spiritual) responsibility to lead the man away from his physical desires, but in marriage it is the man's (spiritual) responsibility to lead the woman away from her limited focus on the material world, especially babies and children.

The "mysterious" nature of sexuality, given so much emphasis in courtship, now gives way to the "natural" orientation women have toward procreation and men's more "intellectual" approach to marriage and the world. Women are encouraged to respond with "total abandon" to their husbands' physical demands,[31] yet it is quite clear that men are the initiators and guides to sexual expression.[32] One of the most frequently mentioned aspects of femininity in marriage is "docility" or "receptivity." Women's "need for authority,"[33] the necessity of fathers to "direct" mothers,[34] woman's nature as "vessel,"[35] and, most important, woman's need to "accept" her femininity,[36] are all essential for a good Catholic marriage. One priest castigates the woman who "refuses to answer the call of self-immolation" that constitutes "a refusal of her very condition of woman."[37] This docility is also physical. Motherhood is the "metaphysical perfection of womanhood,"[38] and mothers are "more truly human than other women."[39] In fact, the "true woman," writes one, "unceasingly desires children."[40]

Men, in contrast, now become spiritual, and this is reflected in their bodies as well. Male "initiative," both intellectual and physical, is highlighted.[41] Men more easily separate the body and the mind, and thus have greater rational control.[42] Men are better philosophers, a skill which requires a high level of abstract thinking,[43] and are better at statistics.[44]

The rhetoric of this literature stresses the "worldly" superiority of the traditionally masculine occupations in emphasizing the importance of motherhood: "Ah! look with pity upon the so-called more important works of your husband—his political, economic, or financial affairs! The poor fellow! Have pity on him and surround him with your tenderness when he comes home in the evening: He has dealt only with lifeless matter, while you have labored over living flesh, over an eternal soul!"[45] Yet mothers are capable only of tending to the physical needs of their children and require fathers for their children's intellectual formation.[46] Men "present the family to the world and...safeguard its rights in the complexity of highly organized civilization."[47] Yet the man is cautioned so that his "physical and intellectual superiority" be "tempered by his vocation to be Christ."[48]

Frequently quoting *Casti Connubii*, these theologians argued for the "different but equal" position of men and women in marriage as ordained not only by civil law but as written by God in natural law. One author exclaims that "the Catholic Church glories in having been the first to proclaim the absolute equality of the sexes and in having drawn all the inferences from this principle,"[49] while repeatedly emphasizing that woman's nature is for reproduction.[50]

This "gendered" understanding of the body allowed Roman Catholic theology to defend itself against charges of being "anti" body, to incorporate sexuality into marriage in a way that did not challenge traditional sex roles, and to prohibit contraception. In short, the body was both a pivot and a bridge between the church and the world. As pivot, the body served as the stabilizing point for sexuality. For men, sexuality meant desire and physical pleasure; for women, it meant procreation and maternal care. Yet, sexual pleasure was clearly subordinated first to the woman's spirituality and then to her maternity. In fact, women's capacity for sexual pleasure was rarely addressed; when it was, it was dependent on male guidance. As bridge, the body functioned as the church's link to the material world. In sacramental marriage, the relationship of Christ to the church is reflected in the relationship of husband to wife. It is the body itself which is a pivot: the male body at first sexual, then spiritual: the female body at first spiritual, then sexual. This careful reconfiguring of the body and of sexuality accomplished a number of purposes. Theologians were able to appeal to the emerging social sciences as well as to the traditional teachings of the church with regard to human, and especially female, sexuality. This allowed Roman Catholic theology to maintain that it held a dialogical, not hostile, relationship with the secular world. The dual significance accorded the female body gave it a pivotal position so that it became one of the most important metaphors in the church's own self-understanding. Yet one new theology of marriage that clearly and unambiguously condemned contraception could not pass the test of orthodoxy. This controversy provides an important clue for understanding the social as well as biological function of the gendered body in marriage.

THE MEANING AND END OF MARRIAGE

In 1929, the German theologian Dietrich von Hildebrand published an essay on marriage (*Die Ehe*) and transformed discussion on marriage by introducing the language of *meaning* as distinct from that of *ends*.[51] According to von Hildebrand, the primary "meaning" of marriage is love and the community that is established by the partners: "Love is the primary *meaning* of marriage just as the birth of new human beings is its primary *end*. The social function of marriage and its importance for the State are something secondary and subordinate."[52] In developing his understanding of marriage, von Hildebrand stressed both its "subjective" and its "objective" nature as existing together. Marriage is "a reality in the objective order...a communion of objective validity...[which] persists as such regardless of the sentiments or attitudes of the partners."[53] The distinction von Hildebrand drew between meaning and end was not a hierarchical one, nor did he emphasize the greater importance of love over procreation. His intent, as he expressed it in the preface to his book, was to combat a "terrible anti-personalism" in the world that threatened the "nature and dignity of the person."[54]

In 1935, the German theologian Herbert Doms took up this distinction and developed it further. In his book *Marriage*, Doms not only emphasized the importance of mutual love in marriage but argued as well that the bond between husband and wife is "stronger" than that between parents and children.[55] Sex, he further argued, "is meant to serve husband and wife at least directly as much as it is meant to serve their children."[56] Doms coined the term *Zweieinigkeit*, "Two-in-Oneship," to describe the community of marriage as it is expressed both sexually and personally. Marriage requires the complete giving of one to another, a "constant ordination" to the other.[57] In this union, procreation is the consequence of this love, not its intrinsic meaning.

Doms's purpose was to define the meaning of marriage as related to but distinct from its final orientation. While this understanding of marriage was deliberately developed in nonscholastic language,[58] Doms's conclusions were not really new (he argued) although they could seem to be so.[59] Doms appealed to the biological sciences in making the point that not all sex acts result in procreation. Because of both the data from the sciences and a contemporary understanding of human relationships, he wrote that "marriage, then, fulfills its primary and secondary *purposes* through the realisation of its *meaning*....The constitution of marriage, the union of two persons, does not then consist in their subservience to a purpose outside themselves, *for* which they marry. It consists in the constant vital ordination of husband and wife to each other until they become one."[60] Therefore, Doms suggests that the language of primary and secondary ends in marriage be discarded, since "one is more important from one point of view, [and] from another point of view it is less so."[61]

Doms made it clear that this theology of marriage prohibited any form of contraception, since the ordination of husband and wife to each other "includes the body."[62] There needs to be a "physical realisation of the marital two-in-oneship"[63] since without it the union of the couple is incomplete. In ruling out any form of contraception for subjective and personal reasons, rather than from a natural law position, Doms intended to expand and develop the prevailing theology of marriage in terms more appropriate to the experience of married couples.[64] But the consequence was that the prohibition of contraception was based now not in natural law but in the free and mutual decision of the couple.

Doms's book aroused considerable controversy among moral theologians. John C. Ford, S.J., for example, argued that Doms failed to make a coherent distinction between "meaning" and "end." He further argued that Doms's interpretation of the secondary nature of the ends of mutual help and remedy for concupiscence was a reaction to an exaggerated emphasis on the part of the Catholic tradition on marriage's procreative end.[65] Doms's concern to include a more personalist orientation could in fact, Ford argued, be reconciled with the more traditional language.[66] Ford argued strongly for the "objective" meaning of marriage apart from the couple's feelings for each other, noting that a marriage remained a true marriage although it might be completely without love.[67]

In a subsequent issue of *Theological Studies*, Bernard Lonergan, S.J., distinguished between "horizontal" and "vertical" finality. Equating a concern for the community of love in marriage with vertical "finality," Lonergan concluded that "the horizontal finality to procreation and education of children is more essential than the vertical finality to personal advance in perfection; and if we take the terms 'primary' and 'secondary' in the sense of more and less essential, we have at once the traditional position that the primary end of marriage is the procreation and education of children."[68] The Vatican concurred with the defenders of the traditional position, and in 1944, Doms's understanding was found to be suspect because he failed to assert that the "primary end of marriage is the generation and nurture of offspring"; his interpretation, according to the Vatican, placed the "secondary ends" as "equally primary" with procreation.[69] Because of this, Doms's work was withdrawn from publication by the Holy Office.

As interpreted in recent literature, this action was taken because of Doms's reliance on personalist rather than scholastic concepts.[70] My suggestion here is that Doms's theology of marriage, in appealing to a non-scholastic conception of marriage and in using personalist ideas and language, was implicitly arguing against a hierarchical conception of marriage. In developing a theology of marriage based on mutuality, in bringing the subjective nature of marriage to the foreground, and in moving the physical and biological nature of marriage to the background, Doms challenged not only the traditional structure of marriage but also of the church, given the reliance on marriage as one of its fundamental metaphors. Yet this challenge was clearly not Doms's deliberate intent. Indeed, in the few places in his book where he speaks specifically of husband and wife, he resorts to very traditional conceptions of gender roles.[71] But a challenge to the natural law categories of marriage is an implicit challenge to traditional gender roles as they are construed theologically.

Yet given Pius XI's invitation to develop the more personal dimensions of marriage as well as its purpose for procreation, it is puzzling that Doms's understanding of marriage received such a severe response. Mackin and Cahill both suggest that Doms was proposing a covenantal-personalist model of marriage that challenged the power of the juridical-legalistic model that had been entrenched in the 1917 Code of Canon Law.[72] Both also note the increasing influence of "personalist" categories that eventually permitted the Vatican to incorporate the language of "unitive" and "procreative" as together comprising the significance of the marital act.[73] Mackin also points out the significance of a changed image of the church in the years immediately preceding Vatican II as helping to make possible a change in the church's understanding of marriage.[74] Here I would concur with Mackin, but I would add that this understanding is incomplete without a consideration of the language of gender. It is not only Doms's challenge to traditional scholastic language but also the absence of a gendered language of marriage that posed such a threat to the church in the 1930s and 1940s; this gendered language was central not only for marriage theology but also for the church's own self-understanding.

BODY AND GENDER: AN INTERPRETATION

To suggest that the roles of body and gender have such a significance requires going somewhat beyond the texts in question and moving into the realms of both ethical and feminist theory. First, it is clear that the understanding of the marriage relationship developed by Doms relies heavily on a "personalist" view of human nature, rather than on the traditional natural law basis. To argue that Doms's lack of a traditionally gendered understanding is significant requires that its importance in natural law be established. Second, to argue for the broader significance of gender roles requires that body and gender be interpreted within their social and historical frameworks. Here the work of feminist theory will prove helpful.

The place of natural law in Roman Catholic ethical theory is firmly established.[75] Although its centrality has been challenged in the twentieth century, certain basic themes remain key. Among these are its reliance on the observable data of nature and their metaphysical significance, its understanding of male and female biological and metaphysical complementarity as rooted in the natural order, and its valuation of procreation as the intrinsic meaning of sexual intercourse. This understanding of human nature and sexuality corresponds well to a juridical conception of marriage, as Mackin has pointed out,[76] since it establishes verifiable criteria for legitimacy. Most important for my purposes, a natural law approach to marriage establishes the fundamental importance of biological sex difference as both metaphysically and theologically crucial. But the shortcomings of natural law theory have received much attention in Catholic theology as well. In the early twentieth century, the centrality of natural law was challenged by a new paradigm, emphasizing the historical and subjective character of humanity. Natural law theory, with its reliance on a historical and, critics claimed, "physicalist" view of the person, failed to take into account the subjective and "personal" character of the human. Doms's project was clearly a part of this movement away from natural law categories. Because of his elevation of subjective criteria for marriage, biological difference no longer played a prominent role; Doms developed a theology of marriage that stressed subjective and personal dimensions of personhood. While there was no explicit challenge to gender roles, there was an implicit challenge, as human beings were understood in marriage and in other endeavors to be free, rational, historical, and dynamic. Gender was seldom mentioned, and the absolute difference between male and female was no longer central. The important issue of birth control became a decision of two free and mutual agents employing their consciences.

Marriage is, however, far more theologically significant than the relationship between men and women: it is one of the primary metaphors for the church, if not the most central. This tradition is ancient, going back to the covenant between God and Israel, described in marital terms, and to the Pauline conception of the Christ/church relationship. Throughout the pastoral and theological literature on marriage, the parallels between human marriage and the church are frequently drawn. My point here is that the redescription of human marriage in dynamic, subjective, and, most important, mutual terms constituted a challenge to the church's traditional self-conception. Only thirty years after the crisis of modernism, the basis for the hierarchical conception of the church remained fragile, and a challenge to the juridical conception of marriage (over which the church exercised sole authority) was also a challenge to the juridical model of the church. Gender relationships and sexuality were and are primary loci for establishing and maintaining power in the Roman Catholic church. The connection between sex and power has been established by such theorists as Michel Foucault;[77] my aim here is to extend this thesis to pre–Vatican II marriage theology.

In her book on gender relationships in Victorian England, Mary Poovey writes that "the location and organization of difference are crucial to a culture's self-representation and its distribution of power."[78] She further comments that, in nineteenth-century England, "so much depended on maintaining the oppositional, gendered organization of social relationships at midcentury that challenges to it seemed to threaten the most fundamental principles of the social and natural orders."[79] A similar dynamic was at work in Roman Catholic marriage theology. It represented a place where the church's hierarchical authority was not only exercised but, even more significantly, symbolized. References to the husband's "Christ-like" authority, the church's nuptial relation to God, and the woman's and the church's receptive and maternal character occur frequently in these texts.[80] When personalist, subjective criteria were proposed for marriage, the consequences for the exercise of church authority were all too clear, and the symbolic basis for this authority was undermined. Hence, despite Doms's repudiation of contraception, his theology was suspect because of the subjective basis for the marital relationship, not natural law. The hierarchical relationship of husband and wife was symbolic of the church's own hierarchical structure. The mas-

culine power of the clergy to lead and instruct the feminine and receptive laity was supported by this "gendered" theology of marriage.
Therefore, the "degendering" of this theology reconceived relationships
between men and women, clergy and laity: no longer hierarchical, but
free and mutual. The threat to church power was clear.

In more recent years, personalist language has made a successful
comeback in the official language of the church. Gender roles, however,
have remained unchanged. By the mid-1960s, when the Pastoral Constitution on the Church in the Modern World (*Gaudium et Spes*) was
being drafted, the critical chapter on marriage was the subject of intense
debate.[81] But because of prior discussions at the council on the nature
of the church and the adoption of different metaphors (such as "People
of God") for the church's self-understanding,[82] it became possible to
adopt language for marriage that stressed the personalist dimension
more than the juridical. Ultimately, an understanding of marriage, and
especially of the "marital act," emerged that defined it as *both* "unitive"
(i.e., an expression of mutual love) *and* "procreative,"[83] thus using both
natural law and personalist language. The symbolic basis for a mutual
and a hierarchical understanding of the church was thus established: the
church is the "People of God," *and* it is organized into a hierarchical
society.

Yet personalism failed to incorporate the experiences of women in
its theology of the person. This failure resulted in an androcentric conception of the person, which defines human nature in rational and hierarchical terms.[84] Recall that Doms saw no conflict in holding to traditional
gender roles alongside his conception of a subjective and mutual relationship. The "person" in personalism is male, and women remain the "other."
Thus a dual-nature anthropology (men and women as equal but different
and "essentially complementary") came to coexist alongside a single-
nature anthropology ("man"—human beings—as free, rational, and subjective creatures). As employed in Roman Catholic marriage theology
since Vatican II, personalism has proven to be inadequate in addressing
the concerns of women, and ultimately inadequate for a theology of marriage. In her recent article on sexual ethics, Cahill concludes that "personalism in sexual ethics coincides with the modern turn to the perspective of
the acting subject. It also reflects a more general phenomenological turn
in natural-law thinking. Hence personalism implies the question of the

evaluation of the subject's 'experience,' which is always partial and socially conditioned."[85] I would concur with Cahill that personalism, as used in official Roman Catholic sexual ethics, remains within the horizon of natural law thinking. Personalist theory, however, has also been developed by theologians such as Bernard Häring to criticize the natural law tradition.[86] But the appropriation of personalism by the natural law tradition permits personalism to assume a traditional configuration of gender differences, albeit on a "subjective" rather than "natural" basis.

In a larger sense, however, the changes wrought by the personalist turn are irrevocable. The conception of a historical, dynamic, relational self developed by the personalist thinkers has changed the way in which marriage is conceived and adjudicated within the church, and despite movements to the contrary, this direction is not likely to change. While failing to address the experiences of women, and holding a conception of the person and history that has potentially dangerous implications for the human relationship with the natural world,[87] the personalist turn has changed the church's self-definition in such a way as to demand a reconsideration of the roles of women and of the laity. The metaphor of Christ the Bridegroom with his Spotless Bride the Church reflects neither the marital nor the clergy/lay relationship for many Catholics. Doms's effort in the 1930s began a major shift by undermining body and gender categories, and contemporary feminist theology is continuing this challenge.

CONCLUSION

It is clear that the body's function in determining biological, social, and theological roles in Roman Catholic marriage theology has been a significant one. The conferral of sacramental status on marriage is intended to underscore the sacrality of the natural order and especially of human sexuality.[88] But the body's symbolic role in human relationships and in society has only recently begun to be recognized.[89] In analyzing the role of the body and gender relationships in this crucial time in Catholic theology, my goal has been to understand their functions within and apart from the rhetoric of mystery which has surrounded them.

The female body served in miniature the purpose that the church understood itself to have: a symbol of the sacred within the secular, the spotless and virginal Bride within the profane world. Yet the church, like the body, also possessed natural functions such as governing and producing. These were symbolized in male and female bodies and were sharply differentiated, as were these functions within the church itself between clergy and laity. The personalist view of marriage, while based on an androcentric conception of the self, reinterpreted the meaning of marriage as the mutual self-giving of *persons* and, thus, challenged the theological significance of male and female bodies. It also implicitly (though not explicitly) challenged the traditional configuration of gender relationships and by analogy threatened the hierarchical stability of the church. It is worth noting that one of the reasons given in *Humanae Vitae* for rejecting the (majority) opinion that recommended the approval of contraceptives was the threat to the authority of the church.[90]

The women's movement in the late twentieth century, by reinterpreting the body from the perspective of women's own experience, has revealed the social and political character of the body and of gender roles. This is no less true for religious institutions, as my analysis has tried to show. Roman Catholicism's continual emphasis on sexual morality as the litmus test of orthodoxy can be interpreted as indicating the privatization of religion into the categories of the bourgeois, as Johannes Metz has argued.[91] It can also be seen, as I suggest here, as undergirding a mystical marriage between Christ (as represented by the clergy) and the church (as represented by the laity): a marriage in which the docile and feminized laity are directed by the strong and masculine hierarchy. That these marriages face a rocky and uncertain future should come as no surprise to anyone.

Notes

1. See Theodore Mackin, S.J., *What Is Marriage?* (New York: Paulist, 1982), pp. 225–47, for a thorough discussion of this debate.

2. Lisa Sowle Cahill, "Catholic Sexual Ethics and the Dignity of the Person: A Double Message," *Theological Studies* 50, no. 2 (June 1989): 122.

3. See Mackin for a helpful survey of the history leading up to the 1917 formulation.

4. Pope Pius XI, *Casti Connubii* (Rome, 1930), no. 24, quoted in Mackin, p. 217.

5. As characterized by Mackin, p. 218.

6. See John A. Gallagher, *Time Past, Time Future: An Historical Study of Roman Catholic Moral Theology* (New York: Paulist, 1990).

7. Cahill, p. 121.

8. See, e.g., E. C. Messenger, *Two in One Flesh. Part One: An Introduction to Sex and Marriage* (Westminster, Md.: Newman, 1948), p. vii; Eugene S. Geissler, *The Meaning of Marriage* (Notre Dame, Ind.: Fides, 1962), p. 34; Pierre Dufoyer, *Maternity: A Baby Is Born*, translated and adapted by David M. Murphy (Staten Island, N.Y.: Alba House, 1964), p. v; A. H. Clemens, "What Our Catholic Couples Need to Know," in *The Cana Conference: Proceedings of the Chicago Archdiocese Study Week, 1949* (Chicago: Cana Conference, 1950), pp. 109–11. The Cana Conference and Christian Family Movements deserve a separate study of their own. My point here is to show these issues were discussed across the board.

9. See Dietrich von Hildebrand, *In Defense of Purity: An Analysis of the Catholic Ideals of Purity and Virginity* (New York: Sheed & Ward, 1940), p. 19; *Man and Woman* (Chicago: Franciscan Herald, 1966), pp. 13–15; T. W. Burke, *The Gold Ring: God's Pattern for Perfect Marriage* (New York: David McKay, 1961), p. 99. Nearly all of the pastoral manuals contained some discussion of male/female differences.

10. Burke, p. 98.

11. John R. Cavanagh, "Psychological Differences in Men and Women," in *Christian Marriage: Some Contemporary Problems*, ed. Vincent J. Nugent, C.M. (Jamaica, N.Y.: St. John's University Press, 1961), p. 26.

12. Geissler, p. 17.

13. Ibid., p. 27.

14. P. Leclercq, *Marriage and the Family* (Louvain, 1947), p. 296.

15. Ibid.

16. Cavanaugh, p. 30.

17. James Kelly, *Love and Marriage* (Dublin: Clonmere & Reynolds, 1957), p. 27.

18. Messenger, p. viii. Chapter 2 is entitled "The Supposed Indecency of the Organs of Evacuation and of Sex"; that chapter concludes by referring to the "*complete*" and "*perfect*" human nature of Jesus (emphasis in the original): "He could not have assumed to his Divine Person any part or organ or function which is filthy or impure" (p. 19). Yet Messenger notes that "not all of the parts of the Sacred Humanity of Christ are suitable as objects of devotion" (p. 10).

19. Dufoyer (n. 8 above), p. v.

20. Geissler (n. 8 above), p. 34.

21. Burke (n. 9 above), p. 9.

22. Jean de Fabregues, *Christian Marriage*, trans. Rosemary Haughton (New York: Hawthorne, 1959), p. 23.

23. Marc Oraison, *Union in Marital Love: Its Physical and Spiritual Foundations*, trans. André Humbert (New York: Macmillan, 1958), p. 66.

24. von Hildebrand, *Defense of Purity* (n. 9 above), p. 17.

25. Daniel Planque, *The Christian Couple: A Guide to Marriage*, trans. Martin and Patricia McLaughlin (Notre Dame, Ind.: Fides, 1963), p. 107.

26. Kelly, pp. 27–28.

27. Ibid., pp. 32–33.

28. See, e.g., Oraison, pp. 84 ff., on "self-abuse"; pp. 81–90 concern male adolescent sexuality; pp. 90–91 (about one and a half pages) concern female adolescent sexuality, and "self-abuse" is not mentioned. The problem for adolescent girls is "self-centeredness" and rejection of their femininity (p. 91).

29. Leclercq (n. 14 above), pp. 298–99. This is echoed by Cavanagh, Dufoyer, Fabregues, and also Herbert Doms, *The Meaning of Marriage*, trans. George Sayer (New York: Sheed & Ward, 1939). Doms's work is treated in detail below.

30. Cavanagh (n. 11 above), pp. 28–30.

31. Planque, p. 107.

32. Ibid., pp. 105–7.

33. Geissler (n. 8 above), p. 26.

34. Dufoyer (n. 8 above), p. 100; on the father: "His intervention will often be desirable to direct the mother in her task of teaching. Following her impulses of the moment, letting herself be sidetracked by preoccupations of every sort, she too often neglects to enforce strictly the child's schedule....She is easily led by an excess of tenderness to spoil her child...to fondle him too much for the slightest hurt" (ibid.).

35. Fabregues (n. 35 above), p. 29.

36. Oraison (n. 23 above), p. 53.

37. P. Parrain, "The Personality of Woman," in *Marriage Is Holy*, ed. H. Caffarel, trans. Bernard Murchland, C.S.C. (Chicago: Fides, 1957), p. 80.

38. Doms, p. 194.

39. Dufoyer, pp. 98–99. Mothers are also "more beautiful" than women without children (who are "prone to fibrous tumours" [p. 95]); Burke (n. 9 above) writes that the "divine plan" calls for six or eight children per marriage (p. 133).

40. Dufoyer, p. 93.

41. Oraison, p. 53.

42. Leclercq (n. 14 above), p. 296.

43. Burke, p. 98.

44. Clemens (n. 8 above), p. 11. Dr. Clemens does make the point that there are exceptions and mentions a "particular nun" who "had an interesting mind and the faculty of making statistics interesting" (ibid.).

45. Dufoyer (n. 8 above), p. 98.

46. Ibid., p. 102.

47. Burke, p. 99.

48. Ibid.

49. Leclercq, p. 312.

50. Ibid., pp. 198–99.

51. See Mackin (n. 1 above), p. 226, on von Hildebrand (no publisher indicated). The book was translated into English as *Marriage* (New York: Longmans, Green, 1942). No translator is indicated.

52. von Hildebrand, *Marriage*, p. 4.

53. Ibid., p. 17.

54. Ibid., p. v.

55. Doms (n. 29 above), p. 7. Doms's book was originally published in German as *Von Sinn und Zweck der Ehe* (Breslau: Ostdeutsche Verlagsanstalt, 1935). A number of commentators relied on the French translation, *Du Sens et de la Fin du Mariage* (Paris: Desclee de Brouwer, 1937).

56. Ibid., p. 36 (English translation).

57. Ibid., pp. 57–58.

58. Ibid., p. xxi.

59. Ibid., p. xxiii.

60. Ibid., p. 87.

61. Ibid., p. 88.

62. Ibid., p. 106.

63. Ibid., p. 168.

64. "One cannot help but asking whether St. Thomas does not here look at the relationship of man and woman very much from the outside!" (ibid., p. 46).

65. John C. Ford, S.J., "Marriage: Its Meaning and Purposes," *Theological Studies* 3 (1942): 353–54.

66. Ibid., p. 352.

67. See ibid., p. 348: "Even a marriage in which there is no mutual help, no life in common, hatred instead of love, and complete separation, both bodily and spiritually, remains a true marriage in the sense that the essence of marriage is still there; that is, the partners are still married and in virtue of the essential marriage bond they are still bound to one another."

68. Bernard J. F. Lonergan, S.J., "Finality, Love, Marriage," *Theological Studies* 4 (1943): 507.

69. Mackin (n. 1 above), p. 235.

70. See ibid., pp. 235 ff.: "The challenge to the morality of inherent ends of the physical act of intercourse was a challenge to an entire moral system"; Cahill (n. 2 above), pp. 126–27. It is certainly the case that both Ford and Lonergan appeal to traditional scholastic language and that *Humani Generis*

(*HG*) in 1950 reiterated the importance of scholastic methodology. Compare *HG*, no. 31.

71. Doms (n. 29 above), pp. 13, 18, 163, 194.

72. Compare n. 73 below. A juridical mode defines marriage in empirical ways, i.e., consummation and mutual consent; a covenantal model uses more subjective criteria, not subject to empirical verification.

73. See Cahill, pp. 120–21.

74. Mackin, pp. 241 ff.

75. For a helpful overview of the role of natural law in Roman Catholic ethics, see James M. Gustafson, *Protestant and Roman Catholic Ethics* (Chicago: University of Chicago Press, 1978).

76. See Mackin, pp. 239–45.

77. Michel Foucault, *The History of Sexuality*, 3 vols., trans. Robert Hurley (New York: Vintage Books, 1980, 1985, 1986).

78. Mary Poovey, *Uneven Developments: The Ideological Work of Gender in Mid-Victorian England* (Chicago: University of Chicago Press, 1988), p. 199. I am grateful to Micael Clarke for bringing this book to my attention.

79. Ibid.

80. Geissler (n. 8 above), p. 26; Burke (n. 9 above), p. xiii, Fabregues (n. 22 above), p. 27.

81. See Mackin (n. 1 above), pp. 248–74, for a very helpful discussion of this.

82. "People of God" became the primary metaphor for the church in *Lumen Gentium*, the dogmatic (as distinct from pastoral) constitution on the church, and the placement of the chapters in that document with "The People of God" (chap. 2) *preceding* "The Church Is Hierarchical" (chap. 3) aroused much debate. See Austin Flannery, O.P., *Vatican Council II: The Conciliar and Post-conciliar Documents* (Collegeville, Minn.: Liturgical Press, 1975).

83. See Pope Paul VI, *Humanae Vitae* (Rome, 1968), nos. 4, 6.

84. One of the primary emphases of feminism is its criticism of rationalism, especially Western Enlightenment rationalism, as the primary defining character-istic of human beings. This constitutes a major challenge to Western philosophical conceptions of the person. For a recent treatment, see Alison M. Jaggar and Susan R. Bordo, eds., *Gender/Body/Knowledge: Feminist Reconstructions of Being and Knowing* (New Brunswick, N.J.: Rutgers University Press, 1989). Similarly, fem-inism rejects a hierarchical conception of society. See Rosemary Radford Ruether, *Sexism and God-Talk: Toward a Feminist Theology* (Boston: Beacon, 1983).

85. Cahill (n. 2 above), p. 150.

86. See Bernard Häring, *The Law of Christ*, 3 vols., translated by Edwin G. Kaiser from the 5th German ed. (Paramus, N.J.: Newman Press, 1966).

87. See William C. French, "Transformationist and Creation-Centered Paradigms in Recent Catholic Thought," *Journal of Religion* 70, no. 1 (January 1990): 48–72, esp. 57–61.

88. This is maintained in every Roman Catholic treatment of marriage. See Edward Schillebeeckx's classic *Marriage: Human Reality and Saving Mystery*, trans. N. D. Smith (New York: Sheed & Ward, 1965). For a more recent treatment, see Michael G. Lawler, *Symbol and Sacrament: A Contemporary Sacramental Theology* (New York: Paulist, 1987).

89. Although much attention has been focused on it recently, e.g., the work of Peter Brown, *The Body and Society: Men, Women and Sexual Renunciation in Early Christianity* (New York: Columbia University Press, 1988); Margaret Miles, *Fullness of Life: Historical Foundations for a New Asceticism* (Philadelphia: Westminster, 1981); Carolyn Walker Bynum, *Holy Feast and Holy Fast: The Religious Significance of Food to Medieval Women* (Berkeley and Los Angeles: University of California Press, 1987).

90. Paul VI, *Humanae Vitae,* n. 6.

91. See Johannes B. Metz, *The Emergent Church: The Future of Christianity in a Postbourgeois World*, trans. Peter Mann (New York: Crossroad, 1981).

5. The Second Vatican Council and *Humanae Vitae*

Theodore Mackin

This chapter first appeared in Theodore Mackin, *The Marital Sacrament* (New York: Paulist, 1989).

One of the most valuable accomplishments of the Second Vatican Council's statement on marriage in *Gaudium et spes*[1] was to gather into a single declaration the wealth of insight and interpretation that had grown up in the Church during the preceding three decades. The council's theological commission, chaired by Cardinal Alfredo Ottaviani, had prepared a document on marriage that in attitude and in form imitated Pius IX's *Syllabus Errorum*. It singled out and condemned the abuses of marriage that the commission deemed the most widespread and grievous, with divorce and contraceptive intercourse principal among them. In its positive parts it reaffirmed the contractual nature of marriage generally and repeated the juridicized theology of the sacrament. It proved so unsatisfactory to the cardinals of the council's preparatory commission that they rejected it in its entirety. The chapter on marriage in *Gaudium et spes* is the product of discussion, composition and argumentation that began only in the council's second year (1963) and came to a climax in its final session during October, November and December of 1965.

The bishops' interpretation of marriage in *Gaudium et spes* was their own. They did not seek to consolidate accepted teaching in detail by repeating earlier magisterial statements. They innovated at crucial points, even to the extent of putting in abeyance Catholic doctrine that had been taught for centuries. The non-doctrinal innovation was their refusal to consider marriage the human relationship as a contract. Nowhere in this declaration does the noun "contract" or the verb "to contract" appear. In view of the centuries-old, universal and taken-for-granted perception of marriage by Catholic authorities as a contract, this omission cannot have been accidental.

The point of doctrine that was called into question was that among the ends natural and inherent to marriage procreation is primary. When interpreting the place of procreation in marriage the bishops did not deny that it is a natural and inherent end thereof. Their exact phrasing of the matter was, in context, "Marriage and marital love are by nature oriented to the begetting and nurture of children. Children are the most valuable gift of marriage....Hence, while not making the other ends of marriage of less value, the true conduct of marital love and the entire meaning of family life that comes from it have this goal, that the spouses be willing to co-work courageously with the love of the Creator and Savior...."[2]

From Augustine's *De conjugiis adulterinis* at the beginning of the fifth century, in which he wrote, "Therefore the propagation of children is the first, the natural and the principal purpose of marriage," through its enshrinement in Canon 1013 of the 1917 Code of Canon Law, this primacy of procreation had been confirmed as recently as October 29, 1951, by Pius XII in his discourse to the Association of Italian Catholic Obstetricians. It is understandable that this calling back of the doctrine can have been done only after long and often impassioned debate in the council.[3]

It is important to note the contextual anxiety of the bishops' statement. By this I mean the real-life concerns that prompted their drafting it and in large measure guided their thinking and their formulation of it. Unlike Leo XIII's *Arcanum divinae sapientiae* and Pius XI's *Casti connubii*, the thematic worry of *Gaudium et spes* was not about any deliberate secularist denigration of the holiness of marriage nor about sins committed by the married. It was about the fragility of family life and of marital love under the duress of economic and political forces that attack stable society at every point. Modern warfare and its byproduct of millions of poverty-stricken refugees and homeless children was only the most obvious such force. It would not be far wide of the mark to read the entire document as a plea for the survival of marriage in the sense of family, and counsel for a strategy of such survival.

So far from being even a précis of the theology of the sacrament, the declaration turns to the sacrament only in a kind of second intention. Probably because they addressed their words not only to Christians but to all persons concerned about the well-being of marriage, the bishops did not make the sacramentality of Christian marriage the theme and guide of their discourse. Nevertheless what they did say contributed richly to understanding the sacrament in the same way that Pius XII's discourses had done so. Again, a principle of sacramental theology makes clear why this is so. Every sacrament has as one of its two major components a creaturely, human matrix—as washing with water is the matrix of baptism. For the marital sacrament the human marital relationship is the matrix. Therefore the bishops' interpretation of marriage was by small indirection an interpretation of the sacrament.

It is helpful to distinguish their interpretation into discrete parts thereof and to examine them in sequence: the nature of marriage itself, the act by which a man and woman create their marriage, and the love that is native to marriage. Along the way we will take note of the place for the sacrament that the bishops saw in each of these.

GAUDIUM ET SPES AND THE NATURE OF MARRIAGE

The first designation of marriage is in the introductory paragraph of the chapter. It is that a marriage is a community of love (*communitas amoris*).[4] It is next called an intimate partnership of life and of marital love (*intima communitas vitae et amoris coniugalis*).[5] It is a sacred bond (*vinculum sacrum*), a marital covenant (*foedus coniugale*), the mutual gift of two persons (*mutua duarum personarum donatio*),[6] a Christian vocation (*vocatio christiana*), an unbreakable covenant (*foedus indissolubile*).[7]

The bishops identified the act by which a man and a woman create their marriage consistently with their refusal to continue designating marriage itself as a contract. They did not call this act a contractual exchange. They called it, as a human act, a personal consent by which the spouses give themselves over to and accept one another (*actus humanus quo coniuges sese mutuo tradunt atque accipiunt*).[8] The term "human act" is not included casually. In scholastic moral philosophy an *actus humanus*—in contradistinction to an *actus hominis*, "the act of a human being"—designates conduct which is the product of reason and will. It involves an informed and free decision. It negates any suggestion that persons can be put into marriage or lured into it in ways that override their freedom. The term "give over" translates the Latin verb *tradere*. Predicated of the self in this context it bespeaks a handing over of one's person. This interpretation is refined a few paragraphs later where the partners are said to create their marriage by making gifts to one another of their persons (*mutua duarum personarum donatio*).[9] The bishops add that this mutual giving over of the self need not end with the act that creates the marriage, and ought not. Where the spouses love one another with love that is genuinely marital, they continue to make gifts of their persons to one another freely and gladly, and with tender affection (*talis amor...coniuges ad liberum et mutuum sui ipsius donum, tenero affectu et opera probatum, conducit*).[10]

That tells something of the nature and role of the love that the bishops see as native to marriage. To begin with, its source is God's love for the spouses. It is covenantal love, one whose substance is reciprocal commitment. Its model is the love union of Christ and the Church. This double-linked love—of God for the spouses and of the spouses for one another—is both the point of entry of the sacrament into their marriage and its place of residence there: "For as in olden times God came to his people in a covenant of love and fidelity [this was the corporate sacrament in which the people Israel lived], so now the savior of men and the spouse of the Church comes to Christian spouses through the sacrament of marriage."[11] To make the historically resonating point that the sacrament is not limited to the religious wedding ceremony, the bishops add immediately, "What is more, Christ stays with the couple. And just as he loved the Church and gave his life for her, so also the spouses by their mutual self-giving may love one another with perpetual fidelity."[12] This means only secondarily that the Christ-Church love relationship is a model for the spouses. It means first that Christ's indwelling in their relationship lends them the strength to love with a love like this.

The insight continues: "The love natural to marriage [*germanus amor coniugalis*] is taken up into the divine love [is joined with it as its instrument] and is there enriched and ruled by the redeeming power of Christ and the saving action of the Church." The effect of this is to lead the husband and wife powerfully to God and to strengthen them in their vocation as parents.[13]

The familiarity of this theological language ought not hide a striking contrast in it with authoritative Catholic statements of past centuries. By the end of the high middle ages the Church's teachers, official and unofficial, were agreed that the sacrament in marriage makes it a means of gracing the spouses. But the gracing they acknowledged was an attenuated kind. It was not "primary grace," not the joining in personal union with God. It was secondary, helping, "actual" grace—the strength to resist temptation to adultery and to resist misuse of sexuality within one's marriage, the wisdom and strength to bring up one's children in Christian goodness.

Gaudium et spes here breaks out of that self-limitation. Clearly it implies that in and by the sacrament the spouses are brought into personal union with God in Christ, or their union there is intensified by it. The clauses that tell this are "...so now the savior...comes to Christian spouses through the sacrament of marriage"; "Christ stays with the couple"; "the love natural to marriage is taken up into the divine love and is there enriched"; "their love can lead them powerfully to God."

The helping function of the grace of the sacrament is affirmed, but it is presented as the effect of the spouses' union with God in Christ.

> Through this sacrament the spouses are penetrated with the spirit of Christ as they fulfill their marital and family obligations. This spirit suffuses their whole life with faith, hope and charity. Thus they grow continually each in his and her perfection as well as in mutual holiness.[14]

This sacramentality exists not only in the one-to-one union of the spouses but in their families as well. The family is the sacrament grown to fullness. Not until the bishops say this do they bring into play the traditional imaging role of the sacrament in marriage. Apparently their intent is to say that the marriage is this image—or is the image most effectively—when it becomes a family.

> Hence the family, because it arises from marriage, which is an image of the covenant of love of Christ and the Church, and a participation in this covenant, will disclose to all the

living presence of the Savior in the world, as well as show also the authentic nature of the Church.[15]

Gaudium et spes devotes an entire section (no. 49) to a descriptive definition of this marital love, and labels the section appropriately: *De amore coniugali*. One may guess why it does so. It has already called marriage a covenant of love. But there are many kinds of love in human relationships, some of them constructive, some destructive. The bishops want to make clear the love they deem marital—marital, again, as the matrix of the sacrament.

They begin by pointing out that the Jewish and Christian scriptures urge the centrality of love in marriage. They also do what centuries of their forebears had refused or had feared to do: they named passages in the Song of Solomon as sources of this urging.[16] How radically they have freed themselves from the past is evident in their holding that the love described in these passages is marital love, and in implying thereby that it is this love that animates the matrix of the sacrament. The passages are 1:2–3 ("Let her kiss me with the kiss of her mouth! More delightful is your love than wine"); 1:16 ("Ah, you are beautiful, my lover—Yes, you are lovely"); 4:16 ("Let my lover come to his garden and eat its choice fruits"); 5:1 ("I have come to my garden, my sister, my bride…"); 7:8–14 (these are the verses that describe in detail the girl's physical beauty).

The bishops describe marital love as fully and authentically (*eminenter*) human. It involves the entire person and seeks the good of the entire person. It is guided and directed to the partner by free decision, by an act of the will. Therefore it makes all bodily expressions of affection fully human—can make them manifestations of marital friendship. It is far from spontaneous, instinctive erotic response, which is by nature self-gratifying and temporary. This love leads to and expresses itself in the spouses' free and willing gifting of themselves to one another in tender and bodily expressions of affection. It suffuses all their selves; it grows continually. It is faithful, constant against all its enemies both inside the souls of the spouses and outside them. It wants to last for the spouses' lifetime together and does so.[17]

The bishops then make a point that is simultaneously psychological, moral and theological, and is a formal rebuff to eighteen centuries of Christian fear and suspicion of sexuality. They identify the conduct in which the exquisite marital love they have described is most typically and fully expressed. This is the spouses' lovemaking completed in sexual intercourse.

> This love is expressed most clearly and comes to its fullness in the conduct that is proper to marriage. The acts by which spouses come together intimately and chastely are good and honorable. Expressed in a way that is authentically human they manifest the spouses' mutual self-giving and impel them to it—the self-giving by which they enrich one another with joyful and grateful wills.[18]

Finally, to return to an earlier element of marital love, by nature it is oriented to children and desires them. In this it strives to co-work with God in his love of creation—in his love to create. By loving in this way the spouses not only co-work with his love, which is essentially creative, but they also manifest its nature to the world. By having children and nurturing them they interpret the nature of God's love correctly to the world.

Note what *Gaudium et spes* has done to a centuries-old thesis in the theology of the sacraments. That thesis said that God made marriage a sacrament at the beginning of history when he created the first human beings as an image—not as images—of himself; when for this imaging he made them man and woman; when he revealed the reason for and used their sexually correlated natures to extend his creation, "to increase and multiply and fill the earth"; when he gave the woman to the man and they joined and became one flesh. That was the primordial sacrament, even before the time of the law of Moses, and centuries before the coming of Christ. But now the bishops say that this essentially creative love of God is the love at work in the marital sacrament in the new law of Christ. Generations of fathers and theologians had insisted that God's love in the latter sacrament is medicinal for and controlling of men's and women's wounded sexuality. But here the bishops say that this love in the new sacrament is principally fertile and creative. In short, family is the filled-out sacrament of marriage—not widowhood, as Tertullian in the morning of Christian history and Pius XII a generation ago would have it.

Paul VI's Encyclical Letter *Humanae Vitae*

It is commonly known that Pope Paul's encyclical letter, *Humanae vitae*, of July 25, 1968, was the completion of a task left over by the Second Vatican Council.[19] The council left it not unfinished, because the bishops never took it up, but left it untouched because Paul took it off the council's agenda. He reserved to himself the completion of the task. This was the reexamination of the Catholic Church's proscriptive moral judgment on artificial control of human fertility. Paul began action in the matter by announcing, on June 23, 1964, between the council's second and third sessions, his expansion of the Pontifical Study Commission on Population Control that his predecessor, John XXIII, had established. The commission was to study the matter and to report its recommendation to him. It did so, and recommended in the spring of 1966 a change toward mitigation of the proscription of artificial birth control. Paul's rejection of this recommendation is well known, as is his renewal of the proscription. This is set forth in *Humanae vitae*.[20]

Somewhat like his predecessors, Pius XI and Pius XII, Paul drew his condemnation of artificial limitation of birth from the nature of marriage. They had said that it contradicts marriage's primary end. But in the meantime, as we have seen, the bishops of Vatican II had voided the major premise of their moral logic that produces this conclusion, had done so by taking away the primacy of procreation among marriage's ends. Consequently Paul had to begin his moral logic with a different premise.

He found this premise in the same moral-anthropological territory in which many Catholic scholars had claimed reasons for the permissibility of contraceptive intercourse. They had drawn this permissibility from the demands of marital love and of responsible parenthood. In order to join issue with them Paul began *Humanae vitae* by setting out his own understanding of "these two great realities of married life." He drew explicitly from *Gaudium et spes* to do this.[21] As its bishop-authors had done, he claimed that for men and women the true source of their marital love is God's love. By this he did not mean primarily that God's love is the model for theirs. He meant something more practical.

> Conjugal love reveals its true nature and nobility when it is considered in its authentic origin, God, who is love....Marriage is

not, then the effect of chance or the product of evolution or of unconscious forces; it is the wise institution of the Creator to realize in mankind his design of love.[22]

Unlike his predecessors over the centuries Paul does not draw on Genesis 1 and 2 as factual sources in order to explain how God's love has produced marriage and how it produces love in spouses. Nevertheless as the bishops of Vatican II did, he insists that God is the source of the spouses' marital love because he is active in their lives—active by his love that is essentially creative, essentially fruitful. This is a point essential to the teaching of *Gaudium et spes* and seems to be taken directly from it. But Paul draws a conclusion from it that the bishops did not. He says, or at least implies, that *because* God's love at work in the spouses' lives is essentially fruitful, their loves too must be fruitful. His love works to make theirs like his. If they keep it from being so, two consequences follow: Their love is not marital, but is something other and less—stunted, self-serving, private. And the spouses have contradicted God's action in their lives. This is in essence sinful.

This essentiality of fertility to marital love is the major premise of the moral logic Paul uses to warrant his condemnation of all artificial limiting of fertility. He expands the assertion of this essentiality into a complex principle. It is a principle about sexual intercourse within marriage. (Whether it is about intercourse prescinding from marriage is aside from Paul's point here.) He makes for it the claim he has made about marital love itself. It has two essential and inherent meanings—not ends, as had been said for centuries by the Catholic authorities, but meanings (not *fines* but *sensus*). These meanings are the procreative and the unitive. They are inseparable—inseparable in the sense that an act of intercourse in marriage cannot have one without the other. It either has both or it has neither.

To claim this is not to claim a moral principle. It is to assert a fact of human psychology. Set out fully it means that no matter the partners' intention and motivation, if they do not leave their act open to the possibility of conception, it is not unitive—it is not an act of love that is marital. Reciprocally, if the act is not unitive, neither is it truly procreative. It is only reproductive. The reason for this last conclusion is unstated at this point but hovers near: God's creation is in essence a loving act.

That teaching ["...that each and every marital act must remain open to the transmission of life"]...is founded upon the inseparable connection, willed by God and unable to be broken by man on his own initiative, between the two meanings of the conjugal act: the unitive meaning and the procreative meaning. Indeed, by its intimate structure, the conjugal act, while most closely uniting husband and wife, capacitates them for the generation of new lives, according to laws inscribed in the very being of man and of woman. By safeguarding both these essential aspects, the unitive and the procreative, the conjugal act preserves in its fullness the sense or meaning of true mutual love and its ordination toward man's most high calling to parenthood....[23]

Because he has made this claim for sexual intercourse within marriage Paul has by implication made it for marriage itself. The two meanings, unitive and procreative, are essential to it and inseparable from it. If these two characteristics are not found within a relationship, at least in intention, it is not a marriage. How the procreative meaning or intention could be in the relationship of a couple marrying after the woman's menopause, or where either is sterile for any reason, is not clear.[24]

The encyclical is not about the sacramentality of Christian marriages since it is about marriage universally and a moral demand assumed to be in it universally. But Paul does not pass the sacrament by. His first mention of it is succinct but traditional: "For baptized persons, moreover, marriage invests the dignity of a sacramental sign of grace, inasmuch as it represents the union of Christ and the Church."[25] His second and slightly longer reference to it contains both doctrine and moral-ascetical counsel. It incorporates his assumption about the inseparability of the procreative and the unitive meanings of intercourse in marriage. It gives to the sacrament the work of manifesting this inseparability—gives it because this inseparability is a demand of God's love at work in the Christian spouses' union, and because this is the work of the sacrament, to manifest God's work in this union.

Christian married couples…must remember that their Christian vocation, which began at baptism, is further specified and reinforced by the sacrament of matrimony.

By it husband and wife are strengthened and, as it were, consecrated for the faithful accomplishment of their proper duties, for the carrying out of their proper vocation even to perfection, and the Christian witness which is proper to them before the whole world. To them the Lord entrusts the task of making visible to men the holiness and sweetness of the law which unites the mutual love of husband and wife with their cooperation with the love of God the author of human life.[26]

It goes without saying that the accuracy of this theology of the sacrament is in direct proportion to the accuracy of Paul's assumption that in marital intercourse the unitive and the procreative meanings are inseparable.

But *Humanae vitae*'s fullest contribution to the theology of the sacrament is of the same indirect kind as that of *Gaudium et spes*. This is by its enrichment of the sacrament's matrix. The encyclical does this by detailing the traits of marital love, and this it does to complete its explanation of the theological principle that because God has designed this love according to the model of his own love, and works in and through human marital love, it must have the same characteristics as his. The description of the first characteristic almost duplicates the thought of *Gaudium et spes*. It shares the latter's negative purpose, which is to gainsay the common persuasion in the Western world that the love germane to marriage is romantic infatuation or an emotional involvement closely akin to it.

This love is first of all fully *human* [italics in the original], that is to say, of the senses and the spirit at the same time. It is not then, a simple transport of instinct and sentiment, but also, and principally, an act of the free will, intended to endure and to grow by means of the joys and sorrows of daily life, in such a way that husband and wife become one only heart and one only soul, and together attain their human perfection.[27]

The second characteristic is almost equally a duplication of the descriptive definition in *Gaudium et spes*. It rejects in passing what the ancients, Aristotle among them, had said, that full and perfect friendship is less possible between a man and a woman because of the inferiority in her of the virtues needed for friendship, whereas full friendship calls for equality of persons.[28] *Humanae vitae* rejects this in saying that it is characteristic of marital love that husbands and wives share everything, that they make gifts of their persons to one another.

The third characteristic of marital love is the most briefly stated. "Again, this love is faithful and exclusive until death."[29] A supporting paragraph adds one of the few instances in the encyclical of fact that could be gathered only inductively: "The example of so many married persons down through the centuries shows not only that fidelity is according to the nature of marriage but also that it is a source of profound and lasting happiness."

The final characteristic that Paul finds in marital love belongs to the thesis of his letter and is the premise of its moral argument. It is that this love is fruitful. But here he adds presumably another point of psychological information, one that can be verified only by experience, namely that marital love cannot attain its full realization if confined within the husband-wife relationship.

> And finally this love is *fecund*, for it is not exhausted by the communion between husband and wife, but is destined to continue, raising up new lives....[30]

This too must have consequences for the marital love in the marriages of the infertile—for whom, we recall, Paul has left the way to marriage entirely open.

...[Elsewhere] I suggested that of all Pope Paul's predecessors (but now the bishops of Vatican II excepted) the German pantheistic idealist, Georg W. F. Hegel, came closest to understanding marriage as Paul would understand it a century and a half later. He said that as couples transcend the earlier and immature stages of their relationship that form only partial unions they approach a total communion of their beings. At least verbally Paul affirms the same:

> By means of the reciprocal personal gift of self, proper and
> exclusive to them, husband and wife tend toward the com-
> munion of their beings in a view of mutual personal perfec-
> tion, to collaborate with God in the generation of new lives.[31]

But differences between Paul's understanding and Hegel's ought to
be noted. For Hegel the communion of the partners was in consciousness
alone. To attain this they must rise above the inferior phenomena of
human interaction, including the bodily. For Paul the communion is of the
spouses' entire beings, physical as well as spiritual.

For Hegel the communion was more perfect the more the distinct
personal consciousnesses disappeared into the one consciousness. For
Paul the communion, while diminishing the separateness of the partners,
must maintain their distinction. This is so because they create the union
by making gifts of themselves to one another, and sustain it by continuing to do so. This is possible only to distinct, free and volitionally self-
possessed persons.

But both Hegel and Paul seem to agree in this, that the man and
wife can reach the fullness, the perfection of their kind of love in this
reciprocally self-giving union. In the degree that they try only to take
from one another they destroy their union and also themselves.

A last reflection on *Humanae vitae* finds that probably without
intending to do so, here in two combined subordinate clauses Paul may
have pointed to the heart of his definition of marriage, and therein to the
heart of the sacrament's matrix: "By means of the reciprocal and personal gift of self, proper and exclusive to them...." "Proper to" in the
traditional vocabulary of this document can mean "intrinsic to,"
"belonging to its essence," "of its nature." Its meaning here is fixed
more accurately by the adjective "exclusive." It indicates a kind and an
inclusiveness of self-giving that only a man and a woman can have. In
it they can work toward the full realization of their persons—but only
together and only by the self-giving. Here we are back beyond Hegel to
Hugh of St. Victor in the twelfth century, who found marriage's finally
distinguishing trait in the inclusiveness, the exclusiveness and the intensity of the love of the husband and wife for one another.

Notes

1. This is the title by which the *Pastoral Constitution on the Church in the Modern World* is popularly known. The constitution is in English translation in *The Documents of Vatican II*, Walter M. Abbott, S.J., General Editor, N.Y. 1966, pp. 199–308. The authorized publication of the constitution is in *Sacrosanctum Oecumenicum Concilium Vaticanum II, Constitutiones, Decreta, Declarationes*, Typis Polyglottis Vaticanis, 1966, pp. 681–835. Hereafter cited as *GS*.

2. *GS*, No. 50, p. 254.

3. The pertinent paragraphs of this discourse are in *Matrimony: Papal Teachings*, ed. Monks of Solesmes, trans. Michael Byrnes, pp. 426–427.

4. *GS*, No. 47, p. 249.

5. *GS*, No. 48, p. 250.

6. *GS*, No. 49, p. 253.

7. *GS*, No. 50, p. 255.

8. *GS*, No. 48, p. 250.

9. Ibid., p. 251.

10. *GS*, No. 49, p. 253.

11. *GS*, No. 48, pp. 250–251.

12. Ibid., p. 251.

13. Ibid.

14. Ibid.

15. Ibid., p. 252.

16. These sources are listed in note 165, p. 252 of the English translation.

17. No. 49, ibid., pp. 252–253.

18. Ibid.

19. A translation of the encyclical in English is on the Vatican website at http://www.vatican.va/holy_father/paul_vi/encyclicals/documents/hf_p-vi_enc_25071968_humanae-vitae_en.html. The authorized Latin Publication is in *Acta Apostolicae Sedis*, Vol. 60 (1968), pp. 481–503.

20. Paul never intended that *Humanae vitae* be a final statement about marriage, sexuality and procreation. About two weeks after publishing the encyclical he said that it does no more than clarify a fundamental chapter in the personal, married, family and social life of men and women; but it is not a complete treatise about men and women in this sphere of marriage, family and their moral probity. He added that this is an immense field to which the Church's *magisterium* could and perhaps should return with a fuller, more organic and more systematic exposition. This statement is recorded in *Origins*, Vol. 10, no. 17, p. 265.

21. *HV*, Par. 7.

22. *HV*, Par. 8.

23. *HV*, Par. 12.

24. Paul did not skirt this difficulty: "These acts...do not cease to be lawful if, for causes independent of the will of the husband and wife, they are foreseen to be infertile, since they are always oriented to expressing and strengthening their union. In fact, as experience bears witness, not every marital act is followed by new life. God has wisely disposed natural laws and rhythms of fertility which of themselves bring about a spacing of births" (ibid., par. 11). But in one sense Paul does miss the point. The question here is not whether infertile intercourse is lawful but whether it is marital.

His solution creates more difficulties. How can a couple leave their intercourse open to conception when they know conception is impossible? Since, when conception is impossible, the strengthening of union by itself keeps intercourse morally good (as he insists), where is the inseparability of the two meanings? Since God and human nature intend the infertility of some and even most acts of intercourse again where is the natural inseparability of their two meanings?

25. Par. 8, *HV*, p. 7.

26. *HV*, Par. 25.

27. *HV*, Par. 9.

28. See Aristotle's *History of Animals*, Book 9, Chapter 1, and his *Nicomachean Ethics*, Book 8, Chapter 12.

29. *HV*, Par. 9.

30. Ibid.

31. *HV*, Par. 7.

6. Pope John Paul II on the Theology of the Body

John S. Grabowski

This chapter first appeared as the "Foreword" in Pope John Paul II, *The Theology of the Body: Human Love in the Divine Plan* (Boston: Pauline, 1997).

Karol Wojtyla, known to the world since 1978 as Pope John Paul II, has always been fascinated by the human person. As a university student in Poland during the dark days of its Nazi occupation, Wojtyla wrote plays which used biblical motifs to explore the suffering and identity of his people. Following the war, while Poland continued to suffer under a now Marxist form of totalitarianism, the newly ordained Fr. Wojtyla wrote still more plays wrestling with the meaning of human existence (*Our God's Brother*). As his ministry grew and deepened, so did the range of subjects he treated in his plays. They extended from happiness and failure in marriage (*The Jeweler's Shop*), to the situation of fallen humanity confronted by God's redemptive love (*The Radiation of Fatherhood*).

At the same time that his skill as a playwright matured, Karol Wojtyla was also honing his skills as a philosopher. His doctoral dissertation in philosophy attempted to explore the new philosophy of consciousness known as phenomenology as the basis for an exposition of Christian ethics. This subject would occupy much of his teaching career at the University of Lublin. It would also form the basis for his synthesis of St. Thomas' philosophy of being and a phenomenological account of human action and experience in the opus *The Acting Person*.

But Wojtyla's laboratory encompassed more than the library and the lectern. He also learned a great deal from his pastoral ministry as a priest, bishop, and finally cardinal. As cardinal of the huge diocese of Krakow, Wojtyla worked to establish programs which would help married couples live the Church's teaching on sexuality and marriage. The experience gained in his extensive pastoral work helped him develop a new philosophical account of Catholic sexual ethics in *Love and Responsibility*.

Especially important in his mind was the articulation of a cogent modern rationale for the Church's position on birth regulation. Whereas Catholic moralists of preceding generations had treated contraception as a violation of chastity or a frustration of the natural law, Wojtyla developed a new personalist approach based on his philosophical work. In this view sexual intercourse in marriage has an inherent meaning of total bodily self-giving. Contraception overlays this meaning with a contradictory language of withholding and refusal. The fertility which is withheld or refused is not simply a superficial, biological component of the person which can be manipulated in the pursuit of other ends, but an aspect of the person as a whole. Contraception therefore violates the dignity of the person because it falsifies the total offering of self which intercourse is meant to express.

Wojtyla's pastoral and philosophical work earned him a spot on the Pontifical Study Commission on Family Population and Birth Problems called by John XXIII and repeatedly expanded by Paul VI during the first years of his pontificate. The Communist authorities in Poland prevented Wojtyla from attending the decisive final meetings of the commission. But his personal consultations with Paul VI and his published work were influential in *Humanae Vitae*'s reiteration of the Church's traditional ban of artificial contraception (1968).

As a bishop in the diocese of Krakow with a budding scholarly career, Wojtyla was also an active participant in the Second Vatican Council. There he helped to draft important sections of the Council's Pastoral Constitution on the Church, *Gaudium et Spes*. At the same time he was deeply impressed by the document's understanding of the human person within the mystery of Christ:

> The truth is that only in the mystery of the incarnate Word
> does the mystery of man take on light....Christ, the new

> Adam, in the very revelation of the mystery of the Father
> and of his love, fully reveals man to himself and brings to
> light his most high calling (*GS* 22 as cited in *Redemptor*
> *Hominis* 8).

Hence the central point of reference for any adequate understanding of the human person is the Incarnate Son of God. This theme would figure prominently in John Paul II's first encyclical, *Redemptor Hominis.*

Since his elevation to the papacy, John Paul II has continued to focus on the human person as revealed in the light of Christ. In this context we can locate his weekly general audiences which comprise the theology of the body. Given between September 1979 and November 1984, these audiences comprise a catechesis on the bodily dimension of human personhood, sexuality, and marriage in the light of biblical revelation.

The point of departure for this catechesis is found in Jesus' response to the Pharisees' question concerning the permissibility of divorce (cf. Mt 19:4–6). When confronted with such a fundamental question about the meaning of marriage and human sexuality, Jesus appealed to "the beginning" described in the opening chapters of Genesis. John Paul II proposes to do the same. While these chapters may be "mythic" in the sense that they are not history as we understand it, they nevertheless offer fundamental theological truths about the embodied human person and can shed light on our own present day experience.

Through this remarkable form of biblical analysis, the Pope locates and develops three such original experiences of humanity in the Garden of Eden: original solitude, original unity, and original nakedness. The first man depicted in Genesis, like all men and women, was aware of himself as a subject, an "I." Yet he also discovered the uniqueness of his existence because, unlike the animals whom he named (cf. Gn 2:19), his body was capable of expressing his subjectivity and freedom. This solitude provided an opportunity to respond in gratitude and obedience to the Creator. Yet it also produced a profound longing for another being like himself (cf. Gn 2:18).

This longing is answered in the creation of woman—another person, equal in dignity, another "I" revealed through the body. Yet this body was wonderfully different from that of the man, revealing a unique and "original" way of being a person. Far from dividing humanity, these differences were intended to summon them together in the unity of love. The body thus has a "nuptial" meaning which points toward the human need for community. The most fundamental and intense form of human community is the unity of man and woman in the covenant of marriage. When this communion is characterized by authentic self-giving love, marriage becomes a "communion of persons" which reflects God's own trinitarian life (cf. the general audience of January 16, 1980; and *Mulieris Dignitatem* [*MD*] 7).

The most intimate expression of this communion with marriage takes place through the bodies of husband and wife. In sexual self-donation the couple indeed speaks a "language of the body," expressing in a manner far more profound than words the totality of their gift to each other. In this embodied dialogue of mutual love the couple continually discovers each other and themselves more deeply. Hence the biblical expression for intercourse—"to know" (cf. Gn 4:1a)—is especially apt since it expresses the knowledge gained in sexual self-giving.

As intended by God, this language spoken by husband and wife through their naked bodies was unattended by shame (cf. Gn 2:25). John Paul contrasts this shameless discovery of the nuptial character of the body with the experience of shame after the fall (cf. Gn 3:7). The experience of original nakedness given to us in the revealed text points to a time of integration within human persons when there was no "interior rupture and opposition between what is spiritual and what is sensible." It also points to a time of harmony between man and woman when there was no "rupture and opposition between...male and female" (cf. the general audience of January 2, 1980).

Sin shattered the original integrity of the person and the unity between male and female. The Pope describes the fall as "a constitutive break within the human person...almost a rupture of man's original spiritual and somatic unity" (cf. the general audience of May 28, 1980). In this fallen state, the body is no longer subordinated to the spirit and so its capacity to express the person is radically diminished. Now the experience of nakedness brings shame and fear (cf. Gn 3:7, 10). The unity between man and woman is also broken and replaced by suspicion and alienation. Rather than self-donation, masculine-feminine relationships are marked by domination and subservience. In the words of Yahweh to the woman following the sin of the first pair, "He shall rule over you" (Gn 3:16b), John Paul II sees a depiction of male "domination" of and discrimination against women (cf. *MD* 10). This domination diminishes the dignity of both sexes, but it has more serious consequences for the woman insofar as she is made the object of male control.

This also points to the heart of what the Pope means when he speaks of lust. It is the propensity of fallen humanity to regard others not as persons, but as objects to be controlled or means to be used for personal gratification. This lust limits both the nuptial character of the body and the ability of the individual to form a communion of persons with others. As fallen, humanity is faced with its own constant inclination to sin known as concupiscence. This inclination is continually played out in the relationship between the sexes (cf. *MD* 10).

But if the Pope's understanding of the person takes account of the ravages of sin, it is even more profoundly marked by hope in the power of the redemption. While it does not erase humanity's history as a fallen race or restore men and women to a state of original innocence, the grace of Christ makes it possible for them to live as God intended "from the beginning." This includes what John Paul calls the "redemption of the body," in which grace enables the body to once again express the person as it did at creation. Such an idea implies that the reality of creation already included humanity's election in Christ (cf. Eph 12:3–4). Hence marriage is a "primordial sacrament" (cf. the general audience of October 6, 1982).

Grace also overcomes the alienation between the sexes, making possible an appreciation of both their equal dignity and their irreducible "originality" as persons. This transformation is especially evident in marriage, where authority within marital communion comes to be understood and lived as "mutual subjection out of reverence for Christ" (Eph 5:21; cf. *MD* 24). When this communion is characterized by authentic self-giving love where each lives for the other, the Christian family becomes a manifestation of the eternal communion within the Trinity.

If the self-giving of marriage is a paradigm for all human community and indeed for the whole of reality, where does religious celibacy fit within the Pope's vision? For John Paul, consecrated virginity or celibacy is also a pre-eminent way of giving oneself to another in which the body expresses the person. Celibacy also points to the marital character of reality since it is a response of the person to the love of the Divine Spouse. Thus celibacy and marriage are two mutually illuminating realities through which human persons can realize their own humanity by being for another.

This catechesis also has practical moral implications, especially in regard to the crucial issue of birth regulation. In this regard, John Paul offers two distinct lines of argument for the Church's teaching. The first is a restatement of his personalist understanding which he developed as a professional philosopher. Contraception violates the language of the body as complete self-giving of the whole person (cf. the general audience of August 22, 1984; [*Evangelium Vitae*] *EV* 13, 42). But here he adds a second line of argument. This teaching is not simply based on human reason (i.e., the natural law), but also "the moral order revealed by God" (cf. the general audience of July 18, 1984). The biblical text itself links the knowledge gained in sexual self-giving with motherhood and fatherhood (cf. Gn 4:1 a–b; the general audience of March 12, 1980; *EV* 43). In so doing he has provided a new source and a more authoritative foundation for the traditional Catholic understanding of this issue.

The common thread which unites all of John Paul's teaching contained in this book is a focus on the human person in the light of the mystery of Christ. While much of the teaching of Paul VI in *Humanae Vitae* was based on an appeal to the natural law, John Paul II consistently bases his teaching, not only on the dignity of the person, but on biblical revelation. Thus it is primarily an exposition of various biblical texts which frames the teaching offered within the catechesis on the theology of the body, *Mulieris Dignitatem*, and *Evangelium Vitae*. This is consistent with the Pope's teaching as a whole. Whether grounding his understanding of morality within the invitation to discipleship which Jesus extended to the rich young man of Matthew 19 (cf. *Veritatis Splendor*), or his theology of work within the opening chapters of Genesis (cf. the social teaching in *Laborem Exercens*), John Paul II has attempted to make the human person revealed in the light of Christ the basis of the Church's teaching in sexual, social and medical morality.

7. Pope John Paul II on Love, Sexuality, Marriage, and Family

Richard M. Hogan and John M. LeVoir

This chapter first appeared in Richard M. Hogan and John LeVoir, *Covenant of Love: Pope John Paul II on Sexuality, Marriage, and Family in the Modern World* (Garden City, N.Y.: Doubleday, 1985).

MAN AND WOMAN (IMAGES OF GOD) AND LOVE

After twenty-five years of thought and reflection on marriage and the family, Karol Wojtyla was called to the chair of Saint Peter. As a theologian in his own right, he developed a new understanding of the moral precepts of Christ. This development can already be seen in his early work, *Love and Responsibility*. Later, as archbishop of Kracow and as a participant in the Second Vatican Council, he proposed his new moral theology to the other conciliar fathers. His new understanding was received by the council and became part of its teaching in the *Pastoral Constitution on the Church in the Modern World*. Now, as the Vicar of Christ, John Paul II has offered the world his fully matured moral theology in his papal addresses entitled *Theology of the Body* and in his *Apostolic Exhortation on the Family*. Since this new development is found in the conciliar documents, John Paul II is teaching us what the Second Vatican Council intended.

The central idea in the new theology of John Paul II is the subjective turn founded on the revelation in Genesis that we are made in God's image. Endowed with a likeness to God, we have been created to act as

78

He does, i.e., to love, to give ourselves as He does within the Holy Trinity. Our dignity lies in our similarity to God. When we fail to act as He does, we destroy ourselves and our dignity. As John Paul wrote in his first encyclical, "Man cannot live without love. He remains a being that is incomprehensible for himself, his life is senseless."[1] Continuing the same theme in his document on family life, the Pope says, "Love is therefore the fundamental and innate vocation of every human being."[2] Thus, the Holy Father insists that we must love. This necessity flows from within ourselves, God does not compel us to love. Rather, the obligation to love is derived from the kind of creatures we are, i.e., persons made in the image of God.

However, God must show us how to love because love is primarily a divine activity in which we, through God's creative act, are called to share. (Thus, Christ, the God-man, is absolutely central to each and every human being. Only in Him can we see how God loves, i.e., how we should love.) We know from revelation, i.e., from the Old Testament and most perfectly from Christ, that God loves through a complete self-donation of Himself. This love is perfectly present in the Holy Trinity where each divine Person totally surrenders Himself to the others. This total self-gift of each Person within the Trinity, while preserving the distinct features of each Person (Father, Son, Holy Spirit), establishes a complete union of wills. The love of each divine Person is a personal choice, a will-act, made by each based on knowledge of the truth. The self-donation of each divine Person to the others unites all three in a *communion of persons*. In effect, there is an attitude, a choice, to act as one. This is what love is: an act of the will to do what another wills.

God's self-gift of Himself is extended to us and made known to us in the creation and most especially in the redemption. In creation, God shared Himself with us and all creation because He shared what He is: existence. He gave Himself to what He created. Of course, in a unique way, He gave Himself to man and woman when He created Adam and Eve in His own image. But His creative act, as much of a self-surrender as it was, is infinitely less precious than the total abnegation of self that is manifested in the incarnation. As Saint Paul wrote, "Though He was in the form of God, [Jesus] did not count equality with God a thing to be grasped, but emptied Himself, taking the form of a servant being born in the likeness of men."[3] The incarnation, God taking the nature of one of

His creatures, shows us how God loves. But even the assumption of a human nature did not completely reveal the full extent of God's love. Only on the cross do we see how far the self-surrender of God extends. He gave Himself for our sakes that we might have life. He gave until He had nothing more to give and He did it totally for us. This is love! Since we are made in God's likeness, we are made to love as He did and does: an all-encompassing self-surrender for the sake of others. Only when we mirror the love of the Trinity in our love do we fulfill ourselves as God created us. Only then is life meaningful.

Wojtyla points out that the vocation to give ourselves in love is a call given to us because we are persons: creatures endowed with minds and wills. In other words, as personal beings, we can know the truth and we can choose to give ourselves to another person or persons. Thus, like the Trinity, we have the capability of entering a communion of persons. We are first called to enter a *communion of persons* with God and then with other human beings. Failure to form a *communion of persons* is an attack, an aggression, against our very persons. We must love. It is a subjective need which every human being has.

Of course, a *communion of persons*, a relationship of love, cannot be established unless there are at least two persons who individually choose through a personal will-act to give themselves to each other. Thus, we cannot, properly speaking, love a thing or even an animal. These beings do not have wills: they do not have the ability to give themselves to others. They cannot love and since love is a reciprocal gift of at least two persons, we cannot love them.

Love is an activity proper to persons. Love is also the *only* way to relate to persons. In one of his early works on love, John Paul teaches that a "person is a good towards which the only proper adequate attitude is love." "This [personalistic] norm, in its negative aspect, states that the person is a kind of good which does not admit of use and cannot be treated as an object of use and as such the means to an end."[4] The dignity of persons as created in God's image makes them superior to the remainder of creation. That superiority gives them a right to be treasured for their own sakes, not as means to an end. We must, then, relate to other persons only through love, i.e., in and through a *communion of persons*. The dignity of other persons and our own dignity require such a stance. Should one person treat another as a means to an end, as someone to be used, the second becomes, for the first, less than a personal being. The first person is reducing the second to a thing. Of necessity, because the first person is equal to the second, the first is also reducing himself/herself to a thing. The dignity of persons, our own and that of others, requires that the personalistic norm always be observed. As human persons, we are not merely spirits. We have bodies and they, as we have seen, are given to us by God as part of the gift of life so that our persons might be expressed in a physical way. Of all the Persons in the universe, the three Persons in God, the angels, and humans, only human persons have bodies. Of all the bodily creatures in the world, only we are persons. Thus, we are unique. Only we can express in the physical world how a person loves. Only we can manifest a *communion of persons* in a physical way. The body is the means by which our love is expressed. But it is also a means by which the love of others may be received. As such, it can only be viewed as an object of love. The body is not an appendage which a person carries around with him/her. To treat the body as a thing is to treat the person as a thing. The body is the expression of the person and it should be loved as the person should be loved. The personalistic norm is not limited to the spiritual aspects of persons. It includes the bodies of persons. We may never exclude the body from the dignity proper to personal beings. Many different practices traditionally taboo in most societies could be justified if the body were divorced from the person. But we dare not permit such an opinion to gain acceptance because it would irreparably harm human dignity.

The Family Is a Communion of Persons

In His creative act, God specified two particular communions which should exist for us when He said to Adam and Eve, "Be fruitful and multiply, and fill the earth and subdue it."[5] We are called, by creation and "from the beginning," to enter into a *communion of persons* so that we may increase and multiply and to enter into a communion so that the earth might be subdued. Of course, the first communion is the family. The second is that found in the workplace. In both communions, the activity of man and woman reflects the acts of God, not only in the self-gift which establishes the communions, but also in the effects of the self-gift. When

God loves, it is life-giving. When man and woman love within the family, new life is brought forth. When people work, they dominate creation. They are acting in a way analogous to God, who, as the Creator, has total dominion over the world. Still, the first communion is the more fundamental. It is the one which reflects God's trinitarian life more closely because it is a total self-surrender of one person to another. In the workplace, we do not give ourselves completely to one another. Second, the communion of persons of the family is life-giving whereas that of the workplace is not. The love of a man and a woman is usually fertile as God's love is fertile. Thus, in this way, the *communion of persons* which is the family reflects God's love more closely. It is appropriate to consider the family as the first and most important *communion of persons* and then to examine the relationships which should exist in the workplace.

"Male and female He created them."[6] If we are called to love one another, as God loves, i.e., to surrender ourselves completely to one another, and if our bodies are to express our persons, it is most appropriate that there be bodily differences which allow us to express our love for one another. By God's holy will, there are such differences: God created us as men and women (although both male and female bodies equally express the human person). The physical gift of a man and a woman to each other is the outward sign, the sacrament, of the familial *communion of persons*. The body, then, is the means and the sign of the gift of the male-person to the female-person. The Holy Father calls this capacity of the body to express the total self-surrender of one person to another the nuptial meaning of the body. In this total physical surrender based on *communion of persons*, the married couple becomes, physically, an image of God. When a married couple acts in accordance with their vows and God's will, they are a sign (a sacrament), a physical manifestation, of the love of persons. They are an image of God in their bodily gift to one another.

The Pope also stresses that the communion of two persons expressed through their bodies is a mutual giving and acceptance. The gift of each spouse mirrors God's gift of Himself in creation. Each spouse gives himself/herself as the Creator did when He created the world, gives himself/herself for the sake of the other. Similarly, the acceptance of the other's gift on the part of each spouse is an act of gratitude to the Creator for the gift. The entire physical creation participates in the gratitude of the man and the woman to the Creator for the gift each has received. The married couple gives as God gives and each responds with gratitude and in that response, all creation responds to the Creator thanking Him for the gift of being. At one and the same time, the couple is an image of God and a sign of creation's response to the Creator.

In his *Theology of the Body* series, the Holy Father defended the ancient biblical terminology for the sexual union of a man and a woman: to know. Of course, since we gain self-knowledge through our acts, the self-gift of a husband and a wife to one another does reveal to each of them more about themselves. But the knowledge gleaned from the gift of a husband and a wife to one another transcends the truth they know about themselves from their other acts because this act of self-surrender is more God-like. The gift of love, acting as God does, expressed through the body, touches the central mystery of the human person in a way in which most of our other acts do not. Therefore, the verb, to know, is most accurate for the self-gift of a man and a woman to one another.

The knowledge gleaned from this act may be specified in three areas. First, there is the knowledge of oneself and the other in the mutual *communion of persons*. In this mutual giving, one experiences and knows oneself as well as the other in a much fuller way than would otherwise be possible. Second, the hidden treasures of humanity are revealed in motherhood and fatherhood. The woman, whose femininity is hidden, is revealed to herself and to others (especially to her husband) in motherhood. Similarly, the new relationship of the male to the child, fatherhood, reveals to the husband and to others (especially to his wife) an aspect of humanity not previously experienced. Third, in the child, both the man and the woman see and know themselves.

Of course, true love, the surrender of oneself to another, is a freely chosen act of a person. Acts of human persons have (or should have) their origins in the faculties of mind and will. The physical union of a man and a woman is not simply an act of their bodies. It is founded on their marriage vows. These vows are choices or will-acts grounded in the dignity of the beloved by which an irrevocable union—a *communion of persons*—is established. This communion can then be expressed in the physical order through their bodies because God gave their bodies a nuptial meaning when He created them male and female.

Marriage vows, then, are freely chosen will-acts. In the vows, each spouse promises to give himself/herself to the other. These vows are not (or should not be) exchanged solely on the basis of sensuality or sentiment. Rather, they should be exchanged because each, perceiving the dignity which God gave the beloved in His creative act, wishes to give himself/herself to the other. Unlike some sensual or sentimental feelings, marriage vows are always under the control of the ones making them. Each spouse promises to love the other forever, i.e., to give himself/herself to the other until death. He/she can always be faithful to that promise, can always give himself/herself to the other, no matter what feelings he/she has or what the other does. Good feelings might cease, but marriage must be founded on a firmer basis than transient emotions. If marriage were only constituted by the feelings of each spouse, there would be a violation of the personalistic norm. In this case, implicitly, each spouse would marry because the other makes him/her feel good. If that good feeling should cease, the marriage would end. In other words, the spouse would have been there to make the other feel good. With such a union, there would be no assurance for either spouse that the marriage would endure. Neither spouse could be sure that he/she would feel good in two months, five years, let alone forty or fifty years. It is quite clear that a union founded on a selfish desire to achieve an emotional high through the spouse is directly contrary to the commitment of marriage, which is based on a God-like self-donation of each spouse to the other. Marriage, if it is to be a *communion of persons*, must originate in the will, must be rooted in the personalistic norm, and must be an imitation of the Trinity. Sensuality and sentiment will then accompany the marital communion instead of determining it.

Marriage reflects God's love within the Trinity and His love for us, because marriage is constituted by the irrevocable choice in the wills of the spouses. In the Trinity and in creation, love is a choice in the wills of the divine Persons. The familial *communion of persons* reflects the trinitarian *communion of persons* because the irrevocable will-acts of the married partners, establishing a mutual self-surrender, mirror the unbreakable fidelity of God to Himself (within the Trinity) and to those whom He loves (us) outside the Trinity. He never will cease loving Himself or us because He has chosen to do so and His will-acts are, as those of married partners ought to be, irrevocable.

An act of the will is within the control of the one who makes it. Neither the spouse, nor even the angels, including the devil, can cause us to alter our own choices. It is within the power of the fallen angels to tempt, i.e., to suggest possible choices contrary to God's will, but they can never actually make us choose what we do not choose ourselves. Only God has such power and He will never choose for us. If He were to do that, it would destroy us because we would be reduced to the status of animals, lacking free will. Of course, through lack of cooperation, sickness, or a variety of other causes, the expression of mutual self-donation in marriage may be hampered. However, that does not alter the gift itself.

Since the love of a husband and a wife should be a *communion of persons* based on the truth of the infinite dignity with which the Creator endowed both of them, it is not offensive, as Sacred Scripture has it, to ask wives to be obedient to their husbands. Nor is it too demanding to ask husbands to be willing to die for their wives as Christ died for the Church. In the exchange of marital vows, both the man and the woman give themselves completely to each other. They each promise, "Not my will, but thine be done."[7] To ask obedience of wives is simply to remind wives of what they have already promised. Obedience, if it is a human act based on a relationship between persons, must be an act of love (personalistic norm). Otherwise, the demand for obedience would be an act of tyranny and the one who is obedient would be acting as a slave. Obedience is the willing cooperation of one with the other because both are united through their freely chosen will-acts. Of course, wives should obey their husbands, i.e., they should be united with them in their wills. That is what was promised on the marriage day through the vows. Similarly, when Saint Paul asks husbands to be ready to die for their wives, he is only reminding them of what they promised. They, in the vows, promised everything they had to their wives: a total self-surrender. In that total gift, they function as creatures made in the image of God. They act as Christ acted. If necessary, husbands must be ready to do what Christ did, surrender everything for the sake of the other. What Saint Paul affirmed of husbands is equally true of wives and what he said of wives is equally true of husbands. Husbands and wives have promised obedience, i.e., a union of wills, to one another. They have voluntarily given themselves totally to one another and each should be ready to die for the other. Seen in the light of John Paul's personalism, Saint Paul's teaching is not sexist. It is the obvious corollary to the total union which husbands and wives are called to form with one another.

The gift of a man and a woman to one another in marriage must be indissoluble as long as both live. Each surrenders himself/herself to the other and receives the gift of the other in return. Once given, the gift may never be withdrawn. Once received, the gift of the other may never be rejected. As the *Apostolic Exhortation on the Family* argues, "The indissolubility of marriage…[is] a sign and a requirement of the absolutely faithful love that God has for man and that the Lord Jesus has for the Church."[8] In other words, God's love is always characterized by perfect fidelity. Human love, since it is to be a reflection of God's love, must also be faithful forever. God is always faithful in His love because anything less would not be a total self-surrender. A gift, if it is total, is not bounded in degree or in time! To give oneself only for a period of time and not forever (at least, for as long as marriage is possible, i.e., until the death of one of the spouses) is to limit the gift. But anything less than a total surrender of oneself for the other is, as we have seen, a violation of the requirement of love, a violation of the personalistic norm. It is, in effect, to use someone rather than to love him/her.

A husband or a wife who has divorced his or her spouse and remarried has treated his or her first spouse as a thing. When the offended spouse ceased to please, he/she was rejected. One may treat cars, boats and even animals as objects to be used, but never may a human person be so humiliated (personalistic norm). Since the offended spouse was presumably sincere in his/her total self-surrender, he/she cannot help but feel totally devastated. First, he/she, believing in the gift of the other party, fell victim to a broken covenant (which is, in itself, devastating) and, as a result, unwittingly allowed himself/herself to become an object of use, a "thing." Second, and even more humiliating, the offended spouse is now rejected even as a "thing" to be used! Objects are at least useful, but the abandoned spouse is not even considered to have a use! No wonder there are such psychological difficulties for those who have been set aside by their spouses! The Pope continually stresses that marriage should be an affirmation of the value of the person. However, when it is no longer indissoluble, it not only ceases to confirm the personal dignity of the individual spouses, it actually has the potential of destroying the sense of self-worth and dignity in the offended spouse. Once that awareness of one's own value is destroyed, it is most difficult to recover it. The spouse has been used as a thing and he/she may believe himself/herself to be just that: a thing (perhaps even a worthless thing).

The indissolubility of marriage is not harmed either by separation of the spouses without remarriage or by the death of one of the spouses and a subsequent second marriage by the surviving spouse. Separation (in practice in the United States, civil divorce without a second marriage) is an evil, but sometimes justified. As John Paul says so descriptively, one or both spouses "may cease to feel that there is any subjective justification for this union, and gradually fall into a state of mind which is psychologically or both psychologically and physiologically incompatible with it. Such a condition warrants separation from 'bed and table,' but cannot annul the fact that they are objectively united, and united in wedlock."[9] Even living apart, they are wedded and bound to one another. Their separation, as all other decisions, should be mutually agreeable. But, even if one unilaterally separates, i.e., moves out, that does not change the union in which they are joined. In separation, the self-surrender of both parties remains intact, but it is not expressed. A second marriage after the death of the spouse does not prejudice the self-surrender in marriage because marriage is both a spiritual and a bodily reality. When one of the spouses dies, i.e., when the body and soul separate, the marital union ceases. A widow or widower is free to remarry.

It should be clear that the conclusions of the foregoing discussion regarding the indissolubility of marriage are founded on the principle that marriage is a total *communion of persons* established by the will-acts of the spouses. Once the self-gift of the man and the woman is made in the marriage vows, it is irrevocable. Even if both cease to feel any stirrings of sensuality or sentiment in the presence of the other, they are still united as husband and wife. They chose one another forever.

REVISIONIST SEXUAL MORALITY: AN ATTACK ON THE FAMILY

The familial *communion of persons* was established by God in Genesis. Through this union of love, man and woman were to fulfill their calling to love as God loves. However, original sin intervened and prevented Adam and Eve from surrendering themselves to each other as God had planned "from the beginning." Indicating that our first parents, by sinning, tottered on the precipice of total self-destruction, the Pope teaches that with the loss of God's grace and the concomitant loss of the dominion of the mind and will over the body, there was a "constitutive break within the human person, almost a rupture of man's original spiritual and somatic unity."[10] Further, there was an "ending of the capacity of a full mutual communion."[11] It is "as if the body, in its masculinity and femininity, no longer constituted the 'trustworthy' substratum of the *communion of persons*."[12] After sin the other (usually of the opposite sex) is often looked upon not for his/her own sake, but for selfish reasons: what can he/she do for me? How can he/she satisfy my selfish desires and inclinations? But, "man indeed, as a person is 'the only creature on earth that God has willed for its own sake' and, at the same time, he is the one who can fully discover his true self only in a sincere giving of himself."[13] Thus, original sin attacked man in his most essential activity, his sincere giving.

Offenses against the sincere giving in the family, i.e., against the first and primary *communion of persons* established by God in His creative act, have been committed by men and women since the fall. For example, in divorce and remarriage, as we have seen, the offended spouse is treated as an object. This is a violation of the familial *communion of persons* caused by selfishness. Selfishness also attacks the family in many other ways, e.g., pre-marital intercourse, polygamy, adultery and lust, abortion, contraception and artificial conception (test-tube babies), and homosexuality. In our age, most of these practices are not only common-place (as they have been in past ages), but they are even defended. Many would like to justify these acts and cease making an effort to resist them. Four different positions are often advanced in favor of this revisionist morality. The first is proposed by those who misunderstand freedom. They mistakenly equate it with a selfish independence, precluding all forms of self-donation. But this attitude, as well as the actions flowing from it, destroys true freedom because only in an unselfish gift of love is our freedom realized. God made us to love and He also made us free. The two are not in conflict and cannot be because we are made in God's image. Just as God loves and is at the same time perfectly free, when we love unselfishly we are perfectly free. Furthermore, failure to love unselfishly destroys us and consequently our freedom. This is the experience of people who have accepted the "do your own thing" attitude. They ruin themselves, leading miserable lives, because they fail to love, the "fundamental and innate vocation of every human being."[14]

Others would justify these selfish violations of the familial *communion of persons* by divorcing the body from the human person. This is a fundamental misunderstanding of how God made us. They would argue that if the body is meant to express the person, then the individual should be able to choose how his/her body should express his/her person. In their eyes, the Christian sexual ethic makes people slaves to the biological functions of their bodies. If we are to be the masters of nature, why can we not govern our own bodies, freely choosing to express whatever we want through them?

But the human person is not the arbiter of nature! The order of nature is the same as the order of existence and depends upon God, the first cause. On the other hand, the biological order is a scientific abstraction from nature: Showing incredible insight, Karol Wojtyla stated twenty-five years ago that our sexuality "owes its objective importance to its connection with the divine work of creation...and this importance vanishes almost completely if our way of thinking is inspired only by the biological order of nature" which "as a product of the human intellect...abstracts its elements from a larger reality."[15] The Holy Father insists that the body expresses the person as it is because God made the body as well as the soul. In other words, people do not govern their bodies absolutely because their bodies belong by God's creative act to the order of nature, not only to the biological order. There is an integral view of the human person in John Paul's thought, i.e., the body, in all of its functions, is a gift from God just as life itself. As we may not tamper with our lives, so we may not tamper with our bodies.

Still others might argue that since the Christian norms are ideals which can never be attained, God would not ask us to live by them. They might point to the seeming unnatural demands made by the Christian ethic on men and women. Therefore, in their view, acts contrary to these teachings are not sins, i.e., subhuman, but rather are normal (read: permissible) for us. Of course, the commandments are impossible for fallen man without God's grace. With God's grace, however, anything is possible. What is natural for man and woman is the state of original innocence where lust and selfishness were not a problem. In a sense, then, our present state is unnatural. Christ calls us to return to our original state. In response to the questions the Pharisees asked Him about divorce, He taught, "Have you not read that He who made them from the beginning made them male and female, and said, 'For this reason a man shall leave his father and mother and be joined to his wife, and the two shall become one'?"[16] The phrase, "the beginning," is a clear reference to the first words in Genesis, to the time before the fall. In other words, Christ told the Pharisees that married people must live the way Adam and Eve did before the fall in a total *communion of persons* without any tinge of selfishness. This is clearly impossible for fallen man left to his own devices. But Christ would never ask us to do the impossible. His victory on the cross makes God's grace available to us and with that it is possible to live as Adam and Eve did.

A fourth objection to the moral teachings of the Church begins with the same premise as the third one: the Christian moral life is comprised of ideals impossible for us to reach. Since we often fall short of these ideals while striving through our best efforts to live by them, some would argue that we must not be burdened with the full force of the moral ideals, but rather congratulated for what we have attained. Thus, they claim there are differences in the application of the law to individuals, what the Pope calls a gradualness of the law.

However, the Holy Father teaches, as we have seen, that the Christian life is possible with God's grace. It is always attainable. Therefore, we are always bound by the moral teachings. But it is quite clear that we find it easier to do things we have done before. As we practice the Christian life, we grow accustomed to it. There is a growth in virtue. The moral precepts always bind, but they become easier for us to practice. This is not a gradualness in the application of the law to an individual. Rather, it is a gradual perfection of the person in his/her practice of the Christian life (or as John Paul labels it, the law of gradualness in human behavior).

The Church is *for* man. It has the optimistic view of man. The Church repeats to each human person the message of Christ, "Yes, you can live as God's image!" Those who wish to justify acts opposed to the teachings of the Church and the nature of man and woman see the difficulties and hardships many people have in living according to Christian norms. Although those opposed to Church teaching seem to be motivated by compassion, in effect they are pessimistic about our possibility of ever overcoming the effects of sin. If their position were to be accepted, we would be reduced to a level beneath that planned for us "from the beginning." The Pope counters the arguments of the critics by an insistence that true compassion is that shown by Christ on Calvary. Through the blood of His cross, we can live as Adam and Eve before the fall, if we are only willing to cooperate with God's grace. As the Pope teaches, "to diminish in no way the teaching of Christ constitutes an eminent form of charity for souls."[17] There is no compassion without the truth. Let us always offer the truth compassionately.

Notes

1. *Redemptor hominis*, no. 10.
2. See *Familiaris consortio*, no. 11.
3. See Phil. 2:6–7.
4. See *Love and Responsibility*, by Karol Wojtyla, translated by H. T. Willetts. New York: Farrar, Straus and Giroux, 1981.
5. See Gen. 1:28.
6. Ibid., 1:27.
7. See Luke 22:42.
8. See *Familiaris consortio*, no. 20.
9. See *Love and Responsibility*, p. 215.
10. See *Theology of the Body*.
11. Ibid., no. 29.
12. Ibid.
13. Ibid., no. 32.
14. See *Familiaris consortio*, no. 11.
15. See *Love and Responsibility*, p. 57.
16. See Matt. 19:4–5.
17. See *Familiaris consortio*, no. 33.

8. Pope John Paul II and Post–Vatican II U.S. Catholic Moral Theologians on Marriage

Charles E. Curran

This chapter first appeared in Charles E. Curran, *The Moral Theology of Pope John Paul II* (Washington, D.C.: Georgetown University Press, 2005), and Curran, *Catholic Moral Theology in the United States: A History* (Washington, D.C.: Georgetown University Press, 2008).

This chapter consists of two parts. The first part will analyze and criticize the approach to sexuality, love, and marriage proposed by John Paul II. The second part will briefly overview the approaches to marriage found in the writings of contemporary U.S. Catholic moral theologians.

POPE JOHN PAUL II ON SEXUALITY, LOVE, AND MARRIAGE

John Paul II has written extensively on sexuality, marriage, and gender. The encyclical *Veritatis splendor* (1993) covers the whole field of moral theology and mentions sexuality and marriage in the process.[1] Other documents deal primarily and extensively with sexuality and marriage—the Apostolic Exhortation *Familiaris consortio* (1981),[2] the Apostolic Letter *Mulieris dignitatem* (1988),[3] the 1994 "Letter to Families,"[4] the 1995 "Letter to Women,"[5] the 1995 World Day of Peace Message, "Women:

Teachers of Peace."[6] The most extensive discussion of sexuality and marriage comes from the talks given at the first general audiences of the pope held weekly from September 1979 to November 1984. Ordinarily a discussion of papal teaching does not focus on the short talks given at the pope's weekly audiences, but...these talks [have been noted] as a source for John Paul II's teaching on marriage and sexuality. These talks have been published in English in one large volume, *The Theology of the Body: Human Love in the Divine Plan*[7] [*TB*].

John Paul II's discussion of sexuality and marriage faithfully follows out his methodology and approach to moral theology as discussed previously. The pope emphasizes that the primary reality is truth and he seeks to teach the truth about marriage and sexuality. *Familiaris consortio* begins by pointing out that many today are "doubtful and almost unaware of the ultimate meaning and truth of conjugal and family life" (1.1). In this context, "Illuminated by the faith that gives her an understanding of all the truth concerning the great value of marriage and the family and their deepest meaning, the Church once again feels the pressing need to proclaim the Gospel, that is the 'good news' to all people without exception, in particular to all those who are called to marriage and are preparing for it, to all married couples and parents in the world" (3.1). The primary question for moral teaching in general and for marriage and sexuality in particular is the question of truth.

John Paul II's teaching on marriage and family uses different sources of moral wisdom and knowledge, but the previous teachings of the hierarchical magisterium hold a central place. *Mulieris dignitatem* begins by citing the recent official teachings that have dealt with the role of women—Pius XII, John XXIII, Vatican Council II, Paul VI, the 1971 and 1987 Synod of Bishops. In his teaching on marriage and sexuality, as in all his teaching, he strongly supports and defends the specific moral norms associated with previous hierarchical teachings.

Theology and Meaning of the Body and Human Sexuality

Karol Wojtyla's training and profession was as an ethicist. His writings before becoming pope dealt primarily with issues of meaning and not primarily with casuistry. As pope, he has had to address many casuistic issues dealing with the moral norms of Catholic hierarchical teaching, but he still continues to probe the deeper question of meaning. His long series of general audience talks at the beginning of his pontificate well illustrates such an approach.

John Paul II develops the meaning and theology of the body and human sexuality in the light of his theological anthropology involving creation, the fall, and redemption of the body (*TB* 25–90).

In the garden, in the state of original innocence before the fall ("In the beginning"), the human person experiences three aspects of humanity—original solitude, original unity or communion of persons, and original nakedness. Thanks to the gift of creation, in the very experience of his body, Adam perceives himself as different from all other creation including the animals because he has a unique relationship with God. The pope often refers to this as the first covenant. Through this covenant given by God, Adam experiences his power of self-determination and self-choice in which he recognizes himself as an image of God. But Adam also experiences that he is alone—he is missing someone to share love and life with him (*TB* 35–42).

The second aspect of creation is the original unity or the communion of persons in and through the body. God made woman—the equal and the partner of man. Human beings now appear as masculine and feminine. This sexual difference makes possible the communion of persons in and through their bodies, which reflects God's own Trinitarian life. This "nuptial meaning" of the body is shown in the sincere gift of one to the other. In this context John Paul II often cites *Gaudium et spes* 24—"Man can fully discover his true self only in a sincere giving of himself" (*TB* 60–66). Here human persons find themselves an even more significant image of the triune God.

The aspect of original nakedness also contributes to the nuptial meaning of the body. This original nakedness signifies the absence of shame or interior division which thus allows Adam and Eve to give themselves totally and completely to one another in the sincere gift of love. There is no holding back and no temptation to treat the other as object (*TB* 57–60).

The fall brought about a threefold break with regard to the human person—a break in the relationship of loving dependence on God which Wojtyla refers to as a breaking of the covenant, the break in the relationship between man and woman, and a break or disunion in the human person brought about by concupiscence. In keeping with the Catholic understanding of the role of sin, the fall does not completely destroy what was present from the beginning but obscures or diminishes the image and likeness of God in the human being (*MD* 9).

The theology of the body puts special emphasis on concupiscence and lust that causes the division within the human person (spirit and body) and thereby affects the community of persons in their one-flesh unity. In this context, Genesis 3:7 is the primary text—"Then the eyes of both were open, and they knew that they were naked, and they sewed fig leafs together and made themselves aprons." Genesis 3:10 adds another element. In response to the call of God after the fall in the garden, Adam replied, "I heard the sound of you in the garden, and I was afraid because I was naked, and I hid myself." Thus, the "man of original innocence" becomes the "man of lust." Lust manifests itself above all in the shame that human beings now experience after the fall. A disquiet exists within human beings. This is the second discovery of sex (*TB* 114–25).

Although John Paul II recognizes that original sin also affects the heart and the spirit (*TB* 122), the emphasis here is on the fact that the body is no longer subject to the spirit. Lust thus affects the relationship of man and woman and the nuptial meaning of the body. Gone is the joyous, spontaneous self-gift of one to the other. The pope mentions at various times three different but interconnected effects of the lust, concupiscence, and shame that affect the nuptial relationship of man and woman. The very fact that Adam and Eve hid themselves from one another behind their aprons shows a lack of trust. Notice how this hiding relates to the fact that they hid themselves from God previously because they knew they were naked (*TB* 121). Second, the husband "will rule over you" (Genesis 3:16). The domination of one over the other thus destroys the original equality (*TB* 122–24). Third, the heart is now a battlefield between love and lust. Concupiscence works against the self-control and interior freedom of the original communion of persons. Now the other is no longer a person but is reduced to an object of sexual gratification (*TB* 125–30). Such are the effects of sin on the nuptial meaning of the body and the sexual union of man and woman.

The pope bases the effect of redemption on the nuptial meaning of the body on a number of different Scriptural texts in contradistinction to his concentration on Genesis in describing original innocence and the fall. Genesis, however, also points toward future redemption with its *proto-evangelium*—the woman (the new Eve) will crush the head of the serpent (*MD* 11). One series of talks from December 17, 1980, to May 6, 1981, bears the title: "St. Paul's Teaching on the Human Body" (*TB* 191–232). The human body is the temple of the Holy Spirit and member of Christ (1 Cor. 6:15–20). 1 Thessalonians 4:4 calls for controlling the body in holiness and honor. Paul in Romans 8:23 refers explicitly to the redemption of the body. This redemption by God's grace overcomes the effect of the fall and makes possible once again the nuptial meaning of the body found in original innocence (*TB* 32–34).

The pope puts heavy emphasis on Matthew 5:27–28—if a man looks at a woman lustfully, he has already committed adultery in his heart. The meaning of adultery is thus transferred from the body to the heart (*TB* 142–44). Redemption thus overcomes the power of concupiscence and lust that sees the other merely as an object of sexual gratification. Concupiscence and lust depersonalize. The commandment forbidding adultery is carried out through purity of heart. Male and female through the redemption of the body now regain the nuptial meaning of the body because of which they can freely give themselves in the total self-gift of one to the other. The Sermon on the Mount calls us not to go back to original innocence but to rediscover on the foundations of the perennial and indestructible meaning of what is human the living form of redeemed humankind (*TB* 175). Through self-control, continence, and temperance man and woman can now live out the nuptial meaning of the body. The power of redemption thus completes the power of creation (*TB* 147–80).

Sacramentality of Marriage

John Paul II devoted a series of his general audience talks from July 28, 1982, to July 4, 1984, with some interruptions, to the sacramentality of marriage. In keeping with his methodology in these talks, he bases his approach on Scripture and in particular on Ephesians 5:21–32. The very first talk begins with the citation of this long passage. This passage in general calls on spouses to love one another as Christ has loved the church. Because of this a man leaves his mother and father to become one flesh with his wife. This is a great mystery in reference to Christ and the church. Note that the English word "mystery" here is a translation of the Latin word "*sacramentum*." Thus the passage lends itself to be understood in a sacramental way. But, of course, to see the contemporary Catholic understanding of sacramentality in this passage, one has to read quite a bit into the biblical passage itself—which John Paul II is very willing to do (*TB* 304–6).

The passage also appeals to the pope for a number of other reasons. Ephesians here cites Genesis about a man leaving father and mother and becoming one flesh with his wife. Thus the passage refers back to the "beginning" to which the pope has paid so much attention in his previous talks. The passage puts heavy emphasis on the body in keeping with his emphasis on the theology of the body. But, in addition to referring to the human body in its masculinity and femininity, Ephesians speaks of the body in a metaphorical sense—the body of the church—and thus provides a basis for the sacramental understanding of the spousal relationship of husband and wife in light of the relationship of Christ to the church. In addition, the liturgy of the church sees this text in its relationship to the sacrament of marriage. Here the prayer of the church tells us something about the faith of the church (*TB* 304–6).

…[Elsewhere it has been] pointed out how the pope interprets away the obvious meaning of the text "wives be subject to your husbands." The mutual relations of husband and wife flow from their common relationship with Christ. They are to be "subject to one another out of reverence for Christ." There is a mutual subjection of the spouses, one to the other, based on their relationship to Christ. Husbands are then told to love their wives which "removes any fear that might have arisen (given the modern sensitivity) from the previous phrase: 'wives be subject to your husbands.'" Love excludes any subjection whereby the wife is a servant, slave, or object of domination by the husband. The communion of husband and wife is based on mutual love and mutual subjection (*TB* 310).

In addition, the pope does not deal with the analogy of Christ to the husband and the church to the wife. Christ is obviously the head of his body, the church. For many Christians, even some today, this means that the husband is the head of the wife and of the family. But the pope's own position is clear—there is a reciprocal and equal love relationship of husband and wife with no one-sided domination by the husband.

In his discussion of marriage as a sacrament, John Paul II uses the term "sacrament" in both a broader and a more narrow or technical sense of one of the seven sacraments of the church. In the broader sense, a sacrament is a sign that effectively transmits in the visible world the invisible mystery hidden from eternity in God (*TB* 333–41). In this sense, creation and redemption are both sacraments. But marriage is the primordial sacrament signifying the loving relationship of God to his people and of Christ to the church. Marriage is the "primordial sacrament instituted from the beginning and linked with the sacrament of creation in its globality" (*TB* 339). Ephesians 1:3–4 tells us of the mystery hidden in God from all eternity. God chose us in Christ before the foundation of the world that we should be holy and blameless before him. "[T]he reality of man's creation was already imbued by the perennial election of man in Christ." The one flesh loving union of the first man and woman in Genesis in their holiness constitutes the sign of the mystery of God's covenant love hidden in God from eternity. The procreative powers of the first couple also continue the work of creation. Thus, marriage is the primordial sacrament of creation itself (*TB* 333–36).

But marriage is also the primordial sacrament of redemption. Although grace is lost after the fall, marriage never ceased to be in some sense a figure of the great mystery or sacrament of God's covenant love for his people. There is a continuity between creation and redemption. The sacrament of creation as the original gift of grace constituted human beings in the state of original innocence and justice. "The new gracing of man in the sacrament of redemption instead gives him above all the remission of sins." Grace abounds even more. Christ's redemptive love, according to Ephesians, is his special love for the church of which marriage is the primordial sacrament (*TB* 337).

The sacrament of marriage in the narrower and stricter sense of one of the seven sacraments of the church, based on Ephesians, understands the relationship between husband and wife on the basis of the relationship between Christ and the church. This analogy operates in two directions. The relationship of Christ to the church tells us something about Christian marriage, whereas the spousal relationship tells us something about Christ's love for the church (*TB* 312–14). The Hebrew Bible prefigured this analogy as found in the Prophets such as Isaiah who rebukes Israel as an unfaithful spouse (*TB* 327–30). John Paul II also appeals to the Song of Songs "found in the wake of that sacrament in which, through the language of the body, the visible sign of man and woman's participation in the covenant of grace and love offered by God to man is constituted" (*TB* 368). The Book of Tobit also tells us about the truth and power of marital love (*TB* 375–77).

The matrimonial consent of husband and wife shares in, signifies, and also tells something about the covenant of Christ with the church and of God with his people. "The analogy of spousal love indicates the radical character of grace." "The analogy of spousal love seems to emphasize especially the aspect of the gift of self on the part of God to man....It is a total (or rather radical) and irrevocable gift..." (*TB* 330–31).

Critical Appraisal

The pope has developed his understanding of marriage especially in the long series of general audience talks at the beginning of his pontificate. One cannot easily describe the genre of these talks. Although they have a homiletical tone at times, they are not homilies. Without doubt the talks belong to the genre of teaching. Here the pope is proposing to the world his understanding of marriage and its meaning for Christians today. The talks occasionally cite philosophers and other secular thinkers; the talks also come complete with footnotes. But the theology of the body is not developed in a systematic and complete way. The very nature of short talks presented every week to a different audience militates against a totally systematic approach. Since the talks are not a complete and systematic presentation of the pope's teaching on marriage, many aspects remain somewhat unclear and certainly less developed than they would be in a truly systematic presentation.[8] I will consider four issues—the theology of the body in general, the spirit-body relationship, the meaning of love, and the role of sexual pleasure.

THEOLOGY OF THE BODY

The nuptial meaning of the body is the basic understanding developed by John Paul II in his approach to marriage and sexuality. The pope has definitely made a positive contribution that has never been found before in papal teaching. On the basis of a theology of the body, he develops his understanding of the meaning and spirituality of marriage. In the process he uses both Scripture and his own personalistic philosophy to develop the nuptial meaning of the body as a foundation for a better understanding of the spirituality of marriage.

The theology of the body as developed by John Paul II, however, cannot serve as a theology for all bodies. In other words there are different theologies of the body. What the pope develops in terms of the nuptial meaning of the body really does not apply to people who are single or those who are widows or widowers. In a later discussion of virginity and celibacy, the pope does try to show how these realities also come under the influence of the nuptial meaning of the body. But there are many people for whom the nuptial meaning of the body as developed here is not appropriate.

Implicitly, John Paul II's theology of the body maintains that heterosexual marriage is the only context for human sexuality. This understanding obviously is based on the contemporary hierarchical Catholic teaching. The discussion of homosexuality is touched on only lightly in chapters 16 and 17, on same-sex marriage. But just as his nuptial theology of the body does not apply to all persons and all bodies so too he would have to prove that heterosexual marital sexuality is the only meaning for sexuality for all human beings. The theology of the body developed by John Paul II gives a very positive approach to the understanding of marriage, but the theology of the body and its accompanying understanding of sexuality does not necessarily apply to all human beings.

SPIRIT-BODY RELATIONSHIP

There is no Manichean dualism in John Paul II's anthropology of human sexuality. The body and sexuality are not bad (*TB* 165–67). The very title of the book in English, *The Theology of the Body*, argues against any kind of total dualism between the spirit and body or matter. Yet in the world of human existence after sin, the pope frequently refers to lust and its effects on the human person especially in terms of the body.

In discussing lust these talks frequently cite 1 John 2:15–16 which mentions the threefold aspect of lust—lust of the flesh, of the eyes, and of the pride of life (e.g., *TB* 116, 127, 165, 203). So lust also involves the spirit and not just the body. But there can be no doubt that John Paul II emphasizes the lust of the flesh. The passage of the Sermon on the Mount (looking lustfully at a woman), which he so often cites, does not condemn the body or sexuality but "contains a call to overcome the three forms of lust, especially the lust of the flesh" (*TB* 165). In another context the talks comment on 1 Corinthians 12:18–25 in which St. Paul refers to the less honorable parts or the unpresentable parts of the body. For John Paul II, Paul here calls for respect for the whole human body with no Manichean contempt for the body. But Paul is conscious of historical man after sin and in using these terms for the sexual parts of the body testifies to the shame that has been present in human experience ever since the sin of Adam and Eve. This shame is the fruit of the three forms of lust with particular reference to the lust of the flesh (*TB* 202–3). As a result of such an understanding, these texts frequently refer to "The Opposition in the Human Heart Between the Spirit and the Body" which is the title of the July 30, 1980, address (*TB* 128). The problem with "the man of lust" after original sin is that the "body is not subordinated to the spirit as in the state of original innocence. It bears within it a constant center of resistance to the spirit" (*TB* 115).

In the light of such an understanding of the effect of lust and concupiscence for redeemed people, "the body is given as a task to the human spirit." This is the spirituality of the body (*TB* 215). For the redeemed person, the emphasis is on self-control. "It is precisely at the price of self-control that man reaches that deeper and more mature spontaneity with which his heart, mastering his instincts, rediscovers the spiritual beauty of the sign constituted by the human body in its masculinity and femininity" (*TB* 173). However, John Paul II is not entirely negative about passion. As the Book of Sirach points out, carnal concupiscence and passion suffocate the voice of conscience. Passion tends to satisfy the senses and the body but such satisfaction brings no peace or true satisfaction. However, through the radical transformation of grace, passion can become a creative force (*TB* 145–46).

No one can deny the role of concupiscence and lust in human sexuality. Self-control and discipline are absolutely necessary. But John Paul II's incomplete discussion of concupiscence, lust, and self-control seems too one-sided. Yes, sin affects the body but it also affects the spirit. Sin does not necessarily bring about an opposition between spirit and body or between the higher and the lower parts of the human person as so often seems to be the case in the words used by John Paul II. The senses and passions are not simply forces that must be controlled and directed by reason. The senses and the passions, despite the influence of sin, still can point to and indicate the true and the good. Reason and spirit are not the only realities that can help us discern the true and the good. And, like the senses and passions, they too can become disturbed by sin. Yes, there is need for self-control with regard to sexual passion, but sexual passion is basically a good that is often disturbed by sin. Its basic goodness should not be denied or forgotten. The impression given by *The Theology of the Body* is that passion and sexual pleasure are totally suspect and in need of control. The pope does not seem to acknowledge a fundamental goodness about sexuality despite the ever-present danger of lust and concupiscence. There is just an occasional remark along more positive lines, but the heavy emphasis of the talks remains on the negative reality of sexual passion and the need for spirit and reason to control it.

MEANING OF LOVE

The lack of a systematic and complete theology of the body in these talks also comes through in the sketchy understanding of human love. The subtitle of the English collection of these talks is "Human Love in the Divine Plan," but there is no in-depth or systematic discussion of human love. The general approach is quite clear but it usually presents just two extremes. Love involves a sincere gift of self to the other—"the personal and total self-giving" (*FC* 20.3). The opposite of love is treating the other as an object or as a means of self-sexual gratification. The contrast is between disinterested giving and selfish enjoyment (*TB* 130). A more complete picture should recognize that the gift of self also involves some human fulfillment and sexual enjoyment.

The primary understanding of marriage as a sign of the covenant love of God for human beings, of Yahweh for the people of the covenant, and of Christ for the church makes the love of giving self to the other the basic meaning of marital love. In his writings on marriage, the pope emphasizes the cross more than the resurrection of Jesus because of his emphasis on God's love for us as total gift. Theological literature refers to this love as *agape*—the total giving of self.[9]

Although John Paul II in his discussion of marriage gives primacy to *agape* love or the gift of self modeled on God's love especially as seen in the incarnation and death of Jesus, the other aspects of love as reciprocity and mutual communion and also some self-fulfillment are mentioned occasionally.

Love as personal communion comes through especially in the loving union of Adam and Eve that overcomes the problem of solitude. The body shares fully in the personal communion of love between husband and wife. Such a love makes Adam and Eve—as husband and wife—images of the love of the Trinity (*TB* 45–48).

The talks also refer to *eros*. Here the pope distinguishes between the common use of the term and the more philosophical use of *eros* going back to Plato. In common language today, the erotic signifies what comes from desire and serves to satisfy the lust of the flesh. This is precisely what Matthew 5:27–28 condemns and what the talks emphasize. But *eros* in the platonic sense has a positive role to play. Here *eros* is the interior force that attracts human beings to what is true, good, and beautiful. In the description of original innocence in the garden, the talks recognize that Adam longed for someone to share love and life with him. The attraction, and even the sexual attraction between man and woman, has a very positive aspect about it. The Song of Songs presents *eros* as the form of human love in which the energies of desire are at work. *Agape* love, as described by St. Paul in 1 Corinthians 13:4–8 (love is patient, kind, not jealous), purifies this *eros* love of the Song of Songs and brings it to completion (*TB* 168–71). Thus, in the talks, there are some indications that *eros* is not completely negative and even has a positive role to play.

At the very minimum, the full meaning of human love in marriage with all its dimensions is not developed in a systematic way in these talks. The emphasis is on *agape* love understood as self-gift. The talks recognize love as communion but fail to develop the mutuality and reciprocity aspects of marital love. In addition, the pope does not integrate love as communion with love as self-gift. John Paul II does not discuss at length the proper love of self in marriage. The focus is on love as self-gift without developing the point that some true self-fulfillment and happiness are achieved in and through this self-gift.

The emphasis on love as a sincere gift of self—the personal and total self-giving—together with a narrow focus on Genesis results in a somewhat romantic, narrow, and unreal understanding of marriage in its total life context. Married people have lives of their own and are involved in many other activities and pursuits. Too often in the past, understandings similar to John Paul II's approach have limited the life especially of married women to the sphere of the home with husband and children. Yes, the marriage commitment is of singular importance for married people, but individual married people have their own lives to live in the various spheres of human existence.

SEXUAL PLEASURE

These talks for all practical purposes ignore the positive aspect of sexual pleasure. One would expect that talks dealing precisely with the body would recognize the role of sexual pleasure in marriage and insist that such pleasure is good. This failure to mention the role and goodness of sexual pleasure is somewhat connected with the previous discussions of lust and love. Lust affects primarily the flesh. All recognize that the drive for sexual pleasure often distorts what the pope calls "the nuptial meaning of the body." But sexual pleasure itself is something that is a good that can and often is abused. The failure to develop the proper role of sexual pleasure seems to be associated with a fear of such pleasure and a tendency to see it primarily in a negative way. If the talks gave more importance to a proper self-love and true fulfillment, they would have furnished a proper context for the discussion of sexual pleasure.

CONTEMPORARY U.S. CATHOLIC MORAL
THEOLOGIANS ON MARRIAGE

Writings on marriage in the Catholic tradition involve a number of different theological disciplines—sacramental, spiritual, systematic, moral, and pastoral theologies as well as canon law. The discussion in the second part of this chapter will be limited to the aspect of marriage touching on moral theology in the writings of post–Vatican II moral theologians in the United States.

Different Perspectives

One perspective for how moral theology views marriage is the scholarly perspective with its intended audience being other scholars and not just students and pastors. Theodore Mackin's triology on marriage in the Catholic Church exemplifies this perspective.[10]...*What Is Marriage?* traces the historical development of the understanding of marriage from the Scripture through the new canon law in the early 1980s. Mackin proposes that the Vatican II understanding of marriage as a covenant of love is much better than the older juridical notion of marriage as a contract. In this book too, he argues that in light of marriage as a covenant of love the church should change its teaching on divorce and remarriage.

The most popular perspective for moral theology to address Christian marriage is the pastoral or pedagogical perspective. The pastoral perspective deals with the realities and issues faced by married couples in their lives while the pedagogical aims at teaching students. Since almost all Catholic colleges taught, and many continue to teach, courses in marriage, many writers approach marriage from this perspective. Until the beginning of the twenty-first century, the pastoral and pedagogical perspectives addressed the moral theology of marriage primarily in light of the internal life of the church especially Vatican II and *Humanae vitae*. The teachers and professors of these courses cut their theological teeth in light of Vatican II and the discussions of *Humanae vitae*. Vatican II's call for a scriptural approach and the emphasis on the person also greatly influenced the approach they took to marriage. In addition, as mentioned earlier, Vatican II specifically understood marriage primarily as the loving covenant between spouses mirroring the covenant love of Jesus for the church and not a contract. The issue of contraception for spouses came up in every marriage class and so did the issue of divorce and remarriage.

The writings of Michael G. Lawler of Creighton University and William P. Roberts of Dayton University, both teachers of marriage courses in Catholic colleges in the last quarter of the twentieth century who have written extensively on marriage, follow this internal church approach. The first sentence of the "Foreword" of the Lawler-Roberts 1996, co-edited volume makes the point very clearly. "Among the paradigm shifts that took place at the Second Vatican Council must be counted the change in the church's theological understanding of marriage." The purpose of their book is to probe the implications of this change.[11]

The article by Gloria Blanchfield Thomas in this book on teaching marriage in a Catholic college well illustrates the perspective.[12] Thomas, a happily married Catholic and grandmother, is obviously a good pedagogue who uses lectures, discussions, journaling, and guest speakers to carry out her method of a hermeneutic circle involving experience, Scripture, and church teaching. Her students are apparently predominantly Catholic although some are alienated from the church. The students find the teaching on artificial birth control incredible. One-third of their parents are divorced. Premarital sexuality is an issue for all of them. The women students definitely want equality in marriage and the freedom to pursue careers and hope that the church will help them to live out their commitments in light of their complex lives. Thus, the moral aspects are an important part but only a part of the course on marriage. A course on Catholic marriage taught by a committed Catholic to Catholic students in a Catholic college will tend to emphasize an internal church perspective.

Lawler's 2002 book, *Marriage and the Catholic Church: Disputed Questions*, by definition looks at things only from the viewpoint of the church.[13] His longest section discusses the bond of marriage and the call for the church to change its teaching on divorce and remarriage. He ends the book with a proposal concerning cohabitation and marriage in the Catholic Church. He proposes bringing back into Catholic practice the ceremony of betrothal as well as marriage. Betrothal could occur between prenuptial cohabiters (not non-nuptial cohabiters) and sexual relations would be church approved as the couple proceeds toward marriage. His earlier book *Family: American and Christian* (1998) recognized the problems and difficulties of marriage in contemporary American life, but his emphasis is more on the need for the church to change some of its approaches.[14] But as will be developed shortly, younger Catholic moral theologians are putting much more emphasis on what the Catholic Church and tradition can and should do to support Catholic marriages in our contemporary society and, at the same time, contribute to the transformation of society.

The pastoral or pedagogical perspective has been primary in Catholic moral theology dealing with marriage, but other perspectives have appeared. James and Kathleen McGinnis are Catholic social activists (but James has a Ph.D. in ethics in the area of nonviolence) who wrote *Parenting for Peace and Justice* which sold over 60,000 copies.[15] Their aim is to show how Catholic parents and families can carry out the call to work for justice, peace, and the transformation of the world.

Rosemary Ruether's *Christianity and the Making of the Modern Family* argues from a broad Christian feminist perspective that the conservative evangelical emphasis today on family values is totally wrong and has no basic support from the Christian Bible or tradition.[16] The concept of family has changed dramatically over the years in light of changing sociological, cultural, and economic factors. The New Testament is quite negative about families. The Victorian or "modern" family is the product of a particular social class and a particular historical period. Ruether advocates a pluralism of family forms in which people live together in mutuality with one another and with sustainable communities and environments.

Lisa Sowle Cahill in *Family: A Christian Social Perspective* (2000) in keeping with her usual style, uses biblical, historical, and contemporary church sources to develop her thesis with special emphasis on the family as domestic church.[17] The family is a school of intimacy, empathy, and love, and the family as domestic church tries to transform society by bringing these values to bear on the life of all others especially those suffering from inequality and injustice because of gender, race, or class. Cahill realistically recognizes that at times the surrounding culture has worked against this vision and ideal of Christian families and has prevented such families from truly carrying out their transformative role. In the process, Cahill also condemns the present American welfare system that tends to blame the individual persons and does not recognize how social structures create many problems for the poor and disadvantaged. One chapter develops how African-American families, even when under duress, show to others the true generosity and help of the domestic church.

Cahill describes her own position as a complex middle position mediating between the evangelical conservative and the mainline feminist. The former extols the existing nuclear family, fails to recognize the transformative role of the family, and even tends to support existing inequalities of gender, race, and class. The mainline feminist approach sees diversity in family forms as true liberation from the patriarchal nuclear family but fails to build up better ideals of kin-derived, spousal, and parental relationships and how all families can better serve the common good. Cahill's mediating position sees the family as created by kinship and marriage as the most basic family form, but it is not the only or exclusively legitimate form. The form has some significant meaning, but the most important criterion is the finality of living out the reality of the domestic church. Cahill also disagrees with the approach of the Religion, Culture, and Family Project headed by Don Browning at the University of Chicago with which she had been connected. In her judgment, that approach too narrowly sees the crisis of families in terms of the expressive individualism so rampant in our society that works against marital commitment, but not enough attention is given to the societal aspects and the transformative role of the family.

Considerations of marriage and family raise the issue of the role of women in these institutions and in the broader society. Catholic feminist theologians have addressed this issue and in the process have analyzed and criticized hierarchical church teaching including the many writings of Pope John Paul II. Christine Gudorf points out the schizophrenia in papal teaching on the role of women in the public and private realms. Papal social teaching stresses basic equality and a just democratic system, but papal teaching on the private realm of marriage and family stresses static institutions rooted in divine and natural law, hierarchy, and paternalism.[18]

Cahill traces the development in papal teaching on the family which has moved away from an earlier emphasis on the husband as the head of the family to a greater emphasis on equality. Pope John Paul II insists on the basic rights and equality of women with a special concern for the poor and deplores both violence and discrimination against women. Within marriage and family, John Paul II nowhere calls for the wife to be submissive to the husband. But John Paul II firmly espouses a complementary model of equality and sees the woman's role primarily as mother. Both the civilization of love and the successful raising of children depend on the father's becoming involved in the motherhood of his wife.[19] Gudorf sees John Paul II as exemplifying the biology as destiny school with regard to women but not with regard to men thus seeing the woman primarily in terms of her maternal role. In addition, John Paul II still demonstrates the romantic approach of putting women on a pedestal.[20]

Aline Kalbian likewise disagrees with the papal emphasis on complementarity. She points out that, in the papal language, sex and gender are used indiscriminately. As a result, gender is based on biology and no role is given to the cultural formation of gender. Kalbian sees a connection between moral order, theological order, and ecclesiastical order in official Catholic teaching. Perhaps the metaphor of the church as mother might destabilize some of the understanding of order in these other relationships, which result in a lack of full equality for women.[21] Not all Catholic women agree with Gudorf, Cahill, and Kalbian. Léonie Caldecott warmly embraces John Paul II's "new feminism" with its emphasis on the maternal role of women and a complementarity model.[22]

Behind the papal emphasis on complementarity is the defense of the Catholic Church's teaching and practice of excluding women from ordained ministry. This issue has deeply troubled many women and men in the church; however, the issue lies beyond the concerns of this chapter.

Twenty-First Century Approaches

In the twenty-first century, moral theologians from a different social location began to write about marriage and family. They were younger, married scholars reflecting on their own experience for whom Vatican II and *Humanae vitae* were part of history and not lived experience. Julie Hanlon Rubio appeals to her own experience, Scripture, the marriage liturgy, tradition, the human sciences, contemporary social sciences and also quotes frequently from the teaching of John Paul II (with a few gentle disagreements on the mothering role of women and the complementary roles of husband and wife) in developing her sacramental understanding of the ideal of marriage and family.[23] Obviously, there are different types of families but she wants to hold up the ideal.

Marriage and family are not based on a romantic love of the partners, but are sacramental communities of disciples related to the broader community of the church with its call to transform the world around it. The New Testament shows an ambivalence—both a suspicion of marriage (it tends to be idolatrous and keep people away from discipleship and also incorporates patriarchal inequality) and a respect for the institution of marriage. The New Testament says little about children in the family, but the early church put more emphasis here. Rubio stresses the dual vocation of parents with their commitment to the good of the family but also their vocation to work in the world and try to transform it. Separate chapters discuss mothering, fathering, and welcoming children in the Christian family. She opposes changing the church teaching on divorce and marriage but supports a pastoral policy that permits the divorced and remarried to share fully in the Eucharist. Rubio does not discuss contraception as an issue or as a problem.

David Matzko McCarthy writes from a similar perspective but gives less emphasis to marriage as a sacrament.[24] In light of his Hauerwasian approach, he sees greater opposition between the culture and the Catholic understanding, and maintains there is no role for the family in trying to transform the broader society and world. McCarthy recognizes his book is not the typical book on marriage and family. He strongly criticizes the understanding of marriage based on romantic love and sexual desire which results in the closed, isolated, suburban family. Such a model is heavily influenced by the capitalistic market economy and merely contractual social relations. For similar reasons, he disagrees with the post–Vatican II Catholic personalism which also narrows the family to an interpersonal place with no room for the politics of neighborhood and the economy of home. He proposes as an alternative to the closed, isolated family based on affectionate or interpersonal bonds the open public family grounded in the social and economic operations of the neighborhood and households. Neighborhood and community relationships extend the open family outwards. Thus, the role of the partners in the household is to cultivate the community and neighborhood relationships that make the family truly open and public. McCarthy affirms gender differences but these differences do not result in different familial or public roles. Marriage, love, and sex must always be seen as part of the venture of a rich social life. In this book, McCarthy does not mention his previously expressed support of *Humanae vitae*'s condemnation of artificial contraception for spouses.[25]

Like Rubio, Florence Caffrey Bourg appeals to the resources of her Catholic tradition, calls upon her own experience as a spouse and mother of young children, and strongly opposes romantic love as a basis for families in her book on Christian families—*Where Two or Three are Gathered.*[26] She uses the metaphor of domestic church found in Catholic Church documents since Vatican II and in some other sources to develop her understanding of the Christian family. Bourg sees ordinary family life as a sphere of grace and as an encounter between humans and God. She insists on the equal role of parents in developing the role of the family as the basic cell of society and of the church in character education, formation of religious identity, and the creation of just social structures. The lives of families as domestic churches constitute the focal point around which she organizes insights about sacramental, virtue, and life ethics theologies. Like her dissertation director, Lisa Cahill, Bourg sees the purpose and finality of the Christian family as more important than the form that it takes as is indicated in her inclusive title.

The consideration of marriage and sexuality in post–Vatican II moral theology exemplifies the tension between those who defend the existing hierarchical teachings and those who advocate some changes. At the turn of the century some younger Catholic moral theologians have attempted to move beyond these divisions and tensions.

Notes

1. Pope John Paul II, *Veritatis splendor*, in Miller, *Encyclicals of John Paul II*, 584–661. Note that all Vatican documents can be found on the Vatican website—www.vatican.va.

2. Pope John Paul II, *Familiaris consortio*, in Miller, *Post-Synodal Apostolic Exhortations of John Paul II*, 148–233. Subsequent references in the text will be to *FC* followed by the paragraph number.

3. Pope John Paul II, *Mulieris dignitatem*, in John Paul II, *The Theology of the Body*, 443–92. Subsequent references in the text will be to *MD* followed by the paragraph number.

4. Pope John Paul II, "Letter to Families," *Origins* 23 (1994): 637–59. Subsequent references in the text will be to *LF* followed by the paragraph number.

5. Pope John Paul II, "Letter to Women," *Origins* 25 (1995): 137–43. Subsequent references in the text will be to *LW* followed by the paragraph number.

6. Pope John Paul II, "1995 World Day of Peace: Women: Teachers of

Peace," *Origins* 24 (1994): 465–69. Subsequent references in the text will be to *WTP* followed by the paragraph number.

7. Pope John Paul II, *Theology of the Body*, 25–432.

8. For a positive appraisal of John Paul II's approach, see Janet E. Smith, *Humanae Vitae: A Generation Later* (Washington: Catholic University of America Press, 1991), 230–65; for a negative appraisal, see Luke Timothy Johnson, "A Disembodied 'Theology of the Body': John Paul II on Love, Sex, and Pleasure," *Commonweal* 128, n. 2 (January 26, 2001): 11–17.

9. Bernard V. Brady, *Christian Love: How Christians through the Centuries Have Understood Love* (Washington: Georgetown University Press, 2003).

10. Theodore Mackin, *What Is Marriage? Marriage in the Catholic Church* (New York: Paulist, 1982); Theodore Mackin, *The Marital Sacrament* (New York: Paulist, 1989).

11. Michael G. Lawler and William P. Roberts, eds., *Christian Marriage and Family: Contemporary Theological and Pastoral Perspectives* (Collegeville, Minn.: Liturgical, 1996), vii.

12. Gloria Blanchfield Thomas, "Teaching Marriage in a Catholic College," in *Christian Marriage and Family*, ed. Lawler and Roberts, 176–91.

13. Michael G. Lawler, *Marriage and the Catholic Church: Disputed Questions* (Collegeville, Minn.: Liturgical, 2002).

14. Michael G. Lawler, *Family: American and Christian* (Chicago: Loyola, 1998).

15. James McGinnis and Kathleen McGinnis, *Parenting for Peace and Justice* (Maryknoll, N.Y.: Orbis, 1981); James McGinnis and Kathleen McGinnis, *Parenting for Peace and Justice: Ten Years Later* (Maryknoll, N.Y.: Orbis, 1990).

16. Rosemary Radford Ruether, *Christianity and the Making of the Modern Family* (Boston: Beacon, 2000).

17. Lisa Sowle Cahill, *Family: A Christian Social Perspective* (Minneapolis: Fortress, 2000).

18. Christine E. Gudorf, "Encountering the Other: The Modern Papacy on Women," in *Feminist Ethics and the Catholic Moral Tradition: Readings in Moral Theology No. 9*, ed. Charles E. Curran, Margaret A. Farley, and Richard A. McCormick (New York: Paulist, 1996), 66.

19. Cahill, *Family*, 85–95.

20. Gudorf, "Encountering the Other," in *Feminist Ethics and the Catholic Tradition*, ed. Curran, Farley, and McCormick, 70–85.

21. Aline H. Kalbian, *Sexing the Church: Gender, Power, and Ethics in Contemporary Catholicism* (Bloomington, Ind.: Indiana University Press, 2005).

See also Cristina Traina, "Papal Ideals, Marital Realities: One View from the Ground," in *Sexual Diversity and Catholicism*, ed. Jung and Coray, 269–88.

22. Léonie Caldecott, "Sincere Gift: The Pope's 'New Feminism,'" in *John Paul II and Moral Theology: Readings in Moral Theology No. 10*, ed. Charles E. Curran and Richard A. McCormick (New York: Paulist, 1998), 216–34.

23. Julie Hanlon Rubio, *A Christian Theology of Marriage and Family* (New York: Paulist, 2003).

24. David Matzko McCarthy, *Sex and Love in the Home: A Theology of the Household* (London: SCM, 2001).

25. David Matzko McCarthy, "Procreation, the Development of Peoples, and the Final Destiny of Humanity," *Communio* 26 (1999): 698–721.

26. Florence Caffrey Bourg, *Where Two or Three Are Gathered: Christian Families as Domestic Churches* (Notre Dame, Ind.: University of Notre Dame Press, 2004).

Part Two

THEOLOGY/SPIRITUALITY
OF MARRIAGE

9. Toward a Post–Vatican II Spirituality of Marriage

William P. Roberts

This chapter first appeared in *Christian Marriage and Family: Contemporary Theological and Pastoral Perspectives*, ed. Michael G. Lawler and William P. Roberts (Collegeville, Minn.: Liturgical, 1996).

Three of the key words that have been stressed in Catholic teaching about marriage since the Second Vatican Council are: Partnership, intimacy, and sacramentality. The term "partnership" represents a dramatic shift from the millennia-old patriarchal view of marriage. "Intimacy" highlights the departure from the earlier view that saw procreation as the primary purpose of married life and underscores the importance of the quality of the friendship that a wife and husband ought to enjoy. Indeed, we have come to see that the quality of parenting itself is deeply influenced by the tone of the marital relationship. The belief that marriage is a sacrament has been a part of Catholic teaching for many centuries, but the focus has broadened to include not just the ceremony as sacrament but the entire married life of the couple together as sacrament. The couple become sacrament to one another.

The purpose of this chapter is not to rehash the theology that has been written around these three aspects of Christian marriage. Rather, presupposing that theology, we will strive to suggest some of the implications that each of these terms has for growth in Christian spirituality for a married couple.

PARTNERSHIP

Whether they realized it or not, when the bishops attending Vatican II called marriage a *partnership* of life and love, they struck a fatal blow to the patriarchal view of marriage.[1] Since much of the past Christian spirituality of marriage had been built on a patriarchal view of the marital relationship (the husband, head of the wife as Christ is head of the Church; the wife obedient to the husband as the Church is obedient to Christ), it is urgent that a "new kind of marital spirituality be encouraged that reflects the partnership model."[2] In this chapter we would like to point to some of the directions this kind of spirituality could take.

1. *Basic to a marital spirituality built on partnership is religious belief and faith.* Do we really believe that God created women and men as equal human beings, and that Jesus reaffirmed this equality?

The insights of the Genesis 1 creation account serve as a basis for viewing the female-male relationship as an equal partnership.

> God created man in the image of himself,
> in the image of God he created him,
> male and female he created them.[3]

God is neither male nor female, but transcends both. Both the female and male enjoy the dignity, given them by God, to be created in God's image and likeness.

But it is not only in imaging God that the female and male are on equal footing. They constitute a partnership in participating in God's creative power.

> God blessed them, saying to them, "Be fruitful, multiply, fill the
> earth and subdue it. Be masters of the fish of the sea, the birds
> of heaven and all the living creatures that move on earth."[4]

The advent of Jesus Christ underscored the divine intent that women and men be on equal footing. His teaching about marriage affirmed the Genesis 2 teaching that the two equal human beings, wife and husband, are called by God to become one. He dispelled the double standard that saw adultery only in terms of a violation of a husband's property rights over his wife. In Jesus' perspective, no one owns another, nor should anyone lord it over another.[5] He also rejected the inequality in the practice of divorce that allowed the husband to dismiss his wife, who was usually deprived of any such possibility. Contrary to the Jewish tradition of the time, Jesus had women disciples and made them the first partners in his ministry of proclaiming his resurrection.

Paul appreciated the significance that Christ has for establishing equality among human beings. Through faith in Christ, Paul insisted, we are all children of God, since all who have been baptized have been clothed in Christ. Accordingly, there is no room for any discrimination on the basis of ethnic background, socio-economic status, or gender. We are all one in Christ.[6]

So, prayerful contemplation on the God who is the One who creates all humans, female and male, in God's image and likeness, is essential to a spirituality that approaches marriage as a true partnership. Equally important is prayerful contemplation on Jesus, the Christ, who wishes to free all humans from the bondage of prejudice and high-handedness, and who calls all to "be one, just as, Father, you are in me and I am in you."[7]

2. *Marital partnership demands dying to sexist attitudes.* All Christian living, rooted as it is in baptism, involves participating in the death and resurrection of Jesus. This means dying to sin, so as to live more fully the life of God in Christ.[8] For the married couple a key aspect of this death and resurrection spirituality is the call to die to sexism so as to live in fuller equality and partnership with one another. In light of the many millennia of patriarchalism to which we are all heirs, this can be a more difficult task than usually imagined. Attitudes of male superiority are embedded deeply in the human psyche of both men and women. These attitudes are manifested in the words, gestures, and actions through which many men attempt to put women down. They are also reflected in the way in which many women have interiorized a position of gender subservience. It is a lifelong challenge for a married couple to come to grips with these deep pockets of sexism within themselves, as they strive to build an authentic partnership of life and love.

3. *True partnership means the mutual acceptance of each other on equal footing in regard to all that constitutes an intimate marital union of life and love.* There is something in the human system that seems to drive humans to create hierarchical structures, to compete instead of cooperate, to build and climb ladders rather than engage in the circular dance.[9]

In the Yahwist account of the advent of sin onto the human scene, the imagery of oneness intended by God in Genesis 2 shifts. After the fall, the male finger of accusation is pointed at the woman, and the husband begins his reign of domination over his wife.[10] To create marital partnership is to surrender both the domination and the acceptance of it.

How is this done?

First, by the mutual respect of the equality in being and in dignity that each has. Both are human beings with gifts and faults, with needs and desires, with fears and dreams. Both have ideas worth considering, but ideas that also need reconsidering and, often, reshaping. Both have sensitivities and feelings that deserve to be taken seriously. Each has equal rights: to be free, to follow conscience, to be treated as becomes a human being, to privacy and personal space, to become the person each is called to be, and to form together this unique partnership called marriage. Respecting these rights, and balancing them in ways that do not infringe on the rights of the other take extraordinary degrees of love, respect, caring, sensitivity, and true regard for one another. Such virtues can never come forth from a mean-spirited individual. They can only be born in the heart of a humble, open, and generous person.

Second, by rejecting the ladder model of marriage, and adopting the circular dance model.[11] On a ladder only one person gets to the top, and often only by stepping on other people's fingers, or by throwing them off the ladder altogether. On a ladder there is always a higher and a lower. In a circular dance, however, people are on equal footing. The better one is, the better the other can be. Competition gives way to cooperation. In a circular dance everyone is enriched by the good performance of the other, and everyone has fun.

A patriarchal approach to marriage falls under the ladder model. The husband is head of the wife. She is to defer to him and be the subservient one. A marital partnership, on the other hand, is consonant with the circular dance model. Marriage is, after all, a dance. It takes two to tango. In a dance both must be very present to each other. They must be aware of each other's movements. They must enter into rhythm with one another. There is a joyful working together. Neither strives to get ahead of the other, "to get the upper hand," to compete. The better they coordinate their energies and their creativity, the more beautiful the dance— and the more enjoyable the experience.

Entering into the marital dance requires surrendering unilateral "headship." Instead, both wife and husband become co-creators of the marital union. They become co-heads, co-authors, of the ongoing nurturing that enables them to become more deeply married everyday.

4. *In a partnership both make the decisions.* In any human relationship, there is a temptation for one to control the other. This sinful tendency entered the history of marriage at an early stage. In patriarchal societies it was the husband who won control. He was the one to make the final decisions. His wife was expected to obey.

An insight of the Pauline author in the Letter to the Ephesians points in another direction. In addressing the married couple he begins, "Be subject to one another out of reverence for Christ."[12]

If marriage is truly a partnership, then neither party makes unilateral decisions that the other must obey. Rather, they reach decisions together in a dialogical way. They both express their ideas, feelings, and viewpoints in regard to the issue to be decided. They both listen to each other and take each other seriously. They both learn from each other and broaden one another's perspective. Then they come to agree on a decision with which both are comfortable, and for which both are equally responsible.

This method of decision-making involves many of the traditional virtues. It requires the humility that is necessary to acknowledge that one does not have all the knowledge and all the answers; we need one another for more balanced judgment. It demands respect for the other as a person with gifts, talents, and insights that can complement what I am lacking. It presupposes consideration for the feelings, needs, and desires of another, and the generosity and self-sacrifice to surrender one's own self-centered interest, and bend out of concern for the other.

5. *In a partnership both render service to one another.* Due to patriarchal influence, people were led to believe that it was fair to distribute the

manifold tasks that constitute family life according to gender stereotypes. The husband was breadwinner, the ultimate disciplinarian of the children, and performed the "manly" jobs of cutting the grass, taking out the garbage, and doing home repairs. Most of the more menial tasks connected with rearing children and maintaining a household were left to the wife: baby-sitting, changing diapers, doing the dishes, cooking, washing clothes—and the list is almost endless.

Another viewpoint is provided in John's Gospel. At the Last Supper Jesus performed for his disciples a task that not even a Jewish slave at the time could be commanded to do. He washed the feet of his disciples and, lest the point be missed, explicitly spelled out the lesson. Do you understand "what I have done to you? You call me Master and Lord, and rightly; so I am. If I, then, the Lord and Master, have washed your feet, you must wash each other's feet. I have given you an example so that you may copy what I have done to you."[13]

If marriage is a partnership, both spouses are equally called to serve one another, the family, and the wider community. Together they are co-responsible for all of the services that need to be rendered. These services are divided not on the basis of sexist stereotypes but in light of the talents, time, interests, and energy each has. They are performed not according to legalistic contract, but in a spirit of loving generosity that seeks to lighten the other's burden.

INTIMACY

The marital relationship, according to the bishops at Vatican II, is to be an intimate one.[14] Intimacy is closeness. It is being dear friends. In marriage it is being best friends, who are always there for one another.

The 1917 Code of Canon Law spoke of marriage as the exchange of the permanent and exclusive rights of one's body for acts of sexual intercourse that were suitable for procreation.[15] The spirituality required to fulfill that definition was quite minimal: remain married, do not commit adultery, and respond to each other's "request" for sexual intercourse (or, as the pre–Vatican II moral theology books put it, "render the debt").

Once one accepts marriage as a call to a unique kind of intimacy with one's spouse, the horizons of one's marital spirituality are dramatically expanded. While the demands of the Code's definition can be easily delimited, the challenge to grow in intimacy has no bounds.

The pursuit of marital intimacy brings one into direct confrontation with human sinfulness.[16] Sin involves alienation from God, from other humans, and from the cosmos. God's redemptive grace through Christ calls humans to a new union with the Divine, and with one another. That in a couple which resists marital intimacy is the same as that which resists personal relationship with God and others. This resistance is rooted in self-centeredness, lack of generosity, fear of facing up to truth, and fear of the loss of self. These barriers to intimacy are broken down only by dying to those pockets of darkness and narrowness that reside deep inside the human and that hinder the kind of mutual self-communication needed for personal closeness. By dying to these barriers that stand in the way of authentic marital love and by surrendering oneself in faith, hope, and love to one's spouse, one also opens oneself up to God and to Christ who communicate the gift of their own presence and love through the uniqueness of marital intimacy.

But, concretely, what does achieving such intimacy involve? At the risk of oversimplifying, we will concentrate on four of the elements that are essential for an intimate relationship between wife and husband.

Self-Revelation

Personal unity is built on self-revelation. God brings us into communion with the Divine by revealing God's self to us, and by empowering us to respond. Christ comes to reveal in human terms who God is for us by revealing himself to us as the One sent by God. Humans are made in the image and likeness of God, and marriage for Christians is a sign of God's love, of Christ's love. The intimacy any couple achieves is founded on their mutual self-revelation.

This communication of self one to the other takes place by being willing to surrender some of our protective hiddenness and take the risk of sharing what is on one's mind and in one's heart. By sharing ideas the couple not only get to know the deeper side of the other but also learn from one another. Feelings are shared so that each can participate more deeply in the lived experience of each other: their joys, sorrows, and depressions, their dreams, hopes, and fears, their love and hurts, their satisfaction and disappointments. Being close to another is being comfortable in expressing how I feel, knowing the other will accept me as I am.

This kind of communication demands humility, that is, being honestly in touch with oneself. One must own one's convictions and admit the way one feels. Such communication also requires an inner security that makes possible taking the risk that the other might not understand or might not accept one's ideas or feelings.

Perhaps more difficult than sharing ideas and feelings is revealing one's inner faith and prayer life. To tell you about my faith and prayer experience presupposes a certain degree of closeness, as well as our ability to share in other ways. It also has great bonding power.[17]

Faith sharing refers here not just to telling each other about the religious dogmas one believes in but to reveal something of the way one relates to God. Who is God for us: a distant supreme being? a law-giver in the sky? a judge who punishes the evildoer? or the Abba of our Lord, Jesus Christ, intimately present to us at the core of our being? How do we feel toward this God: fear? trust? love? anger? ambivalence? What meaning does Christ have for us as the Way through whom we can relate to God? How personal is our relationship to Christ? What are our hopes, dreams, fears, doubts about the afterlife, and our final destiny? And when the couple share in this way, are they able to listen to each other in a non-judgmental way, and support each other where they are in their faith journey?

The sharing of prayer is far more than merely reciting prayers together. While joint prayer recitations can be mutually beneficial, the exclusive use of prayers composed by someone else can serve as an escape from revealing one's own prayer life. When a couple pray together spontaneously, in their own words and style, each gives the other a glimpse into one's faith-filled heart and soul. Such sharing helps seal the intimacy experienced in so many of the other moments of married life.

Love

Becoming personally intimate in marriage involves a process whereby the couple evolve from having fallen in love to growing in love.[18] Falling in love is something that happens to the couple. Growing in love takes place as a result of the couple's willful intent to commit themselves to become increasingly one in mind and heart. While falling in love is effortless, growing in love demands determination, dedication, and work.

To love is to be sensitive to another: to be aware of who the other is; to understand what it is like "to walk in the shoes" of the other; to be able to feel with the other. To love is to be responsive to the needs and desires of the other; to be willing to put oneself out in order to help the other grow intellectually, psychologically, and spiritually. Two people grow in love by attuning themselves to each other.

Authentic spousal love brings the couple together in a oneness that enhances, rather than negates, the individuality and identity of each. It binds them in an interdependence that leaves each independent. As they grow in love, they belong increasingly to each other, without either owning, possessing, or dominating the other.[19]

Personal Enjoyment

At the Last Supper, after admonishing the disciples to remain in his love, Jesus added: "I have told you this so that my own joy may be in you and your joy be complete." He then immediately proceeded to exhort them again to "love one another, as I have loved you."[20] Love and joy go hand in hand.

Unfortunately, in our work-oriented society, where too few take time to see and smell the flowers, joy may be, in the minds of most people, one of the last qualities associated with Christian spirituality. The advice of Paul to the Philippians still needs to be taken to heart. After urging Euodia and Syntyche to come to agreement with each other, "in the Lord," and asking Syzygus to really be a partner and help them, Paul reminded his readers: "Always be joyful, then, in the Lord; I repeat, be joyful."[21]

With its preoccupation with celibacy, and the exclusion of married couples from the official teaching authority of the Church, Roman Catholicism has had a difficult time preaching the fullness of the good news in regard to marriage. For centuries prior to Vatican II, the couple's enjoyment of one another was seen as only "a secondary end" of marriage.[22]

In light of this past lack of preaching the virtue of enjoying each other in marriage, combined with the workaholic tendencies of present American culture, it is no wonder that marriage is often depicted more in terms of work, duty, or burden, than of joy. Do many couples even become restless or feel guilty if they take too much time to just bask in the enjoyment of each other's presence? "There are just so many other things that need to get done."

This kind of joy, however, is essential to creating marital intimacy. Close friendship is not just built on love; it also depends on liking the other, on having fun just being together. But enjoying each other's presence requires at least three things. First, a couple must set their priorities straight. Do they really believe that creating personal relationship is more redemptive than making money, or climbing to the top of the career ladder, or "accomplishing" many things?

Second, it is necessary to take the time. It takes time to spend time together, and the fruitful results are far less immediately measurable than when one is busy about many things. To take this kind of time often means sacrificing the "sacredness" of one's own schedule. It means putting other things that one is anxious to get to on the back burner. It means putting oneself out for the sake of the relationship.

Third, I must often be willing to share with the other what I like to do, and, at other times, I ought to be willing to surrender what I would prefer to do, so as to share in what the other likes. While there is joy in doing what I want, there can often be greater joy in doing what the other wants. The key is mutuality.

One final note is in order. To enjoy being with the other implies being able to enjoy sometimes being alone.[23] Too much togetherness can smother. To be in touch with oneself, and to be able to draw on one's own personal resources provides one with the independence needed to create a healthy interdependence. To be able to rest comfortably in one's own self-presence is a precondition for being able to rest comfortably in the presence of the other. To step aside and take the time to fill one's own well, one's own inner storehouse, enables one to share more deeply of one's own personal riches in those moments together.

In a healthy marriage, there is a time to retreat, to be alone, and a time to be together. Mature couples provide both kinds of opportunity.

Sexual Intimacy

There is wisdom to be found in the fact that the ancient Israelites referred to sexual intercourse as "knowing" another. If intercourse is performed in a human way, that is, with mind and heart and soul, as well as with body, then the spouses, indeed, reveal themselves to each other in all of their nakedness, physical, spiritual, intellectual, and emotional. Such intimate exchange catches up all the intimate sharings in the rest of their marriage, and, in turn, enhances and enriches them.

In the not too distant past, it was just about unheard of to speak of the spirituality of sexual intimacy. The life of celibacy was perceived as the "higher state." It was seen as a precondition for real holiness. In fact, "celibacy" became, in common usage, synonymous with "chastity."[24] While Augustine's pessimistic view of marital intercourse had been abandoned, marriage continued to be widely viewed as a second-class way of Christian living, suitable for those who were not generous and courageous enough to embrace the celibate state. Even today, despite the many positive things that the Church has recently said about sexual intimacy, most ecclesiastical justifications of the celibacy mandate for priests contain, by implication, a putting down of marriage and marital intercourse.[25]

For our purposes here we can reflect on four dimensions of a Christian spirituality of sexual intimacy.

1. *Marital sexual intimacy is as valid an expression of Christian chastity as celibacy.* Chastity consists in taking all of one's sexual energies and directing them in personal commitment and love for the personal growth of oneself and others. In marriage this is done by giving all one is as an active sexual being to one's spouse for the personal enrichment of the lives of both as well as the continued life-giving for any children who come from the marriage and the wider community whom the couple serve. Marital chastity consists in being for the other in sexual love rather than using or exploiting the other. Marital chastity involves

abstinence: abstinence from all extra-marital sexual activity; and abstinence from the genital expression of love with one's spouse when that would not be to the benefit of the other or of the relationship.[26] Chastity for married couples means daring to take the risk and expose oneself in all one's vulnerabilities, so that the personal bonding between the two will be forever deepened. It means giving freely of oneself with the firm belief that neither will betray the trust and both will ever remain faithful to this covenant of sexual intimacy.

2. *Achieving healthy sexual intimacy implies grateful acceptance of the gift of human sexuality.* Each is comfortable with her/his own body and sexuality. Each accepts the gift of the unique sexual being that the other is. Both see sexual intimacy in its beauty and goodness as a gratuitous, graceful, and grace-filled gift from the Creator.

3. *Sensitivity, caring, concern, and empathy toward one's partner are essential ingredients for a mutually satisfying sexual relationship.* Such qualities, however, can only be present in this intimate exchange to the degree that they are present in all the other details of the marriage.

4. *Belief that marital sexual intimacy is a sacrament, a sign of the intimate love that God and Christ have for us adds a further transcendent dimension.*[27] The love of God and Christ both serve as a model for the way the spouses manifest their love for each other, as well as enable them to experience God's and Christ's healing and redemptive love through the expression of their own sexual love.

SACRAMENTALITY

Three inadequacies have manifested themselves in much of the common perception of marriage as a sacrament. First, despite the official position of the Latin Rite of the Roman Catholic Church that the couple are the ministers of the sacrament of marriage, the way most Catholics talk and write about wedding ceremonies seems to attribute that role to the priest or deacon. Second, until recently at least, the common view tended to limit the sacrament to the ceremony, rather than see the totality of the Christian couple's marriage as a sacrament. Third, the sacrament of marriage is often not sufficiently perceived in the context of the other sacraments. In this final section of the chapter, we examine the sacramental dimension of marital spirituality by viewing the married life of Christian spouses in the context of all of the sacraments.

Marriage and Baptism/Confirmation

The Christian is baptized into the crucified and risen Christ.[28] By the power of the Spirit s/he dies to sinfulness and participates now in the life of the risen Christ and in Christ's union with the God whom Jesus calls Abba. By virtue of baptism s/he is called to the fullness of Christian holiness, that is, the perfection of love.[29] As one explicitly and consciously relates to the Christian community, s/he is called to share in the ongoing mission of Christ in the Church to promote God's Kingdom, God's reign. In confirmation both the baptismal gift and the person's intent to live out one's baptism are confirmed.

The sacramental life of Christian marriage ought to be chosen as a particular way in which the couple see they can best grow in Christian holiness and participate in Christ's mission. In marriage they renew their baptismal commitment and give it new direction. They will continue to share in Christ's death and resurrection by dying to all the sinful obstacles that can stand in the way of marital partnership and intimacy, and by growing in union with Christ through their growth in oneness with each other. They will strive to grow in the perfection of love by nurturing each other, their family, and those outside the household whom they are called to serve. They will deepen their relationship to the church by creating a domestic church, that will both nourish and be nourished by the wider Church.

Marriage and Eucharist

The night before he died Jesus took bread and wine, gave them to his disciples with the invitation to take and eat, take and drink, for this bread is his body given for them, and this cup of wine is his blood (his life) poured out for the forgiveness of sin. He then added the admonition to do this in memory of him.[30]

Christian married couples are called not only to celebrate the Eucharistic liturgy but also more significantly to live Eucharistically, indeed, to become Eucharist, especially for one another.[31] What does this mean? How can it be done? For our purposes here, three of the ways in which a married couple's spirituality can be Eucharistic will be addressed.

First, one can appreciate and experience the Eucharistic dimension of shared family meals. In the Eucharist Christ, through the giving and sharing of the bread and the wine, enters into communion with us. There are two critical questions for married couples. Do we arrange our schedules and take the time to eat together often enough? When we do, are we just eating side by side, or are we sharing the meal as a way of entering into deeper personal communion with one another?

Second, in the Eucharist Christ gives us bread and wine as a sign of the gift of himself in personal presence and intimate friendship to us. What redeems, what transforms, what enriches the life of the Christian is not the bread and the wine in themselves, but Christ's self-gift in nurturing love. In marriage the couple give and do many things for each other. A crucial question to be asked is: Are the things they give and do a sign of their gift of themselves to one another in intimacy and love, or are they cheap substitutes for the sacrificial gift of being personally present to each other, and being for each other?[32]

Third, in the Eucharist Christ gives us his body and blood, that is, all he is as a living person. This giving in Eucharist is sign of his self-giving in all the other moments that constitute human living. The Christian's openness to Christ's gift in Eucharist, in turn, deepens one's awareness and receptivity of this gift in the totality of one's life. Marital sexual intercourse can parallel this dynamic. Through their bodily expression of love the couple can communicate the gift of themselves to each other. They, thus, can celebrate in this present moment the gift they have been for each other in the history of their relationship, and reaffirm their pledge to be gift for one another in all of the tomorrows they have together on this earth. In light of this experience, and in light of their faith experience of Eucharist, they can come to see that at the core of the meaning of the sacramentality of marriage is this: that through the mutual gifts of themselves Christ communicates the gift of himself.

Marriage and Reconciliation

What do the paralytic, the woman caught in adultery, Zacchaeus, the woman who anointed Christ's feet, and the disciples in the room on Easter Sunday evening have in common?[33] They all experienced the forgiveness of Jesus. Christ's ministry of forgiveness is not merely a reality of the past. It is a reality of the present. Christ's ministry of forgiveness continues in the community of the forgiving and the forgiven.

Where does the sacramentalizing of this ministry of forgiveness begin? In personal relationships. Of all relationships marriage is uniquely intimate. When two people become that close, vulnerabilities are made naked. Hurts, misunderstandings, mistakes are inevitable. The need to say "I am sorry," "I forgive" is imperative. Through all these little rituals of sorrow and forgiveness, the couple mediate to each other the healing forgiveness of Christ. These sacramental rituals can then be more formally celebrated in what is called the sacrament of reconciliation.

Marriage and Healing

No one is perfectly whole. We are all, as Bernard Bassett indicated a few decades ago, "slightly neurotic."[34] One of the important aspects of a loving, mature marriage is its power to heal some of the things that ail us. Three areas of marital healing can be cited here. A loving couple can help heal in each other some of the obstacles that can stand in the way of growing more fully in the relationship. By their mutual love they can heal some of the wounds in their self-image that cause them to think poorly of themselves, and to lack belief in their innate strengths and gifts. As their self-image is healed, their inner security is strengthened and they are gradually freed from some of the fears of rejection that prevent them from getting closer to one another. In a good marriage a couple can also heal each other from the hurts and scars inflicted in their transactions with the "outside world." Their mutual understanding strengthens them when they are misunderstood by relatives, friends, and colleagues at work. Their belief in one another helps them overcome their self-doubts when they are challenged by new opportunities that at first seem beyond their capabilities. Their acceptance of each other is a salve when they "fail" in a pet enterprise, or in getting a job or a promotion.

Finally, a caring couple contribute to the health and well-being of each other. They do this by creating an environment that provides happiness, a sense of self-fulfillment, and the kind of diet, leisure, and general life style that promotes psychological and physical health. This nurturing of the health of one another takes on special meaning when an ill spouse is nursed by the other and either helped on the road to recovery or enabled to deal with a terminal illness in a constructive way.

Priestly Ministry

Through baptism all Christians are called to share in the priestly ministry of Christ.[35] Married couples exercise this priestly ministry in a variety of special ways. They minister the sacrament of marriage to each other. They exercise a leadership role in forming the family, which Vatican II calls the domestic church. They are teachers and nurturers of the faith, especially in regard to their children. They also call the family to worship and are leaders of family prayer.

In conclusion, partnership, intimacy, sacramentality: these are three key notions that are an integral part of a post–Vatican II theology of marriage. One approach to a contemporary Christian spirituality of marriage is to engage in the prayer, the self-assessment, and the pursuit of the human qualities (or, virtues, if you will) necessary to achieve, to an ever increasing degree, a marriage that is truly an intimate, sacramental partnership. If this is done, the couple will not only have achieved a high degree of oneness, they will also have journeyed along that path to perfection to which Jesus says we are all called.[36]

Notes

1. Pastoral Constitution on the Church in the Modern World, 48. All references in this chapter to the teachings of the Second Vatican Council are to Walter M. Abbott, S.J., ed., *The Documents of Vatican II* (New York: America Press, 1966).

2. A literalist reading of Ephesians 5:21–33 would seem, on the surface, to support a patriarchal approach to marriage. In chapter 2 of *Marriage: Sacrament of Hope and Challenge* (Cincinnati: St. Anthony Messenger Press, 1988), I have shown how this text, interpreted in context, does not endorse such a view.

3. Genesis 1:27. All Scripture quotations in this chapter are taken from *The New Jerusalem Bible* (Garden City, N.Y.: Doubleday & Company, 1985).

4. Genesis 1:28.

5. Matthew 20:24–28.

6. Galatians 3:25–28.

7. John 17:21.

8. See Romans 6:1–11.

9. I am borrowing here from imagery that is employed in the writings of Matthew Fox. See, for example, "Sexuality and Compassion: From Climbing Jacob's Ladder to Dancing Sarah's Circle" in *A Spirituality Named Compassion and the Healing of the Global Village, Humpty Dumpty and Us* (Minneapolis: Winston Press, 1979), 36–67.

10. See Genesis 3:12 and 16.

11. My reflection here is very much influenced by Matthew Fox's treatment of this imagery, referred to above.

12. Ephesians 5:22.

13. John 13:13–15.

14. Pastoral Constitution on the Church in the Modern World, 48.

15. T. Lincoln Bouscaren, S.J., and Adam C. Ellis, S.J., *Canon Law: A Text and Commentary* (Milwaukee: Bruce Publishing, 1957), canon 1081.

16. I am influenced here by the reflections of Theodore Mackin in his essay, "How To Understand The Sacrament of Marriage," in William P. Roberts, ed., *Commitment to Partnership: Explorations of the Theology of Marriage* (Mahwah, N.J.: Paulist Press, 1987).

17. The research done by Andrew Greeley and the National Opinion Research Center at the University of Chicago supports the link between sharing religious devotion and prayer and achieving romantic intimacy. See interview with Andrew Greeley, *Catholic Telegraph*, November 2, 1990, 10.

18. See Christopher C. Reilly, *Making Your Marriage Work: Growing in Love After Falling in Love* (Mystic, Conn.: Twenty-Third Publications, 1989), especially 6–21.

19. Three helpful descriptions of love are found in the writings of M. Scott Peck, Louis Evely, and Segundo Galilea. Love, M. Scott Peck says in *The Road Less Traveled* (New York: Simon and Schuster, 1978), is "the will to extend one's self for the purpose of nurturing one's own or another's spiritual growth," 81. Evely writes in *That Man Is You* (Westminster, Md.: Newman

Press, 1966): "To love someone is to bid him to live, invite him to grow," 102. About love, Galilea has this to say in *Spirituality of Hope* (Maryknoll, N.Y.: Orbis Books, 1989): "The mandate of love is to let others be what they are in their deepest identity," 18.

20. John 15:11, 12.

21. Philippians 4:4.

22. As witnessed to in canon 1013 of the 1917 Code.

23. For an excellent treatment of creative solitude, as opposed to empty aloneness, see Edward R. Dufresne, *Partnership: Marriage and The Committed Life* (Mahwah, N.J.: Paulist Press, 1975), ch. 3, "Solitude in Marriage," 39–54.

24. For example, the second vow of the three taken by members of religious communities was commonly—though, inaccurately—referred to as the vow of chastity. Such language ignores the fact that all Christians, including the married, are called to a life of chastity. The marriage vow is nothing if it is not a commitment to marital chastity.

25. This is especially true of the argument that says the priest must be unmarried in order to "fully dedicate himself to God"; as if baptism did not already call each of us to such a dedication, and the sacrament of marriage, lived sincerely and authentically, cannot be an expression of this kind of commitment.

26. For example, because of illness, fatigue, or because it is not the opportune moment.

27. This point is further explained in my booklet *Sex Is Sacramental* in the *Faith Notes* series (St. Meinrad, Ind.: Abbey Press, 1991).

28. Romans 6:3–4.

29. Dogmatic Constitution on the Church, ch. 5, "The Call of the Whole Church to Holiness."

30. Matthew 26:26–29; Mark 14:22–25; Luke 22:19–20; 1 Corinthians 11:23–26.

31. For further treatment of this theme see my *Marriage: Sacrament of Hope and Challenge* (Cincinnati: St. Anthony Messenger Press, 1988), ch. 6, "Bread Broken, Body Given."

32. I use the word "sacrifice" here in its root meaning from the Latin *sacer* (sacred) and *ficare* (to make). What sanctifies a couple's relationship, and renders them increasingly sacred to each other is the gift of their personal presence to one another in all of the routine dealings that constitute married life.

33. Luke 5:17–26; John 8:1–11; Luke 19:1–10; Luke 7:36–50; John 20:19–23.

34. Bernard Bassett, S.J., *We Neurotics* (Fresno: Academy Guild Press, 1962).

35. Dogmatic Constitution on the Church, 10. Also see 1 Peter 2:5–9.

36. Matthew 5:48.

10. The Nuptial Mystery

Angelo Scola

This chapter first appeared in *Communio* 25 (Winter 1988).

In the present context, it is not possible to develop a full account of the analogical levels—if I may use the technical term—characteristic of the nuptial mystery. I will therefore limit myself to reflecting on some anthropological implications which might be of help on the personal and ecclesial paths that each one of us is called to tread. Concretely, I intend to highlight the three elements implicated by the nuptial mystery; but I will consider these on the basis of the daily experience of those who strive to live their lives in Christ, or, if they have not yet received the grace of an explicit encounter with Christ, those who, at the very least, are permeated with a religious outlook on life.

For convenience's sake, I will give you the titles first. First of all, I would like to dwell on the general meaning of nuptiality, understood as the interconnection of sexual difference, love, and procreation. Secondly, I will endeavor to show how the human experience of nuptiality lies at the heart of the Church according to God's original plan. Thirdly and finally, I will look at the task the nuptial mystery implies for the married faithful.

As a side note, it bears remarking that it matters little for our purposes whether we speak of male/female sexual difference, or—to use the Anglo-Saxon vocabulary—"gender." These expressions are not altogether synonymous. In fact, there are nuances of difference implied in these variations in vocabulary. As has been recently pointed out, it is not the same thing to talk about gender rather than sexual difference or maleness/femaleness.[1] A difference in expression can be a way of insinuating an ideological reduction of the reality of things. Thus, for example, the category of gender, especially when it is transposed into the context of a Latin mentality, may lend itself more easily than that of maleness/femaleness to nullifying the weight of physiological evidence that establishes differences between masculinity and femininity.[2] Nonetheless, on a general level such as ours, these differences do not significantly affect the meaning of things, and we may thus use the terms interchangeably.

THE GENERAL MEANING OF NUPTIALITY AS THE INTERCONNECTION OF SEXUAL DIFFERENCE, LOVE, AND PROCREATION

We have already said that, by the expression "nuptial mystery," we mean first of all the concrete experience of the man-woman relationship that lies at the very origin of the phenomenon of nuptiality in all its various types, and thus forms its constitutive nucleus. Using the language of analogy, we might say that this relationship represents the *analogatum princeps*. We see in this affirmation one of the most fundamental exigencies of the history of thought in general and of the tradition of Christian thought in particular, namely, its realism.[3] Human thought is made to grasp reality. It therefore communicates with reality. It is on this basis that human thought becomes capable of knowledge and at the same time of language, that is to say, of communication with others.

Today, however, thought's elementary capacity to relate to reality is very often ignored. I am convinced that, in the concrete situation that besets Christianity today, conversion (*metanoia*) is necessary also in this respect. This is the invitation extended by the motto first used by Husserl, a motto that turns up in every aspect of the Anglo-Saxon culture. I am referring to the urgency of turning (*cum-vertere*) to things just as they are, to reality in itself. What we need today is a conversion "to the real." Only thus will it be possible to grasp the mystery of which reality itself is always the *sign*. A *real sign*—it is exactly this! In more technical terms, we could say that reality presents itself as an event (*e-venio*)[4] that calls on our freedom to adhere to it. Allow me to have recourse to Chesterton in order to express this structural listening to the real which, as it happens to us (this is what "event" means!), sets in motion the creativity of the "I." In the novel *The Napoleon of Notting Hill* we find the following paradoxical dialogue:

> "And then something did happen. Buck, it's the solemn truth that nothing has ever happened to you in your life. Nothing has ever happened to me in my life."
>
> "Nothing ever happened!" said Buck, staring. "What do you mean?"
>
> "Nothing has ever happened," repeated Barker, with a morbid obstinacy. "You don't know what a thing happening means? You sit in your office expecting customers, and customers come; you walk in the street expecting friends, and friends meet you; you want a drink and get it; you feel inclined for a bet and make it. You expect either to win or lose, and you do either one or the other. But things happen!" and he shuddered ungovernably.
>
> "Go on," said Buck, shortly. "Get on."
>
> "As we walked wearily round the corners, something happened. *When something happens, it happens first, and you see it afterwards.*...It happens of itself, and you have nothing to do with it."[5]

This is the primacy of reality as an event that calls on our freedom!

Entering now more directly into the mystery of the man-woman relationship, let us once again set forth the question that—in a simple and unparalleled manner—John Paul II posed in the striking catechesis on spousal love (theology of the body) at the beginning of his pontificate. I am referring to the following assertion: "The definitive creation of mankind consists in the creation of unity of two beings. Their unity above all denotes the identity of human nature; the duality, on the other hand, manifests what, on the basis of this identity, constitutes the masculinity and femininity of created man."[6] John Paul II took this theme up again even more explicitly in the third part—which still has not been studied in depth—of *Mulieris dignitatem*: "It is a question of understanding the reasons and the consequences of the decision of the Creator that the human being would always exist only as female or male."[7]

Going back to things in themselves—listening to the real—when speaking about nuptiality means answering the demand to welcome the data that offers itself directly to the consciousness of each one of us. Every man and woman in fact comes into the world as a sexual being (man or woman), in the context of a parental relationship, and in most cases, at least until recently,[8] born out of a conjugal act that involves the love of a man and a woman (two persons of a different sex), regardless of the couple's intention. Because I am born from a father and mother, I thus stand within a constitutive relationship which our tradition identifies with the term "marriage," as the basis of the reality of the family. What does all of this mean?[9]

I will respond briefly using a somewhat technical expression, but one that until now has seemed the most effective to bring to a point all of the data concerning nuptiality. Nuptiality, in its interconnection of sexual difference, love and fruitfulness, manifests a reciprocity between me and another. This reciprocity bears a very peculiar characteristic which I call "asymmetry." *Asymmetrical reciprocity* (this is the technical term!) is thus the meaning of nuptiality.[10]

Let us begin with the category of reciprocity: its immediate meaning is quite clear. There exists another modality other than my own for embodying the total identity (*corpore et anima unus*) of the human person, namely, that of the woman. My existence as a sexual being means, in some sense, that I am placed from the beginning in relation to another. The other is presented to me as being identical in her own being as a person but, at the same time, because of sexual difference, she reveals to me a radical difference that distinguishes her from me at all levels. Thus if my way of embodying the identity of person is masculine, the feminine mode that stands before me is a *different way* of being a person. The reciprocity that springs from sexual difference thus shows that the "I" emerges into existence from within a kind of constitutive polarity.[11] In order to be able to say "I" in the fullest sense, I need to take the other into account; I have the possibility of (that is, the resource for) taking the other into account. Therefore, the expressions "male-female," "sexuality" or "gender" identify in concise terms wherein the difference lies. A difference that comes to light within a unity[12] never destroys the unity of human nature, which belongs to each of the two.

This is why the pope, like Balthasar, speaks of a *dual unity*. It is worth saying that man, as he exists here and now (*Dasein*), is not a purely spiritual subject. We do not find spiritual subjects walking in the street; when we look at our son or daughter, we always see a male or female human being. We are dealing with a relationship that is intrinsically connected with the fundamental experience of the self-awareness of our "I," to such an extent that it is coessential with it. There is no reason to waste words here: it suffices to recall our mother's smile when we were children and how decisive this smiling and friendly "*thou*" was for us to be able to say "*I*" with greater force and energy.[13] It happens, for example, when we enter into a friend's house, that a child who does not know us might hide in his mother's skirts. Then, when a conversation begins between his parents and the "stranger," the child enters the circle of communication; he detaches himself from the mother and moves towards the friend. In a certain sense the child realizes that the other is quite different, and this at first puts him on his guard. But then this diversity is eventually revealed to him as something good, as a resource that makes the "I" grow. The example shows us in passing that the "other" is obviously a category broader than that of the "other sex." Nevertheless, it is undeniable that the original and basic experience of otherness is founded on sexual otherness. It is not necessary to get involved in depth psychology to see this.[14]

Why in fact do we qualify this reciprocity as *asymmetrical?* I will explain by making reference to a significant passage from Plato's *Symposium*, in which Aristophanes imagines that sexual difference—the existence of people as male and female—is due to the jealousy of a god who cut into two halves a being who initially formed a unity. Sexual difference would therefore indicate the path that the two halves would have to follow in the almost always failed attempt to recover the much desired original unity.[15] This androgynous vision of things, widespread today, is profoundly erroneous.[16] The error lies in the fact that reciprocity is "thought" as simple complementarity. On the contrary, sexual reciprocity is not simple complementarity, but possesses, rather, an important asymmetry, and this for at least two reasons. The first reason is quite obvious: every male and female lives simultaneously and as if in his or her very foundations, a plurality of relationships with the other sex. My "I" is simultaneously a point of reciprocity for different persons of the other sex, each of whom has a different *status*. I am immediately related to my mother, sister, a female friend, and so on, and when I relate to someone of the other sex, I am not at all polarized in a search for a fictitious other half of myself.

It is important to see, however, that this is nothing but the macroscopic expression of the true, radical meaning of asymmetry (*asimmetricità*). Asymmetry consists in the fact that sexual difference, in a significant and immediate way, testifies that the other always remains "other" for me. One can even say that "the aspiration to overcome the duality of the sexes is more than just a tragic illusion: it is the death of love itself and of those who love."[17] We find a confirmation of this point in depth psychology (which is certainly not likely to "connive" with the Christian vision of things). Psychoanalysis, for example, clearly affirms that sexual difference, in a certain sense, cannot be overcome. It cannot be deduced, that is, it cannot be translated into concepts, because it is precisely the decisive practical point in which the "I" experiences that the "other" always stands before him as "other." At the very moment in which the "other" presents himself as the condition and the occasion for the fulfillment of the "I," this same "other" leaves the "I" at a distance, by saying repeatedly "I am another for you."[18] This occurs even in that special place of unity between man and woman, in marriage, which is called the conjugal act. In this instance, to use the great expression of the Judeo-Christian tradition, the "one flesh" comes into being; and even in the "one flesh" the "other" remains "other" for me (asymmetrical reciprocity). Why is this?

The reason lies in the fact that the *difference between the two* (the man and the woman) *makes space for a third*, and this once again speaks of otherness. The reciprocity does not cancel the difference because it is asymmetrical, since it exists not for the sake of androgynous union of two halves, but for the procreation of the child. This is the fruit that is essentially connected to the love of the two persons. To avoid misunderstanding, this assertion requires a few words about love. Asymmetrical reciprocity, which we have been discussing, is rooted in man's instinctive nature, draws this instinctive desire from the unconscious, accompanies it in the preconscious, and manifests it as the ontological value that leads St. Thomas to define desire as *amor naturalis*.[19] Therefore asymmetrical sexual reciprocity forms the anthropological foundation that makes the experience of love possible.

An author whom I know is dear to you all, C. S. Lewis, comes to our aid. In his beautiful Anglo-Saxon style full of subtle irony, he presents the theme of love. I am referring to his wise and delightful essay, *The Four Loves*.[20] Lewis rightly rebels against the idea of using different words to describe the complex forms of the phenomenon of love. According to many thinkers, even some Christian ones, we should not use the word "love" for describing physical love, and at the same time for speaking about spiritual or ecstatic love, which implies a going out of oneself. By contrast, Lewis maintains that all expressions of love fall under the same category, "love." Even the most degraded form of commercialized love, which he calls *Venus*, no matter how debased and disfigured it may be, does not cease to possess the traits of love and should be called "love." The fact that love is realized in degrees that are enormously different does not prevent these different degrees from retaining the name "love." For this reason Lewis contests the opposition of so-called "Need-love" and Gift-love": "It would be a bold and silly creature that came before its Creator with the boast 'I'm no beggar. I love you disinterestedly.' Those who come nearest to a Gift-love for God will in the next moment, even at the very same moment, be beating their breasts with the publican and laying their indigence before the only real Giver. And God will have it so."[21]

The passage from Lewis is related to what I said earlier about the necessity, which we can ill-afford to give up today more than ever, of starting with things as they are. Now, human love has to take into account the constitutive dimensions of human nature, which is made up both of soul and body. Love should not be thought of as something angelic, any more than it should be reduced to mere animal instinct. There must always be a unity, even at its highest level, between the instinctual, psychological, and spiritual dimensions. Nature is not opposed to freedom, but, as St. Thomas teaches us when he talks about natural inclinations as one of the orienting foundations of natural law and ethics,[22] it offers freedom guidelines that the latter is called on to choose, and thereby personalizes them. This is why we cannot talk about love without involving sexual difference and what this objectively signifies, namely, the objective orientation of the conjugal act towards procreation! In this respect, sexual reciprocity means "love" and at the same time, by reason of its asymmetry, it means an openness to the fruits of love, to fecundity, and procreation. This is not the occasion to work out in detail the intrinsic link that connects sexual difference, love, and procreation; it suffices to emphasize that the asymmetry that characterizes sexual reciprocity is necessary because of the fact that the two persons who come together in "one flesh," regardless of the degree of awareness with which the act occurs (although this is of course also important), are taken up into a dynamic that opens them to the procreation of a child who is the very fruit of love according to the vision that has quite rightly permeated the whole Western world: *amor est diffusivum sui*.[23]

THE NUPTIAL MYSTERY: "ONE FLESH," OR THE LOGIC OF THE INCARNATION (SACRAMENT)

It is possible at this point to understand how the structure of human sexuality is part of a design in which we are called to participate. Welcoming this call belongs to the religious sense that characterizes humanity. The person who perceives the dimension of mystery connected to nuptiality recognizes in its constitutive factors signs through which Mystery itself calls on the person. Whoever, on the other hand, claims to deny this religious sense will be led to read the phenomenon of nuptiality (sexuality, love, fecundity) as something closed in on itself. This person will constantly be tempted to reduce nuptiality to the realm of the inner-worldly and will not be able to see how our nuptiality could contain in itself that remarkable openness of nature, with all of its biological and psychological laws but also its reason, toward the transcendent. The experience of sexuality gives rise to an interaction between nature and culture which not only contributes to fulfilling the history of each "I," but at the same time the history of humanity as a whole, allowing also for an authentically ecological relationship, that is, a fully healthy relationship, with the universe.

Religious man finds it natural to let this threefold asymmetrical reciprocity call on him and provoke him to ask why things are as they are: we only need think of the amazement that a new-born child stirs up in the hearts of its parents. This is an amazement full of humility because of the disproportion of such a gift, as it were. It is a humility that raises the heart toward the Author of life and causes us to fall on our knees in adoration and at the same time fills us with awe for being so unworthy of the gift received.

For the religious person who is a Christian, that is to say for the one who has encountered in the person of Christ a powerful and adequate response to religious yearning, the provocation that arises from the asymmetrical reciprocity of sexuality marks only the beginning of an exhilarating road that leads, by grace, to the heart of the Mystery himself.

In this regard, revelation, as manifest in Scripture and as abiding in "the place of practice and experience" that Blondel called Tradition—the place that joins us in unbroken continuity to the group of friends who lived with Jesus by the lake of Gennesaret, who participated in the important and dramatic final events in Jerusalem and who were able to touch the wounds of the Risen One[24] with their own hands—proposes the nuptial mystery as the key for understanding (by analogy, of course) the salient aspects, the dogma, of our faith.

It is useful here to list in order the three most fundamental aspects. First of all, there is the relationship between Christ and the Church that is presented, particularly in chapter five of the Letter to the Ephesians, as a relationship between a Bridegroom and a Bride.[25] Then there is the existence of the two natures in the one person of Jesus Christ as the foundation[26] that makes possible the "one flesh" of the two spouses that stems from the sacrament of marriage. Finally, there is the nuptial dimension within the Trinity[27] where the difference between the Divine Persons lives in perfect unity as the cause and reason for the possibility of unity in difference which is proper to the man-woman relationship.

As I have already said, it is not my intention in this forum to go into too much detail concerning nuptiality in all its aspects. I will simply limit myself to looking at two anthropological considerations which carry an important practical significance. In the first place, the meaning of our chapter's title should now be clearer. In fact, to reiterate, when we talk about the nuptial mystery at the heart of the Church, we are not only referring to the experience of asymmetrical reciprocity which is given to us in the love between a man and a woman, but we are moved by faith itself to inquire into the relationship between Christ and the Church, the event of Christ, and the mystery of the Trinity. The mystery of nuptiality shows itself to be harmoniously unified and complex at the same time!

The question now arises: how is it possible to hold all these meanings in a unity and justify them, without becoming vulnerable to the objection that we have thereby left the field of the verifiable experience of human sexuality to end up prey to arbitrary constructions, perhaps the fruit of the fervent imagination of some particularly well-versed theologian, but alien to everyday practical human existence? To address this objection, we have to penetrate deeply into the logic of Christianity and grasp its profound nature. *This is the logic of the Incarnation or of the sacrament.*[28] I believe that one of the most serious temptations that besets Christians today is that of spiritualism. What I mean is the often unintentional but nevertheless serious way that some people have of looking at Christ's ascension as a disincarnation. It is fairly common, even among Christians, to find the practical belief that, ultimately, the event of Christ does not succeed in being present materially in the here and now of history. Jesus Christ is not considered effectively present to every person of every age. He is treated like a fact of the past! If this is so, then Jesus Christ ceases to be an event! Even if he could be considered as the paradigmatic model for human behavior, he will invariably be reduced to a hypothesis. Thus his truth and his substance will be lost. In my opinion, we have here one of the most insidious objections to Christianity.[29] Arising with the Enlightenment, this unresolved challenge continues to surface, as forcefully as ever, both in the experience of the individual and of the Christian community, especially in the inter-religious and multi-cultural context which today characterizes the mission of the Church. Christ is treated like a fact of the past, a noble metaphor that inspires our conduct. By contrast, the logic of the Incarnation is the logic of the real sign which, according to the form of the sacrament, makes the event of Christ present to the freedom of modern man, calling him to follow. This logic leads us to read every circumstance, every relationship, as a sign of Christ's happening for me here and now. It is only in this perspective that the fundamental experience of being human is flooded with light at every level, including that of the asymmetrical reciprocity found in the man-woman relationship.

Here the "I" is called not only to make space so that the other may say "I," but the two spouses are moreover led, in a certain sense, to transcend themselves as unity-of-two (a dual unity) so as to welcome a third person, the child. This reveals that, in the reality of the very love that unites the two, there is an inherent moment of ascent towards a mysterious "*Quid.*" Thus the question concerning what lies behind this ascending dynamism becomes even more acute. Balthasar helps us to find an answer. He asks himself: "When the trinitarian God...creates the couple, what does he create? What is the original couple in the mind of God?"[30] According to the theologian from Basel, God first had in mind the perfect archetype of the couple, namely, Christ the Bridegroom and the Church his Bride. The experience of the man-woman relation thus encounters its fullest meaning, which is its final (eschatological) and for this reason its primordial meaning, only in reference to this original relation. The truth of nuptiality is thus contained in the modality by which Christ generates his Bride in the total self-gift of the cross, and continues his relationship with her according to the logic of the sacrament.

From this perspective, it becomes clearer what it means to speak of the family as the domestic Church. In the first place, the expression does not mean that the family is a particular cell in a large diocesan community in the formal-juridical sense. If it did, then we would be left with the difficult task of determining the particular prerogatives of this familial domestic Church (are the spouses the "ministers" of the domestic Church? What is involved in such a ministry? Should the Eucharist be celebrated in the family?). The Council, referring to the Fathers of the Church,[31] sought instead to call the members of the family to take joy in the creative depth of the relationship between a man and woman founded on the sacrament of marriage. What is at issue here is the possibility of living every day more deeply and thus participating in the sacramental sign of marriage, which is the total and joyous gift of oneself to the other, whose goodness and beauty redounds back to and thus fulfills the "I." The sacrament of marriage, or rather marriage in as much as it is a sacrament,[32] puts at the disposal of the spouses' freedom the great resource of the perfect love by which Christ, who gave his life for his Church, makes her his Bride and preserves her from wrinkle or stain. As paradoxical as it may seem, on a pastoral level, the category of the domestic church emerges more, in its full effective reality, when we look at the Church as a family,[33] than at the family as a Church. Here we see the great power of the vision of the Letter to the Ephesians, where the relationship between Christ and the Church is described in the light of the man-woman relationship and vice versa. Far from chasing after fantastic theories and abandoning the realm of experience, this choice permits an unparalleled concreteness which demonstrates the persuasive force of the experience and the logic of the Incarnation. Balthasar affirms that the fullness of the mystery of man and woman "is only attained in the mystery of Christ and his Church (Eph 5:27,33)."[34]

Having opened the horizon of conjugal and family life to Christ's boundless love for his Bride, we cannot help but pursue the question further. The asymmetrical logic of the reciprocity that characterizes nuptiality does not allow us to rest content; it urges other questions.

On what basis can we legitimately speak of Christ as the Bridegroom of his Bride the Church, without falling into a fruitless parody of the eros relationship, analogous to that which many writers see in the material world, if not even more dangerous since it is applied to the most noble reality of our faith, a reality we pray to and adore?[35] We are given the possibility of speaking in these terms because of the profound nature of the singular event of Jesus Christ. In him, two natures exist in one person, according to the modality wonderfully described by the Council of Chalcedon (*inconfuse, immutabiliter, indivise, inseparabiliter*).[36] With the revelation of Jesus Christ, the original experience of dual unity appears in history. The unity of the person of Christ (true God and true man) is communicated sacramentally through his powerful authority over humankind and the cosmos (miracles); moreover, there is Christ's greater Lordship over himself which enables his supreme, spontaneous ("*sponte*" according to St. Anselm) abandonment to the Father on the cross. "The Son of Man has the power to lay down his life and to take it up again." Such is the self-rule of the Crucified Risen Lord! This powerful unity of the "I" of Jesus Christ (the perfect *Ich-Mitte*) is not sundered by the duality of natures. On the contrary, it is rather strengthened by virtue of their interconnectedness. Christ, in fact, is one, because he is the bearer of a single human nature—the unique and unrepeatable humanity of the Son of God.[37] He (true God and true man) binds himself to a precise moment in time and to precise and particular circumstances, and becomes involved in the lives of certain men and women in particular. But in the humanity of the Son of God and through the power of the Resurrection, Jesus Christ embraces all moments of time and all circumstances in space, thus making himself contemporary to every man and woman in every place and in every period in time. Concretely speaking, how can this be so? Through the sacramental dynamism (the full experience of *logos*) by which the Risen Lord who dwells bodily with the Trinity, and through all moments in time and space with his body, the Church, which has her foundation in his mystical body (the Eucharist).[38] In this way, the dual unity of the two natures in the one person of Christ appears as the source from which spring the dual unity between Christ the Bridegroom and his Bride the Church. The believer who has formed his thoughts in meditation on the nuptial mystery of the two natures in the one person of Jesus Christ will not be surprised that the four adverbs from the Council of Chalcedon serve to illuminate the meaning of the original biblical commandment to man and woman to become one flesh. Thus a strict link is established between the man-woman relation, the Christ-Church relation, and the man-God relation. Here, our fragile freedom receives the unexpected possibility of finding a firm foundation in the experience of a tenacious and faithful love.

We said before that this represents the culmination of the experience of dual unity within the horizon of the human; but, once again, the fruitful asymmetry by which the Church Bride is born from the two natures in the one person of Jesus Christ requires a basis. Our ascent continues toward its final goal. Where does the unity of Jesus Christ come from and what is the reason for it? First of all, let us address its purpose. It comes from the mysterious decision of God the Father to send his only Son, and through him the Holy Spirit, to make men and women exist as autonomous creatures and nonetheless "capable" of participating at that supreme level of love which consists in being his adopted sons and daughters. We are called to be *sons in the Son* so that we can call on God as "Abba," an expression both tender and dramatic.[39] It is a name more familiar than "father" because of the tones of gentleness running through it.[40] The familiarity of God the Father with us is fulfilled in his unconditional fidelity to the original plan (which is another decisive factor for the man-woman relationship and for the family). Not even sin breaks this pact; instead, it becomes an occasion for the Father to reveal, in the Crucified Risen Lord who pours out his Spirit on us, his true face: mercy. This is the bond (another nuptial word!) of perfect love. We can now see more precisely where the ultimate root of nuptiality lies, the root that illuminates every level of the reality, because it reveals the full sense of the asymmetrical reciprocity that is the fruit of dual unity. It is the event of Jesus Christ that allows us to catch a glimpse, however inadequate, of the fact that the Trinity presents an experience of love in its most complete form, according to the perfection that consists in a difference between the three persons which does not destroy, but rather exalts, the unity of the one God. For this reason, the triune God is the ultimate explanation of all possible difference, and therefore also of dual unity. God's triunity is the ultimate guarantee that difference does not do away with the contingent being. On the contrary, difference exists for the sake of its truth and fulfillment. In this sense, difference within perfect unity, which characterizes the triune God, tells us who God truly is: He is purest love. The love of the Father for the Son is so perfect that the Holy Spirit is at once the bond (*nexus*) and the fruit of this love.[41]

We can now grasp the importance of Balthasar's striking analogy between the life of the Trinity and the conjugal act of man and woman in relation to the begetting of a child. Balthasar is not afraid to assert, even going against Augustine and Thomas,[42] that man, woman and child are the most adequate natural analogy of the Trinity. In this sense, even in the Trinity there exists a nuptial relationship made up of a reciprocity. We are dealing here with a reciprocity which maintains, in a certain sense, the element of asymmetry because it rests on the exchange (each Person simultaneously relates to the other two) between the three in the one nature of God, but this perfect difference lies within perfect unity. The one and the three are the ultimate driving force of every nuptiality. In fact, in God, the third person is no longer hidden as he is in the various relationships between man/woman (child), Christ-Bridegroom/the Church-Bride (Jesus Christ), the divine and human nature of Jesus Christ (Father), because the Father, Son, and Spirit are identically manifest as the one God. At the same time, the dynamism of nuptiality is revealed in all its fullness: the reciprocal love between the Father and the Son is the perfect bond which begets a perfect fruit, the Holy Spirit, who is himself God. To bring the different aspects described in this section together, it is worth quoting in full a passage from Balthasar which shows the link between the Trinity and the family:

> We have already noted the impossibility of approaching the Holy Spirit except from two directions at once: as the (subjective) quintessence of the mutual love of Father and Son, hence, as the bond (*nexus*) between them; and as the (objec-

tive) fruit that stems from and attests to this love. This impossibility translates into a convergence of the poles. Imagine for a moment that the act of love between a man and woman did not include nine months pregnancy, that is, the aspect of time. In the parents' generative-receptive embrace, the child would already be immediately present; it would be at one and the same time their mutual love in action and something more, namely, its transcendent result. Nor would it be a valid objection to say that the diastasis we have described just now has to do simply with man's gendered nature, and that in some higher form of love there would be no reproduction (a view that turns up not only in today's common distinction between the ends of marriage, but also in the notion of eros that we find from Plato to Soloviev: cf., G3).We must say, in fact, that this form of exuberance and thus fruitfulness (which can be spiritual) is part of every love, and that includes precisely the higher kind of love. In this sense, it is precisely perfect creaturely love that is an authentic *imago Trinitatis*....What follows from this, as Adrienne von Speyr explains (*Welt des Gebetes*: Einsiedeln, 1951), is mutual admiration, indeed, adoration, infinite mutual thanksgiving (the Father thanks the Son for allowing himself to be generated eternally, the Son thanks the Father for giving himself away eternally), mutual petition (the Father asks the Son to fulfill all of his, the Father's, wishes, the Son asks the Father for permission to carry out the Father's utmost wishes). This mutual indwelling would seem to be eternally self-sufficient, but it is intrinsically superabundant, so much so that it produces "unexpectedly" (one is tempted to say) and precisely *as* superabundance something that is once more One: the proof that the loving interpenetration has been a success, just as the human child is at once the proof of the reciprocal love of the parents and the fruit of their love. "The third," says Tertullian, "is the fruit from the root of the fruit tree" (*Adv. Prax.* 8 [PL 2,163)].[43]

The ascent has reached its goal, and, well beyond the weak stammering of our poor concepts, the mystery of the Christian God at work in the lives of Christian spouses and the Christian family finds a way to become manifest in an attested manner. Supporting this assertion, we find not only the trinitarian prophecies in the Old Testament, where the Trinity's visit to a man or woman almost always leaves as a sign a son (for example, Sarah or Manoah) but also and especially the incomparable event of the Annunciation with the gift of the Word, who became a child for us and for our salvation.

THE NUPTIAL MYSTERY AND THE CHRISTIAN STATES OF LIFE

If up until this point we have kept to the essential arguments, we can now ask ourselves how *nuptiality*, developed in the total vision of God's plan, enters concretely into Christian life. The Church traditionally deals with this question by means of the theme of Christian states of life.[44] Returning to the beautiful works of Balthasar and Adrienne von Speyr for a reflection on the genesis, meaning, and variety of the states of life,[45] I feel compelled, on this occasion, to highlight two often neglected aspects of nuptiality as a dynamic of the life of the faithful in the two states of marriage and virginity.

Nuptiality and the Indissolubility of Marriage

Indissolubility is ultimately what makes Christian marriage a sacrament, that is, an objective and subjective expression (*ex opere operato et ex opere operantis*) of nuptiality.[46] In fact only by its being indissoluble does marriage participate in the nuptial sacrifice that the Word Incarnate makes of himself on the Cross to his Immaculate Bride, thereby revealing the essence of the spousal love that circulates in the Trinity. This offering is the absolute expression of the Father's fidelity to his plan of covenant with humankind precisely because it is irreversible. Here we have the root of the indissoluble nature of the Christian marriage (and ideally of "natural" marriage as an expression of the man-woman relationship[47]). This is possible for man and woman as a result of the grace of the sacrament (the objective dimension—*ex opere operato*) which calls on freedom (the subjective dimension—*ex opere operantis*) to adhere to it. The most elevated human sign of this subjective obedience in the objective grace of the sacrament is the fiat of Mary (the image of the Church), who by her Immaculate Conception was able freely to receive the gift of the Word in the Incarnation. The unconditional and immaculate "yes" of the Virgin Mary becomes the permanent guarantee of the reciprocity of the Bride in relation to Christ the Bridegroom.[48] Incidentally, it should be noted that indissolubility, with all of the dramatic trials of life it entails, corresponds to the constitutive desire of love as it is given in basic human experience.[49] A genuine declaration of love cannot keep from saying "forever." The sacrament of marriage, which by grace enables an act of indissoluble proportions, offers a sure and objective path for this deep-rooted exigence of the human heart.

Nuptiality and Virginity

The second observation that I would like to make regarding nuptiality and the states of life lies in the somewhat provocative affirmation that virginity is the culmination of nuptiality—even for spouses.[50] In the end, virginity is the ultimate meaning of indissolubility. In fact, it is impossible to love the other as "other" if one does not love the other in his or her own destiny.[51] There is no real love between a man and woman, between a husband and wife, if there is no detachment (which is traditionally called "chastity"), through which the other is welcomed as a sign of Mystery, a sign of the Trinity. In this possession in detachment, the husband and wife can live indissolubility, whose ultimate guarantee is forgiveness. A similar type of relationship has rightly been called Christian virginity. We are dealing here with a virtue that is eminently Christ-like, because it finds its most perfect expression in the way in which the God-man took possession of people and things. Christian virginity, which springs from Baptism and develops as a virtue through sacramental grace, the gifts of the Holy Spirit, and ascetic effort, can find special help in the Virgin Mary and St. Joseph. Mary is a virgin precisely because she is a mother and a mother because she is a virgin. And the putative fatherhood of Joseph, far from being a disincarnate love, demonstrates that the ultimate depth of every human nuptiality is possession in detachment (virginal). This is the reason for the prophetic value of virginity in the life of the Church, whose special value was reconfirmed by the Council of Trent. This assertion, far from disincarnating marriage, shows its constitutive complementarity with the choice of virginity. The two states of life mutually recall the fullness of nuptiality.[52] The fact that love is always spousal, illustrates the paradigmatic nature of marriage.[53] The other state of life, virginity, expressing the full modality of possession—possession in detachment—prevents love and the affective life from closing itself up in the inner-worldly, and opens it beyond the implacable link between sexuality, begetting, and death.[54] We can now grasp the pedagogical force of the following assertion: "The more the charism of virginal life is present and affirmed in Christian life, the more marriage will be called to its true nature and will be helped to conform to its ideal."[55]

Notes

1. Cf. P. Donati, ed., *Uomo e Donna in Famiglia* (Cinisello Balsamo, 1997).

2. Cf. G. Rossi, "Genere e sesso: Chi ha paura dell'identità femminile?" *Nuntium* (1998).

3. St. Thomas reminds us that while divine knowledge is the measure of reality, reality is the measure of human knowledge: "Veritas autem quae est in intellectu humano…non comparatur ad res sicut mensura extrinseca et communis ad mensurata, sed vel sicut mensurata ad mensuram, ut est de veritate intellectus humani, et sic oportet eam variari secundum varietatem rerum" ["But the truth that is in the human intellect…is not related to things as an exterior and universal measure to what is measured, but as what is measured is related to the measure, as it is in the case of the truth of the human intellect, and so this truth has to vary according to the variety of things" (St. Thomas Aquinas, *De veritate* 1.4.1).

4. In this regard, one can speak of "symbolic ontology": cf. G. Colombo, *La ragione teologica* (Milan, 1995); A. Bertuletti, "La 'ragione teologica' di Giuseppe Colombo: Il significato storico-teoretico di una proposta teologica," *Teologia* (1996): 1, 18–36; id., *Il concetto di esperienza*, in *L'evidenza e la fede* (Milan, 1988), 112–81.

5. G. K. Chesterton, *The Napoleon of Notting Hill*, 127–28.

6. John Paul II, *The Theology of the Body*, 45.

7. John Paul II, *Mulieris Dignitatem*, 1. See in this regard *Dignità e vocazione della donna: Testo e commenti* (Vatican City, 1989), with the partici-

pation of M. Sales, A. Scola, L. and S. Grygiel, I. de la Potterie, V. Grossi, E. Scabini, C. Lubich, G. Blaquière, J. Burggraff, A. Vanhoye, G. Chantraine, G. Honoré-Lainé, M. Hendrikx, and D. Tettamanzi.

8. Cf. P. Morande, "La imagen del padre en la cultura de la postmodernidad," *Anthropotes* (1996): 241–59.

9. A great difficulty undermines the educational capacity of parents towards their children, but also that of the ecclesial body—parish, diocesan church or the Universal Church—towards engaged couples preparing for marriage. It is a question of their incapacity to give good enough reasons for the moral injunction, the "ought." With respect to responsible procreation, contraception, and premarital relations, this incapacity often comes from not beginning with things as they are, which in our case means starting with the real experience of the man-woman relationship: we come into the world as a man or woman within a familial context. We are the children of a modernity which, having separated the individual dimension from the social dimension of ethics, has ended by bracketing the foundation of reality as it presents itself, setting in its place and otherwise compensating for it by laying emphasis on the "ought," and having lost the capacity to give (ontological) reasons for acting. By contrast, in the inevitable weaving together of the "is" and the "ought," only the perception of how "things are"—the perception of being—can guarantee the truth and the creative freshness of the "ought."

10. P. Vanzan speaks of asymmetrical reciprocity ("Uomo e donna oltre la modernità," *Famiglia oggi* 10 [1997]: 25–31), and quotes Rosetta Stella ("Il Papa e la crisi della modernità: Una reciprocità asimmetrica" *Prospectiva Persona*, December 1996). I reached the same formulation myself around 1987 in the context of my teaching at the Pontifical John Paul II Institute for Studies on Marriage and the Family.

11. On constitutive polarities, see H. U. von Balthasar, *Theo-Drama*, vol. 2, 346–94; A. Scola, *Hans Urs von Balthasar*, 84–100; R. Guardini, *L'opposizione polare* (Brescia, 1998).

12. It is useful to note that the dramatic anthropology alluded to here might perfect, without destroying, the classical anthropological conception of the individual, only bringing out the influence of the man-woman and individual-community polarities, as coessential with the body-soul polarity, which, as in classical anthropology, maintains its own priority. Cf. A. Scola, *Hans Urs von Balthasar*, 89.

13. Cf. H. U. von Balthasar, *L'accesso alla realtà di Dio, in Mysterium salutatis*, vol. 2, 5th ed., ed. J. Feiner and M. Löhrer (Brescia, 1980), 19–57; id., "A résumé of my thought," in *Communio* 15 (Winter 1988): 468–73.

14. With regard to psychoanalysis and the Christian *Weltanschauung*, it is remarkable how often those who accuse Christian education of inflicting severe psychological damage are not so quick to recognize how similar the two approaches are in their assertion of the irreducibility of sexual difference. It seems

to me that a similarly unobjective attitude can be seen in some of Beattie's reflections in T. Beattie, "A Man and Three Women—Hans, Adrienne, Mary and Luce," *New Blackfriars* 79 (February 1998): 97–105.

15. Cf. Plato, *The Symposium*, 189d.

16. This androgynous mentality which is dominant nowadays is not the least reason for the spread of homosexuality and transsexuality and explains at the same time why these might be presented as legitimate sexual alternatives. Our judgment here is ontological not ethical (cf. *Anthropologia cristiana e omossessualità* [Vatican City]).

17. G. Zuanazzi, *Temi e simboli dell'eros* (Rome, 1991), 76.

18. The publications of the Jesuit Beirnaert are noteworthy on this point (L. Beirnaert, *Aux frontiers de l'acte analytique* [Paris, 1987]; id., *Expérience chrétienne et psychologie* [Paris, 1966]).

19. Cf. St. Thomas Aquinas, *Summa Theologiae* 1–2.26.

20. C. S. Lewis, *The Four Loves* (New York: Harcourt and Brace, 1960); id., *Mere Christianity* (London, 1996), 84–100.

21. Cf. C. S. Lewis, *The Four Loves*, 14.

22. Cf. St. Thomas Aquinas, *Summa Theologiae* 1–2.91.2, A. Scola, *Questioni di Antropologia Teologica* (Rome, 1997), 131–38.

23. Cf. A. Scola, *Identidad y diferencia* (Madrid, 1989), 39f. The original axiom in St. Thomas speaks of *bonum diffusivum sui* for example in St. Thomas Aquinas, *Summa Theologiae*, 1–2.1.4. Cf. J.-P. Jossua, "L'axiome *bonum diffusivum sui* chez saint Thomas d'Aquin," *Recherches de Science Religieuse* (1966): 127–53.

24. The following passage from Mauriac's *Life of Jesus* gives eloquent testimony to the continuity between the first group of apostles and the life of the Church: "Those who were 'his own' could go through life with their eyes closed, having no longer anything to fear of men. Nothing more to fear, nothing more to expect. They had given everything in order to attain all, so closely identified with their love that those who received them received Love also. These words of Jesus spoken in the hearing of the Twelve carried the germ of the bravery of thousands of martyrs, the joy of those who would suffer for Christ. Thenceforth, and no matter what horrible thing might happen to them, the friends of Jesus had but to lift up their eyes to see the open heaven" (F. Mauriac, *Life of Jesus* [New York, 1939], 62).

25. Cf. A. Vanhoye, "'Il grande mistero': La lettera di Ef 5, 21–33 nel nuovo documento pontificio," in *Dignitá e vocazione*, 146–53; H. U. von Balthasar, *Explorations in Theleology*, vol. 2, *Spouse of the Word* (San Francisco: Ignatius Press, 1991), 143ff.

26. Cf. C. Giuliodori, *Intelligenza teologica*, 194–97.

27. Cf. ibid., 117–33.

28. Cf. A. Scola, *Questioni di antropologia*, 43–53.

29. "How is it possible for a contingent historical truth to become proof of the truth of necessary reason?" (G. E. Lessing, "Sopra la prova dello Spirito e della forza," in M. F. Sciacca and M. Schiavone, *Grande ontologia filosofica*, vol. 15 [Milan], 1557–59).

30. Cf. I. de la Potterie, "Antropomorfismo e simbolismo del linguaggio biblico sulla elezione uomo-donna," *Dignità e vocazione*, 110–16.

31. Cf. *Lumen Gentium*, 11; *Familiaris consortio*, 21.

32. Cf., A. Scola, *Questioni di antropologia*, 51–52.

33. "According to the Council, the Church is the Bride of Christ and our mother, the holy city and the first fruits of the coming Kingdom. It will be necessary to take into account these suggestive images, according to the suggestions of the Synod, in order to develop an ecclesiology centered on the concept of the Church as the family of God" (John Paul II, *Ecclesia in Africa*, 63).

34. Cf. H. U. von Balthasar, *Theo-Drama*, vol. 3, *Dramatis Personae: Persons in Christ*, trans. Graham Harrison (San Francisco: Ignatius Press, 1992), 289.

35. Cf. G. Loughlin, "Sexing the Trinity," 18–19.

36. Cf. *DS* 302.

37. On the singularity of Jesus Christ, see G. Moioli, *Cristologia: Proposta sistematica* (Milan, 1978), 223–55; A. Scola, *Questioni di antropologia*, 11–27, 107–30.

38. Cf. H de Lubac, *Corpus Mysticum* (Milan, 1982), 33–59.

39. Cf. Gal 4:6.

40. Cf. J. Jeremias, *Abbà* (Brescia, 1968).

41. Cf. H. U. von Balthasar, *Theologik*, vol. 3, 144–50.

42. This spousal illustration of the mystery of the Trinity seems no less valid than that of St. Augustine (Father: *Mens*; Son: *Notitia*; Spirit: *Amor*, whose traces are fixed in the spirit of man as intellect, memory, and will) or that of Hugh of St. Victor, taken up again by St. Thomas who defines the Father as Power, the Son as Wisdom, and the Spirit as Love" (C. Giuliodori, *Intelligenza teologica*, 121).

43. H. U. von Balthasar, *Theologik*, vol. 3, 145–47.

44. Cf. Antoine, "Etats de vie," in *Dictionnaire de Théologie Catholique*, vol. 5 (Paris, 1913), 905–11; there is another bibliography in G. Lesage and G. Rocca, "Stato di perfezione," in G. Pelliccia and G. Rocca, eds., *Dizionario degli Instituti di Perfezione*, vol. 9 (Rome, 1997), 204–15.

45. Cf. H. U. von Balthasar, *The Christian State of Life*, trans. Sr. Mary Frances McCarthy (San Francisco: Ignatius Press, 1983).

46. Cf. A. Scola, "Spiritualità coniugale nel contesto culturale contemporaneo," in *Cristo Sposo della Chiesa sposa*, ed. R. Bonetti (Rome, 1997), 49–52.

47. Cf. id., *Questioni di Antropologia*, 51–52.

48. Cf. id., *Spiritualità coniugule*, 49.

49. Cf. H. U. von Balthasar, *The Christian State of Life*, 58–60.

50. Cf. A. Scola, *Spiritualità coniugale*, 52–54.

51. Cf. L. Giussani, *Il tempo e il tempio* (Milan, 1995), 11–35.

52. Cf. A. Sicari, "Diversità e complementarità degli stati di vita nella Chiesa," *Communio* 135 (1994): 8–24. See also *Christifideles laici*, 55.

53. Cf. John Paul II, *The Theology of the Body*, 277ff.

54. Cf. *DS* 1810. This concerns the fruitfulness which springs from consecrated virginity. See also, A. Scola, *Hans Urs von Balthasar*, 115–16.

55. G. Biffi, *Matrimonio e famiglia: Nota pastorale* (Bologna, 1990), 12.

11. The Family as Domestic Church and the Romantic Model of Love

Florence Caffrey Bourg

This chapter first appeared in Florence Caffrey Bourg, *Where Two or Three Are Gathered: Christian Families as Domestic Churches* (Notre Dame, Ind.: University of Notre Dame Press, 2004).

> "Baptism brings all Christians into union with God. Your family life is sacred because family relationships confirm and deepen this union and allow the Lord to work through you."[1]

When I give a lecture on the theme of domestic church, the first question I usually get from my audience is, "What counts as a domestic church?" Most people who pose this question to me seem concerned that "domestic church" not be used in a way that ranks some families as more "Christian" than others, based on quantifiable characteristics such as a certain number of children, a particular division of labor among spouses, or a canonically valid marriage.

The ranking of marriages (or lack thereof) is an especially delicate issue, one that often creates obstacles for families trying to worship together. For instance, celebration of a child's first Communion becomes awkward when parents in canonically invalid marriages are asked to refrain from receiving the Eucharist.[2] Prisca Wagua reports that in Africa, most local churches refuse to baptize children of unwed mothers.[3] Similar obstacles can be experienced in interchurch Christian families, even though Catholicism teaches that any valid marriage of two baptized Christians is sacramental. The web site of the Association of Interchurch Families is replete with stories of families who wish for more opportunities for the Eucharistic sharing.[4] Some testimonials report that teenagers raised in interchurch families find themselves torn when the time for confirmation approaches. Sarah Mayles in England wishes that an ecumenical confirmation service could be developed. In the meantime, she says, "I am an interchurch child; my father is an Anglican and my mother a Roman Catholic. I have grown up as an active member of both denominations and have attended confirmation classes both in the Anglican and the Roman Catholic traditions. I feel an equal member of both churches, and I have decided not to be confirmed to this date. I do not want to affirm publicly my allegiance within one particular church if in so doing I have to discard my commitment to the other."[5]

SACRAMENTAL FOUNDATION OF THE DOMESTIC CHURCH

In a global context, where such sensitive cases are increasingly common, we are faced with a theological question: what is the sacramental foundation of a Christian family or domestic church? Is it shared baptism and/or confirmation, shared Eucharist, sacramental marriage, all of the above, some of the above, or none of the above? Because I am still sorting out my thoughts on issues of shared Eucharist and confirmation for interdenominational families, I will confine this chapter to an examination of how domestic churches are formed by the sacraments of baptism and marriage....

Even before I began lecturing on domestic church, I was sensitized to these questions by my own family history. On the one hand, I am the product of what might be considered the ideal model of a domestic church. Both my parents are Catholic; they were married in the Catholic Church and have been married for forty years. I am one of five siblings, all of whom went through Catholic schools and through the usual childhood sacraments. My mother, a math teacher, quit her profession when her first child was born and didn't resume it till the youngest started kindergarten. On the other hand, I knew from the beginning of my research on domestic church that not all Christian families look like my immediate family. I knew this because neither of my parents had grown up in a family that fit the so-called traditional demographic model. My parents were both raised, for the better part of their childhood, by single mothers. I have never known either of my grandfathers. My paternal grandmother was widowed at a young age. She was left to care for six children ranging from two to thirteen years old. She had only an eighth grade education. She was blessed with my grandfather's brothers, who helped her keep my grandfather's pub in business and acted as surrogate fathers until five of the six the children were on their own. (Sadly, one of the children died in a car accident when he was twenty-one years old.) My grandmother never remarried. For her last few years, when she was no longer able to live alone, her children took turns taking her into their homes for a few months at a time. She died at my Uncle Jack and Aunt Betsy's house when she was ninety-four years old.

My maternal grandmother has an equally remarkable story. When she was four years old, she sailed from Ireland to America with an aunt, leaving her parents behind. Eventually her mother and brother joined her. Because my great-grandmother Katherine supported herself as a nanny for another family's children, my grandmother grew up in a "blended" family, with surrogate sisters and brothers along with her blood brother. My grandmother eventually married and had three children. However, her marriage was not happy. Her husband was often away on military duty. When he was home, he drank too much. Eventually my grandmother packed up the three kids and left, a daring thing to do in her day. She sought an annulment, but it was denied, and she never remarried. She raised my mother, aunt, and uncle with the help of my great-grandmother Katherine. She managed to send her children to Catholic school by working at the school as a gym teacher. She never earned enough money to buy a home or a car. My aunt, as it turned out, developed mental illness as a teenager and was never able to live independently, so she and my grandmother lived together until my grandmother died, also at the age of ninety-four.

Although on paper both my grandmothers had a sacramental marriage, in practice neither could draw upon a sacramental marriage for the strength needed to raise their children to adulthood. Neither had an easy life, but despite these hardships both kept their faith. This faith was passed on to my parents, and from them to me and my siblings, and now to our own children. Because it was so clear to me that my faith derived from Christian families that did not fit the so-called traditional model, I knew when I began work on the theme of domestic church that I'd need to give careful thought to the "marriage or baptism" question and the "nuclear family" question.

The State of the Question

The "marriage or baptism" issue is one on which we find significant differences of perspective, sometimes within a single text. At times the lack of clarity is not so much in the authors' intention as in their consistency of presentation. For example, in *Christian Families in the Real World*, Mitch Finley and Kathy Finley define domestic church in their introduction as "a community of baptized Christians." Chapter 4, somewhat misleadingly titled "Marriage: Foundation for the Domestic Church," attempts to clarify that the most basic of all sacraments is baptism and that marriage, a specification of baptism, is the smallest authentic form of church. But later, chapter 7, titled "Spirituality and the Single Parent," states, "The single-parent family is a true family and a legitimate form of domestic church." Here it appears that baptism, not marriage, is the sacramental foundation of domestic churches.[6]

Beginning with the documents of Vatican II and continuing in the writings of John Paul II, most magisterial reflections on the domestic church's sacramental basis or its practical duties are derived primarily from theology of marriage. (Recent statements of the U.S. bishops are a significant exception, to be discussed shortly.) Marriage theology tends to be based on natural law rather than on scripture—it revolves around marriage as God's institution for the procreation and education of children and the perpetuation of human society. Baptism is mentioned in connection with domestic church, but not as often as marriage. Sometimes sacraments of marriage and baptism are cited in close proximity with each other as grounding for domestic church, without much clarification of their relationship—*Lumen Gentium* #11 is one example; another is the *Catechism of the Catholic Church*, which includes discussion of domestic church within its treatise on the sacrament of marriage, but comments that "members of the family exercise the priesthood of the baptised in a privileged way" (#1657).

Paul VI takes the opposite approach, introducing the idea of domestic church in a section of *Evangelii Nuntiandi* describing the family's share in the evangelizing apostolate of the laity. Evangelization is not construed solely as the parents' duty flowing from the natural and sacramental purposes of marriage. Rather, "[i]n a family which is conscious of this mission [as domestic church], all members evangelize and are evangelized." Indeed, in families resulting from a "mixed marriage" the duty remains because it is a consequence of common baptism. These families have "the difficult task of becoming builders of unity" (#71).

Familiaris Consortio gives varying explanations of the sacramental grounding of the domestic church's mission. In section #49, which begins formal reflection on the Christian family as sharing in the life and mission of the Church, the pope states that he will "examine the many profound bonds linking the Church and the Christian family and establishing the family as a 'Church in miniature' (Ecclesia domestica)." Surprisingly, baptism is not included as one of these bonds. (The closest is an explanation of the Church as Mother.) The sacrament of marriage, however, does get attention as a point of entry in the Church's saving mission:

> [T]he Christian family is grafted into the mystery of the Church to such a degree as to become a sharer, in its own way, in the saving mission proper to the Church: by virtue of the sacrament, Christian married couples and parents "in their state and way of life have their own special gift among the People of God." For this reason they not only receive the love of Christ and become a saved community, but they are also called upon to communicate Christ's love to their brethren, thus becoming a saving community.

The quote in this passage comes from *Lumen Gentium* #11; the "sacrament" referred to is marriage, not baptism. It is difficult to understand why baptism is not cited as the sacrament by virtue of which Christian families become a saving community, since it is this sacrament, not marriage, that all Christians share and which is most directly indicative of new life in Christ. It appears as if only sacramentally married members of a Christian family are full-fledged members of a domestic church.

The puzzle becomes more perplexing when we consider other sections of *Familiaris Consortio*. Section #52 describes the Christian family's mission as an evangelizing community. We read, "This apostolic mission of the family is rooted in Baptism and receives from the grace of the sacrament of marriage new strength to transmit the faith, to sanctify and transform our present society to God's plan."[7] But an earlier section, #36, entitled "The Right and Duty of Parents Regarding Education," asserts that "[t]he task of giving education is rooted in the primary vocation of married couples to participate in God's creative activity." Are evangelization and education so different as to be rooted in different sacramental vocations? Perhaps one could argue that evangelization is a specifically Christian activity rooted in baptism, while education is a separate, secular, or natural activity rooted in marriage, understood in natural law terms. But this view seems at odds with the Church's post–Vatican II agenda of removing the dichotomy between sacred and secular life, and with some of the pope's statements elsewhere regarding education.[8] Section #38 of *Familiaris Consortio*, entitled "The Mission to Educate and the Sacrament of Marriage," continues the argument begun in section #36 and goes to great lengths to ground Christian parents' educational ministry in the sacrament of marriage:

> The sacrament of marriage gives to the educational role the dignity and vocation of being really and truly a "ministry" of the Church at the service of the building up of her members. So great and splendid is the educational ministry of Christian parents that Saint Thomas has no hesitation comparing it with the ministry of priests: "Some only propagate and guard spiritual life by a spiritual ministry: this is the role of the sacrament of Orders; others do this for both corporal and spiritual life, and this is brought about by the sacrament of marriage, by which a man and a woman join in order to beget offspring and bring them up to worship God."[9]

While no one would question that married parents have a solemn duty to educate their children, or that education is a creative activity, it is not clear why the sacrament of marriage, rather than baptism, gives parental education its character as a "true ministry of the Church." In my mind, any Christian education should be considered, first and foremost, a reflection of the general baptismal vocation to "preach the gospel to all nations, teaching them everything I have commanded you" (Matthew 28:18–20). This passage in *Familiaris Consortio* leaves us wondering whether single, divorced, widowed, or foster parents can consider their education of children a Christian ministry. It would seem much simpler and more theologically consistent to link all Christian education with the apostolic mission of evangelization, rooted in baptism.

Turning to the gift of evangelical discernment, which surely must be a crucial task of any domestic church, the "marriage or baptism" muddle becomes even muddier. We are told in *Familiaris Consortio* #5 that "[t]his discernment is accomplished through the sense of faith, which is a gift that the Spirit gives to all the faithful." One might assume the charism for evangelical discernment is given by the Holy Spirit in baptism, and perhaps in other common experiences shared by the faithful, such as hearing the Word of God and using it to interpret everyday experiences. But neither is mentioned as a source of evangelical discernment; instead, we are told that "Christian spouses and parents...are qualified for this role by their charism or specific gift, the gift of the sacrament of matrimony." The pope does not convincingly explain how people like my two grandmothers (let alone the countless Christian single parents who have never married) might have the capacity for evangelical discernment in raising their children to be mature Christian adults.

One may ask whether the sacraments of baptism and marriage, singly or in combination, are the sole or sufficient source of a domestic church's discernment of its nature and mission, or its capacity to fulfill them. Even for domestic churches that do arise from sacramental marriage, a more complex explanation of the capacity for evangelical discernment seems demanded by common sense. Isn't the capacity for discernment a growing thing, linked not only to experiences of sacrament ritual, but also to broader life experience? It seems odd to think that a lifetime supply of discernment skills is given all at once to a young bride and groom, or to a person being baptised. Most any parent will acknowledge that wisdom in raising a Christian family comes from trial and error, and also from the borrowed wisdom of persons who have had similar experiences. A simplistic, deductive explanation of sacraments as the source of a domestic church's evangelical discernment capacities would eliminate the need for permanent catechesis, which John Paul II promotes.[10] Two options present themselves: either sacraments of marriage and baptism must be understood as including some element of continual process, or some experiential foundation for domestic churches' evangelical discernment must be added.[11]

John Paul II's writings do not completely settle the question of how baptism and marriage are related in forming domestic churches or in indicating their mission. He gives no argument for the domestic church's existence in anything other than a traditional nuclear family—a happily and, most importantly, sacramentally married husband and wife raising young children. He does not satisfactorily explain how members of a family whose relationship is not marital or parent-child participate as agents of the domestic church's ministry.[12]

The U.S. bishops present a significantly different picture. Beginning in their 1992 colloquium on domestic church and continuing in *Follow the Way of Love*, the U.S. bishops regard the sacrament of baptism as the most important source of insight into the nature and mission of domestic churches. *Follow the Way of Love*'s introductory discourse on the meaning of domestic church focuses on gifts and missionary tasks given in baptism. In this pivotal section of the document, the sacrament of marriage is not mentioned at all in the first few pages (8–10) as the foundation of either family or domestic church. Instead, we are told, "Baptism brings all Christians into union with God. Your family life is sacred because family relationships confirm and deepen this union and allow the Lord to work through you." "Family" is defined as "our first community and the most basic way in which the Lord gathers us, forms us, and acts in the world," and "church" is defined as "two or three gathered in [Jesus'] name....We give the name church to the people whom the Lord gathers, who strive to follow his way of love, and through whose lives his saving presence is made known." Later, page 11 introduces sacramental marriage as a sign of Christ's promise to be faithful to those he has chosen. Note that the bishops do not introduce marriage until they first clarify that Christ's promise to be faithful is the "firm foundation" on which "every" Christian family, "like the whole Church," rests. This clarification is noteworthy because the bishops immediately turn their attention to God's gracious presence in the love among members of families that may not arise from sacramental marriage—single-parent, blended, and inter-religious families, along with childless families. They conclude, "The church of the home can live and grow in every family."

The bishops' rationale for this novel approach to domestic church is spelled out candidly in the proceedings of their 1992 colloquium:

> The theology of marriage is a major source of our theology of family as domestic church. In fact, the term is first used by St. John Chrysostom in his homilies on the "marriage passage" in the Epistle to the Ephesians. In *Lumen Gentium* and other documents the term is consistently linked with Christian marriage. The family (domestic church) is regarded as proceeding from, or being rooted in, marriage. Marriage is the origin of family and, therefore, of the domestic church. This is the position taken in official church teaching.
>
> But there are tensions and limits. On the one hand, this position emphasizes the importance and dignity of marriage. On the other hand, it exposes an apparent weakness in our theologizing. There are "families" in our society that are not rooted in marriage. For example, a woman may have a child, never marry the child's father, and then raise and care for her child (sometimes with the help of other family members) in a loving and stable manner. Then, too, there are many families who are no longer united by marriage, e.g., a divorced parent raising children alone. Single-parent families in our society are customarily regarded as families. But are they domestic churches in the same way as families which are rooted in marriage?
>
> A question was raised...about the relationship of baptism to the domestic church. Our baptismal vocation is basic and antecedent to any other. Matrimony specifies and gives focus to our baptismal commitment. To what extent does Baptism bring the domestic church into being? If this sacrament is also foundational for the domestic church, is the possibility left open for unmarried persons to create a domestic church?[13]

The difference in the current approach of the U.S. bishops, compared to Roman magisterial statements, stems largely from inductive versus deductive reasoning. It corresponds with the two perspectives on the gap between ideals and reality described earlier: ideally all domestic churches might arise from an intact, sacramental marriage, but in fact, many families that seem to deserve the name do not.

The U.S. bishops display conscious, consistent commitment to contemporary Catholicism's upholding of baptism as the foundational sacrament of the Church (universal and domestic), and the mark of every Christian's call to holiness—whether that person is ordained or lay, single or married, adult or child. The pope, by contrast, appears to straddle two worldviews—one being that of the U.S. bishops, and the other an older perspective that attends more to the separate spiritualities of lay and ordained Christians than to their sharing in the one Spirit of God, and that sees marriage as a sacrament primarily directed toward procreation and education of children. Thus marriage appears related to baptism as the means of future enlargement of the ranks of baptized Christians, rather than as a specification of baptism directed equally to deepening the faith of spouses themselves. For this reason, the pope seems bound to maintain the pattern of situating domestic church only within sacramental marriage and, moreover, only those with children.[14]

The Primacy of Baptism

While theology and practice of sacramental marriage are surely not peripheral to understanding domestic churches, there are many reasons why baptism must be considered a domestic church's primary sacramental foundation. Such a perspective has several advantages. It affirms baptism as the root of every Christian's vocation to holiness. It can appeal to any Christian denomination, and especially to interchurch families whose members participate in more than one Christian tradition. Reflection on domestic church as founded upon shared baptism can be extended to incorporate families wherein one spouse is already Christian and the other spouse or children are exploring Christianity or formally preparing for baptism, a process that can take several years.[15] This approach can speak to Christian couples whose "irregular" marriages are regarded canonically as "invalid" but whose shared, valid baptism is not called into question by Catholicism. This approach better accommodates bonds of family members (such as siblings) not related by marriage. It creates a door for welcoming ordained and other unmarried adults—who are not sealed off from family life—into reflections on domestic church. It acknowledges that just as the role of "child" is our first entrance into family at a human level, the one permanent and universal role among humans, baptism, which marks us a "child of God," is the first, permanent, and universal experience shared by Christians.[16] For all these reasons, baptism as the sacramental foundation of domestic churches deserves more attention in theological and magisterial literature.[17]

There is a further reason why baptism as the sacramental foundation of domestic church deserves more attention; it has to do with the concept of imago dei in connection with the tensions inherent in family life. When marriage is seen as the sacramental foundation of domestic church, the message often conveyed, especially by John Paul II, is that a family is sacramental (i.e., conveys God's image or makes God present) to the extent that it models the reciprocal sort of love often called "communion." Though marriage is often said to image the love between Christ and the Church, the way that love is described often sounds more like the perfect communion within the triune Godhead.[18] But there is an equally important aspect of God's love which is especially apparent when it engages humans. Here the love relationship is decidedly less reciprocal. It entails suffering, dying to the self, and struggling to rise again and again to offer love in the hope that maybe this time it will be accepted and returned. This is the "paschal" sort of love best symbolized in baptism. It is this sort of love that many lay authors find neglected in literature I have categorized as deductive and idealistic.

It seems most accurate from a practical and theological perspective to consider marriage and baptism as an interwoven sacramental foundation of domestic church, with baptism being primary.[19] If the domestic church is interpreted as "two or three gathered together in my name,"[20] one can view baptism as that which symbolically marks persons with Jesus' name and invites them to commit to his mission. Sacramental marriage can be seen as that which often (though not always) gathers persons into families, giving them a unique vocation and a bond that distinguishes one group from another. Like other sacraments family members share, sacramental marriage is a public renewal and specification of one's baptismal commitment. Participation in a domestic church engages members in both the reciprocal, joyous love that is a foretaste of heavenly communion, and the earthly, painful, dying-and-rising, hopeful love celebrated at Easter. A domestic church is a case study in the eschatological image of God's kingdom as "already but not yet."

Is a Romantic Model of Love Appropriate for Domestic Church?

"A theology of domestic church, properly understood, should be a counter-cultural statement. It should radically challenge certain postmodern and Western notions about what a family is for, e.g., a safe haven, a unit of consumerism, an overly-affective domain."[21]

The nuclear model of family is often linked with a "romantic" model that understands the purpose of marriage and family as providing love among members. Love is understood in a way that emphasizes emotional intimacy, affirmation, and companionship. This model has become so prevalent in our culture that some of my students have a hard time grasping the fact that people in many times and places, even today, have not seen finding a "soul mate" as the primary mark of a good marriage.[22] When we study Scripture, especially the Old Testament, the first reaction of many students is that people in ancient times did not think love was important for marriage and family life. (Surely this must have been true in some cases, and is probably still true in some cases today.) What takes time for these students to appreciate is that the Bible speaks frequently of love, but love is often understood with different emphases. Ancient Jewish women hoped that their husbands would be reliable providers for their families and respected members of their community. Texts like Proverbs 31 show that a man would praise his wife for her skill and diligence in managing a household, for caring for the children, who would carry on his family name, and even for her "wisdom" and "kindly counsel." These efforts, and the praise attached to them, should be understood as expressions of marital love. While literature such as the Song of Songs reveals that a romantic, passionate sort of love was not unknown, this aspect of love was typically of secondary concern, as Michael Lawler explains:

> Love between spouses was not exclusively romantic love rooted in feeling and passion; it was the love required in the Torah injunction cited by Jesus, "You shall love your neighbor as yourself" (Lev. 19:18; Mk. 12:31; Mt. 19:19). Though feeling is sometimes part of neighbor-love, it is not always part of it and it is never all there is to it. Neighbor-love is more radical than feeling, romantic or otherwise. It is…a love rooted in the will and expressed in active "loyalty, service, and obedience." The neighbor-love and, therefore, the spousal love the Bible requires is loyalty/fidelity, service, and obedience or availability to another person.[23]

Rosemary Haughton traces historical development of family patterns, particularly nineteenth-century development of the bourgeois ideal whereby romantic love is considered the cement that holds families together. Noting economic and psychological needs served by various models of family at the times they developed, Haughton says it is appropriate that the nineteenth-century middle-class romantic ideal has retained such a prominent place in Christianity today, even if family love is not always as sincere as it is made out to be, and even if economic forces still steer decisions to marry and have children. She says it "matters to Christians" that families be places where people learn how to love. Indeed, this purpose ought to be the standard by which Christians evaluate and adapt cultural variations of family life: "[F]or most ordinary Christians, now as previously, the Christian family will be formed according to whatever sociological pattern happens to form family life in general at the time. Christians need only refuse to accept the general pattern when either they have a special vocation to do something different, or the prevalent pattern makes the growth of love and holiness virtually impossible. This is certainly not the case in our society. Like the first Gentile Christians, we do not need to alter the normal pattern so much as transform it."[24]

For Christians trying to assess the romantic model of family life, accepting the normal cultural pattern, and yet transforming it to align it with Christian priorities, is key. Christians should welcome an emphasis on companionship as a balance to models that have viewed marriage and family as simply economic institutions or legal contracts—with women and children often regarded as property. Still, the romantic model can distort the reality of family life, even serving as a rationalization to jump ship when the going gets tough, under the presumption that family life is not good simply because all one's perceived needs are not being met.

To provoke my students to scrutinize this model, I tell two stories of marriages within my own extended family. The first story is about a nephew I inherited from my husband's side of the family. My nephew has been married twice. In his first marriage, both the bride and the groom came from wealthy families. The wedding was picture perfect, with a bishop officiating. There were at least four showers before the wedding day; once the couple opened their wedding gifts, they had a fully furnished home. It would appear that this young couple didn't want for anything. And yet, about five months after the wedding, my nephew came home to find a note on the kitchen table; it said, "I'm not having fun anymore." His wife wanted, and got, a divorce. Soon after this disaster, my nephew told my husband, "I don't know what happened—we hadn't even been married long enough to have a fight!" Years later, my nephew's mother told me that the young bride apparently had doubts about getting married, but went through with the wedding because it seemed impossible to back out. Given the lavishness of the wedding preparations, this explanation seems plausible. Here, it seems the romantic model provided the impetus to enter a marriage that probably shouldn't have happened, and to leave once it was clear that one spouse "wasn't having fun anymore."

The second story I tell my students is about my aunt Joan and my uncle Tom, who have three adult children and three grandchildren. About twenty years ago, my uncle Tom was doing some home repairs and fell off the roof of his house (surprising, since he was a firefighter). He went into a coma. If my memory serves me correctly, it lasted several weeks, perhaps months. When he emerged from the coma, he was a very different person. He had to relearn almost everything. He has never again been able to work professionally, and has many permanent disabilities. I suspect that over the years there have been days when my aunt has said to herself, "I'm not having fun anymore." Yet, she took her marriage promises at face value; she and my uncle have been married over forty years. Despite the difficulties she has endured in taking care of her husband and children, my aunt has a reputation as a very optimistic person.

When I tell my aunt and uncle's story, I ask my students to question not only the romantic model of marriage and family, but also the related presumption that these are private affairs. The 2001 "State of Our Unions" report from the Rutgers National Marriage Project says that 80 percent of young adults surveyed agreed that "marriage is nobody's business but the two people involved." Taken together with the 94 percent rate of young people who see marriage as a relationship with a soul mate first and foremost, the portrait of marriage embraced is, in the words of the report's authors, "emotionally deep but socially shallow."[25] A theology of domestic church, in keeping with the best of Christian tradition, reminds us that marriage and family are always public affairs. Far from being nobody else's business, the family's role of teaching people how to love and keep commitments is a matter with many public repercussions, as is the role of providing for material needs of immediate family members and the surrounding community. Sometimes the public significance of marriage and family is not apparent until we consider the social costs (e.g., foster care, substance abuse and mental-health treatment, a judicial system to handle divorce and child custody disputes, restraining orders, etc.) that are traceable to broken or unhealthy family life. Recent social scientific research published by the Rutgers University National Marriage Project, the University of Chicago Family, Religion, and Culture Project, and the Creighton University Center for Marriage and Family confirms that marriage and family life inevitably have a public impact—especially on children—whether we intend this or not.[26] The question is not whether marriage and family have a public impact, but what sort of impact this will be, i.e., helpful or destructive.

From a theological perspective, a sacramental marriage is meant to be a public sign, witnessing God's covenant with humans and Christ's love for the Church. Covenant love doesn't disappear simply because one party "isn't having fun anymore." I tell my students, "My aunt Joan is not only an example of a loyal wife. She is an example of what it means to be a Christian, and that means being an example of how much God loves us. That's what 'marriage as a sacrament' is all about." The public witness of her domestic church was verified at my brother's wedding. At the reception, there was a series of eloquent toasts. One of the loveliest was when my brother toasted my aunt Joan and uncle Tom, thanking them for their presence and saying that he had them in mind when he pledged to marry his wife "for better or worse." I suspect my aunt's fidelity to my uncle in his time of need was not motivated explicitly by a desire to teach her nephew a countercultural lesson of what marriage is about. And yet, providentially, that is how her marriage functioned.

Set in a cultural context where privacy and freedom of choice are celebrated almost as ends in themselves, the romantic model of family love can be interpreted such that it prescribes no particular obligation toward persons not mutually chosen. Christian heritage should provoke domestic churches to regard immediate and extended family members, whether chosen (i.e., spouses and "planned" children) or unchosen (i.e., everybody else) as a blessing, with some gift to offer, rather than a mere burden or untimely inconvenience. The romantic model can be interpreted to permit opting out of obligations toward persons with unforeseen special needs, or who change in ways that we do not choose—especially in ways that affect their ability to provide us affirmation and emotional companionship. For instance, one might argue that my uncle Tom is no longer the same person my aunt Joan married. Care for him has imposed countless physical, emotional, and financial sacrifices on her; moreover, he has not been able to fulfill her emotional and sexual needs as she had hoped, so her marriage promises can be considered void if she chooses. Apparently, my aunt thinks differently.[27]

The romantic model of family has evolved to a point where deliberately-chosen companionship and emotional affirmation are depicted as the "love" that makes family life worth living. Ironically, this model can fuel new forms of the contractual understanding of marriage and family that proponents of romantic love have historically critiqued. The contracts may not be of the same terms as those of a previous era, but nevertheless the relationships are contractual in character, for they are commitments to relationships on specified terms. Serial marriages and divorces among individuals who "go their separate ways" as their "interests change" are one example.[28] Another example is seen in advertisements that have become increasingly common in Ivy League campus newspapers, seeking "generous" female students (with stipulated heights, ethnicities, and SAT scores) to provide eggs for "loving" infertile couples (in exchange for tens of thousands of dollars). The desire to parent a child of one's own at any cost, which at first glance seems an expression of pride in one's heritage, self-sacrifice, or altruism, can become distorted when infertility therapy becomes a lucrative commodity, but the distortion is shrouded by romantic language of love and generosity.[29] Thus, the danger of conceiving family in romantic terms is that we may completely miss an important message conveyed in the symbol of domestic church—a call to solidarity among all children of God and brothers and sisters in Christ, not simply those to whom we are related by blood, marriage, or carefully screened adoption.

Notes

1. USCC, *Follow the Way of Love*, 8.

2. Karen Sue Smith and Sarah Randag, "Please Pass Down the Faith," *U.S. Catholic* 63, no. 11 (November 1998): 17–21.

3. Prisca Wagua, "Pastoral Care for Incomplete Families: A Forgotten Ministry in Africa," *African Ecclesiastical Review* 38, no. 2 (April 1996): 118.

4. See http://www.aifw.org.

5. Sarah Mayles, "My Experience as an Interchurch Child," at http://www.aifw.org/journal/ 2000jul05.htm.

6. Mitch Finley and Kathy Finley, *Christian Families in the Real World* (Chicago: Thomas More Press, 1984), 20, 48, 86.

7. Similar statements appear in *Familiaris Consortio* ## 54, 56.

8. We read in *Letter to Families* #16, "Through Christ all education, within the family and outside it, becomes part of God's own saving pedagogy, which is addressed to individuals and families and culminates in the paschal mystery of the Lord's own death and resurrection. The 'heart' of our redemption is the starting point of every process of Christian education, which is likewise always an education to full humanity." I prefer this formulation to others described above.

9. However, section #38 goes on to connect baptism, teaching, and the domestic church: "Thus in the case of baptized people, the family, called together by word and sacrament as the Church of the home, is both teacher and mother, the same as the worldwide Church."

10. *Familiaris Consortio* ## 9, 55, 65, 69; *Catechesi Tradendae* ## 22, 23, 43.

11. Both options appear to have, at first glance, much common-sense value, but theoretical difficulties arise from each. "Process" explanations of

sacraments have trouble dealing with the traditional doctrine that sacraments give grace *ex opere operato* (see *Familiaris Consortio* ## 67, 68). *Ex opere operato*, Latin for "from the work done," is a concept used to specify how a sacrament achieves its effect "not because of the faith of the recipient and/or the worthiness of the minister, but because of the power of Christ who acts within and through it" (Definition from Richard McBrien, *Catholicism* [San Francisco, Harper Collins, 1994], 1239). With reference to marriage in particular, a process explanation of sacramental effectiveness opens the door to liberal attitudes toward divorce and the granting of annulments. If sources other than the experience of sacramental marriage are acknowledged as the root of evangelical discernment pertaining to family life, this means that families not rooted in sacramental marriage can be acknowledged among the ranks of domestic churches. While the U.S. bishops and many lay writers seem comfortable with this idea, I have not found any clear statement from John Paul II in *Familiaris Consortio* or *Letter to Families* saying that he accepts it.

12. In *Familiaris Consortio* #21 (cf. #19) John Paul II explains these relationships as follows: "Conjugal communion constitutes the foundation on which is built the broader communion of the family, of parents and children, of brothers and sisters with each other, of relatives and other members of the household. This communion is rooted in the natural bonds of flesh and blood, and grows to its specifically human perfection with the establishment and maturing of the still deeper and richer bonds of the spirit: the love that animates the interpersonal relationships of the different members of the family constitutes the interior strength that shapes and animates the family communion and the community." Germain Grisez makes a similar argument in "The Christian Family as Fulfillment of Sacramental Marriage," 33: "Since children participate in their parents' marriage insofar as they come to be and are nurtured in it, Christian children participate in the sacrament of marriage insofar as their parents bring them up as members of Christ." These statements are problematic; both suggest that other familial bonds are somehow not direct or immediate, but rather channeled through the marital bond.

13. NCCB, "A Theological and Pastoral Colloquium," 10–11.

14. For example, John Paul II states that "[w]hen children are born, the married couple becomes a family in the full and specific sense" (*Familiaris Consortio* #69). He repeatedly uses the expression, "a community of life and love," interchangeably to refer to marriage or family, whereas *Gaudium et Spes* #48 and #50, the source of the citation, use it only to define marriage. While it is not wrong to say that family is a community of life and love, the pope's use of the citation suggests that, in his mind, marriage, parenthood, and family/domestic church must necessarily exist together. William May's chapter on domestic church in *Marriage: The Rock on Which the Family Is Built* and Germain Grisez

in "The Christian Family as Fulfillment of Sacramental Marriage" provide similar arguments. An exaggerated formulation is found in Caffara, "The Ecclesial Identity and Mission of the Family":

> It is obvious that we set out from the pre-suppositions: 1) that only marriage containing the elements of *unity* and *indissolubility* can form the basis of the *family*; and 2) that the family community is an expansion of the *husband-wife* community. In fact, we can uncover the identity of the family by beginning precisely with the following question: In what does this very expansion of the *husband-wife* community into a *family* community consist? What does this expansion consist of in its *specific* identity and nature? How, precisely, does the husband-wife community get *transformed* into a family community?
>
> The answer is so obvious and simple that it might make us wonder if beginning with this question in order to uncover the identity of the family is perhaps *too* simple to put us on the right track: for the answer is the *child*. It is the *child* who transforms the husband-wife community into a family community, and it is therefore the act of *procreation* which expands the husband-wife community so that it becomes a family community. (6)

15. In fact, we might revise the statement from *Follow the Way of Love* cited in the epigraph at the start of this chapter: "Baptism brings all Christians into union with God. Your family life is sacred because family relationships confirm and deepen this union and allow the Lord to work through you" (8). We could say, "Family life introduces Christians to union with God. Baptism is sacred because it confirms and deepens this union and helps you recognize the Lord working through you."

16. Reflections on family and domestic church should give more attention to childhood, along with marriage and parenthood. Mary Mulligan raises this issue in "Family, Become What You Are," *New Theology Review* 5, no. 2 (May 1992): 6–19, at 12. A valuable essay on the subject of perpetual childhood is Karl Rahner's "Ideas for a Theology of Childhood," *Theological Investigations*, vol. 8 (New York: Seabury Press, 1977), 33–50. In this essay Rahner argues, "[C]hildhood is not a state which only applies to the first phase of our lives in the biological sense. Rather it is a basic condition which is always appropriate to a life that is lived aright." See also Rahner's "Christmas, the Festival of Eternal Youth," *Theological Investigations*, vol. 7 (New York: Herder & Herder, 1971), 121–126, and Bunge, *The Child in Christian Thought*.

17. Grisez acknowledges some limits in interpreting marriage as a sign of the Church: "[I]t seems to me, though the couple's one-flesh union aptly signifies the union of Christ with his Church considered as a whole, the Christian family completes the sacrament by more aptly signifying the union of Christ with his Church considered as a gathering of many members—God's 'large family,' in which Jesus, the Father's natural Son, is 'the firstborn'" ("The Christian Family," 33).

18. See Frederick Parrella, "Towards a Spirituality of the Family," *Communio* 9, no. 2 (Summer 1982): 127–141, at 132–137. There is some truth in this perspective. As Parrella notes, "Christ reveals a God of infinite love, one who relates infinitely and whose very nature as Person is constituted by such infinite relation. Therefore we are God's image only in so far as we stand in relation to others."

19. With the caveat, introduced earlier, that the effect of these sacraments not be understood simplistically and legalistically, apart from active faith and ongoing fruitful participation in Christian living. Singly or in combination they are not sufficient, in isolation, to create a Christian domestic church.

20. In his argument for children as the fulfillment of a sacramental marriage, Grisez adapts this definition to suit his purposes: "The three or more family members are gathered in Jesus' name, and he lives in their midst. Thus, the family is a community called together by God, an *ekklesia*, a church" ("The Christian Family as Fulfillment of Sacramental Marriage," 33).

21. NCCB, "A Theological and Pastoral Colloquium," 12.

22. The 2001 "State of Our Unions" report published by the National Marriage Project at Rutgers University finds that in a sample of 1003 persons aged twenty to twenty-nine, 94 percent of never married persons agreed that "when you marry you want your spouse to be your soul-mate, first and foremost." The report is available at the web site http://marriage.rutgers.edu.

23. Lawler, "Towards a Theology of Christian Family," 59 (emphases added).

24. Haughton, *The Knife Edge of Experience*, 102–103, 111–112.

25. See http://marriage.rutgers.edu.

26. See the web site for the National Marriage Project, cited above; the Family, Religion, and Culture Project can be found at http://divinity.uchicago.edu; the Center for Marriage and Family site is http://www.creighton.edu/MarriageandFamily. The web site for the Emory University Center for Interdisciplinary Study of Religion's forthcoming projects on sex, marriage, and family and on children is http://www.law.emory.edu/cisr.

27. In their anthology of readings pertaining to courtship and marriage, *Wing to Wing, Oar to Oar* (Notre Dame, IN: University of Notre Dame Press, 2000), Amy Kass and Leon Kass include a selection of traditional religious wedding vows and contemporary vows. None of the contemporary vows includes a promise to maintain the marital commitment "for better or worse, in sickness and in health, as long as we both shall live." None of them includes a promise to accept children into

the relationship, let alone a promise to be of service to the Church or community. Instead, the vows implicitly suggest that the couple promise to remain married as long as they both are "happy" and "fulfilled"—however the individuals choose to define these terms. One vow reads, "I love you because you are the one person with whom I can be totally myself. You have accepted me as I am. I will try, in every way possible, to make you as happy as you have made me." Another reads, "I want for you that which brings you the greatest personal fulfillment. I promise to encourage and support you as you strive to attain the finest of which you are capable." A third says, "I will try never to do anything which will embarrass you, for I want you always to be proud of me and our relationship. I will care for my body so that my good health will be an asset to our relationship. I will strive for intellectual growth so that I may be an interesting and mentally stimulating companion" (525).

28. I must bracket for now the heartbreaking cases of persons who divorce, sometimes more than once, because they discover that their spouse is abusive. For now, I have in mind what behavioral scientists label as "low-level conflict," such as "emotional distancing, boredom, or a change in one spouse's priorities"—in other words, "not having fun anymore." According to research summarized in Stephen Post's *More Lasting Unions* (Grand Rapids, MI: William B. Eerdmans, 2000), "[Paul] Amato and [Alan] Booth emphasize that about 70 percent of divorces terminate low-conflict marriages that have some shortcomings but are still reasonably tolerable for spouses and far better for children than divorce. Unprecedented and excessively high individual expectations make many good marriages not 'good enough.' While low-conflict marriages now routinely become divorces, this was not always the case....Although estimates vary somewhat, divorces resulting from high-level, persistent conflict make up, at most, one fourth of all cases. It seems possible, then, that many marriages could be saved if parents were better prepared for the realities of marriage, regularly supported in marriage (for example, in conflict resolution), and better educated about the consequences of divorce for their children" (15, 17).

29. In their feminist critiques of the infertility therapy industry, Maura Ryan and Lisa Sowle Cahill wisely raise concern about commodification and exploitation of children along with women, both pleasantly packaged in language of "personal fulfillment." While many older children, non-Caucasian children, and handicapped children wait for "loving" families to adopt them, couples might mortgage their homes, max out their credit cards, and endure painful and intrusive therapies with low success rates in the quest to create a certain type of child to love. See Maura Ryan, "The Argument for Unlimited Procreative Liberty: A Feminist Critique," in *Perspectives on Marriage*, ed. Kieran Scott and Michael Warren (Oxford: Oxford University Press, 2001), 187–201; Lisa Sowle Cahill, *Sex, Gender, and Christian Ethics* (Cambridge: Cambridge University Press, 1996), 217–254; and Amy Laura Hall, *Conceiving Parenthood* (Grand Rapids, MI: Eerdmans, 2008).

12. The Dual Vocation of Christian Parents

Julie Hanlon Rubio

This chapter first appeared in *Theological Studies* 63 (2002).

Flannery O'Connor's wonderful story, "The Lame Shall Enter First," is not often read by literary critics as a "family values" story, but ordinary readers often hear it as a warning to parents who sacrifice their children for the sake of important work. In their view, this story calls for a reexamination of what it means to be a parent. Sheppard, the father in the story, is a respectable middle-class widower who works as a city recreational director and volunteers as a counselor at a reform school for boys on the weekends. He has a burning desire to help disadvantaged children improve themselves and he eventually invites a difficult boy named Rufus to come and live with him and his eleven-year-old son. Gradually it becomes clear that Sheppard is entranced with his own good mission to Rufus, so entranced that he allows his son to grieve his dead mother alone. One morning at breakfast, in an attempt to inspire some compassion in his son Norton, Sheppard tells him that he is lucky his mother is not in the state penitentiary like Rufus' mother. Norton dissolves into tears, saying, "If she was in the penitentiary, "I could go to seeeeee her."[1] His father tells him to stop being selfish and grow up. Throughout the story, Sheppard puts a great deal of effort into saving Rufus, while ignoring the silent grieving of his own son. Near the end of the story, when faced with Rufus' ultimate rejection, he claims, "I have nothing to reproach myself with....I did more for him than I did for my own child,"[2] and fails to see the irony. For most readers, the failure of a father to care for his own son is obvious. Norton is left alone to make sense of his mother's death, Rufus is brought into the house to take away what is left of Sheppard's attention, and, at the end of the story, Sheppard finds Norton hanging in his room. This story of an ordinary, fallen, or lame human being is a perfect illustration of Flannery O'Connor's famous pessimism about human nature.[3]

Students in my classes read the story and find it easy to see parallels with their own lives. Many speak of parents who put their children second and their work first. The anguish in their voices is unmistakable. They know well the failures of parents to love their children. Suicide may be an extreme response, but the pain that inspires it is apparently widespread. Perhaps then it is legitimate to take O'Connor's story as a prophetic word about the duties of parenthood.

However, it seems to me that the story is not really about the importance of sacrificing social responsibilities for one's family. Rather, O'Connor is telling a story about a man who fails to connect with two boys—one, his own, and one whom he tries to adopt. Ultimately, he can save neither boy. Like most of O'Connor's tragic characters, Sheppard is not a good Christian. Sheppard's sin is not failing to put his family first; it is failing to be Christ-like. He ignores Rufus' concern with the state of his soul, forfeiting his trust, *and* fails to comfort his suffering son, forfeiting his life. He does not meet Christ or put on Christ at home or in the world.

If this interpretation is correct, why do my students so often read the story as a cautionary tale for parents who fail their children? Something in American culture makes it easy to see Sheppard's failings as a parent in the home but difficult to see his failings as a parent in the world. In America today, "family first" is nearly a sacred value. Most people agree that prioritizing family is the moral thing to do. One often hears the adage, "Nobody on his deathbed wished he had spent more time at the office." Media accounts of executives leaving corporate life to be with young children receive a great deal of attention. Ordinary families mourn their business and long for the time to put their own families first. Even in the presidential campaign of 2000, both Al Gore and George W. Bush were lauded as good fathers who put their families first. In fact, those who gave their nomination speeches emphasized the fatherly qualities of the nominees over and above their political positions, accomplishments, and goals. More recently, a popular billboard reads, "There's a reason most people don't have pictures of the office at home." That the sign is part of a "values" campaign by a large corporation apparently is an irony lost on most admirers. At any rate, the idea that family first is a claimed American value seems reasonable enough.

More comprehensive evidence for the prevalence of the "family first" ideal is available in the recent book, *Ask the Children: What America's Children Really Think about Working Parents*. Ellen Galinsky of the Families and Work Institute published there the results of a national survey of over 1000 third to twelfth graders and 600 parents. Galinsky reports that most working parents whom she and her colleagues interviewed claim to put their families first. A small percentage of parents admit that they do not, but Galinsky suggests that children of these parents are more likely to be dissatisfied.[4] According to her study, parents can avoid problems by prioritizing family.

What does this mean? It is not always clear, for the value "family first" is not connected to a specific practice. Certainly, for most Americans, prioritizing family does not mean quitting work. Galinsky argues, "It is not *that* we work, but *how* we work." In other words, the problem is not that parents have commitments other than their children; it is that children are not their top priority. Children, according to Galinsky, need to feel that their parents' work is not more important than they are. As one girl interviewed by Galinsky wrote, "I think the thing that goes on with kids is: 'Wouldn't you rather be with me than do this other thing?' I want my mother to like her job, but not more than she loves me."[5] According to Galinsky, children are more likely to give their mothers high grades when they feel that they are managing the work-family balance successfully and putting their families before their jobs most of the time.[6] Sacrificing everything for the sake of one's children is not necessary. One simply has to put them first.

On the other hand, one could argue that Americans do not seem to put family first in any meaningful way, for they spend much of their most precious commodity—their time—away from their children. Even when parents are around, they are often not fully present. The image of a family trying to eat dinner while cell phones and beepers compete for attention has become a cliché. This image is a powerful illustration of how much Americans have allowed work to invade their family lives. Despite the near universal acceptance of family first as a value, clearly, families do not always come first in the lives of most Americans, and most parents are aware of this inconsistency. The Flannery O'Connor story works as a guilt-inducer because it taps into both the "family first" value and the justifiable parental fear that they are selling their kids short.

As a Christian theologian, I am interested both in the vigor and frequency with which Americans claim this value (even those who work long hours rarely say they put family second) and in widespread parental worries that they are not doing enough (even parents who profess confidence in their choices often fear that they have not sacrificed enough for children). Most Americans parents want to work, yet they also want to have the kind of strong emotional ties to their children that will ensure enduring relationships. They do not want to end up like Sheppard.

Part of the problem may be the lack of a language for expressing the pull of dual responsibilities that most parents feel. It seems there is a choice. One may take the moral high ground and value "family first," or one may join the undistinguished ranks of inattentive parents glued to their offices and cell phones by valuing work first and family second. I would argue that the Christian tradition, exemplified by O'Connor correctly read, offers a different way of talking and thinking about parenting. The tradition points toward the ideal of a dual vocation for Christian parents that calls parents to be Christians at home and in the world. In this chapter, I will (1) show that the concept of dual vocation is implicit in the work of contemporary theology but in need of explication; (2) explore both sides of the dual vocation (nurture of children and work for the common good); (3) ask whether the idea of a split vocation is more compelling; and (4) conclude with cautious advocacy of dual vocation.

DUAL VOCATION IN THE WORK OF PRESENT-DAY THEOLOGIANS

While the concept of dual vocation is assumed in much of contemporary Christian theology, a full articulation remains necessary because theologians tend to emphasize one aspect of the dual vocation at the expense of the other, thereby impoverishing their family ethics. Methodist theologian Stephen Post is a good example of a theologian who focuses his energy on calling parents back to their nurturing role. In response to what he characterizes as a current crisis of the family, he asserts that parents must own their vocation to parenting. Implying that men and women will play different roles, he writes: "My own parental experience tells me that the relationship that my daughter and son have with their mother is qualitatively different from their relationship with me."[7] While affirming the existence of differences, Post does not give them a central place in his parenting ethic. Rather, his emphasis is on the need for parents to care for their children and in arguing for "models of co-parenting, in which both mother and father are deeply bonded with their children."[8] Post's ideal of co-parenting with different but significant roles for men and women is a key part of his attempt to restore family to its proper place in society.[9]

In choosing this emphasis on the nurturing half of the parenting vocation, Post leaves himself vulnerable on two counts. First, although he obviously wants to argue for a progressive family model, his stress on parenting and his acknowledgement of gender differences can be read as advocacy of a more traditional family model. Without the idea of dual vocation for both parents, a parent's (especially a mother's) choice to take up socially important work seems harder to justify. Second, the stress on nurture of one's own over service to others has the effect of making parenting more of a private vocation. Although Post does write also of the Christian family's responsibilities to those outside the family circle, he is more concerned with the right ordering of loves. Citing his own failure to put second his work with Alzheimer's patients when his young son needed him, and discussing the problems of other overcommitted parents, he seeks to reemphasize the duty to care for kin.[10] The overall effect is to minimize the responsibilities of parents (especially mothers) to non-family members.

Women theologians writing on parenting tend to question the idea of role differences more deeply than Post and to devote more energy to arguing for dual-career marriages in which both spouses have significant commitments outside the family. In her book *Family: A Christian Social Perspective*, Catholic ethicist Lisa Sowle Cahill does this in a subtle way by focusing less on parenting and more on the social responsibilities of the family, the other half of the dual vocation. While acknowledging the Catholic tradition's emphasis on "permanent marriage and the two-parent family nurturing children," she insists that families become domestic churches by carrying out "the social mission of compassion and service in spirit of Christian love."[11] She holds up African American families as role models for more privileged families, calling attention to their concern for each other across family lines.[12] Because her primary concern is calling parents and children to embrace key roles in society, beyond a brief acknowledgement that the tradition focuses on parental responsibility for children's character formation, she gives little attention to parental nurture.[13]

This reluctance to talk more fully about parenting limits Cahill's work, in my view, because the responsibilities of parents to care for their own can seem unimportant in comparison to weighty social duties attributed to families. In the context of Cahill's work, it would seem difficult to justify a choice to forgo a socially important job in order to spend more time with young children. Moreover, it is unclear how families themselves can live out the social justice Church's teachings at home. Even the idea of domestic church, which is central to her book, is primarily discussed in terms of social policy rather than in terms of what families might do together.[14] Although this it is obviously not Cahill's intention to devalue parenting, her emphasis on social commitment seems implicitly to diminish the weight of the parental vocation to nurture.

Thus, while both Post and Cahill assume that parenting involves work inside and outside the home for both men and women, Cahill sees the family differently than Post (as including the stranger rather than reaching out to the stranger) and thus she places the social mission of the family at the center of its existence. While not dismissive of parental duties, unlike Post (who places permanent marriage and care for children at the center of his project) Cahill is more focused on opening Christian families to the fullness of their social responsibilities. She claims that while care for one's own may be a universal family ethic, "the ultimate tests of a distinctively *Christian* ethics of family life go beyond the well-being of family members and the successful accomplishment of family roles. The Christian family defines *family values* as care for others, especially the poor."[15] Thus primary care for children by parents is not the primary mission of the Christian family; care for others is. Post argues, in contrast, that in the Christian biblical family ethic, "familial love is placed at the very center of the entire spiritual universe, and thereby sets the example for universal solicitude. Only secondarily is the family focused outward."[16] He seems far more aware of the limitations of human beings and of the neglected children of well-meaning, but over-committed parents.

Post and Cahill are representative of two important strains of contemporary Christian thought on parenting. Post believes the contemporary family crisis is a crisis of values which leads to diminished parental investment in children. He sees in the Christian tradition a strong valuing of family and concludes that today's Christian parents must retrieve a sense of the centrality of family commitment. Cahill roots the contemporary crisis in the insularity of families and in their diminished investment in the poor. She sees in the Christian tradition a strong emphasis on social concern and calls today's families to reach outward. Both assume that parenting involves work and nurture for men and women, but each emphasizes one part of the dual vocation and unwittingly diminishes the fullness of the call to parent.

Catholic and Protestant feminist theologians also assume that parenting involves responsibilities to others as well as one's own, but they, too, often fail to reckon with the full meaning of dual vocation. Methodist theologian Bonnie Miller-McLemore, for instance, develops psychologist Erik Erikson's concept of generativity and argues that this should not be seen as a stage of life during which an adult is productive or creative, but rather as an ongoing dimension of adult life involving both productivity in the world of work and nurturing children at home.[17] Contending that the first chapter of the Book of Genesis gives to both men and women the responsibilities to fill the earth (have and care for children) and to subdue it (work), she believes that living in a fully human way means being creative in both tasks.[18] Miller-McLemore carefully distinguishes herself from radical feminists who seem to diminish the work of parenting, though she clearly seeks to respond to their writings. As well, she writes out of her own experience as a mother who struggles to balance teaching and writing with caring for her family.[19] She argues quite powerfully that women and men need assistance from the church and society as they strive to be "good enough" parents and workers.[20]

The limitation of McLemore's work is that despite her interpretation of Genesis as a call to two kinds of work early on in the book, and despite her own obviously socially important work as a theologian, minister, and teacher, she spends most of the book speaking about work as fulfillment rather than duty. While she appropriately describes care for children both as gift and task, she speaks of work as that which a mother must do *for herself* in order to be capable of giving to her children.[21] While the emphasis on the self is significant and has been important in feminist work, it is not sufficient to ground a Christian ethic of work. The dual vocation idea allows for the recognition of dual responsibilities that avoids stereotyping work as pleasureful escape from the gratifying but demanding work of childcare. One can find echoes of Miller-McLemore's argument in many other feminist writers.[22] All share an interest in defending women's right to work and underlining their need to work. Like Post and Cahill, these Christian feminists do not ignore the importance of parenting. In fact, many are among the strongest voices calling for a renewed attention to children in a world that often ignores them. Yet, few make explicit the idea that Christian women and men are called (not just entitled) to serve both at home and the world. The following section aims to do just this.

A CHRISTIAN PARENT AT HOME: NURTURING ONE'S CHILDREN

Sacrificing one's own needs in order to nurture one's children is a large part of parenting. Pregnancy in particular is in some ways a paradigmatic experience of sacrificial love, for the mother's body is taken over by her child, who eats from her food, drinks from her drink, moves within her, causes her pain and discomfort, and distorts the shape of her body. In some important sense, pregnancy requires sacrifice of mothers whether or not they consciously choose it. Pregnancy itself pulls women into the sacrifices of parenting, readying them for (or at least warning them of) what is to come. In addition, all parents know that sacrifice is a necessary part of raising children. Believing this allows parents to go without sleep and change diapers in the early years, to give up the leisurely weekends of their pre-child existence in exchange for weekends spent watching youth athletic games and cleaning the house, to give up relative tranquility for teenage years of rebellion and challenge. Those who are not willing to engage in significant sacrifice are not ready for parenting.

Moreover, most Christian parents feel that their children are worth all the time, energy, and love they have to give; nurture is what parents are called to do. This parental instinct can be justified in ethical terms by exploring the implications of natural connections between parents and children. It seems intuitively correct to say that children deserve parental care because of their physical connection to their parents. One Catholic theologian argues that

> If we really believe bodies matter, and are prepared to follow this insight where it takes us, we cannot help but acknowledge the fact that a child is produced by the bodily union of its mother and father, that the mother carries it in her body for nine months, that the child usually shares many of its parents' bodily features and bears their genetic inheritance, is of enormous significance and provides a uniquely firm foundation for a relationship of love.[23]

This is not simply a concern for today. Vigen Guroian, an Armenian Oriental Orthodox theologian who teaches in the United States, has shown that fourth-century theologian John Chrysostom would call today's parents back to their primary duty to care for their children because they are connected. Guroian shows how Chrysostom puts the souls of children in parents' hands, and argues that "whether a child inherits the kingdom of heaven relies upon the care he or she receives from parents."[24] This strong sense of parents' ultimate responsibility comes from Chrysostom's belief that a child is intimately linked to her or his parents as is stated in *On Marriage and Family*:

> The child is a bridge connecting mother to father, so the three become one flesh....And here the bridge is formed from the substance of each! Just as the head and the body are one, so it is with the child. That is why Scripture does not say, "They shall be one flesh." But they shall be joined together "into one flesh," namely the child.[25]

Chrysostom's belief that one-fleshness connects parents and children and links their lives and destinies together is echoed in the writings of Thomas Aquinas, who uses natural law to connect children and parents. He posits that because the child comes from the parents, they are best able to care for him. As Christina Traina puts it, for Aquinas, "the affective love of parent for child is appropriately among the most intense, intimate, long-lasting human attachments. No one is nearer to us than our children, whom we love 'as being part of' ourselves."[26] Given this assumption, Aquinas's insistence that "[n]urture by the family—specifically the mother—is appropriate for children at [the] pre-rational stage" makes sense.[27] Biological ties weigh heavily in the writings of Aquinas and Chrysostom on childhood. Both of these key historical figures believe that because children and parents are bodily connected, they have special commitments to each other. Most contemporary parents would readily agree that this commitment is simply there when a child is born, thus it seems a natural, and good thing to fulfill it.[28]

However, physical connection does not always lead to emotional connection. Stories of young women leaving newborn babies they never wanted in trashcans or hospitals are but one indication that pregnancy is not always a bonding experience for women. Stories of the many men who leave women when they are pregnant are one indication that genes are not enough to hold parents and children together. Writings by feminist mothers have revealed the un-naturalness of the parental bond for many women. In Adrienne Rich's seminal text *Of Woman Born*, she writes of how she broke out in a rash several days before her first son was to be born. The rash was diagnosed as "an allergic reaction to pregnancy."[29] A mother allergic to having children! Here, and throughout the book, Rich gives testimony to the difficulty she had embracing her role as mother, for to be a mother she had to give up her vocation as a poet. Though she struggled to complete the sacrifice she knew she was supposed to make, she found herself incapable. This profound discomfort with the sacrifices of parenting compels Rich to begin and end her book with reflections on the true story of a mother of eight "who had recently murdered and decapitated her two youngest on her suburban front lawn."[30]

One can take this seriously as a warning that parental love is not always natural and still affirm that though many parents would acknowledge experiencing moments of extreme anger with their children, for most, love and a profound desire to care for children in their vulnerable, dependent state win out. Theologian Sally Purvis speaks for many parents when she writes of how "the most sustained and trustworthy embodiment of agape in my life is my experience of being a mother to my two sons."[31] Like many, Purvis is overwhelmed by how much she is capable of giving to her children. Over and against Kierkegaard's claim that love for the dead is the criterion for universal, disinterested Christian love, or agape, Purvis suggests the model of a mother, who loves within an intense special relationship with her children.[32] She argues that mother-love is inclusive in that it extends to all of her children, no matter who they are as individuals, that it is connected and focused on the needs of others, and that it is unconditional.[33] She then contends that her model better fits the scriptural stories from which Christians are supposed to take their understanding of love. Jesus told the Parable of the Good Samaritan and this story, Purvis argues, is about love that does not have limits, about a man who behaved not like a neighbor, but like a lover.[34] Mothers, too, are like lovers in that they care intensely for others, regardless of what is given back. It is the intensity to which Christians are both drawn and called.

Popular Christian writing also testifies to the importance of the parent-child bond in the lives of Christian families.[35] For instance, many journals for pregnant women ask women to use their pregnancy as a way to deepen their understanding of divine sacrifice and of the sacrifices they will make as parents. As mother and author Carrie Heiman writes:

> I'm giving up my old body; I'm giving up my old world. My world seems to revolve more and more around this child. When I bring this child into my life, my life will not be the same again. There is so much I'm giving up so I can receive this new life. But maybe I shouldn't be so surprised; that's what Jesus did for me, isn't it? He gave and gave until his body was changed almost beyond recognition—as it hung on the Cross. And finally he gave his very body and blood in order to bring me to spiritual birth.[36]

For Heiman, the giving or self-sacrifice is very physical, and yet also spiritual.

Her physical transformation has spiritual import. As she becomes a mother, she is learning to give and thus becoming more Christ-like. Like Sally Purvis, who came to understand agape by reflecting on her mothering, Heiman comes to understand the Cross by reflecting on her pregnancy. Both women affirm the power of the experience of mothering, the connection between mother and child, and the importance of sacrifice. As Miller-McLemore points out, pregnancy is but one part of being/becoming a parent. Men, too, can experience profound connections to their children. Still, the experience of pregnancy is unique and revelatory, for, "In the pregnant body, the self and the other coexist. The other is both myself and not my self, hourly, daily becoming more separate, until that which was mine becomes irrevocably another. In the pregnancy moment, I am one but two."[37]

According to Miller-McLemore, the knowledge women gain from carrying and nursing babies is not "privileged knowledge. It is knowledge that must be shared."[38] Moreover, it can be shared and appropriated by others who have not become mothers. It is also not learned or appropriated by all who do become mothers. Because human beings are not determined by biology, they experience things differently and learn in unique ways. If not all biological mothers learn connection and empathy from pregnancy, many fathers can and do. They, too, experience the pull of their children upon their energies. They want to sacrifice for them and nurture them.

The experience of Christian parents affirms that the duty to nurture one's children is rooted in the physical connections between parent and child. The Christian tradition testifies to the experience of Christian parents when it recognizes that children deserve parents' time and attention. This claim reflects the ongoing discernment of the Christian community as its members reflect on their experiences and come to understand their intense love for those closest to them. Clearly, care for one's own is a crucial part of the Christian moral life.[39]

BEING A CHRISTIAN PARENT OUTSIDE THE HOME: PUBLIC WORK

The value of nurturing one's own children does not provide an adequate basis for a full discussion of the Christian calling to parenthood. Historically, the Christian tradition has had more to say about the family than this. In the Gospels, what stands out is a suspicion of the family, a concern that it will be difficult to live a truly Christian life if one stays within the traditional family structure. Ambivalence about the family continues throughout the Christian tradition. All of this suggests the necessity of rethinking the centrality of nurturing one's own children and considering the importance of caring for those outside one's own family.

Jesus and the Early Christians as Models

It is not possible here to give a full account of the scriptural witness on families, but it should be possible to show that discipleship in the Gospels requires going beyond love of one's family. The Gospel of Mark provides a good example of a conflict between family and discipleship in Jesus' own life. Jesus is teaching a large crowd that follows him everywhere he goes. His mother and brother hear about this and go to find and "seize" him (Mark 3:20–22). When the crowd tells him that his family has come to see him, he asks: "'Who are my mother and my brothers?' And looking around on those who sat about him, he said: 'Here are my mother and my brothers! Whoever does the will of God is my brother, and sister, and mother'" (Mark 3:33–35). Jesus rejects his family's attempt to take him away from his disciples. He might have simply told his family that he had pressing work to do. Instead, he uses his rejection of their request to call the whole nature of the kinship bond into question. He says very plainly that those he has gathered around him are his new family, and he seems to deny loyalty or duty to his family of origin. The author of the Anchor Bible commentary claims that this state-ment, "exemplifies the radical demand of Jesus upon those who are set in a new framework in which bonds of fellowship in a common obedience to God are placed above the bonds of kinship."[40] Another commentator simply says that Jesus tells his disciples here that, "spiritual kinship surpasses the accidents of birth."[41] When confronted with the demands of his family, Jesus proposes a new radical moral standard that threatens the most basic family loyalties and engenders the most difficult conflicts between family and reli-gious commitment.

In a related story in the Gospel of Luke, Jesus tells a man who wants to follow him that he must not stop to bury his dead father. "Leave the dead to bury their own dead," Jesus says, "but as for you, go and proclaim the kingdom of God" (Luke 9:60, parallel in Matthew 8:21–22). Luke shows Jesus asking for devotion to the work of kingdom of God, understanding that his command will call into question even ordinary family affection. According to Joseph Fitzmyer, Jesus "knows...that the demands of the kingdom are bound to rupture even ordinary family life."[42]

As in the Markan story, Jesus' words grate against the most basic moral sensibilities. What can Jesus possibly have meant by this? It seems that he cannot have been speaking literally. Still even a figurative interpretation leaves one with an extreme family-denying ethic. Perhaps, some have argued, Jesus is speaking only to those with a special calling to leave everything for him. Or perhaps this and other similar passages date from early strains of the oral traditions ("Q" and "proto-Mark") that were gathered and edited by the wandering charismatics who made up the core of the Jesus movement.[43] However, it is more likely that this saying of Jesus is not a literal command addressed to a special group (there is no indication that it is), but rather a command pregnant with symbolism that is intended to address a general need for disciples of Jesus to place their commitment to Jesus above their commitments to their families. Richard Horsley makes this point precisely and further claims that Jesus' radical anti-family message was rooted in his commitment to his mission: "the revitalization of local community life."[44] This mission required some to leave their families and spread the word, while others opened and restructured their families at home. The goal, according to Horsley, was a society in which people treated each other with compassion, forgave each other's debts, shared their property, and refused to lord power over each other. Some rejection of the traditional family was necessary in order to move toward the goal of a renewed and restructured family and community life in which discipleship had priority for all.

Yet, Jesus does not altogether reject marriage. Rather, in his refusal to sanction divorce, he reaffirms the importance of the marital commitment in the lives of the people he has gathered around him. He recalls the Genesis account, and claims that "from the beginning of creation, 'God made them male and female.' 'For this reason a man shall leave his father and mother and be joined to his wife, and the two shall become one flesh.'...What therefore God has joined together, let not man put asunder" (Mark 10:6–9). This saying is widely viewed as support for marriage as a holy union. It should allay any fears that "marriage or the nuclear family (was) rejected or even devalued."[45]

So if marriage is not rejected altogether, what is? Certainly, the patriarchal structure of the family—both the absence of fathers in the new kingdom and Jesus' admonition to "Call no one father" (Mt. 23:8)—attest to this. But it is difficult to deny a more far-reaching anti-kinship message in this crucial set of Jesus' sayings, for he does not simply target fathers. Mothers, children, and siblings are implicated as well. It is the bond of kinship itself and all the ethical priority that comes with it which is being called into question, because the Jesus of the Gospels preaches that family, like money and power, can be dangerous to the person who is trying to live a holy life. He taught that those who would serve God must resist the temptation to make care of their own their only mission in life.

This emphasis on going beyond family makes sense if one understands the historical context. In the Greco-Roman world in which Jesus lived, family was a weightier matter. It was the primary reality, more important than individuals certainly, and significant in its relation to the state because through the family, more citizens for the Roman Empire were produced.[46] For this reason, the early Christians were derided, and even persecuted for their anti-family views.[47] Greco-Roman ideals of marriage in Jesus' time emphasized the ethical duty to marry. Marriages came into existence via private compacts between two persons who intended to become husband and wife.[48] However, children were a crucial part of marriage. In fact, "[p]rocreation was regarded as a civic duty, and all citizens of marriageable age were expected to contribute."[49] Because life expectancies were so short and the survival of the society was so crucial, through law and social pressure, "young men and women were discreetly mobilized to use their bodies for reproduction."[50]

Historical sources are replete with examples of cultural and ethical conflict between the Romans, who believed the family to be the prime sacred duty, and the early Christians, who affirmed other priorities. Stories of women who sneak out of their husbands' beds at night to join in Christian worship in other rooms, or stories of disciples of Christ who come together despite diverse backgrounds, or of women who give up their high status as wives to "slave of God" are common in Christian literature of the time.[51] Moreover, the early Christian text The Acts of Paul and Thecla portrays Thecla as a heroine because she leaves her fiancé to preach the gospel with Paul.[52] She and other early Christian celibates contributed to the Christians' reputation in Palestine as "'homewreckers,' initiators of a message not of household order but disorder."[53]

This is all the more shocking because among the Palestinian Jews, marriage was expected as a matter of course.[54] The Hebrew Bible presents us with "a religious community built upon the patriarchal family."[55] Unlike Roman society, in which family loyalty is linked to state and cult, the family in Jewish culture is directly tied to the faith. The Jews as a people have a covenant with God, and each Jew becomes a part of the covenant in and through the family. Marriage went largely unquestioned in the lives of Palestinian Jews, until Jesus of Nazareth came onto the scene.[56]

The marriage ideals of both Jewish and Roman cultures were sweeping in scope and demanding in expectations. It is not difficult to understand that Jesus of Nazareth, who, like other radicals of his time, wanted to give himself totally to God, questioned the marital ethos of the time. The demand for so much loyalty to family seemed to him idolatrous. He did not want family to function as an idol in his life, or in the lives of his followers, so he asked them to go against the cultural mores of their time and put God first. The early Christians heard this message, as is evident in New Testament and early Christian texts.

Of course, the New Testament also contains affirmations of marriage like the well-known words from Ephesians 5:22–23 ("Wives submit to your husbands as to the Lord....Husbands love your wives as your own bodies"). There are two strains in the Christian tradition, both of which strive to be true to Jesus' message. One, represented by Paul and his followers, represents an attempt to build upon Jesus' affirmation of marriage and the experience of married Christian men and women that marriage is good and even godly. This is the strain that eventually triumphed, and it is the one that is most often preached today. However, even today, there are echoes of the more radical early strain which questions the possibility of harmoniously combining love for God (and its accompanying public vocation to spread the gospel) with the more private vocation of giving oneself in marriage. Historian Peter Brown notes that this strain is rooted in the ancient belief that a good person must achieve "singleness of heart," or total commitment to one good. He argues that this vision "is the great hope which, in all future centuries, would continue to flicker disquietingly along the edges of the Christian

Church."[57] It can be heard today in the Catholic Church's assertion that celibacy is a higher calling than marriage.[58] It is also heard in the quiet lives of priests, monks, and women religious that say to married Christians: "There is more to life than family. God may sometimes be more deeply known and loved by those who are free from other passions." The higher valuing of the non-married life is a constant challenge to Christian families.

If this tradition is taken seriously, the idea that parental sacrifice for children must take precedence over the public vocations of men and women must be brought into question. Jesus' followers are called first and foremost to discipleship in community. He tells them that discipleship with him means *not* putting their families first. He asks them to break out of traditional roles, especially traditional family roles, in order to realize the radical meaning of his message. The Christian tradition, at least in its early stages, is no more encouraging. Contemporary Christians who want to be true to Scripture and tradition have to reckon with the centrality of the Christian's public vocation as it is attested to by these sources.

If discipleship is the fundamental calling of Christians, discipleship to Jesus of Nazareth presumes a public vocation. Certainly one can practice Christian virtue, keep the many of the commandments, and obey God's will at home in one's family. Perhaps the Gospels and early tradition were insufficiently attentive to this reality, which contemporary Christians know so well. However, I would argue that one cannot fully realize the demands of discipleship to Jesus unless one also has a public vocation. The public nature of discipleship is evident in the life of Jesus. Jesus himself acknowledges the conflict between serving God (in his public preaching) and serving his family. Jesus' mission is primarily public, so public that he is eventually crucified (given the death of a political criminal). Those who were his earliest followers sought to continue his mission by traveling to spread his message, forming new kinds of families that were radically inclusive, and refusing to participate in many mainstream political practices and institutions. Discipleship to Jesus must involve some form of public vocation.

Work in the Present-Day Catholic Tradition

The Catholic tradition affirms the importance of a public vocation and presumes that work is an important aspect of that vocation. Pope John Paul II writes in *Laborem Exercens* that "work is a fundamental dimension of man's existence on earth."[59] Work is not simply something that one does to fill a day, or what one has to do in order to eat. According to the Pope, work is commanded by God in Genesis 1:28 ("Be fruitful and multiply, and fill the earth and subdue it"), and therefore it must be fundamental to humanity. The subject of work is the human person.[60] Work is something persons choose. The work a person does must "serve to realize his humanity, to fulfill his calling to be a person that is his by reason of his very humanity."[61] A person's work is her vocation. In her work, she realizes herself as a person. Work is both an obligation and a right of all persons.[62] It is a share in the work of the Creator.[63]

Two important ethical implications can be drawn from John Paul II's theology of work. First, all persons have a calling that must be answered, an invitation to share in the shaping and molding of the world. Work is a right, not simply because all persons have a right to the basic necessities of life, but because all persons have something important to do in this world by which they will realize themselves. Second, the work that persons do is crucially important. It is not something to be thought of lightly, or not thought of at all in relation to one's Christian vocation. Work is a fundamental part of the moral life. The Fathers of Vatican II stated that Christians must not separate faith and life.[64] What people do is an important part of who they are. A Christian cannot choose to engage in work in a less than fully human way.

Nevertheless, no specific kind of work is ruled out. The Pope claims that it is the person who works, not the work itself that is crucial.[65] This qualification is important in that it affirms that people can work in a variety of jobs while living out their Christian vocation. However, it is also important to acknowledge that people are easily persuaded not to look closely at what kind of work they do. Clearly, too, not all work can be considered Christian work.[66]

Dorothy Day's insistence that work is prayer is a helpful qualifier to the Pope's general vision. Day values work that truly benefits needy human beings. In her book *Loaves and Fishes* Day writes about the quiet commitment of a woman named Marie who each night sweeps the floor of the Catholic Worker house and sees her work as a prayer.[67] The sweeping of the floor allows life to go on in a shelter for some of the most disadvantaged in the city. Surely it is important to Day that she sweeps this floor and not another. Day herself struggled until she found meaningful work that was in accord with her faith. Writing was not enough; she wanted to be a part of a Christian community committed to the poor. In this context, writing, cooking, and sweeping the floor are important work. Day's example is a reminder that all Christians are called to find significant work; only this work constitutes prayer.

For Christian parents who are trying to live as disciples of Christ, this means that work ought to be seen as more than a means to an end, more than a way to support a family. It makes little sense to spend ten to fourteen hours a day getting ready for, driving to, doing, and driving home from something less than meaningful in order that the other, more meaningful two to six hours of a day are possible. It makes little sense to spend the majority of our time doing something unrelated to who we really are. For if work is not a part of what we are, what are we? In his theology of work, the Pope forces this question, because he affirms that work is fundamental to the development and fulfillment of human beings and insists that human beings can and must choose humanizing work.

If work is all this, it does not seem that Christian parents can avoid the fulfillment of a public vocation or work during their parenting years. Work is a part of a Christian's commitment to live an ethical life. It cannot be put aside when children arrive, nor can the needs of children be allowed to completely shift the focus of work from humanity to providing the best for one's own.

Family in the Contemporary Catholic Tradition

The same Catholic tradition that sees work as a part of one's public vocation also claims that family life is, in part, public. It views the family not simply as a private haven, but as a community with a mission that goes beyond itself. In the Catholic tradition, family life is a part of the public vocation of parents.

In John Paul II's 1981 post-synodal apostolic exhortation *Familiaris consortio (On the Family)*, he defines the family as "a community of life and love" that has four major tasks. Each of these tasks has public dimensions. The first task is the most obvious. The family must "guard, reveal and communicate love."[68] He distinguishes himself from earlier popes by the inspired way in which he describes married love and demands that it rise to the heights for which it is destined. His personalist language represents an attempt to take seriously the importance that modern men and women give to spousal relationships. Love among family members is primary not because it is most important, but because it is the foundation for the rest of what the family does. This is the beginning, not the end.

The second task is that of "serving life." According to the pope, this means that parents have a responsibility to serve life by nurturing children *and* by bringing life to the world.[69] Having children is only the first step. Education is an important responsibility, and it includes the task of instilling in children, "the essential values of human life," especially the idea that possessions do not make human beings what they are and the responsibility to adopt a simple lifestyle.[70] The pope also affirms that when mothers and fathers teach their children about the gospel, "they become fully parents, in that they are begetters not only of bodily life but also of the life that through the Spirit's renewal flows from the cross and resurrection of Christ."[71] This seems to indicate that passing on the Christian faith is even more important than the admittedly awesome process of passing on life. Here, as in the gospel itself, the spiritual and public duty is placed above (but in relation to) the private duty. This emphasis on the spiritual is made clear when the Pope claims that families have a "spiritual fecundity" by which they share with others the self-giving love they nurture within.[72] Families are called to respond especially to all of God's children with compassion. Serving life is much more than having babies.

The third task to which the pope calls families further indicates that families are not oriented simply toward their own good. Families are called to participate in the development of society, for "far from being closed in on itself, the family is by its nature and vocation open to other families and to society and undertakes its social role."[73] This means that families "cannot stop short at procreation and education";[74] they have distinct and fundamental social and political duties.[75] Specifically, the pope asks families first, to practice hospitality, opening their table and their home to those who are not as fortunate as they are, second, to become politically involved, assisting in the transformation of society, and third, to practice a preferential option for the poor, manifesting a "special concern for the hungry, the poor, the old, the sick, drug victims and those with no family."[76] All of this is part of the social mission of the family. It is not optional, nor is it an add-on that families are to do after the really important tasks are done. It is, according to John Paul II, a fundamental part of a family's identity and calling. This activity might be described as a crucial part of a family's public vocation. It is what it does, as a community of love, in the world.

Finally, to describe the fourth task the pope uses the "domestic church" imagery which received renewed attention at Vatican II to suggest that families must serve the church as well as one another.[77] As a "church in miniature," the family evangelizes its members, witnesses to the world, uses its home as a sanctuary (for rituals of prayer, sacrament, and sacramentals) and serves the broader community—for like the Church, the family is a servant of humanity.[78] Here again, the emphasis is on the public role of the family.

At each point in his description of the ideal family, the pope implies that families are about more than themselves. They are communities of love, but they are not inwardly focused. They serve life by giving birth, physically and spiritually. They serve society, especially the poorest members. They are the church in their home, and as such contribute to their ecclesial mission. John Paul II's emphasis on the social responsibilities of the family implies that Christian parenting requires something different of parents than focusing on the family. The genius of Catholic teaching on the family is that it refuses to limit families by telling them just to take care of their own. It calls into question the ethic of parenting in American culture that centers on the duty of parents to sacrifice for their children. His definition of family seems to require instead that parents serve their children and the world.

Both the earliest strains of the Christian tradition and contemporary Catholic teaching indicate that all Christians have a duty to engage in public work. While neither full-time work nor work for pay is obligatory, some kind of commitment to the good of others or the common good seems required. In the Gospels and the papal teaching on work, this obligation extends to all Christians, including parents, but it is specifically linked to parents as family members in John Paul II's prophetic teaching on the family.

A SPLIT VOCATION?

While the papal teaching stresses that families have private and public vocations and calls all persons to humanizing work, it continues to call women to full-time motherhood. One might ask whether this teaching advocates a split vocation for families, with women covering the "private" realm and men taking care of "public" dimensions.

Papal teaching clearly states that women are the primary parents who bear the cross of parenting most directly. In *On the Family*, John Paul II claims that women's work in the home ought to be celebrated and made more possible by society. If women must work outside the home, the pope asks that they make sure that their family life comes first.[79] In his 1994 *Letter to Families* written for the International Year of the Family, he calls raising children "a genuine apostolate," but differentiates between the primary role of mother, and the secondary role of father, who must "become willingly involved as a husband and father in the motherhood of his wife."[80] The nuclear family is presumed to be the ideal place for childcare. Recent writings have included more acknowledgment that women have the right to work and bring distinct gifts to public life.[81] Still, the current plurality of family situations in the contemporary world is not viewed positively. For example, in a recent speech, the acknowledgment of women's gifts is followed by a prayer to entrust the Virgin Mary with the challenge that working women present. The Holy Family, in which "Mary, like any good housewife, was busy with domestic tasks while Joseph, with Jesus beside him, worked as a carpenter," is still the ideal.[82] More significantly, the idea that parents might struggle to balance nurture for children with a vocation in society is not taken up as a moral dilemma. All of this seems to indicate that the Catholic tradition sees men and women as responsible for only half of the dual vocation of the family.

On the other hand, the pope claims that women's care for their families is work and has social import because it is crucial to society that children are loved and nurtured.[83] He rightly acknowledges that the work of parenting contributes to the good of society and is in that sense public work.[84] He also acknowledges that fathers care for their families by working, and are (secondarily) directly responsible for their children.[85] It seems that the papal teaching advocates dual vocation, but with an imbalance. Mothers fulfill private and public vocations by mothering, with an emphasis on the private, while fathers fulfill private and public vocations by working, with an emphasis on the public. Does this division of vocation square with contemporary experience?

Feminist Mothers

Feminist writing of the last three decades reveals that those who do caring work often experience this work as isolating and they long to participate in the larger society. Many women who are very committed to parenting nonetheless speak about the need for work that involves them in the lives of individuals who are not their own. Many feminist mothers have expressed their frustration with the limitations of work that is concentrated in the home and involves a great many tasks that are necessary and valuable, but also mundane, repetitive, and seemingly unconnected to the larger world. Feminist writers claim that many women need public work in order to be fulfilled as persons, and this claim fits nicely with Catholic teaching on the right and duty of public participation. Both Catholic thought and feminist thought affirm the importance of public vocation, while still upholding the importance of the work of parenting.[86]

Feminist literature on mothering is different from the idealistic portraits of motherhood which appear in popular culture and even in academic writing. This literature is unintelligible to many who are new to it. For instance, in Stephen Post's discussion of parental love, he criticizes a feminist essay entitled, "Motherhood: The Annihilation of Women," claiming that although in some extreme cases, motherhood is seriously problematic for women, "were most mothers asked whether motherhood has 'annihilated' them, they would find the question extreme and even peculiar."[87] However, feminist mothering literature gives voice to the very real feeling of many mothers that parenting, while exhilarating and fulfilling in many ways, is not enough to fill a life.

In 1969, Betty Friedan called it "the problem with no name," and chronicled a generation of women's feelings of emptiness, lack of self-worth, and incompleteness.[88] Since then, feminist writers have struggled to explain the ambivalence of their experience of motherhood. Adrienne Rich is perhaps the best known and most articulate. Rich writes in *Of Woman Born* that when she thought back upon her early mothering years, she "could remember little except anxiety, physical weariness, anger, self-blame, boredom, and division within myself: a division made more acute by the moments of passionate love, delight in my children's spirited bodies and minds, amazement at how they went on loving me in spite of my failures to love them wholly and selflessly."[89] Rich gave up her vocation as a writer in order to be with her children full-time. She writes that she struggled to have some life of her own, and recalls that she "was fighting for my life through, against, and with the lives of my children."[90] She longed for more time for her work, for the realm of poetry, "where I lived as no one's mother, where I existed as myself."[91] Out of this experience of suffering, Rich wrote a book examining the roots of motherhood as an institution. In the book she takes pains to establish she has great hope for motherhood as an experience, but she believes that it must be freed from the trappings of the institution that make it women's whole identity. Rich's poignant writing is a testimony to women's need to be something other than mothers. It is testimony to women's need for public vocations.

Current feminist writing has often given voice to the reality that working women long for more time to fulfill the responsibilities of their private vocation to their children. They do not see their financial support of their family as fulfilling their duty to care for their own. Instead, they want more time to play with, teach, and care for their children. As Peterson-Izer and Ravizza put it, "children and parents can benefit enormously from more time spent together—reading stories, playing games, kissing and hugging, talking to one another; most children and parents alike long for more of this kind of presence."[92] Unsatisfied with the way men have embraced public work, contemporary feminists struggle to define new ways of working that allow for the fulfillment of both public and private vocations.

Modern Fathers

Feminist literature indicates that parenthood is not fully a public vocation for women. Some of the new popular work on fatherhood parallels this literature in its support for the notion that public work is crucial to men's self-fulfillment. Pioneers in the field of fathering argue that men should not feel guilty about their work outside the home because work gives them a sense of accomplishment, emotional fulfillment, and a chance to make a difference.[93] Despite the fact that they encourage men to spend at least a little more time at home, the authors are careful to affirm men's efforts to care for their children by providing for them, and to let men know that their own happiness at work contributes to their children's quest to be independent and successful persons.[94] New writers on fatherhood advocate more interaction with children for men, while affirming the important, even crucial, place of public work in men's lives.

Even writers such as Robert Griswold, author of *Fatherhood in America*, who question the dominance of work in men's lives, do not suggest that men abandon work altogether. Griswold argues that women's entry into the labor force has changed all the rules for men. He asserts that: "Nothing has posed a greater challenge to the ideology of male breadwinning and traditional male prerogatives than this transformation in the household economy."[95] Griswold welcomes this challenge because he sees breadwinning as an inadequate platform around which to build a whole definition of fatherhood, let alone a whole identity. On the other hand, he speaks at several points about the "boring, repetitious, and vexing work of child care."[96] He closes his book with the hopeful claim that one day mothers and fathers will be both workers and caregivers.[97]

Perhaps it seems unremarkable that no one is urging men to become full-time parents. When the average man spends so little time per day with his children, it may be ridiculous to ask for more than additional "quality time" or, at most, a sharing of roles. Still, it is significant that most people are aware enough of the limitations of parenting work to know that asking men to embrace that work full-time is not the best option. Men are not asked to become fathers in the same way that women have been mothers. On the other hand, men are being asked to extend their conception of fathering beyond breadwinning, and a growing number of co-parenting fathers are coming to rejoice in the delights of child rearing.

Thus fathering literature, in its insistence that men's public work is valuable for men, is the flipside of the feminist mothering literature which insists that women's total investment in work in the home may be detrimental to women. Both sets of writings point toward the idea that persons have a need to participate in work which is in some important sense larger or more far-reaching than the work of parenting, even as they affirm the duties and joys of caring for children.

Serving in Two Realms

The need to engage in public work is sometimes characterized as a need for fulfillment, in opposition to the duty to sacrifice that the work of parenting is founded upon. However, this kind of dichotomizing is inaccurate and unhelpful. Many parents speak with intensity about the joy of being with their children or with guilt about how much fun they are having at home. Studies of stay-home mothers indicate that when women want to stay home, their experiences can be quite positive.[98] Thus, parenting is not wholly self-sacrificial, but the desire to work is not wholly self-serving either. Most working parents speak of their work at least in part as a calling, a way to use their talents in service to society. Perhaps what women long for and what men refuse to give up is the very connection to the world, the very same vocation to serve that the pope writes about. Perhaps what parents are saying is that they want to serve and enjoy life both at home and in the world. They want to be a central part of both realms of life—the private and the public.

DUAL VOCATION WITH CAUTION: LAME PARENTS SLOUCHING FORWARD

I have argued that Christian parents are called to balance nurture of children with a willingness to take up the work of Christ in the world. Both the Christian tradition and the experience of Christian parents testify to importance of rearing one's own offspring and to the desire to serve others. The Gospels and the early Christian tradition witness both to the importance of care for children and to the primary obligation of adult Christians to discipleship, which presumes a public vocation. The contemporary Catholic tradition speaks to the importance of work and family as dimensions of one's public vocation and of the importance of parental nurturance. Thus a fully Christian discussion of parenting will emphasize ethical obligations of men and women to realize their Christian calling both at home and in the world. Christian parents have important public responsibilities inside and outside the boundaries of their families.

However, the idea of public vocation is not meant to be a justification for high-power jobs that do not allow for adequate time with children. Galinsky's *Ask the Children* provides powerful testimony from children themselves that some parents take their work commitment far too seriously. When children are asked what they want to tell the working parents of America, many talk about time. They say: "You don't know how it hurts when you think your parents love their job more than you," or "I wish you would stop working so much and spend more time with us," or "Spend time with your children, because when you're gone, there is a big hole in our hearts that makes some or most of us want to cry."[99] A Christian understanding of the dual vocation of parenting must not contribute to the rationalizing of parents who do not spend enough time with their children.

Still, the Christian tradition does point toward the notion that parenting is both a public and a private calling. Implied in the notion of public vocation is the idea that the full self-realization of a Christian requires involvement in private and public life. This understanding of the human person is assumed both in Catholic teaching on work and in Catholic teaching on the family. It implies that focusing on one's family is not enough for Christian parents.

Flannery O'Connor's story "The Lame Shall Enter First" can be read as a portrait of a man who fails as a Christian in both his public and private vocations. In private, he ignores his son's feelings and is crassly ignorant of his son's needs. He attempts to make his family life "public," but ends up failing to convince his son of the importance of unselfishness because he does not truly model it at home. He fails in his public life because he tries to remake Rufus in his own image instead of listening to what the boy truly needs. He is more in love with the idea of himself as savior than with the work and worker of salvation. He does not fully comprehend the scope and limits of his dual vocation as a parent.

All of these failings should give parents pause, but should not send them back to "focus on the family." Sheppard sins, finally, not because he fails to put family first, but because he, like all of Flannery O'Connor's characters, is finite or lame, limited by his very humanity in his quest to be a good parent and a good citizen, or, in Christian terms, a good disciple. However, O'Connor did not write her gloomy stories to convince her readers to give up the struggle to go beyond their limits. Instead, she hoped that those whom she called "lame beasts slouching toward Bethlehem"[100] would not fail to take up humbly the challenge of being Christ for others. Her story suggests, as any good Christian story would, that this must be done at home and in the world.

Notes

1. Flannery O'Connor, "The Lame Shall Enter First," in her *The Complete Stories* (New York: Noonday, 1946), 445–82, at 447.

2. Ibid., 480–81.

3. In the story, Rufus is physically lame, but it is clearly Sheppard, who lacks faith and compassion, who is truly lame. The story's title refers to the biblical idea that the last shall be first.

4. Ellen Galinsky, *Ask the Children: What America's Children Really Think about Working Parents* (New York: William Morrow, 1999), 251.

5. Ibid., xviii.

6. Ibid., 251.

7. Stephen Post, *More Lasting Unions: Christianity, the Family, and Society* (Grand Rapids: Eerdmans, 2000), 108.

8. Ibid.

9. Ibid., 196.

10. Ibid., 177–96. Post acknowledges that the Christian tradition today must necessarily focus here because parents are not committed enough to children.

11. Lisa Sowle Cahill, *Family: A Christian Social Perspective* (Minneapolis: Fortress, 2000), 129.

12. Ibid.

13. Ibid., 81.

14. Ibid., 95–110.

15. Ibid., 135. My own earlier work on family is similar in emphasis; see "Does Family Conflict with Community?" *Theological Studies* 58 (1997), 597–617.

16. Post, *More Lasting Unions*, 62.

17. Bonnie Miller-McLemore, *Also a Mother: Work and Family as Theological Dilemma* (Nashville: Abingdon, 1994), 49.

18. Ibid., 36–37.

19. Ibid., 109–30.

20. Ibid., 185–95.

21. Ibid., esp. 121–25. In this section, Miller-McLemore describes the book's cover image of a mother reaching up for her work of her own in order to be capable of reaching down to her child. The concept of generativity which grounds the book's central argument is discussed in terms of fulfillment (realizing desires to work and to parent) or authentic self-development rather than obligation. See also 175–85.

22. See Jule Dejager Ward, *La Leche League: At the Crossroads of Medicine, Feminism, and Religion* (Chapel Hill: University of North Carolina, 2000); Maria Riley, *Transforming Feminism* (Kansas City: Sheed & Ward, 1989); Carol Coston, "Women's Ways of Working," in *One Hundred Years of Catholic Social Thought: Celebration and Challenge*, ed. John A. Coleman (Maryknoll, NY: Orbis, 1991); Christine Gudorf, "Western Religion and the Patriarchal Family," in *Perspectives on Marriage: A Reader*, ed. Kieran Scott and Michael Warren (New York: Oxford University, 2000) and "Parenting, Mutual Love and Sacrifice," in *Women's Consciousness, Women's Conscience: A Reader in Feminist Ethics*, ed. Barbara H. Andolsen, Christine E. Gudorf, and Mary D. Pellauer (Minneapolis: Winston/Seabury, 1985); Rosemary Radford Ruether, "Christian Understandings of Human Nature and Gender," in *Religion, Feminism, and the Family*, ed. Anne Carr and May Stewart Van Leeuwen (Louisville: Westminster, 1996); and Christina Traina, "Papal Ideals and Marital Realities: One View from the Ground," in *Sexual Diversity and Catholicism: Toward the Development of Moral Theology*, ed. Patricia Beattie Jung with Joseph Andrew Coray (Collegeville: Liturgical, 2001).

23. Linda Woodhead, "Faith, Feminism, and the Family," in *The Family*, ed. Lisa Sowle Cahill and Dietmar Mieth, *Concilium* 1995/4 (Maryknoll, NY: Orbis, 1995), 45.

24. Vigen Guroian, "The Ecclesial Family: John Chrysostom on Parenthood and Children," in *The Child in Christian Thought*, ed. Marcia Bunge (Grand Rapids: Eerdmans, 2001), 69.

25. Ibid., 67.

26. Traina, "A Person in the Making: Thomas Aquinas on Children and Childhood," in *The Child in Christian Thought*, 121.

27. Ibid., 115.

28. Stephen Post affirms this insight in his book *Spheres of Love: Toward a New Ethics of the Family* (Dallas: Southern Methodist University, 1994). He argues that "the first sphere of love is the one where our natural sympathies lie" (146).

29. Adrienne Rich, *Of Woman Born: Motherhood as Experience and Institution*, Tenth Anniversary ed. (New York: W. W. Norton, 1986; orig. ed. 1976), 26.

30. Ibid., 24.

31. Sally Purvis, "Mothers, Neighbors and Strangers: Another Look at Agape," *Journal of Feminist Studies in Religion* 7 (Spring 1991): 19.

32. Ibid., 21. Purvis, like Post, questions the agape tradition of Kierkegaard, Gene Outka, and others.

33. Ibid., 26–27.

34. Ibid., 30.

35. See, for instance, Mitch Finley, *Your Family in Focus: Appreciating What You Have, Making It Even Better* (Notre Dame: Ave Maria, 1993).

36. Carrie J. Heiman, *The Nine-Month Miracle: A Journal for the Mother-to-Be* (Liguori, MO: Liguori, 1986), Week 24.

37. Miller-McLemore, *Also a Mother*, 143.

38. Ibid.

39. See also, Karen Peterson-Iyer and Bridget Burke Ravizza, "The Price of Christian Motherhood: Are Christian Universities Willing to Pay It?" unpublished paper, presented at the annual meeting of the Society of Christian Ethics, Vancouver, Canada, January 13, 2002. Peterson-Iyer and Ravizza root the obligation to care in the dignity of the child and in the magisterial teaching upholding of the "lofty calling of parenthood" (*The Church and the Modern World*, no. 47).

40. C. S. Mann, *The Gospel according to Mark*, The Anchor Bible, vol. 27 (Garden City, NY: Doubleday, 1986), 259. See also relevant commentary on parallel passages (Luke 8:19–21, Matthew 12:46–50).

41. Ezra P. Gould, *Mark*, International Critical Commentary (New York: Charles Scribner's Sons, 1961), 68.

42. Joseph Fitzmyer, *The Gospel according to Luke*, The Anchor Bible, vol. 28 (Garden City, NY: Doubleday, 1986), 834.

43. Gerd Theisen, *Sociology of the Early Palestinian Christianity* (Philadelphia: Fortress, 1989), makes this claim about the makeup of the early church.

44. Richard Horsley, *Sociology of the Jesus Movement* (New York: Crossroad, 1989), 117.

45. Ibid., 123.

46. Peter Brown, *The Body and Society: Men, Women and Sexual Renunciation in Early Christianity* (New York: Columbia University, 1988), 5–7.

47. Ibid.

48. David Hunter, *Marriage in the Early Church* (Minneapolis: Fortress, 1992), 6.

49. Ibid., 7. Hunter notes, however, that around the time Christianity was developing, there was in Roman thought a move toward seeing marriage more as a friendship. This trend influenced early Christian writers. See 7–8.

50. Brown, *The Body and Society*, 6.

51. Andrew Jacobs, "A Family Affair: Marriage, Class, and Ethics in the Apocryphal Acts of the Apostles," *Journal of Early Christian Studies* 7 (1999): 105–38.

52. Ibid., 106.

53. Ibid., 107.

54. See Horsely, *Sociology of the Jesus Movement*, 113.

55. Cahill, *Family*, 142.

56. The exceptions here are radical groups like the Essenes and Therapeutae who did live in celibate communities, before the advent of Jesus' ministry. However, though these groups were well-respected, they do not represent mainstream Jewish or Greek thought or practice. See Stephen C. Barton, "The Relativisation of Family Ties," in *Constructing Early Christian Families: Family as Social Reality and Metaphor*, ed. Halvor Moxnes (New York: Routledge, 1997). Barton claims that the evidence of alternatives and the praise of these groups indicate that Jesus is continuing a tradition rather than breaking it. However, his evidence centers largely on elite groups, while the early Jesus movement is a broad-based family-questioning movement. Thus, in my view, Jesus does begin something quite new, though it does have some roots in radical strains of his tradition.

57. Brown, *The Body and Society*, 36, 53.

58. John Paul II, *On the Family* (Washington: United States Catholic Conference, 1981), no. 16. The pope argues that uplifting celibacy confirms the goodness of marriage, because it is the sacrifice of something that is very good. I would argue that the celibacy tradition paradoxically affirms and questions the goodness of marriage.

59. John Paul II, *On Human Labor* (Washington: United States Catholic Conference, 1981), no. 4.

60. Ibid., no. 6.

61. Ibid.

62. Ibid., no. 16.

63. Ibid., no. 25.

64. *Gaudium et spes*, no. 43; translation by Austin Flannery, O.P., *Vatican Council II: The Conciliar and Post Conciliar Documents*, rev. ed. (Northport, NY: Costello, 1988).

65. *On Human Labor*, no. 6.

66. This pope's recent statement denying the legitimacy of Catholic lawyers' work on divorce cases is a case in point.

67. Dorothy Day, *Loaves and Fishes* (New York: Harper & Row, 1963), 221.

68. *On the Family*, no. 17.

69. Ibid., no. 28.

70. Ibid., no. 37.

71. Ibid., no. 39.

72. Ibid., no. 41.

73. Ibid., no. 42.

74. Ibid., no. 44.

75. Ibid., nos. 44, 47.

76. Ibid., no. 47.

77. Ibid., no. 21.

78. Ibid., nos. 49–64. Lisa Cahill also attests to this emphasis in recent Catholic teaching on the family; see her *Family*, 89–91.

79. *On the Family*, no. 23.

80. *Letter to Families* (Washington: United States Catholic Conference, 1994), no. 16.

81. See especially his *Letter to Women* (Washington: United States Catholic Conference, 1995), nos. 2, 5, 6, and 8. Throughout the letter, the pope lauds the contributions of women to public life while reiterating the idea that men and women have complementary roles in society, the family, and the Church.

82. "Equal Opportunity in the World of Work" [August 20, 1995] in *The Genius of Women* (Washington: United States Catholic Conference, 1997), 32–33.

83. *On the Dignity and Vocation of Woman* (Washington: United States Catholic Conference, 1988), no. 19.

84. See Peterson-Iyer and Ravizza, 12 (see above n. 39).

85. *On the Family*, no. 25.

86. When Catholic thought addresses the worker or the parent generally, this is true. This insight gets lost when women or men are specifically addressed as is evident above.

87. Post, *More Lasting Unions*, 59.

88. Betty Friedan, *The Feminine Mystique* (New York: Norton, 1963), 15–17.

89. Rich, *Of Woman Born*, 15.

90. Ibid., 29.

91. Ibid., 31.

92. Ibid., 30.

93. Mitch and Susan Golant, *Finding Time for Fathering* (New York: Ballantine, 1993), 28–29.

94. Ibid., 61–62.

95. Robert Griswold, *Fatherhood in America: A History* (New York: Basic, 1993), 220.

96. Ibid., 2.

97. Ibid., 269.

98. Galinsky, *Ask the Children*, 49, 54. She notes that the mother's feelings about what she is doing, whether it is working or staying home, make the difference.

99. Ibid., 343–44.

100. Flannery O'Connor, *The Habit of Being*, edited and with an introduction by Sally Fitzgerald (New York: Noonday, 1979), 90. The original phrase is from W. B. Yeats' poem, "The Second Coming."

13. Two Households

David Matzko McCarthy

This chapter first appeared in David Matzko McCarthy, *Sex and Love in the Home: A Theology of the Household*, 2nd ed. (London: SCM, 2004).

A few years ago, my wife, children, and I moved into our current home. The move was a trial that we do not care to repeat: a new teaching position for me, a job search for my wife, strange schools, unfamiliar people, and almost four hundred miles separating us from our former lives. One of the more difficult tasks of the move was looking for a house to buy. We thought that we knew what we wanted; apparently we did not.

In the old neighborhood, we were used to spending our evenings talking over the fence with neighbors. In fact, our yards and houses were modest enough to allow conversations with neighbors a few houses away without raising our voices. We had to get along, and we did. We shared meals, took care of neighborhood children, bought groceries for others if they needed something when we were going to the store. I could water my next-door neighbor's tiny garden from my own backyard, and I often did. With this family, we started a tradition of gathering together for Easter dinner, along with whatever extended family we had with us that year. Certainly, there were problems in the neighborhood (e.g., noise and roaming dogs), but on the whole we lived well as neighbors. Nevertheless, when we moved, we vowed that we would settle only for a house with a sizeable yard, to give us a little more space of our own.

We took great pains over our search for a new place to live. In *Helping Ourselves: Family and the Human Network*, Mary Howell articulates well our apprehensions. She notes that community "is feared as much as it is sought....For many of us the idea of 'community' is tied to a fear of losing what little control we seem to have over the business of our own lives....Thus, family has become the agency of our independence."[1] We were looking for a friendly neighborhood without the need for everyday contact or inter-dependence. Contrary to our original plan, we bought an old row house. It came within our price range, and its well-formed character appealed to us, its odd-shaped doors, high ceilings, and random layout of rooms. The price of character, we have discovered, is not monetary. For instance, our narrow backyard has a long wood-frame apartment building bordering its entire length. Children in the second-floor tenements next door often tease each other by throwing one another's belongings into our backyard. The older children taunt our little ones. The back of our house extends beyond the row of houses, and creates a peculiar situation where we could, if we cared to, converse with some of our neighbors from dining room to dining room. On the other side of the house, I have become used to the uncomfortable practice of waving at our neighbor through the closed kitchen window. This is not the home we were looking for.

This chapter has a biographical subtext about our being pulled into relations based on proximity and mutual concerns. The underlying story is not my own; it is about the life of neighborhoods and networks of households amid a dominant grammar of self-sufficiency and independence. Howell's *Helping Ourselves* will figure prominently in the chapter. I discovered the book after following through on a passing reference by Christopher Lasch in the posthumous *Women and the Common Life*.[2] Lasch notes with regret that this work by Howell, published in 1975, has not been taken seriously if it has been read at all.[3] This lack of interest is understandable. Howell proposes, as will I, that ordinary practices of local interdependence are the substance of a complex system of interchange and a rich community life. Howell's proposal might appear uninteresting because we are accustomed to trivializing the social character of home. When taken seriously, neighborhood systems may be too adventurous for most of us, as Howell suggests. In any case, the little things in the neighborhood are likely to usher in great social change. The chapter begins with an inquiry about where the home is located in contemporary life. After an extended discussion of Howell's picture of the open family, I will conclude with an account of home economics as a complex system of exchange that deepens and extends common life.

A TALE OF TWO HOUSEHOLDS

Ours is an age of contradictions. Although close to 50% of marriages end in divorce, the number of couples vowing never to part is strong and steady.[4] Parenthood is honored more than ever, not only by mothers but by fathers as well; yet, successful people minimize time spent with their children.[5] In response to this confusion, it is tempting to locate the home in some ideal time and place, among ancient Christians, European nobility, the American homestead, peasant farmers, the rising middle class at the turn of the century, or "Leave it to Beaver" reruns.[6] Even if we could will ourselves into a different era, our ideal family may not turn out to be bearable, or supportable as a practical reality. In his *Making of the Modern Family*, Edward Shorter begins with a blunt reference to the "Bad Old Days" of the pre-industrial age, when family was still "held firmly in the matrix of a larger social order."[7] While we might be wistful for days gone by, for inter-generational continuity and the stable home, we ought not overlook the ease with which the household has given way to cultural change and broader social and economic structures. The family we have fits who we are.

Shorter points to three basic moorings of the traditional family: a sphere of kinship, local community, and a historical continuity of habits and social practices. In contrast to the moorings of old, he refers to the modern family as a "free-floating dyad" that creates and dissolves itself at will and is characterized by its adaptability. According to Shorter, the traditional family was constrained by its attachments:

> One set of ties bound it to the surrounding kin, the network of aunts and uncles, cousins and nieces who dotted the old regime's landscape. Another fastened it to the wide community, and gaping holes in the shield of privacy permitted others to enter the household freely and, if necessary, preserve order. A final set of ties held this elementary family to generations past and future. Awareness of ancestral traditions and ways of

doing business would be present in people's minds as they went about their day. Because they knew that the purpose of life was preparing coming generations to do as past ones had done, they would have clear rules for shaping relations within the family, for deciding what was essential and what was not.[8]

Shorter's description of traditional ties is illuminating, but his image of the modern home as a "free-floating dyad" is deceptive if we assume that we can simply cast our lines to the dock in order to secure ourselves, once again, to networks of kin, community, and time.

Like other historical and contemporary studies, Shorter's history of family indicates that traditional links have not really been cut; rather, they are dangling free, still dragging around fragments of what once was their moorage. Generations past are still remembered. Walking about as a McCarthy, I know that cultural heritage is often cause for Irish Americans to think of each other as kin, at least vaguely. This kind of generational continuity, although part of our lives, seldom has practical consequences. Most of us carry on our heritage through rituals that distinguish us (e.g., St. Patrick's Day parades); yet, we have little practical memory or tolerance for what ruled the daily lives of our ancestors.

Among its wide variations, the household and marriage did, at one time, have important social and economic functions, from treaty-making among European nobility to financial agreements and civic/religious commitments among seventeenth-century Puritans.[9] From the New England farm to the Boston tenement house, from plantation to the urban estate, the household sustained an economy, structured the wider social relations of its members, and provided the basic outlines of their identity and future, by passing on land, trade, wealth and station—or not. Today, the household still has powerful influence in determining a son or daughter's cultural literacy and prospects for social mobility.[10] The modern formula, in this regard, is a purely economic one: "It takes money to make money." In order to protect and promote the economic advancement of their members, middle-class families, for instance, have reduced family size and increased hours of work outside the home.

Like its precursors, the modern middle-class household has an economic strategy. It differs from its predecessors insofar as it has been dissociated, at least in theory, from our common language of economic utility. The family's economic strategy is structured outside the home. At the same time that the modern family seems unable to resist invasion by market rationality and utilitarian contracts, it is defined in contrast to dominant forms of social relationships and economic canons of growth and profit.[11] Although as economically minded as ever, family, most assume, ought to lack an economy.

With the progress of modern industry and market rationality, "affection and inclination, love and sympathy, came to take the place of 'instrumental' considerations in regulating the dealings of family members with one another. Spouses and children came to be prized for what they were, rather than for what they represented or could do."[12] When money-making and social position take leave of home, sentiment fills the conceptual void, providing a rationale for marriage, in romantic love, and for our relationships to offspring, in the intensity of the mother-child relationship.[13] With the rise of industry, the world of production and politics comes to be located in the public life of men, while women are thought to sustain the emotional and moral sphere of home.[14] At the same time that the social and economic character of the household is degraded, family is honored for its non-economic, non-utilitarian relationships.

In the process of becoming "non-economic," however, the household becomes a center of consumption. Relationships between spouses and between parent and child become product- rather than production-oriented. Domestic life, on its own dull terms, is considered inhospitable to romance and must be remade and enlivened by floral scents, whiter laundry, and skin that challenges time, by leisure, exotic vacations, and expensive nights out without the kids.[15] At the same time, the focus of the household becomes its children, who take advantage of a protracted childhood, require high emotional investment, and are considered priceless to the degree they are beyond calculation of financial investment and return.[16] For those with means, monetary expense may in fact be a measure of emotional assets, not in a vulgar sense of buying love, but in a more systemic orientation that puts the benefits of wages out to the service of the consumptive household. Growth capitalism provides ever-increasing standards for good parents and the expanding plenty of the family. Affection, for all classes, carries a financial burden; monetary resources are the making of harmony at home.

Contractual social relations and market utility shape the dominant narrative of home, but on this standard, many households do not succeed. The ideal suburban home brings the benefit of social autonomy and various pleasures of leisure, but many aspiring families do not attain self-sufficiency and security. The middle-class family, by and large, is motivated and structured by a therapeutic individualism that advances the economic interests of its members while cultivating love and compatibility through non-utilitarian activities (i.e., fun).[17] But there are households (perhaps most) that occupy spaces outside the dominant narrative, on the fringe, or at an intermediate point between failure and success. The aspiring homes are bound to networks of dependency but always looking forward to the freedom of contractual arrangements. Such households continue to sustain informal and subsistent economies, and these networks of exchange lie between contractual arrangements, on one hand, and the sentimental home, on the other.

One example is the family farm, where the household is structured as a productive rather than consumptive set of relationships.[18] On a farm in Rocky Ridge, Maryland, Dennis "Buck" Wivell was raised as the youngest of thirteen children. When asked why his parents had so many children, Buck does not reply with comment about their love for children or their preference for large families. He points out, laconically, that his parents needed a lot of help on the farm. Buck's dry response does not indicate that he has had a better childhood and that his family enjoys a deeper bond. On the contrary, he is more likely to evoke sympathy than envy or admiration from his classmates. After graduation, he will leave them scratching their heads when he does not take his degree in accounting to a high paying job in the city. At this point in his life, he will tell you, he prefers manual labor. Buck's life on the family farm may not survive the market privileges of mass production and corporate farming, and Buck himself stands within the economic and social world of other American twenty-two-year-olds. But he is outside of it as well, and it is this other side of the household that, by necessity rather than lifestyle choice, pushes beyond the sentimental character of the modern home and represents a different kind of social formation.

Some analogies can be drawn from research on informal economies. Through her ongoing study of New York City's informal economy, Saskia Sassen-Koob proposes that the conditions of late capitalism, with its polarization of high-and-low-paying jobs and its devaluation of labor, actually "induce the growth of an informal economy in large cities."[19] The middle-class boom after World War II brought a standardization of consumption and production. Now the impetus for uniformity is waning, along with the manufacturing industry and its capacity to afford a middle-class wage. The formal economy, in other words, depends upon an availability of resources and level of wages that it cannot sustain. These tensions within the formal economy create favorable conditions for the cheap, flexible work of unlicensed enterprises and informal labor arrangements.

The ugly side of the informal economy is the exploitation of workers in sweatshops and the like. The positive side is the strength of neighborhood sub-economies, usually found among immigrant communities, that provide local goods and services for a local price. According to Sassen-Koob, "certain aspects of the informal transportation system are illustrative, notably gypsy cabs servicing low-income immigrant areas...[as well as] certain aspects of the construction industry, especially renovations and small-store alterations or construction."[20] Often these enterprises will expand, from their local base, to a wider constituency in response to outside demand.

Community and kinship seem to be the difference between sweatshop abuses and advantageous illegal work. Outside the formal economy, household and neighborhood appear to make the difference between exploitation and mutually beneficial agreements, between economic captivity and cooperation. Unregistered workers who enter the work force in an "individuated and dispersed manner...[are] extremely dependent on the labor market supply and demand forces entirely beyond their control."[21] They have few protections and suffer the lawlessness of the informal economy. The economically privileged exploit the weak. Immigrant and ethnic enclaves, in contrast, tend to shield their members from the forces of the wider economy. Workers outside the rule of law are sustained by the rule of community and home. The household, in this regard, functions as a structured (albeit "non-public") economy where laborers and entrepreneurs, as husband and wife, brother and sister, share work and profits as they share a home.[22]

The relationship between the formal and informal economy suggests that we may not have to look outside the narrative of the upwardly mobile household in order to find a different kind of home. In the way that pressures of the formal economy create conditions for informal arrangements, the market conditions of the contractual, affective home produce conditions for different kinds of household economies based on establishing ties to neighborhood and wider networks of productive association. The narrative of suburban isolation and self-sufficiency will continue to be attractive, but for many, practically unattainable. The example of the immigrant enclave is interesting because it points to practical bonds of proximity and necessity, rather than lifestyle choice. In a similar way, many households are faced with the necessity of defining themselves as part of a neighborhood that must cooperate for mutual benefit and common ends. Between the dominant languages of the disinterested market and private, sentimental attachments, there are spaces where a social fabric of reciprocity, roles, vocation, apprenticeship, and practical wisdom is sustained. These spaces are not suited to replace the dominant economy, and by their nature they will not become national or global systems. Neighborhood economies, inasmuch as they are restricted, offer a different grammar and richer possibilities for personal identity, common life, and an ordering of love. It is a mistake to champion an alterative economy as productive of romantic harmony and cheery affections at home. Because more profoundly social, this kind of household diverges from the ideal of the placid suburban home. As interdependence increases, more occasions arise for disagreements, hurts, and unresolved disputes. Those who have attained suburban autonomy will cringe at the noise, the demands of neighbors, and the annoyances of depending upon others. Family members may aspire to upward mobility, but these households will function, in large part, in terms of a local or subsistence economy.

In order to sustain themselves, members of these "subsistence" households establish and maintain informal connections, bartered agreements, and relationships of mutual benefit. There will be a local currency of skills, like welding or sewing, and informal standards of exchange, such as pies for plumbing. Many of these associations are asymmetrical and interpersonally difficult, and they will be tolerable only if balanced by a broader network and a wider sense of reciprocity between households. For balance to be maintained, these informal systems need the passage of time. Differing once again from the suburban dream, these homes will not provide a self-sufficient emotional economy. Spouses and children will look beyond the walls of their homes for friendship and intimacy, not when the family system breaks down, but as a matter of its good working order. I will use Mary Howell's simple designation of these kinds of households as open families rather than closed.[23]

CLOSED FAMILIES

Closed families represent what Howell calls "the mythical standard of the 'ideal' for contemporary U.S. life."[24] The closed family understands its health and well-being in terms of emotional and financial independence. Pointing to the same kind of household, I have used the spatial image of the ideal suburban development: homes set apart in a neighborhood tied together by recreational interests and practically oriented to the outside world through contracted services, salary/wage-earning, and consumption.[25] Another useful conception is the ideal of the nuclear family, defined by narrow lines of kinship and a clear boundary between inside and out. For nuclear households, most kinship relations, grandparents to grandchildren for instance, are considered either positive or unacceptable intrusions, but always as external relationships. The nuclear structure also allows for a simplification of roles, such as father as breadwinner and mother as homemaker, or spouses simply sharing the two roles. In either case, housekeeping as a "role" is clearly divided from productive activity. Children are, in effect, accidental to the system; they have no operative role except as objects of investment (of time, money, emotions). The average nuclear family of four considers at least half its members as irrelevant to its practical maintenance. Its independence is sustained from the outside.

The closed family's self-sufficiency is largely dependent on professional expertise and bureaucratic managers. A principal goal of contractual government in the modern state is to make families independent. Contracting services from professionals and government agencies offers task-oriented, temporary relationships that are free from unpredictable entanglements. I would rather hire a professional to paint and repair my windows than the teenager down the street. In the latter case, I risk involvement in the project. I will have to give detailed instructions to the adolescent along with an avuncular sponsorship of her work. Making demands of a professional painter is less risky because our relationship is limited to a contract. With the teenager, we would have to develop something akin to friendship or an uncle-niece relationship, and I would probably end up making an alliance with her parents whether or not the job goes well. They would walk by the house attempting an innocuous look as they examine my windows with pride. If there is trouble, I am likely to find a parent planted in my yard for an interminable "teaching moment." Worse, it might be me out there teaching basic skills and a good work ethic.

If my car will not start, and my neighbor offers to help replace the starter, I will wonder what his help will cost me, not in dollars but in time, patience, and some future-but-not-yet-conceived payback. At the least, I will owe him gratitude. I might grumble when I write a check to a mechanic for a couple hundred dollars, but the nature of the transaction is clear and formal. My neighbor's offer is not businesslike and self-contained; it is an open-ended neighborliness. It is a risky gesture of friendliness between people who are close enough to see each other and to depend upon one another every day. If I had been stranded on the side of the road, I would gladly accept assistance from a good samaritan who, after helping me, would drive off never to be seen again. Intercourse between neighbors is different. My neighbor's benevolence is part of an ongoing relation, or it might establish a relationship. We will get to know each other with our hands under the hood, and not only that, he will eat up time with incessant jabber about something about which I have little interest (like cars or car racing). I become vulnerable: we will have a relationship that is not mutual, set out in terms of his giving and my receiving. I surely would prefer the independence offered me by the professional mechanic.

Professional expertise and bureaucratic management are also attractive because they present themselves as neutral and scientific.[26] Nowhere is the professional more prominent in day-to-day life than in matters of child-care and education.[27] A family therapist, childcare supervisor, teacher, and social worker have professional certification, and because detached from their clients, they are expected to have more skills and better judgment. Professionals do have a great deal to offer, but their social position privileges bureaucratic knowledge. A woman with a high school education, who has been taking care of children for twenty years, has much less currency and credibility than a young professional, especially if the older woman is not articulate and has not been paid (or paid much) for her twenty years of work. In any respectable business or public institution, the twenty-five-year-old with a degree in social work will be managing the forty-five-year-old wage-earner. This older woman knows children, while the younger has certification as an expert.

In addition, bureaucratic neutrality and detachment give priority to controlled space. Certified day care is often assumed to be more trustworthy than informal home care. There is something reassuring about dropping off one's child at an authorized facility as opposed to a living room. More importantly, the public space socializes children into public life. In his pre-kindergarten program, our son learns that sharing is fun and makes a person feel good inside. This might be true in places where sharing is optional, a matter of amiable relations, or in a contractual setting where social agents are assumed to have a prior and more fundamental independence. At home we teach our children that sharing is necessary (because at home it is), whether they like it or not, whether it feels good or not. At home, sharing a toy is not a matter of happy recreation as much as it is an instance for learning the habits of sharing a bedroom, a kitchen, burdens, and responsibilities. Sharing is a basic grammar of common life. Sometimes it feels good and sometimes not. Sometimes if it makes us feel good inside it is not sharing: sharing, for example, vulnerability or suffering. Sharing in the household is difficult because it is a concession that we are not in control, that our personal possession is limited by common goods.

Sharing is a benign example. Another is the effort to encourage children to take great pride in being unique as though uniqueness *per se* were an achievement and a social contribution. If the student who is uniquely disruptive in class were equally as clever, she would raise an interesting objection from the time-out chair. "I was just being me." Sharing-as-fun and uniqueness-as-essential-value are simply methods of bureaucratic management. They are means of managing relations between individuals who do not share substantive goods and common ends. It is interesting that our public (contractual) socialization depends heavily on cultivating a moral psychology predicated on the isolated self and a pre-social conception of self-interest. I am my own unique category of person, and my motivation to engage in common life (to share) precedes a social conception of the self and personal benefit.

Amid a household economy, it seems to me, constraints are far less psychologically intrusive and personal identity far richer. I do not have to like what I must do, so that I have far more emotional and psychological latitude. When forced to reconcile, I remember the disdain with which I would say, "I am sorry," to my brother. Such contempt is out of bounds at school. In the home, my identity is shaped within a distinct economy of relationships and functions, and as a neighborhood becomes more functionally complex, the system cultivates distinctiveness. Households are similar only by analogy. Bureaucratic management, on the other hand, attempts to make social relationships uniform. In this regard, uniqueness must be emphasized as a counterweight to the systemic uniformity. The closed nuclear family, with its simplified roles, allows for the same kind of bureaucratic regularity. Family comes to mean clearly specified duties of parents to their children, so that there will be hand wringing when no one is present to play the "father" or "mother." Some of the best people I know are psychologically askew. The closed family helps to standardize emotional health, and it certainly makes theories of family therapy easier, where personal character and psychological maladies, for instance, can be identified according to birth order or to the personality types of one's parents.

Bureaucratic management and professional expertise fit with the polity of nation-state individualism and the dream of the suburban home. By assuming a neutral stance, bureaucrats can offer services without overt encroachment, while at the same time reinforcing the family's implied contract with the state. The government's requirements are minimal and usually appear to be benign. They amount to complying with professional guidance offered through the schools, from standards for vaccinations to definitions of abuse and neglect. Most parents manage to steer clear of trouble, and are left alone. Some argue that the state's relationship to the family is a subtle but pernicious management of child rearing and the like.[28] Such arguments are disquieting in their own right when they suggest that family ought to be an autonomous space. The intrusion of impersonal management is precisely this movement toward self-sufficiency. Contractual politics reduces the home to a private place, and in doing so, undermines the possibility of alternative social forms. Taking public servants at their word, we ought to worry that aid to families through public schools and other programs is oriented to the independence of the home. Professional and contractual services allow us to control our associations through contracted and thin social agreements and clearly defined tasks. The contract reduces conflict and the logic of ongoing, day-to-day dependence. It keeps social complications at a minimum, along with coinciding networks of reciprocity and informal relationships of interdependence, subsistence, and mutual aid. The threat of dominant forms of political and economic exchange is that they are inhospitable to the hospitality of home.

The closed household simply shifts its system of dependency to shallow, episodic relationships and deeper monetary (consumptive) demands. The closed family perpetuates a state of affairs where contractual arrangements, bureaucratic management, and professional expertise appear more dependable and available because informal dependence and reciprocity are, by definition, a challenge to the closed home. When I hire a painter rather than apprentice my neighbor's child, she will be inclined to believe that scraping, puttying, and painting are esoteric tasks. Will she ever know what a putty knife looks like? Or the difference between paint and primer? Or what her car's starter looks like? How to make flaky crust and apple pies? Replace screens and window panes, extend the life of her mattress, ground electrical outlets, grow string beans, or know when to plant potatoes? After generations of suburban advancement, when contractual services begin to characterize the home, everyone will become an expert, a professional. The skills and habits of household management will come from outside the neighborhood and home.

HOUSEHOLD NETWORKS

Open families have loose and porous boundaries, whether they are thought to be nuclear, extended, traditional, or untraditional.[29] If the closed nuclear family is a cultural ideal, failure to succeed is likely to necessitate an openness. For example, the closed structure of one middle-class family was destabilized by divorce. After the father left, the mother decided and her teenage children agreed to take in a boarder in order to maintain their home. The teenagers were embarrassed about such an undignified arrangement. To make matters worse, the most promising tenant (an older man and friend of a friend) found their house attractive because he hoped to run a part-time upholstery business out of their large garage. As compensation, he kept track of repairs around the house. After a protracted adjustment period, the family members came to accept their household composition, even with their tenant's eccentricities, phone calls from a guy who knew a guy who needed upholstery work, and an occasional stranger in the kitchen. Sometimes an annoyance, sometimes full of good humor, home life began to take on a formative story of its own, the kind worth telling generations to come. It is interesting that we tend to think of such arrangements as part of the failure, rather than the success, of the home.

When Mary Howell, in *Helping Ourselves*, accounts for the expanding network of the open home into kinfolk, friends, and neighborhood, she focuses upon unpaid services and non-monetary (but still economic) exchange. In this regard, the tenant mentioned above began to be seen as an odd uncle, who paid rent but whose relation to the home's economy could not be reduced to a monthly check. So when the oldest child was married, she was not quite sure what to do with him. Should he sit in one of the family pews? Doesn't he count at least as much as Aunt Esther who is coming up from Florida? Kinship is fraught with these kinds of functional ambiguities and arbitrary preferences. When a friend sold me a dependable car for three hundred dollars (almost a gift), I gave my old car to my second cousin whom I hardly knew and who lived, my mother told me, about ten miles away. Later, he decided to give the car to his sister, whom I knew a little better. Sometime after, while visiting my mother, I was surprised to see my cousin pull up into the driveway in my old car. To tell the truth, I was happier to see my car than her, but even happier to see my beloved brown Toyota and my cousin together. I was happier still to know that she was keeping track of my mother (her great aunt), and it dawned on me that my mother had plotted out the series of exchanges long before. My second cousin drives out to see my mother in my old car; certainly a mutually beneficial relationship.

Howell defines kinfolk as "persons with whom we feel a bond of long-term commitment."[30] My relationship to my second cousins is an interesting case. We do not see each other often or know each other all that well, but we have a strong obligation to each other for mutual assistance. We understand ourselves within a network of interdependence, however distant and infrequently used. I would, for instance, open my home to them and their children, and I cannot account for this commitment simply out of fond affection. We are family, and family implies a kind of material (along with an emotional) exchange. Howell notes that mutual aid expands our circle of kinfolk. "Sometimes a friendship is so stable over time that it seems like a kin bond; friends sometimes act as if their commitment to each other to exchange services were as firm an obligation as it would be for a brother or sister [cousin, aunt or uncle]."[31] Howell observes that it is not an intensity of feeling that distinguishes mere friends from kin, but practical dependence and patronage.

Relationships to kinfolk (not merely blood relations) are "part pleasure and part prickles," part shared history and part misunderstanding, but definitely a web of commitment to mutual service over time. Howell continues:

> With kinfolk we are close to, we most often exchange such services as child care, loans or gifts of money, nursing care for those who are ill at home, visiting and cheering for those who are ill in a hospital, sharing sorrow and giving comfort at times of death, preparing food for special occasions or as a gesture of help. We also exchange special knowledge and skills—plumbing or carpentry, know-how about medical, legal, or educational problems, access to work opportunities, and experienced savvy about the manipulation of bureaucratic agencies like the telephone company, the school system, the outpatient clinic of the local hospital, or the welfare office.[32]

Kinfolk also gossip. Either in day-to-day conversation or while gathering for birthdays and holidays, they repeat shared stories and keep up with who is doing what and who is having a tough time with whom and with what. This gossip, albeit not always charitable, provides the lines of communication for the "exchange-of-service network." It is not idle talk; it is different from pernicious "office gossip" that is not directed to practical help and the good of others. Kin keep track of each other, and in such a network a person's identity is shaped by a web of relations that exceeds private or isolated household units.

Howell's definition of kinfolk includes lasting commitments of friendship, but she identifies "friends" as those with whom we have more temporary relationships. As with kinfolk, she points to the practical nature of friendship, to mutual service and unpaid work, to cooperation and common life. For Howell, friendship differs from kinfolk insofar as "exchanges of service" are more variable, less clearly defined, more voluntary, and more vulnerable.[33] Friendship has a greater dependence on proximity and accessibility. When we change jobs or schools for instance, friendships from the old setting are likely to fade. They do not survive the distance and are crowded out by people and responsibilities in our new life. This "occasional" quality of many friendships has its advantages. We build relationships that correspond to practical matters of everyday life, at work, at school, in task-oriented associations, and while coaching football. To this degree, friendships are clearly based in mutual service, and they link us to even wider networks. "Because all our friends bring us into potential contact with their own networks of kin and beyond, our access to an informal system of exchange of unpaid services is greatly increased through our friendships."[34] The challenge of friendship, in terms of mutual help, is to carry on the means and standards of exchange that tend to have a more natural feel among kinfolk. What is the point at which we ask for fair return, before we start feeling used?

Howell also locates practical exchange in the neighborhood. If kinfolk are defined by enduring commitments and friends by shared activities, neighbors are those with whom we share a place. "Their proximity allows an enormous potential for exchange, and opportunities for repeated contact make it possible to develop trust. The varieties of service that can be exchanged between neighbors are almost endless."[35] Neighbors may or may not be kin, and they may or may not be friends. However, they have a common standpoint: their common neighbors, houses, yards, streets, sidewalks, and soil. Neighborhoods depend upon a common respect for habitat. When families or individuals dishonor the place, through neglect or violence, they breed distrust and fear, and they destroy a neighborhood. Some housing environments are constructed with a disrespect for the human habitat, when families are crowded into projects and when parks are paved over so that no one needs to take responsibility for upkeep. Other environments are built to circumvent trust, by spacing houses a safe distance apart, by fencing and gating the development, or by achieving a (de facto) economic or racial segregation.

If a neighborhood is a habitat, then it is a joint endeavor. Some neighbors make their cooperation formal, through neighborhood associations, food cooperatives, and community centers. Some neighborhoods rally around specific goals, like closing down the drug dealers or raising money for playground equipment. The day-to-day activities of the house-hold are cooperative as well, such as shoveling snow, mowing lawns, keeping track of children, rides to school and choir practice, fixing flat tires and dead batteries, moving furniture, borrowing tools, finding a use for hand-me-down clothes and old desks from the attic, sharing storage space, gardening, finding a good dentist or an electrician who will work outside normal hours. Neighbors reprimand each other's children, and they keep spare keys at each other's houses. They gossip as well. This is how they will know that Mr. Cameron was admitted to the hospital and that they will have to mow his lawn, pick up his mail, and get the bills to his daughter. Neighbors get reputations for cutting hair well, for generosity or stinginess, and for drinking too much. Neighbors know who needs what and who can be depended upon for something else.

Kinfolk, friends, and neighborhood are three distinct, but sometimes overlapping, kinds of networks. Each open household is dependent upon all three, in different ways and configurations. One household might lack relationships of extended family and have more contact with neighbors and friends who function as kin. Another family might have neighbors who are kinfolk or who are co-workers and friends. In any case, the critical feature of the open home is its practical dependence on a wider network of exchange, particularly in relation to a dominant cultural and economic narrative that gives privilege to the isolated, self-sufficient home. To this degree, the distinction between open and closed family is more definitive than distinctions between nuclear and extended or one- and two-parent families. Open families, whether single-parent, extended or nuclear, have a similar orientation to the household economy and are able to minimize the dependence on salary/wage earning, professionals, and constraints of the formal economy.

HOME ECONOMICS[36]

Last January, we in the mid-Atlantic United States were hit with a few unusually heavy snow storms, and we enjoyed the media hype and hysteria usual for areas unaccustomed to deep snow. Grocery shoppers descended upon milk and bread like locusts, and just about every business and institution that could close did. Sitting in our front room while our children made use of their deliverance, from school, I caught a glance, through the window, of snow spraying upward. With a closer look, I discovered our neighbor from about five doors down pushing his snow-blower up and down the sidewalk. As far as I could tell, our neighbor, Carl, was clearing the walk from corner to corner, providing a service for at least seven families. I should add that our town council has mandated sidewalk snow removal. There were about ten inches of snow on the ground, so Carl's task was formidable and much appreciated by all, I was sure.

I began to wonder about his motives. Was Carl just looking for something to do since he could not go to work? Was the snow-blower a new toy? Were we doing him a favor by letting him play on our section of the sidewalk? Was he happy to have a heavy snow in order, finally, to justify the purchase (to his wife perhaps)? Was he simply being neighborly? Would he feel used if we did not thank him, and how much thanks did he need? What, I wondered, could I do for him? His generosity just hung in the air obliging me to respond, but I was not sure how. So I peeked my head out the door and gave him a self-conscious smile and nod. I gave a similar nod and a hello the next day along with a thanks, but the magnanimity of his act still hung in the air. Our good neighbor's benevolence had a similar effect on others. The next day, after a dusting of snow, another neighbor was out clearing the same stretch of sidewalk with his leaf-blower. Like the first neighbor, his preference for a display of mechanical force blurred the line between play and work. His abuse of the power tool created a situation where it was unclear whether or not he was performing an altruistic act. A few days following, after another few inches of snow, enough to cancel school but not work, a third neighbor's two boys were sent out, shovels in hand, in order to take responsibility for the corner-to-corner expanse of walkway. I began to wonder if clearing only one's own section of sidewalk would now be taken as an offense.

When would my turn come, and would my turn mean shoveling snow or doing something else? Both of these questions, first about timing (when?) and next about the form or opportunity for my own expression of neighborliness (what benefit might I bestow?), are key to a basic pattern of household exchange between kinfolk, friends, and neighbors. No one responded to our good neighbor by writing him a check or by dashing out of the house to help him. In either case, he rightfully would be offended. If he were obviously struggling with a shovel, that would be a different matter. Given his mastery of his task, our duty as neighbors was to accept and appreciate his kindness. What would I be saying to him if I rushed out of the house to clear the snow with my shovel before he was able to finish my section of the sidewalk?

There would be no insult, of course, when Pam Kavanaugh sent over a dozen cookies the next day, not as payment but because she happened to have made a double batch. Sam, her eight-year-old boy, told me the story as though it were an adventure. He had helped his mother make cookies. He arranged them on a plate. He wrapped them in cellophane, and he walked them over to Mr. Carl's house with the message (obviously rehearsed) that he and his brother had been making cookies, just for something to do, and wanted to know if Mr. Carl would like to have some. No offense would be taken after the two following snows, when Mr. Carl would return from work to find his own walk cleared, first after just a dusting of snow and then after an inch or two. I expect that when the next heavy snow falls, we will expect to see him out with his snow-blower. Our expectations will have the character partly of a hope and partly of an unarticulated obligation. Carl is now the heavy snow remover (among other things). In one sense, his benevolent use of his snow-blower will always be understood as a gift; yet in another, it would become part of a pattern of reciprocity, part of the neighborhood equilibrium whereby we sustain a certain status among others and exchange benefits.[37]

This kind of neighborly gift exchange is distinguished from buying, selling, lending, and leasing by its temporal structure and by its lack of standardized currency.[38] The counter-gift is deferred, so that, through the lapse of time, a kind of forgetfulness and a shift in context allow the return-gift to take on a gratuity of its own. Baking cookies with one's children in order to occupy them during an idle day establishes an occasion where the excess of cookies (rather than snow removal) is reason for the gift. This means of exchange might appear to conceal the payback; on the contrary, it reveals exchange as social (that is, mutual) self-interest and, in the process, names the social self as a gift. A gift comes back to the original giver not as payment or compensation, but as a social gesture and benefit that carries with it the mark of the giver. Social reciprocity is maintained, weaving a social bond, cultivating standards of neighborliness, and shaping the status, identity, and particular niche of the good neighbor. Gift exchange is not leveled to a common currency, but is sustained by difference and by an inequality of exchange that has its equilibrium within a wider social network. One to one, single party exchanges are rare. Instead, a series of overlapping non-identical gifts take on value and balance in an intricate constellation of wedding showers, baptisms and first communions, three-bean casseroles for grieving families, rides to work, babysitting, informal childcare, and hand-me-down clothes.

We may give our gifts as unmerited and unconditional, but it is a mistake to confuse gratuity with a lack of reciprocity.[39] The temporal structure of gift exchange and the non-identical gift hold gratuity and reciprocity together, and by doing so, make gift-giving a *continuing* possibility. Put another way, the gift is expressed fully only when it mediates shared life. A gracious overture to a stranger, for instance, is truncated if he or she remains outside. Full gratuity is oriented to inviting the stranger to sit at one's table as a guest. Although highly regarded, the anonymous gift is giving cut short and controlled. Giving implies preferential treatment, a being-chosen, that either comes as an invitation or confirms an existing relationship. Gift exchange, reciprocity, doing something for another, and accepting assistance are media through which relationships take shape, through which they take on their particular character. The birthday gift is a common example. Birthday gifts among adult siblings are reciprocal, even though gifts are not given with the intention of securing a gift in return, and there is never a moment of parity. There is no end point at which someone tallies the score. As one birthday follows another, one imbalance is overturned by another (or sometimes not). The gift exchanges, like the ongoing relationships, are never complete. Gifts are not identical or comparable, and sometimes no gift is given at all. Some asymmetries remain and reflect different roles and stations within the network of kin. Seen over time, the cycle of gifts will represent the particularities of that specific circle of reciprocity: who's the glue, who's on the periphery, who makes more money, who likes to spend, who gives the thoughtful gift, and who depends upon whom for what. The same can be said about relationships between spouses or friends. We do not offer identical contributions to our relationships; we are not identical people, and our relationships will be characterized by asymmetries particular to us, which amount to our own personal equilibrium. Likewise, on a theological level, God's grace establishes a distinct kind of reciprocation. Grace is utterly gratuitous, and it is the basis for sharing not only communion with God but the love of God, which makes possible an active, loving return to God and love for others, even one's enemy, for God's sake.[40]

Networks of kin, friends, and neighbors have their own internal logic and course of development. Unpaid services and reciprocity of the household should not be taken as merely an informal imitation of paid and contracted services. The nature of the transaction is different. The exchange of work and assistance may take the form of bartered agreements or monetary compensation, but the base from which these arrangements emerge, insofar as they are set within the open household and neighborhood, is the reciprocity of the gift. The household economy has its foundation within the temporal structure of common life and the ad hoc currency of the non-identical gift.

One day last Spring, my neighbor Chris strolled over while I was putting in replacement windows. He wanted to know if I planned to replace any more windows. I did. He wanted me *to let him* find a good deal on windows *for me*. That was how he put the matter. I would be doing him a favor by letting him help me. He suggested that he would be offended if I went off and bought the rest of the windows retail. He had a friend who had a contractor's license and could get me the windows wholesale. He was persistent (I suspect that he appreciates the hospitality we show to his children). It seems that Chris' offer was part of neighborly reciprocity, but with an interesting economic twist. He was offering me a privileged route around retail, undermining the rules of trade and taxation. The transaction would be much like the neighborhood's support of part-time labor, and services. If you need a carpenter, you ask around for someone who will work in the evening after work. You pay cash. The down side is that you might have to wait a few weeks or months, and you will have to do some of the work. The informal system can be painfully casual.

An interesting question is whether or not these transactions violate basic rules of economic exchange. Does informal work violate union rules? Is the wholesale window connection something like insider trading? Insider trading is wrong because it contradicts the proper functioning of the market. If I act on privileged information about the future of a company and its stock, I disregard the very rules of fairness that make the market work. In fact, my success depends upon those rules in the same way that the effectiveness of a lie depends upon principles of truthfulness. If lies were the rule, not even truth would be trusted. Insider trading works precisely because it is a deception.

The household economy is different. The offer of wholesale windows and black-market carpentry is consistent with our neighborhood reciprocity. The neighborhood is a network of privileged access, personal favors, and most of all, gratuity. Access and gratuity might in fact work in the other direction. If a neighbor or cousin were starting her own business, I might give her more work than I need, pay her more, and encourage others in the network to do so. In this case, we would be giving her a privileged step up in relation to the wider market (something that seems equivalent to price fixing). In this way, the open household cultivates a sub-economy underneath the contractual, impersonal, and individualist constraints of the dominant system. It is natural for networks of kinfolk, friends, and neighbors to do so inasmuch as their social bond and rules of exchange have an entirely different character. On the one hand, the bond is personal and requires preferential treatment and trust. On the other, exchange must always be incomplete and therefore have the quality of a gift that holds the social body together in a temporal sequence of reciprocity.

HOUSEWORK

In our capitalist economy, housework makes people, primarily women, vulnerable.[41] Housecleaning, grocery shopping, cooking, caring for children, mowing the lawn, and organizing community endeavors constitute the housekeeper's long hours of unpaid labor. Housework is not productive in the dominant economy. No distinct product is manufactured, nor does monetary compensation accrue by punching a clock, by position or salary, or by service rendered. To the degree that value is determined by the market, housekeeping is nearly meaningless. Housekeepers acquire little worth, few assets, and scant means for economic independence. In a world where power and cultural capital are structured outside the home, housework diminishes one's personal and social standing. The homemaker is left with no means of self-sufficiency, no credit rating, and no résumé.

Modern economic life has developed along gender lines and between different spheres of activity, between male productivity and a woman's work in the home or home-like work, such as nursing care, any work with children, and housecleaning. Empirical evidence continues to bear out the vulnerability of women and the home. Working women continue to earn considerably less than working men; twice as many elderly women are poor, and more than half of the households in poverty are maintained by single mothers.[42] The compromised status of the home and homemaker is matched, ironically, by the vulnerability of modern work, of salary and wage earning. The working class has no control over the availability of work and secures little or no loyalty from employers, unless employers are willing to make non-economic commitments. Even the professional or successful modern household is supported by a very shallow foundation, by one or two incomes without which the family's home and lifestyle cannot be sustained.

The upwardly mobile family responds to wage vulnerability by narrowing and closing off its borders, by minimizing the household economy, and by redoubling its focus on wage earning and contractual arrangements. The aspiring home is sustained and advanced by minimizing entanglements at home: its time-consuming tasks, its peripheral (non-nuclear) relationships, and the less efficient system of neighborhood reciprocity. However, except for a rare few, this strategy of narrowing boundaries is self-defeating. The home is secured, but there is little time or reason to be there. Household management, then, loses its legs, loses its rationale, and the housekeeper is no longer interdependent but simply dependent and socially inconsequential. The market economy makes voracious demands upon our time, whether we are wage earners or salaried professionals, and home life becomes a competing interest.[43] Except for special occasions or planned quality time, the household becomes part entertainment center (i.e., oriented to leisure), part bedroom, part closet, and a place to heat (but not prepare) food. Housekeeping begins to look more like working as a dispatcher or air traffic controller, managing arrivals and departures.

...I worry, as we come to...[the chapter's] end, that its content seems trivial. Such matters as snow removal and hand-me-down clothes are hardly exceptional practices. The apparent insignificance, however, reveals a great risk. Ordinary practices of community threaten to draw us in and bind us within everyday practices of a richly shared life. My examples are modest because the encroachment of market utility and its thin social relations is so clear. Upward mobility and the promise of contractual politics are nothing if not safe. The open household requires a sense of adventure and a willingness to welcome the unknown and to entertain the unmanageable. If we let down our guard, neighbors will be entering our homes as though they belong there. An interesting contrast to suburban mobility is a recent downward movement among the middle class. Malia McCawley Wyckoff and Mary Snyder, for example, offer a self-help guide, *You Can Afford to Stay Home with Your Kids*.[44] The movement's focus on child rearing is not new, as it is basic to the conception of the closed family. The book's suggestion that the household can be something other than a locus of consumer capitalism is not new either. Many of the authors' practical suggestions are common knowledge (and necessity) in working-class homes and for homemakers who continue to work for wages and sustain their homes through an informal economy, reciprocity, and frugality.[45] The interesting aspect of *You Can Afford to Stay Home* is its theme of conversion, not only converting the consumptive household into a subsistent one, but also a conversion of a family's "worldview." We will be transformed by the way of home.

Notes

1. Mary C. Howell, *Helping Ourselves: Families and the Human Network* (Boston: Beacon Press, 1975), p. 71.

2. Christopher Lasch, *Women and the Common Life: Love, Marriage, and Feminism*, ed. Elisabeth Lasch-Quinn (New York: W. W. Norton & Company, 1997).

3. For a more recent book by Howell, see *Serving the Underserved: Caring for People Who Are Both Old and Mentally Retarded: A Handbook for Caregivers* (Boston: Exceptional Parent Press, 1989).

4. The U.S. Bureau of the Census (1997) puts the marriage rate at 8.9 per thousand in 1995 and the number of divorces at 4.4 per thousand.

5. Arlie Hochschild, *The Time Bind: When Work Becomes Home and Home Becomes Work* (New York: Metropolitan Books, 1997), pp. 15–24, 45–52.

6. Stephanie Coontz, *The Way We Never Were: American Families and the Nostalgia Trap* (New York: Basic Books, 1992).

7. Edward Shorter, *The Making of the Modern Family* (New York: Basic Books, 1997), p. 3.

8. Shorter, *Modern Family*, p. 3.

9. Christopher N. L. Brooke, *Marriage in Christian History* (Cambridge: Cambridge University Press, 1977); Edmund S. Morgan, *The Puritan Family: Religion and Domestic Relations in Seventeenth-Century New England* (New York: Harper & Row, 1944).

10. Stephanie Coontz provides an interesting account of changes in family, among different classes, that were directed toward sustaining its members socially and economically. *The Social Origins of Private Life: A History of American Families 1600–1900* (New York: Verso, 1988).

11. Sharon Hays, *The Cultural Contradictions of Motherhood* (New Haven: Yale University Press, 1996); Robert Bellah, et al., *Habits of the Heart* (Berkeley: University of California Press, 1985); Christopher Lasch, *Haven in a Heartless World* (New York: Basic Books, 1977).

12. Shorter, *Modern Family*, pp. 5–6.

13. Shorter, *Modern Family*, p. 5; Hays, *Cultural Contradictions of Motherhood*, p. 64.

14. Jean Bethke Elshtain, *Public Man, Private Woman* (Princeton: Princeton University Press, 1981).

15. Eva Illouz, *Consuming the Romantic Utopia: Love and the Cultural Contradictions of Capitalism* (Berkeley: University of California Press, 1997), pp. 25–78.

16. Hays, *Cultural Contradictions of Motherhood*, pp. 8–10, 64–68.

17. Hays, *Cultural Contradictions of Motherhood*, p. 68.

18. Wendell Berry, *Home Economics* (San Francisco: North Point Press, 1987); *Sex, Economy, Freedom, and Community* (New York: Pantheon Books, 1992).

19. Saskia Sassen-Koob, "New York City's Informal Economy," *The Informal Economy: Studies in Advanced and Less Developed Countries*, ed. Alejandro Portes, Manuel Castells, and Lauren A. Benton (Baltimore: The Johns Hopkins University Press, 1989), p. 61.

20. Sassen-Koob, "New York City's Informal Economy," p. 71.

21. M. Patricia Fernandez-Kelly and Anna M. Garcia, "Informalization at the Core: Hispanic Women, Homework, and the Advanced Capitalist State," Portes et al. (eds.), *Informal Economy*, p. 260.

22. Fernandez-Kelly and Garcia, "Informalization at the Core," p. 262.

23. Howell, *Helping Ourselves*, pp. 75–76.

24. Howell, *Helping Ourselves*, p. 72.

25. The image of the suburbs is not just a trope but key to the history of the middle-class family. See Lasch, *Haven in a Heartless World*.

26. Alisdair MacIntyre offers an interesting critique of the therapist, expert, and manager in *After Virtue*, 2nd ed. (Notre Dame: University of Notre Dame Press, 1984), pp. 75–78.

27. In *Helping Ourselves*, Howell adds work (pp. 95–118) and healthcare (pp. 169–94) to childcare (pp. 119–45) and education (pp. 146–68) to the list of professionalized areas of family life.

28. James L. Nolan, *The Therapeutic State: Justifying Government at Century's End* (New York: New York University Press, 1998).

29. This account depends partly on Immanuel Wallerstein's contributions to *Creating and Transforming Households: The Constraints of the World-Economy*, ed. Joan Smith and Immanuel Wallerstein (Cambridge: Cambridge University Press, 1992), pp. 3–23, 253–62.

30. Howell, *Helping Ourselves*, p. 76.

31. Howell, *Helping Ourselves*, p. 77.

32. Howell, *Helping Ourselves*, pp. 77–78.

33. Howell, *Helping Ourselves*, p. 80.

34. Howell, *Helping Ourselves*, p. 82.

35. Howell, *Helping Ourselves*, p. 82.

36. The following account of place and the idea of a home economy is gleaned from the wide-ranging writings of Wendell Berry. See, for instance, his *Home Economics*.

37. Alvin W. Gouldner, *For Sociology: Renewal and Critique in Sociology Today* (New York: Basic Books, 1973), pp. 241–42.

38. Pierre Bourdieu, *Outline of a Theory of Practice* (New York: Cambridge University Press, 1977), pp. 4–6; D. Stephen Long, *Divine Economy: Theology and the Market* (London: Routledge, 2000), pp. 144–46.

39. John Milbank, "Can a Gift Be Given? Prolegomena to a Future Trinitarian Metaphysic," *Modern Theology* 11, no. 1 (January 1995), pp. 119–61.

40. Thomas Aquinas, *Summa Theologiae* I.2, qq. 109–14, Blackfriars ed. vol. 30 (New York: McGraw–Hill Book Company, 1972); II.2, qq. 23–7, Blackfriars ed. vol. 34 (1975).

41. Susan Moller Okin's arguments in *Justice, Gender, and the Family* (New York: Basic Books, 1989), pp. 134–69.

42. Okin, *Justice, Gender, and the Family*, p. 3.

43. Peter Meikins, "Confronting the Time Bind: Work, Family, and Capitalism," *Monthly Review* 49, no. 9 (February 1998), pp. 1–13.

44. Malia McCawley Wyckoff and Mary Snyder, *You Can Afford to Stay Home with Your Kids* (Franklin Lakes, NJ: Career Press, 1999).

45. Studies of working-class women are interesting in this regard. Christine Stansell, *City of Women: Sex and Class in New York 1789–1860* (Chicago: University of Illinois Press, 1987); Julie A. Matthaei, *An Economic History of Women in America: Women's Work, the Sexual Division of Labor, and the Development of Capitalism* (New York: Schocken Books, 1982).

14.   A Christian Family Vision

Lisa Sowle Cahill

This chapter first appeared in Lisa Sowle Cahill, *Family: A Christian Social Perspective* (Minneapolis: Fortress, 2000).

A biblical text that begins to define what is required for a family to be domestic church is the so-called parable of judgment in Matthew 25. In its resounding lines, "the Son of Man" proclaims "to those on his right hand":

> "Come, O blessed of my Father, inherit the kingdom pre-
> pared for you from the foundation of the world; for I was
> hungry and you gave me food, I was thirsty and you gave me
> drink, I was a stranger and you welcomed me, I was naked
> and you clothed me, I was sick and you visited me, I was in
> prison and you came to me....Truly I say to you, as you did
> it to one of the least of these my brethren, you did it to me."
> Then he will say to those at his left hand, "Depart from me,
> you cursed, into the eternal fire prepared for the devil and his
> angels, for I was hungry and you gave me no food, I was
> thirsty and you gave me no drink...." Then they also will
> answer, "Lord, when did we see thee hungry or thirsty or a
> stranger or naked or sick or in prison, and did not minister to
> you?" Then he will answer them, "Truly, I say to you, as you
> did it not to the least of these, you did it not to me. And they
> will go away into eternal punishment, but the righteous into
> eternal life." (Matt. 25:31–46)

The disciple finds and serves Christ in "the least of these" by recognizing them as Christ's true family, to whom he refers as "my brethren." To be one in the family of Christ is to "welcome" compassionately those whose suffering is within our reach, taking care of their basic needs for food, clothing, and assistance in time of sickness and travail. The family of Christ includes not only the "stranger" but even the criminal—the one who stands convicted of wrongdoing.

If the family is a school of intimacy, empathy, and love, then the family as little church schools these virtues in attentiveness to the least of Christ's brethren. The virtues of compassion, mercy, and service are not merely held up as distant ideals or supererogatory forms of perfection. Those who fail to find Christ in active love of neighbor must "depart from" him on the day of his glory. Moreover, the text operates on the assumption that those to be cast out are "the righteous," who have not seen that being upright includes active identification with the miseries of those whom they consider less worthy.

Although the passage from Matthew underwrites the preferential option for the poor that provides the social framework for the lives of all Christians, its examples are personal. Its direct appeal to personal response and responsibility gives this parable its moral impact and motivating power. Modern Christians will understand the commanded virtues to result in structural change, empowerment of the poor, and ecumenical cooperation in a public forum and in civil institutions, none of which were very realistic possibilities for disciples at Christianity's point of origin in the first century. In her book on virtue, Diana Fritz Cates makes the case that friendship is a school for compassion and that moral virtue consists in choosing to develop, expand, and extend compassion by training our cognitive, affective, and imaginative capacities appropriately. Moreover, compassion can and should take institutional form, because mediating institutions enable us to recognize and respond to the situations of other persons with whom we are not in immediate, personal contact.[1] Thus, a Christian ethic of compassion and other-concern must be fulfilled through an institutional component, in which sacrificial altruism is extended to distant persons and communities. This institutional extension of co-responsibility with and for other human beings in concentric and overlapping communities from local to global is the essence of social ethics.

Empathy in the face of need is a fundamental human response, learned in the intimate associations of family first of all, then educated toward a wider range of further recipients.[2] Sometimes the needs of family members and of nonmembers will conflict. As Stephen Post poignantly illustrates with instances from his own family life, it can be difficult to know when and how to exercise the preferential option for the poor in the concrete.[3] But the point of the parable of judgment is that Christians must always be aware of neighbors and strangers who suffer as making real claims on them. It is the distinctive contribution of Christian ethics to define prophetically and redefine the identity of the "deserving poor." The religious symbolism of Christianity (and of other religions) that evokes identity with and compassion toward those who suffer has potential to stimulate the imagination and widen the moral outlook of all persons and groups so that natural human emotions are trained toward a generosity that can temper, if not entirely overcome, egotism and fear.

The needs depicted as objects of Christian other-concern in Matthew 25 direct our attention toward the kinds of essential goods that all persons and cultures experience to be necessary. Precisely because the needs and goods identified in the parable are basic to human well-being, our common human condition makes recognition of another's deprivation a human and not only a Christian possibility. Therefore, Christians can cooperate with others in civil society, politics, and government to pursue ends recognizable by all as good and worthy. The gospel text does present Christian virtue as embodying a radical and distinctive orientation toward these universal needs and goods. Those who look upon the needy in Christian faith will see them as Christ and as members of one's own family in Christ. Thus the preferential option to seek goods for kith and kin becomes the preferential option for all those wanting for the material and social necessities of human well-being, including stranger or wrongdoer. Christians have the obligation to heighten the visibility of these priorities in the public domain, making social structures more just.

ECUMENICAL CHRISTIAN COMMITMENT TO FAMILIES TODAY

In their book about the family debate in North American culture, Don Browning and colleagues offer a vision of family as domestic church that distinguishes what they take to be Protestant and Catholic features of this analogy.[4] Their definition provides a way to recapitulate some themes of the present work, while offering an opportunity to examine how different conceptions of the Christian family are at variance or are complementary.

Browning et al. identify prayer and religious catechesis in the home as one of the most crucial characteristics of family as "little church," practices that they allow have not been consistently pursued in mainline Protestant families of recent decades. Importantly, they note that Christian prayer together can and should lead to the sort of transformation of family hierarchies that they surmise to have occurred when inclusive eucharistic rituals were practiced in the house churches of Christianity's first generations.

The key difference that these authors see between Catholic and Protestant understandings of domestic church is that the former is *sacramental*, while the latter is *covenantal*. By this they mean that Catholicism holds that the presence of God in the family is mediated through the sacramental system of the *institutional church*, while Protestantism sees God as present in the family through the parents' own *personal relationship* or covenant with God and God's covenant with the family, existing in dialogical relation to God's covenant with the church. This definition reflects and builds on the Reformation prioritization of individual faith and the responsibility of conscience over ecclesiastical structures. It also represents the biblical and Reformation insight that persons' relations to God and to others in God require and are founded on personal decision and conversion (covenant).

From another angle, however, the emphasis on choice and personal commitment does not completely capture the importance of parental responsibility to children that Browning et al. want to stress. Part of their agenda is to clarify the duty of fathers and mothers to care for their offspring (and co-parents) whether or not that particular responsibility is one parents (especially fathers) would prefer to choose. In other words, biological parenthood morally constitutes a responsibility and morally demands a commitment on the basis of a preexisting, natural reality. The idea that moral relationships arise in important and compelling ways from biological and material forms of human interdependence ("creation") is captured more explicitly in the incarnational view of human existence symbolized in the Catholic sacramental system.

This system not only gives sacramental events an institutional orientation, but also equally importantly identifies human experiences like birth, death, and marriage as occasions of the inbreaking of the divine. God is incarnate and redemptive in nature and natural realities, including natural human relationships and associations that are capable of being sanctified and raised into communion with God. Since persons are by nature social, their family relations are also socially extensive or extenuating, making the family interdependent with other institutions, all of which open out onto the common good. Thus participation in the family as a social institution interwoven with the other institutions of civil society is also an opportunity for divine presence. Browning and co-authors move on in subsequent sections to discuss very perceptively the importance and possibility of ecumenical cooperation for the transformation of civil institutions that support family life.[5] But the coexistence of Christian families with other families in the common good is a more integral and foundational theme of Catholic teaching about families, as is the service character of the Christian family. Human relationships and institutions, in Catholic perspective, are not so corrupted by sin that they scarcely function as mediations of divine presence unless explicitly disciplined by Christian norms that reject ordinary human values. Sin, in fact, is identified in terms of violations of human nature, not so much as capitulation to human drives and desires.

From the Protestant, covenantal side, however, returns the equally necessary caution that nature is corrupted by sin and fails to serve as a ready norm for human behavior. On the issue of family specifically, a covenant perspective holds up prayer in the family as a way of cultivating personal sacrifice as part of a relationship with God. Family spirituality is also important in Catholic teaching about the family as domestic church. But a Protestant, biblical approach will be acutely aware of the difficulty of enacting the relationships of human empathy and sharing that our genuine and natural interdependence would demand. It refuses to be as sanguine about the healing of social life and institutions as recent Catholic social teaching about the common good, including welfare reform. Protestantism identifies a family covenant with God over and above or outside sinful human relationships and worldly structures and tends to stress that personal commitments are prior to and more important than the reformation of social structures. Thus the covenant model of family can help advocate reconfiguration of the natural family to meet Christian ideals. Within this model, a strong critical stance toward Christian family values will be essential to ensure that family ideals and aspirations are genuinely Christian, not just cultural or "natural" familism justified in religious terms.

The Christian family and its family values are not the same as the natural family with its often exaggerated values of family security and advancement; nor is the Christian family the same as the family of modern liberal individualism, where commitments are decided and defined by individual choice. Understanding the family as domestic church requires understanding "church" properly. The primary values defining the Christian family are the same values that define the "new family in Christ": other-concern and compassionate love that overlooks socially normative boundaries and is willing to sacrifice to meet the needs of others. These values are more important in defining the Christian family than is a particular family structure. This does not mean that all structures are equally valid, since some more than others—especially long-term fidelity to mates and children—will serve human growth and happiness and contribute to a more humane society. But it does mean that structure alone is not the key criterion of Christian identity, and it opens up the possibility that even "nontraditional" families may exhibit the most important Christian family values, and for that reason be authentic domestic churches.

Today, in the era of globalization of media, economics, education, politics, and legislation, concern and sacrifice for others take institutional forms, extending personal commitments into consistent social support and allowing broad-based collaboration in marshalling forms of support that include the poor and empower the poor themselves to realize a more humane existence. Certainly civil institutions that support all members of society to realize their potential, meet their obligations, and fully participate in both the domestic and public spheres of the common good must take shape at the local level, tailored to meet local needs and to capitalize on local opportunities. But solidarity as a social virtue also requires that resources be collected and redistributed in regional, national, and international networks, both private and public, so that individuals and families can exercise their responsibilities even toward those to whom they do not feel a close personal tie or with whom they do not enjoy a mutually beneficial immediate relationship.

There are certain family structures and relationships that would serve individual, family, and social well-being in virtually every culture. These include the faithful, long-term personal commitment of sexual partners; their mutually respectful cooperation in domestic life, including participation in institutions such as religion and the economy that link families to society; the equal dignity of women and men; the permanent commitment of parents to nurture and educate children together; sharing material and social resources in the family so that the human needs of all are met; and care for the elderly, the sick, and other vulnerable members. Christian identity confirms these relationships, roles, and values, at least to the extent that they do not overshadow the Christian's duty to extend empathy and care beyond family membership and to support social institutions that serve the needs of other families, groups, and individuals.

But the ultimate tests of a distinctively *Christian* ethics of family life go beyond the well-being of family members and the successful accomplishment of family roles. The Christian family defines *family values* as care for others, especially the poor; it appreciates that truly Christian families are not always the most socially acceptable or prestigious ones; it values and encourages all families who strive earnestly to meet the standard of compassionate action; and it encourages both personal commitment to and the social structuring of mercy and justice.

A PROGRAM FOR CHRISTIAN FAMILIES

We may conclude with five constructive recommendations for Christian family life, along with a word about the likelihood, even inevitability, of failure to follow them fully. The first two of the five address the natural, human functions and importance of families; the latter three address the Christian conversion of family bonds and roles.

1. Christian families should be grounded in the kinds of human relations that promote family well-being in general. Key among them are sex-

ual relationships characterized by faithful commitment and responsible procreation, including long-term shared dedication to the welfare of children; equality, dignity, respect, and reciprocity among adults and between adults and children in ways appropriate to their age and maturity; affection, intimacy, empathy, and mutual support among family members.

2. Family roles should promote social well-being by educating for economic and political participation, including respect for the rights and fulfillment of the responsibilities to others that are part of the common good.

3. The kinship family's well-being is for Christians integrated with and to some extent relativized by the inclusive nature of the Christian community as "new family in Christ." Christ's new family potentially reaches out to all those who are weary and heavily burdened, whether Christian or non-Christian.

4. The natural pro-social role of families is shaped for Christians by a *preferential* option for the poor. In institutionalizing just treatment and just access to goods across society, those who have been previously excluded must be first included. Although justice in its own right may be interpreted as having such a preferential or remedial component, the Christian imagination will be formed to highlight this priority in a special way and to sustain its importance in the face of conflicting practical claims.

5. Christian families will place their moral commitments in the context of a relationship to God and will train the moral imagination to see human relationships in the light of the reign of God. Adults should serve as models to children, including them in the life of a faith community, through liturgy, eucharist, social events, and service activities. Such practices form Christian identity within family life, embodying the meaning of Jesus' command to love God and neighbor in practical relationships in the church, in a circle of family and friends, and in the larger community and society. It must be acknowledged that while it is simple and obvious to state that Christian families will incorporate Christian "spirituality" and prayer, it may well be difficult to re-create a contemporary Christian family spirituality in culturally available, meaningful, and powerful symbols and rituals. This is a place in which the churches can learn from the experience of families and in which the white middle-class families typifying mainline Protestantism and Catholicism can learn from Christians of other ethnic groups and social classes.

As all of us who aim to be Christian families struggle to achieve even one or two of these goals, we realize that the Christian life is truly the way of the cross as well as a journey to redemption. Sometimes our aspirations are ridiculed or rejected by our culture or simply considered unrealistic or irrelevant. Worse, the process of trying to live as Christian families makes us all too acutely aware of sin and failure in our own lives and in those of persons whom we love. Every family experiences situations that cause fear, anger, grief, guilt, and shame. Few continue for long without developing hurtful patterns of insensitive, manipulative, or angry behavior; few parents can honestly say they have loved their children unselfishly and with wholehearted acceptance of their children's independent needs and identities. Many marriages and families break apart; sex is often exploitative, even within marriage; violence and abuse break out more frequently than we will openly admit. Children do not receive all the care and understanding they deserve from parents; elderly parents do not receive the patient devotion and respect their years, if not behavior, have earned them. Christian parents too often fail in attempts to pass on their faith in a vital way to children; children, in turn, cause parents pain by abandoning or betraying their most treasured moral and spiritual ideals. Even without notable disasters, family life over the years invariably brings with it stresses and strains, hurts and disappointments, that too often become hardened into bitterness and alienation.

Even when family life seems rewarding and successful in itself, the social concern of Christian families can be very hard to sustain. At most, it seems, we can teach ourselves and our children to look with greater understanding on different kinds of families undergoing their own trials and seeking their own rewards and to offer our time and resources rather sporadically to help other families in trouble or to make community life better. We are too consumed with our own family's well-being, which for some of us seems very, very difficult to secure.

Our own sins and our need for forgiveness should make all Christian families slow to judge others and quick to offer support, even while we persistently and courageously speak up for the family relationships and social conditions that we believe will enhance family life for all. The Christian family is not the perfect family but one in which fidelity, compassion, forgiveness, and concern for others, even strangers, are known. In striving to embody these virtues, however imperfect its success, a family lives in the presence of God and begins to transform its surroundings. A Christian family is such a family.

Notes

1. Diana Fritz Cates, *Choosing to Feel: Virtue, Friendship and Compassion for Friends* (Notre Dame, Ind.: University of Notre Dame Press, 1997).

2. On this point, see Barbara Deveny Redmond, *The Domestic Church: Primary Agent of Moral Development* (Ph.D. diss., Boston College, Ann Arbor, Mich.: UMI, 1998).

3. Stephen G. Post, *More Lasting Unions: Christianity, the Family and Society* (Grand Rapids, Mich.: William B. Eerdmans, 2000), 178–79.

4. Don S. Browning, Bonnie J. Miller-McLemore, Pamela Couture, K. Brynolf Lyon, and Robert M. Franklin, *From Culture Wars to Common Ground: Religion and the American Family Debate* (Louisville, Ky.: Westminster John Knox Press, 1997), 308–9.

5. Ibid., 309–34. They suggest, for example, that social scientific evidence indicates that both spouses or co-parents will be more satisfied and fulfilled if they have opportunities to engage in domestic work and in some form of paid employment outside the home. They also conclude that a sixty-hour *family* work week should be the norm and should be supported by appropriate employment flexibility and child care. Moreover, single parents, including those receiving public assistance, should only be expected to devote thirty hours to outside work and should receive the necessary funding to make this possible, in cases in which the co-parent is not contributing to family support.

Part Three

SPECIFIC ISSUES

Interchurch Marriage

15. Interchurch Marriages: Theological and Pastoral Reflections[1]

Michael G. Lawler

This chapter first appeared in *Marriage and the Catholic Church* (Collegeville, Minn.: Liturgical, 2002).

For the past thirty years I have taught a course on the theology of marriage at a Catholic university. As a result, I have been called upon regularly to give advice to young couples planning to marry, some thirty-five percent of them these days in the United States of two different Christian denominations. Like all young people in the culture of divorce in which Americans now live, they have questions about commitment, lifelong marriage, divorce, and children. If they are of two different denominations, they also have particular questions about the interchurch marriage they are planning, for they have heard that heterogamous marriages are less stable than homogamous marriages.[2] Two approached me last semester, I shall call them Sarah, who claimed to be a Catholic, and Philip who was a Presbyterian. What follows is a brief resume of our conversations.

THEOLOGICAL CONSIDERATIONS

An important first item is how to talk about their marriage. At our first meeting Sarah and Philip used a traditional term, *mixed marriage.* In 1917, the Catholic Church's Code of Canon Law proscribed mixed marriages. "The church everywhere most severely prohibits the marriage between two baptized persons, one of whom is a Catholic, the other of whom belongs to a heretical or schismatic sect" (Can 1060). No one in 1917 could be in much doubt: in the eyes of the Catholic Church, and many other Churches, a mixed marriage was something evil and to be avoided. In 1983, however, the Code was specifically revised in the matter of "mixed marriages." It now reads: "Without the express permission of the competent authority, marriage is prohibited between two baptized persons, one of whom was baptized in the Catholic Church...the other of whom belongs to a Church or ecclesial communion not in full communion with the Catholic Church" (Can 1124). The softening of the language was obvious to Sarah and Philip, especially the language referring to Philip. No longer is he described negatively as a heretic or schismatic; he is now described positively as a Christian of another Church. This softening of the language furthers the matter of terminology.

Several terms are used to describe religiously heterogamous marriages. The broadest are *interreligious marriage*, which emphasizes the different religions involved, and *interfaith marriage*, which emphasizes the different belief systems involved. I believe that both terms are not specific enough to describe the marriage of a Christian married to another Christian of a different denomination and are best reserved for the marriage between a Christian and someone of another religion. The Code's description of Philip as a Christian belonging to another Church points toward a term which has become common, namely, *interchurch marriage*. This term describes the marriage between spouses from two Christian denominations, in which each spouse participates in her or his own Church and, to some degree, in the spouse's Church, and in which both spouses take an active part in the religious education of their children.[3] This definition has the disadvantage that it embraces only a small percentage of interchurch couples, those at the high end of the religiosity spectrum,[4] but it has the advantage of being the term coming into common usage. Interchurch marriage is the term I will use throughout this chapter. I will use it in its broadest sense, however, to embrace every marriage in which the spouses belong, however loosely, to two different Christian churches or denominations.

When I explained to Sarah and Philip the Code's abandonment of the term *mixed marriage*, they asked what caused such a sea-change. The answer to this question is the answer also to another question: what do a

Catholic woman and a Presbyterian man have in common that might provide a good basis for a Christian married life together? The answer to both questions is their Christian baptism. Baptism is no longer looked upon as an exclusively confessional matter in the divided Christian churches. No one is baptized exclusively into the Catholic Church or the Presbyterian Church; one is baptized into the one, holy, catholic (universal), and apostolic church of Jesus Christ. In spite of intense pressure to repeat the teaching of Pope Pius XII that this Church of Christ is identical with the Roman Catholic Church, the Second Vatican Council in 1964 refused to accept that identity and taught instead that the Church of Christ "*subsists* in the Catholic Church."[5] The Church established by Christ, that is, is imperfectly embodied in but is not identical with the Catholic Church; it is also imperfectly embodied in but is not identical with the Presbyterian Church or any other Protestant Church. While each and every Christian is incorporated into and nurtured in the Church of Christ through faith and baptism in a specific Christian denomination, baptism is never to be thought of as incorporating them into only that denomination. Though, in ecumenical theology, each local Church or denomination is wholly Church, none of them is the whole Church.

Today all the major Christian denominations accept that those who believe in Christ and have been properly baptized are brought into a certain union with the Catholic Church, and with the Presbyterian Church, and so on. They accept baptism in one another's churches as incorporation into the one, universal church of Christ, and hence they do not re-baptize anyone who changes religious affiliation from one Christian denomination to another. The degree of communion between believers of different denominations may not be perfectly clear in any given case, any more than the degree of communion within any given denomination is clear, but it is certain, and has been recently reaffirmed by Pope John Paul II: "All those justified by faith through baptism are incorporated into Christ. They therefore have a right to be honored by the title of Christian, and are properly regarded as brothers and sisters in the Lord by the sons and daughters of the Catholic Church."[6] No longer does the Catholic Church look on Presbyterian Philip as a heretic or schismatic; he is a Christian and a brother. There is a foundational Christian union in the Lord between Sarah and Philip that results from their shared baptism and their shared Christian faith. This foundational communion shared in the Christian Churches through baptism is one reason the Catholic Church has radically mitigated its language about "mixed marriages." One mutual resolution Sarah and Philip should make is not to permit their Christian, faith-filled, and baptismal unity to be obscured by less foundational confessional divisions.

The union in Christ between Sarah and Philip through their shared faith in and baptism into Christ, the Christian bond between them if you like, is further solidified by three other bonds. Their mutual love unites them in an interpersonal bond of friendship; their wedding unites them publicly and legally in the bond of marriage; their celebration of their marriage in the Lord unites them in a religious bond of sacrament. Their marriage in very deed becomes, to paraphrase the Second Vatican Council, "an intimate partnership of love, life, and religion,"[7] which establishes them in a union so close that the Bible describes it as "two in one body" (Gen 2:24). I choose to describe their union as a coupled-We, to intimate the bonds which bind Sarah and Philip together. So close is their communion of love, life, and religious faith that the Catholic Church has established their marital communion as the sacrament or symbol of the steadfast communion between Christ and his Church. The unity Sarah and Philip achieve in their church-blessed marriage places them under the gospel injunction, "What God has joined together let no one put asunder" (Matt 19:6). It was reflection on their blessed communion and on this gospel injunction that drove Presbyterian Philip to raise a question. "If Sarah and I are united in baptism and marriage blessed by both our Churches," he asked, "how can those same Churches separate us for the Holy Communion of the Lord's table?"

Shared Communion

I let this section stand by itself because the question of shared communion is the neuralgic question for many interchurch couples. They argue exactly as Philip did. We are made one in Christ in faith and baptism; we are made one body in Christ in marriage; we desire to celebrate and enhance our unity and one-bodiness in Christ in the sacrament of communion, Holy Communion with the Lord and one another at the Lord's table. How can the Churches who have celebrated our oneness turn around and say we are not and cannot be one in Holy Communion? For many interchurch couples, the inability to share communion is a serious challenge to their Christian life together and sometimes a challenge also to their marital life together. That creates a serious pastoral challenge for the Churches.

There are two major Catholic documents relevant to the question, the Code of Canon Law (1983) and the *Directory for the Application of Principles and Norms on Ecumenism* (1993). No Christian, Protestant or Catholic, should expect any Catholic minister to go beyond the principles and norms embodied in these two foundational documents, for no Catholic minister can go beyond them and still claim to be giving a distinctively Catholic witness. Neither, however, should any Catholic, clerical or lay, impose restrictions beyond what is embodied in these two documents. The main text of canon law sounds not only prescriptive but also restrictive. "Catholic ministers may lawfully administer the sacraments to Catholic members of the Christian faithful only and, likewise, the latter may lawfully receive the sacraments only from Catholic ministers with due regard for 2, 3, and 4 of this canon" (Can 844.1). Due regard for Can 844.2, 3, and 4 requires understanding of the exceptions and conditions enunciated therein and serious interpretation of their possible application in any given case.

> "Whenever necessity requires or a *genuine spiritual advantage commends* it...Christ's faithful for whom it is physically or morally impossible to approach a Catholic minister, may lawfully receive the sacraments of penance, Eucharist, and anointing of the sick from *non-Catholic ministers in whose churches these sacraments are valid*" (Can 844.2).
>
> "Catholic ministers may lawfully administer the sacraments of penance, Eucharist, and anointing of the sick to members of the oriental churches which do not have full communion with the Catholic Church, if they ask on their own for the sacraments and are properly disposed. This holds also for members of other churches, which in the judgment of the Apostolic See are in the same condition as the oriental churches as far as these sacraments are concerned" (Can 844.3).
>
> "If there is a danger of death or if, in the judgment of the diocesan Bishop or of the Episcopal Conference, there *is some other grave and pressing need*, Catholic ministers may law-

fully administer those same sacraments to other Christians not
in full communion with the Catholic Church, who cannot
approach a minister of their own community and *who spontaneously ask for them*, provided that they *demonstrate the
Catholic faith in respect of these sacraments* and are properly
disposed" (Can 844.4).

The *Directory* is just as clear. "In certain circumstances, by way
of exception, and under certain conditions, access to these sacraments
[including Holy Communion] may be permitted, or even *commended*,
for Christians of other churches and ecclesial communities" (n. 129).
The *Directory* raises the question of shared communion with non-Catholic
Christians, thereby suggesting, *ipso facto*, that extraordinary shared communion is a possibility. The conditions under which a Catholic minister
may administer the Eucharist to a baptized, non-Catholic Christian are
specified as fourfold: "the person be unable to have recourse for the sacrament desired to a minister of his or her own church or ecclesial community, ask for the sacrament of his or her own initiative, manifest Catholic
faith in this sacrament, and be properly disposed" (n. 131). Catholics
may ask for the sacrament of Eucharist "only from a minister in whose
church these sacraments are valid or from one who is known to be
validly ordained according to the Catholic teaching on ordination" (n.
132). All of these conditions are the ones I have underscored at various
points in the above discussion of Canon 844.

What is to be noted here is that exceptions and conditions, though
carefully defined and delimited, are listed and never retracted. The problem
is that not all official Catholic interpreters interpret the exceptions and conditions in the same way. Some interpret them rigidly to the letter; others,
equally competent, interpret them more broadly. Predictably, this difference of interpretation causes discontent, confusion, hurt, and frequently
anger among both Catholic and Protestant spouses. That anger, and the
division induced among interchurch families at the Lord's table, as the
German Bishops note in their document on Eucharistic Sharing (1997),
can easily lead to "serious risk to the faith life of one or both partners"; it
can "endanger the integrity of the bond that is created in life and faith
through marriage"; it can lead to "an indifference to the sacrament and a
distancing from Sunday worship and so from the life of the Church."[8]

These considerations highlight shared communion as a specific example of what Pope John Paul II said to interchurch couples gathered in York Cathedral in 1982: "You live in your marriage the hopes and the difficulties of the path to Christian unity." They highlight also the interchurch marriage as a situation requiring special pastoral care.

Since I have introduced the German Bishops' document on Eucharistic Sharing, we can start there in our examination of how principles must be, can be, and are interpreted. The document, as the title indicates, is focused on the sharing of communion in interchurch marriages, and because of that focus gets immediately to concretizing the principles of Canon 844 and the *Directory*. "Families in interchurch marriages may experience '*serious (spiritual) need*' in certain situations…[and] in situations of pastoral need the married partners living in interchurch marriages may be admitted to receive communion in the Catholic Church under certain conditions."[9] Everyone familiar with the Code and the *Directory* will know the provenance of that statement.

The practical question is how is "spiritual need" to be assessed and who is to assess it? The Bishops give a pastoral and obvious answer.

> Since pastorally the establishment of objective criteria for "serious (spiritual) need" is extremely difficult, ascertaining such a need can as a rule only be done by the *minister* concerned. Essentially, this must become clear in pastoral discussion. Does the couple concerned (and any children) experience being separated at the Lord's table as a pressure on their life together? Is it a hindrance to their shared belief? How does it affect them? Does it risk damaging the integrity of their communion in married life and faith?[10]

It is a good pastoral rule [to have] a discussion between the couple and the minister on the spot, usually a priest, who might best understand their situation. There are many interchurch families who could establish their "serious (spiritual) need" in such an open pastoral discussion.

Two years earlier, in 1995, the Catholic Archbishop of Brisbane issued a document entitled *Blessed and Broken: Pastoral Guidelines for Eucharistic Hospitality*, which contained a section on interchurch marriages. Noting that "the Directory of Ecumenism states that Eucharistic sharing for a spouse in a mixed marriage can only be exceptional," the Archbishop agrees with his German brothers that the verification of the required conditions and dispositions is best assessed in pastoral discussion. "It is sufficient for the presiding priest to establish, by means of a few simple questions, whether or not these conditions are met." Of great moment in the Brisbane document is the recognition that some interchurch couples "could well experience a serious spiritual need to receive communion each time he or she accompanies the family to a Catholic mass,"[11] and that this need can be met. Though the Roman *Directory* states that shared communion for interchurch spouses can only be exceptional, a spouse in an interchurch marriage could well experience exceptional ongoing need for shared communion. There is, in some though probably not all interchurch marriages, not only the exceptional, one-time case but also the exceptional, ongoing case. The ongoing spiritual need in this ongoing interchurch case, again, can be assessed in pastoral discussion between the local priest and the couple, but has to be referred to the Archbishop for the authorization of exceptional, but ongoing, shared communion.

An example of a different interpretation of the foundational principles, exceptions, conditions, and circumstances is the document published jointly in 1998 by the Catholic Bishops of Great Britain and Ireland under the title *One Bread, One Body*. This document does not focus exclusively on interchurch marriages and the question of shared communion. As its subtitle asserts, it is a teaching document which, sets forth, first, "the teaching of the Catholic Church on the mystery of the Eucharist" (n. 2) and, then, norms "to govern sharing of the sacraments between Catholics and other Christians in our countries" (n. 8).[12] I cannot deal with the first part here, since focus and space prohibit it, but it is a rich exposition of the contemporary Catholic theology of Eucharist in an ecumenical context. It should be read meditatively by everyone, Catholic and Protestant alike, who wishes to understand the Catholic approach to the Eucharist and why that approach mandates shared communion as an exceptional, rather than a normal, reality for the Catholic Church.

The second part of the document, the norms on sacramental and Eucharistic sharing, is of major interest to us. The Bishops adopt two interesting strategies. While acknowledging the general norm which allows shared communion in exceptional circumstances "when strong desire is accompanied by shared faith, grave and pressing spiritual need, and at least an implicit desire for communion with the Catholic Church" (n. 77), they introduce a shift from the category of *need* to the category of *pain*. This enables them to point out, correctly, the brokenness of the Body of Christ, the pain that results from a broken body, and the fact that taking away the pain (in this case by the palliative of shared communion) does not necessarily achieve healing. Healing is achieved only by dealing with the underlying problem.

In the case of interchurch families, however, the pain of being unable to share communion is not the point. The point on which all the discussion of shared communion turns is the more radical *serious (spiritual) need* felt by interchurch spouses who already share communion in baptism, communion in marriage, and, above all, communion in the intimate partnership of life, love, and faith. Their shared communion in all these facets of life, inchoate and imperfect as it may sometimes be, creates the inter-spousal need for the shared communion of Eucharist. When unfulfilled, that need certainly causes pain, as unfulfilled hunger causes pain. But it is the need not the pain, as it is the hunger not the pain, that must be satisfied. It is not palliative but authentic pastoral care that is required.

The second strategy the Bishops adopt is one found nowhere in the Code, the *Directory*, or any other Vatican document, the transposition of the exceptional case to the exceptional *unique occasion*, "an occasion which of its nature is unrepeatable, a 'one-off' situation which will not come again" (nos. 106, 109). Examples of such unique occasions are baptism, confirmation, first communion, ordination, and death. Though they have earlier employed the classical Catholic language about marriage, "a partnership of the whole of life (*consortium totius vitae*)," the Bishops betray no understanding of what that might mean in practice in the case of committed married couples, interchurch or same-church. The Christian "partnership of the whole of life" is not about unique and occasional events; it is about the seamless whole of life.

The *consortium totius vitae* language derives from ancient Roman definitions of marriage, like the one found in Justinian's *Digesta* (23.2.1), which controlled every discussion of marriage in the West. "Marriage is a union of a man and a woman, and a communion of the whole of life, a participation in divine and human law." The phrase *communion of the whole of life* (*consortium totius vitae*) is ambiguous, open to two separate but not separable interpretations. It can mean as long as life lasts ("until death do us part"), and then implies that marriage is a life-long covenant. It can mean everything that the spouses have ("all my worldly goods"), and then implies that nothing is left unshared between the spouses. Over the centuries in the West, the two meanings have been so interwoven that marriage is considered the union of a man and a woman embracing the sharing of all goods, material and spiritual, as long as life lasts.[13]

A marriage which lasts as long as life lasts is certainly a unique event in the modern world, but it is a diachronic unique event. Any couple journeying through life together can attest to the fact that marriage is an ongoing situation, much more than a one-off wedding, much, much more than a "one-off" baptism or ordination. A marriage is not a one-off wedding; it is, to repeat, a partnership of the whole of life. The "unique (one-off) occasion" confuses wedding and marriage, legal ceremony and diachronic, life-long partnership. If married people allow it to stand unchallenged, there can be no exceptional but ongoing sharing of communion, though the German, Australian, and South African norms, which I have not yet mentioned,[14] all interpret such ongoing exception as possible because of ongoing "serious (spiritual) need." Again, discontent, confusion, hurt, and anger, possibly damaging to both marital and ecclesial communion.

To conclude this section, I wish to return to the four conditions under which a Catholic minister may administer communion to a baptized person: the person is unable to have recourse to a minister of his own church, must ask for communion on his or her own initiative, must manifest Catholic faith in the sacrament, and must be properly disposed. Since these conditions are required of all Catholics for the reception of Eucharist, it is not surprising to find them required also of all non-Catholics. The requirement of proper disposition, required of all who approach Holy Communion, needs no comment; the other three do.

The South African Directory explicates the inability to have recourse to a minister of one's own church. This inability "need not be one that exists over a period of time but could arise out of the nature of the situation in which the petitioner finds himself or herself." They offer as example "when spouses in a mixed marriage attend a Eucharistic celebration together."[15] It is a good and obvious point. Again, it is not about a unique occasion, but about an exceptional but ongoing situation in which an interchurch wife and husband participate together in the Lord's Supper, have a serious need to share communion together, and cannot have recourse on that situation to his or her own minister. If all the other conditions are fulfilled, then on each and every situation, by authoritative interpretation of the norms, the non-Catholic spouse may share communion in the Catholic Church. It is worth noting that the first version of this South African Directory did not obtain Vatican approval and that Roman "suggestions" were incorporated into a revised version released in January 2000. The language of the second version is more precise, more accurately reflects the present discipline, but yields nothing on exceptional practice. What was in the original version explicitly continues to be in the new version implicitly.

This leads to the requirement that a person ask for communion on his or her own initiative? Why, we may ask, establish such a requirement? To respect individual conscience and, in these ecumenical times, to avoid all suspicion of proselytizing. In earlier times, it was common for some Churches to *invite* all baptized Christians who shared their faith in Eucharist to share communion with them. Others suggested this approach could be taken as an invitation to the person to disobey the rules of his or her own Church. When my mother, for instance, "invited" me to do the dishes, I always knew I was in trouble if I did not accept the "invitation." It is difficult to argue that I was completely free. It has become common, therefore, to replace *invite* with *welcome* to the Lord's table, as is done, for instance, in most Anglican Churches world-wide today. *Welcome* does not invite anyone to go beyond the rules of his or her own Church to share communion, but it does respect the consciences of those who believe they can and must go beyond those rules. The initiative is always with the person involved; there is no proselytism; all that is offered is Christian hospitality and welcome when a person has come to his or her own decision.

And what of the requirement to share Catholic faith in the sacrament? The German Bishops summarize that faith briefly: "The crucified and risen Lord Jesus Christ gives himself to us in person in the Eucharist as Giver and Gift in bread and wine and so builds up his Church" (n. 4). Three essential Catholic elements are contained in that summary: the connection between Eucharist and the paschal sacrifice of Christ, the real presence of Christ in Eucharist, and the connection between Eucharist and Church. Any Christian who accepts those three realities in faith is manifesting Catholic faith. Christoph Cardinal Schönborn, Archbishop of Vienna, has offered a short-form statement of the Catholic faith required for sharing communion in a Catholic Church. "Everyone who can in good conscience say 'Amen' to the Eucharistic prayer of the Catholic mass may take communion in a Catholic Church."[16] There are many Protestant Christians, and specifically many interchurch spouses, who can readily say "Amen" to that.

A final point is essential in this discussion. With respect to the requirement of sharing Catholic faith, the South African Directory, citing without acknowledgment Pope John XXIII's instruction to the Fathers at the opening of the Second Vatican Council,[17] notes the "crucial distinction between the substance of the faith and the way in which it is expressed."[18] Believing in the substance of defined Catholic Eucharistic *faith* is one thing; accepting the undefined Catholic *theology* which seeks to explain that faith is quite another. The British and Irish Bishops employ this distinction in their own way by explaining Catholic faith in the Eucharistic presence of Jesus without any reference to the word which was once the touchstone of Catholic explanation, *transubstantiation*, a word they relegate to a footnote.

Contrary to popular unwisdom, this word was never part of Catholic faith about Eucharist. The Council of Trent, frequently cited as defining *transubstantiation* as Catholic faith, simply asserted that the change that takes place in bread and wine is "most aptly (*aptissime*)" called transubstantiation.[19] The Bishops acknowledge the non-substantive nature of the word by relegating it to a brief footnote. The South African bishops insist that, when it comes to judging the substance of the faith that is present, "due cognizance must be taken of those ecumenical agreements that display the existence of a substantial agreement in faith." They offer as an example the agreement reached by the Anglican Roman Catholic International Commission (ARCIC) regarding the Eucharist and have no hesitation in stating that, "in the light of that agreement, members of the Anglican communion may be presumed to share the essentials of Eucharistic faith with us [Catholics]" (n. 6.3.8).

We began this section with a quotation from the Code of Canon Law, noting that it "sounds prescriptive." After our journey through the Code, the Roman *Directory on Ecumenism*, and various authoritative interpretations of both, it now appears as much permissive as prescriptive. "The purpose of every law in the Church," asserts Father Ladislas Örsy, one of the Church's most distinguished canon lawyers, "is to open the way for God's unbounded love." For that to happen, he notes, quoting Pope Paul VI, "we need not so much new legislation as a 'new attitude of mind.'"[20] That new attitude of mind, I suggest, needs to be ecumenical, it needs to realize that there are other Christians besides Catholics, that all of them are united to the Catholic Church through the bonds of baptism, and that some of them are further united to the Catholic Church through the bonds of sacramental, covenantal marriage to a Catholic.

The Catholic tradition about sacraments is that they not only signify grace but they also cause it instrumentally.[21] The aphorisms are well-known; sacraments "effect what they signify," "cause by signifying," are "efficacious signs of grace." The full and intimate communion achieved in marriage between a non–Catholic Christian and Catholic spouse, and the communion achieved directly and indirectly between them and the Catholic Church, can be signified in shared Eucharistic communion. More importantly, those two interconnected communions can also be "caused," effected, enhanced, deepened, and broadened in shared communion. Sacraments, the Second Vatican Council taught, "not only presuppose faith, but by words and objects they also nourish, strengthen, and express it."[22] That they do this, and do the same with love and communion, is a frequently ignored factor in the debate over shared communion. The Council taught, with its usual care that "the expression [or signification] of unity generally forbids common worship. Grace to be obtained sometimes commends it."[23] The overall argument of this section, and of authentic Episcopal teachers of the Church, is that the serious spiritual need experienced by interchurch couples is an exceptional but ongoing "sometimes" that commends it.

PASTORAL CONSIDERATIONS

When I explained to them that their growing communion in love had been long preceded by their baptismal communion in Christ, Sarah and Philip told me this was the first time they had ever heard that. This points to a serious problem that contemporary couples in interchurch marriages frequently have to face, namely, their ignorance of the beliefs not only of their partner's church but also of their own church. In a recent ecumenical group with Pastors from six different Christian denominations, I was horrified to hear Pastors admit openly they did not know much about the teachings of one another's churches. If Pastors do not know what their brothers and sisters in Christ believe, how will their congregations ever know? But Sarah and Philip, and every other interchurch couple, must know if they hope ever to grow together religiously in marriage. Each must understand not only her and his own tradition but also that of the other, so they can come to understand and appreciate one another as fully as possible and respond to their children's questions about their two churches. For this to happen, both need to be educated ecumenically, not just in the few weeks preceding their wedding but also throughout their married life together. As the incidence of interchurch marriage continues to increase, the demand for this kind of religious education will increase accordingly. Mutual ignorance is not a good basis for any marriage, least of all an interchurch marriage.

It is now widely recognized that theology cannot be done in isolation from the cultural context in which it is done; a contemporary theology of interchurch marriages cannot be done without hard scientific data about interchurch marriages. To obtain this data, a national, randomized study of same-church and interchurch marriages was conducted by the Center for Marriage and Family at Creighton University in 1997. Approximately one-third of all respondents were in interchurch relationships at the time of their engagement,[24] a significant percentage. Fewer interchurch than same-church respondents reported they had any marriage preparation and, of those who had marriage preparation, fewer interchurch reported it addressed religious issues related to their relationship and the raising of their children. In an earlier Center for Marriage and Family study of the impact of marriage preparation, interchurch couples, who randomly comprised 39% of that study population, complained that the marriage preparation offered to them minimally sought to prepare them for the challenges of a specifically interchurch marriage.[25]

Marriage preparation is a key learning moment, a natural rite of passage, in a couple's life. It can also be a key religious moment. In the culture of divorce which presently holds sway in the western world, the Churches are challenged to make interchurch couples, now a significant number of all marrying couples, a priority population. Only twenty-four percent of interchurch respondents who reported that religious issues were addressed in their marriage preparation reported having received specific material dealing with their different religious backgrounds. Those engaged in the marriage preparation of interchurch couples must do better to tailor their educational approach to the interchurch character of a couple's relationship. Programs should highlight religious faith and practice as an important part of marriage, as indeed it is,[26] and provide couples with strategies to deal with their religious differences. Such marriage preparation may be done best when the denominations of the two partners are both represented. The continuing and scandalous Christian problem is not that Christians of different denominations are falling in love and marrying in large numbers, but that the Christian Church continues to be rent into different, sometimes unseemly competing, denominations. Only when Protestant and Catholic congregations come to understand and truly respect each other's faith and teachings will they be in a position to provide the marriage preparation interchurch couples require for their marriage to be successful.

In his 1981 letter *On the Family*, Pope John Paul II urged the Catholic Church to "promote better and more intensive programs of marriage preparation to eliminate as far as possible the difficulties many married couples find themselves in, and even more to favor the establishing and maturing of successful marriages" (n. 66). All the churches, not just the Catholic Church, are challenged to promote marriage, to prepare young people for their marital vocation, and to do all in their power to uphold the permanence of marriage. They are specifically challenged by interchurch couples to create preparation programs that make diverse Christian faith and practice an ongoing part of their marriages. That this is an important challenge for the Churches is evident from the fact that the faith of parents is a critical factor in the religious education of their children. It is an even more critical factor in the religious education of interchurch children.

One other factor obliges the Churches to a greater commitment to interchurch marriages. The Creighton interchurch study joined a growing list of studies demonstrating that interchurch couples are at greater risk than same-church couples for marital instability. Same-church respondents had a statistically significant lower percentage of divorce (12.7 percent) than interchurch respondents (20.3 percent). Two things, however, are to be noted here. The first is that, though the percentage of divorce was higher for interchurch than for same-church respondents, both percentages were significantly lower than the percentages commonly reported for the study's time frame, that is, approximately 40 percent.[27] Since every respondent in the study identified with a Christian denomination at the time of engagement, the sample may be more religiously oriented than the general married population. Since religious affiliation is associated with a lower risk of divorce,[28] the greater religiousness of the sample may account for the lower percentage of divorce. There is another message here for marriage preparation providers: religion makes a difference in a marriage, even when there are two different churches involved, as there are in an interchurch marriage. Religion can be a bonder in a marriage, binding the spouses together as a coupled-We; or it can be divisive, keeping the spouses apart from the joint religious activities they ought to share. Here is another place where genuinely ecumenical marriage preparation can help.

The second thing of note in the divorce statistics above is that, when a long list of other variables were taken into account, being in an interchurch marriage per se was not a major predictor of marital instability. This suggests that it is not interchurch marriage per se that puts interchurch couples at greater risk for marital instability but other factors that may accompany the interchurch status of the marriage. Three such factors were found to be major: the religious differences between interchurch couples, the limited, joint religious activities they shared, and their families' approval or non-approval of their choice of spouse. If Churches wish to contribute to the improvement of the declining attractiveness, quality, and stability of marriage, these findings suggest three concrete areas where they might profitably concentrate their efforts in marriage preparation and enrichment programs: the managing of religious differences, the promotion of joint religious activities, and the managing of parental influence. Religious differences and joint religious activities are areas of focus for both same-church and interchurch couples, but they are especially critical for interchurch spouses since they tend to report greater religious differences and fewer joint religious activities.

Two other findings by the Creighton study should be noted by the Churches. The first is that interchurch respondents had, on average, lower religiosity scores than same-church respondents.[29] Religiosity, or level of religious attitude and practice, was assessed by a variety of factors: personal faith, personal church involvement, joint religious activities, sense of belonging to a local congregation, strength of denominational identity, religion as a strength in the marriage, emphasis on religion in raising children, commitment to Christ, and having participated in adult religious education. The *average* scores of interchurch respondents on all these items, both individually and collectively, were lower than the average scores of same-church respondents. I underscore *average* here to introduce an important caveat. Neither same-church nor interchurch individuals are homogeneous groups. Not all churches are alike, not all lawyers are alike, and not all interchurch or same-church individuals are alike. When respondents were divided into groups of high, medium, and low religiosity, there were inter-church individuals in the high religiosity group and same-church respondents in the low religiosity group, though only 15 percent of interchurch were in the high religiosity group compared to 40 percent of same-church respondents. It is evident, nevertheless, that the pervasiveness of religiosity differences show that Churches have much work to do to bind inter-church families to them.

The preceding conclusion is supported by the second item to be noted. Fewer interchurch than same-church respondents were very satisfied with the clergy with whom they came in contact. Satisfaction with clergy was related to clergy awareness of needs, sensitivity to people of other denominations, and commitment to helping interchurch couples deal with their marital and religious lives, and this suggests three areas where Churches and their clergy need to examine their attitudes and behaviors. Clergy need to welcome interchurch couples when they attend Church services or other activities, and they need to invite them to attend more than simply Church services.

The family is the first and most vital cell of any society; the Christian family is the first and most vital cell of the Church. The future of both society and Church, in John Paul's felicitous phrase, "passes through the family."[30] It is in the family, which Chrysostom urged spouses "to make a church"[31] and Augustine called "domestic church" and "little church,"[32] that children learn to value or not to value Christ, Christ's gospel, and Christ's church. If for no other reason than the honest religious nurture of their children, interchurch couples need to strive to understand and respect each other's faith as fully as possible. Only when they mutually understand and respect both faiths can their children consult both of them on both faiths, eliminating the divisive strategy of consulting mother on one faith and father on the other. Understanding and respecting the other spouse's faith might also ensure that nothing explicitly or implicitly derogatory about that faith will ever be said around the children. There are enough sources of potential conflict in marriage without multiplying them.

When we were talking about the children they hoped one day to have, Sarah surprised me with a sudden outburst of anger, blurting out that she would not agree to have Philip sign any document promising their children would be raised Catholics. Her father, she added, who was and still is a Lutheran, had to sign such a document when he married her Catholic mother and had been very angry at the Catholic Church, and her mother, ever since. She was astonished when I told her that neither she nor Philip would have to sign anything. When her parents were married in 1969, it was the law of the Catholic Church that such a written promise be given by the Protestant partner. It is no longer the law. In 1970, Pope Paul VI freed the non-Catholic partner of every declaration and promise concerning children born of the marriage. The Catholic partner is now required to promise *orally* "to do all in my power" to share her (his) faith with the children by having them baptized and raised as Catholics. This promise is simply an assurance given by the Catholic partner that she (he) understands her obligations, it makes explicit in a human fashion, *humano modo*, an obligation already existing by the fact that they are Catholics. Sarah retained a certain amount of anger and unease at the fact that such a promise is required, but both Pope Paul VI and Pope John Paul II have words to soothe her.

After having stated that the Catholic partner in an interchurch marriage is obligated "*as far as possible* to see to it that the children are baptized and brought up" in the Catholic faith, Paul VI added what the Catholic Church takes for granted, namely, the question of the children's faith is not a question for the Catholic partner alone. Their children's education is a responsibility of both parents, "both husband and wife are bound by that responsibility," Paul VI teaches, "and may by no means ignore it."[33] John Paul II reiterates the difficulty that arises here between interchurch couples and reaffirms the Catholic Church's modern celebration of religious freedom. This freedom could be violated, he teaches, "either by undue pressure to make the partner change his or her beliefs or by placing obstacles in the way of the free manifestation of these beliefs by religious practice."[34] John Paul here is simply repeating the Second Vatican Council's reaffirmation of an ancient Catholic teaching that "parents have the right to determine, in accordance with their own religious beliefs, the kind of religious education their children are to receive."[35]

The Catholic Church acknowledges the education of children is the right and duty of both parents and is not to be reserved to one parent over the other, even if that parent happens to be a Catholic. The promise now required of a *Catholic* partner in an interchurch marriage specifies that she (he) "*will do all in my power*" to ensure that children are raised Catholic. It does not, because it cannot, guarantee that they *will in fact* be raised Catholic. Every decision about children in every marriage, including the decision about their religious upbringing, is a decision, the Catholic Church teaches, for both parents, never for the Catholic parent alone. Why then, Sarah wanted to know, did she still have to promise to do all in her power to ensure the children were raised Catholic? So that both she and Philip would be fully conscious of her obligations as a Catholic, not so that Philip would be required to surrender his parental rights.

There is another group of people to be considered in the project of an interchurch marriage, namely, the parents of the prospective bride and groom. All of us derive from a family of origin and all of us are marked by that family, no matter how free and individual we believe we are. I cannot tell you how often I have heard the comment, "My parents would never approve me marrying a Catholic or Presbyterian or a whatever." This perceived tension between parents and an adult child frequently is one more source of stress in pre-marital decisions, and marriage, interchurch or not, is not a state that needs any more stressors in this modern age. Something must be done to reduce that stress before it becomes intolerable. Parents may have concerns about the differences between churches and, therefore, also between their child and the one she or he is marrying. They may fear loss of faith through change of religious affiliation or indifference. They may worry about where the wedding will take place, what church the couple will attend, what faith their grandchildren will be reared in. They may cause great irritation, both before and after the wedding, by trying to convert the spouse not of their denomination. They need a good talking with to dispel their doubts, their fears, their worries, their tensions.

Since they do not always keep up with change, parents frequently need to have explained to them the change in attitudes between the Christian Churches. They need to have explained to them the importance of their different faiths to the prospective spouses and that each not only loves the other but also respects the faith of the other. They need to know their children have already discussed the things that are bothering them, have come to mutually acceptable and respectful decisions about them, and want their parents to join them and support them in the project that is their marriage. Sarah told me that, when she told her parents she was going to marry Philip, they responded that she was facing a difficult task but they would do everything they could to be supportive. Philip, on the other hand, told me his father was very unhappy he was planning to marry a Catholic. Their very different levels of tension provided me with concrete evidence of the importance of embracing families of origin into the process of choosing an interchurch partner.

If there is one thing I have learned over the years of working with couples, it is that a stable and successful marriage takes time. It takes time for two individuals to come to know, appreciate, and respect one another; it takes time for them to come to value one another; it takes time for them to attain mutual love and communion; it takes time for them to become one body. If I was given the opportunity to offer one piece of advice to an interchurch, or any other, couple, it would be this: give your marriage time. I once asked a Missouri Synod Lutheran woman, who had been married to a Catholic for thirty-eight years, what was the most rewarding or most difficult time in her marriage. Her reply surprised me: "it depends what stage of marriage you are talking about." She explained that in the beginning of their marriage, she and her husband had wasted endless hours trying to convert one another, then had gradually come to understand and respect one another's commitment to religion, and had finally come to love one another precisely as *Lutheran* and *Catholic*. "I grew to understand," she said, "that loving John meant loving a Catholic." There is a wise message for all of us, and perhaps also for all of our churches, in that comment.

I have already cited Pope John Paul's 1982 comment to interchurch couples in York cathedral, "you live in your marriages the hopes and the difficulties of the path to Christian unity." His comment can stand as overall summary of everything that can currently be said about interchurch marriages. Marriage is always a time of hope and difficulty, a time of gift and challenge, a time when families lovingly unite or angrily divide. John Paul suggests that interchurch marriages mirror the hopes and the difficulties of the churches as they come to know, appreciate and respect one another as Catholic, as Presbyterian, as Baptist. I agree they do that and suggest they also do more. Interchurch couples who take the time required to know, appreciate, love and respect one another, and thus become one "coupled-We," not only mirror the paths of the churches as they too seek to become one but they also mark out the path by which the churches can reach their goal. The path is not an easy one, for it is not a path that leads necessarily to the conversion of one spouse to the denomination of the other, though about 43 percent of spouses in the Creighton study did change religious affiliation to become same-church. Rather, it is a path that leads to mutual respect, mutual appreciation, mutual trust, mutual love, and mutual unity in diversity. That is the only path that will lead to the fulfillment of Jesus' great prayer for humankind: "That they may all be one" (John 17:21). Oneness for all couples, all churches, all nations is a challenging goal; it is a goal that takes time. It is also a goal towards which many interchurch couples are now mapping out the way. "He who has ears to hear, let him hear" (Matt 11:15; Mark 4:9; Luke 8:8).

Abbreviations

AAS   *Acta Apostolicae Sedis* (Rome: Typis Polyglottis Vaticanis).

DH   *Dignitatis Humanae* (Declaration on Religious Freedom).

DS   *Enchiridion Symbolorum Definitionum et Declarationum de Rebus Fidei et Morum*, ed. H. Denzinger and A. Schoenmetzer (Fribourg: Herder, 1965).

FC   *Familiaris Consortio* (On the Family).

GS   *Gaudium et Spes* (Pastoral Constitution on the Church in the Modern World).

LG   *Lumen Gentium* (Dogmatic Constitution on the Church).

SC   S*acrosanctum Concilium* (Constitution on the Sacred Liturgy).

UR   *Unitatis Redintegratio.*

Notes

1. This essay is a revised version of one that appeared in *INTAMS Review* 6 (2000), 199–214.

2. Howard M. Bahr, "Religious Intermarriage and Divorce in Utah and the Mountain States," *Journal for the Scientific Study of Religion* 20 (1981), 251–61; Dean R. Hoge and Kathleen M. Ferry, *Empirical Research on Interfaith Marriage in America* (Washington, D.C.: United States Catholic Conference, 1981); Tim B. Heaton, Stan L. Albrecht, and Thomas K. Martin, "The Timing of Divorce," *Journal of Marriage and the Family* 47 (1985), 631–39; Tim B. Heaton and Edith L. Pratt, "The Effects of Religious Homogamy on Marital Satisfaction and Stability," *Journal of Family Issues* 11 (1990), 191–207; Larry L. Bumpass, Teresa Castro Martin, and James A. Sweet, *Background and Early Marital Factors* (Madison, Wisc.: Center for Demography and Ecology, 1989); Evelyn L. Lehrer and Carmel U. Chiswick, "Religion as a Determinant of Marital Stability," *Demography* 30 (1993), 385–404.

3. See George Kilcourse, *Double Belonging: Interchurch Families and Christian Unity* (New York: Paulist Press, 1992).

4. See Center for Marriage and Family, *Ministry to Interchurch Marriages: A National Study* (Omaha: Creighton University, 1999), 20–34.

5. *LG* 8.

6. John Paul II, *That All May Be One* n. 13.

7. *GS* 48.

8. "Eucharistic Sharing in Interchurch Marriages and Families: Guidelines from the German Bishops," *Journal of the Association of Interchurch Families* 6 (1998), 10.

9. "Eucharistic Sharing" n. 2. My emphasis.

10. Ibid., n. 5.

11. *Blessed and Broken: Pastoral Guidelines for Eucharistic Hospitality* (Brisbane: Archdiocese of Brisbane, 1995), 7.

12. *One Bread, One Body: A Teaching Document on the Eucharist in the Life of the Church and the Establishment of General Norms on Sacramental Sharing* (London: Catholic Truth Society, 1998).

13. See Michael G. Lawler, *Marriage and Sacrament: A Theology of Christian Marriage* (Collegeville: Liturgical Press, 1993), 7–12.

14. *Directory on Ecumenism for Southern Africa*. This document may be found at http://www.aifw.org/aif/confer/sadirecu.htm.

15. Ibid., n. 6.3.7.

16. *The Tablet*, October 16, 1999.

17. *AAS* 54 (1962), 792.

18. *Directory on Ecumenism for Southern Africa,* n. 6.3.8.

19. *DS* 1652.

20. Ladislas Örsy, "Interchurch Marriages and Reception of Eucharist," *America,* October 12, 1996, 19.

21. Peter Lombard, *Liber Sententiarum* 4, dist. 1, cap. 4; Thomas Aquinas, *Summa Theologica,* III, 60, 1; Michael G. Lawler, *Symbol and Sacrament: A Contemporary Sacramental Theology* (Omaha: Creighton University Press, 1995), 33–35; *LG* 1.

22. *SC* 59.

23. *UR* 8.

24. *Ministry to Interchurch Marriages,* 15.139. This percentage was replicated in the more recent Center for Marriage and Family study, *Time, Sex, and Money: The First Five Years of Marriage* (Omaha: Creighton University, 2000). See also *Catholic Engaged Encounter Renewal: 1999 Follow-Up Project* (Washington: Georgetown University, 1999), 3.

25. *Marriage Preparation in the Catholic Church: Getting it Right* (Omaha: Creighton University, 1995).

26. S. L. Albrecht, H. M. Bahr, and K. L. Goodman, *Divorce and Remarriage* (Westport, CT: Greenwood Press, 1983); Vaughn R. A. Call and Tim B. Heaton, "Religious Influence on Marital Stability," *Journal for the Scientific Study of Religion* 36 (1997), 382–392; Tim B. Heaton and Edith L. Pratt, "The Effects of Religious Homogamy on Marital Satisfaction and Stability," *Journal of Family Issues* 11 (1990), 191–207; Evelyn L. Lehrer and Carmel U. Chiswick, "Religion as a Determinant of Marital Stability," *Demography* 30 (1993), 385–404.

27. Theresa Castro Martin and Larry Bumpass, "Recent Trends in Marital Disruption," *Demography* 26 (1989), 37–51; Andrew J. Cherlin, *Marriage, Divorce, Remarriage* (Cambridge: Harvard University Press, 1992); Norval D. Glenn, *Closed Hearts, Closed Minds: The Textbook Story of Marriage* (New York: Institute for American Values, 1997).

28. See the works cited in Note 26.

29. This finding was replicated independently for a different sample population in Center for Marriage and Family, *Time, Sex, and Money.*

30. *FC* 75.

31. Chrysostom, *Homiliae in Genesim (Hom. Gen.)* 6, 2, *PG* 54.607.

32. Augustine, *Epistola 188,* 3, *PL* 33.849.

33. *Matrimonia Mixta, AAS* 62 (1970) 259.

34. *FC* 78.

35. *DH* 5.

Same-Sex Marriage

16. On the Impossibility of Same-Sex Marriage: A Review of Catholic Teaching

William E. May

This chapter first appeared in *National Catholic Bioethics Quarterly* 4 (2004).

Why are homosexual acts always gravely immoral, and why is it simply impossible for persons of the same sex to marry? To answer these questions I will first review the teaching of the Church. I will then argue that human persons, by choosing to engage in homosexual acts, harm the great goods of marriage. They also harm their own bodily capacity for the marital act as an act of self-giving which constitutes a communion of bodily persons—the good that Pope John Paul II calls the "nuptial meaning of the body."[1] Since this argument's intelligibility depends on a proper understanding of these great goods, I will prepare its way by considering the intrinsic goodness of marriage and the marital act. I will then conclude with an argument to show why it is simply not possible for persons of the same sex to marry.

RELEVANT MAGISTERIAL TEACHING

Magisterial teaching is found in the *Catechism of the Catholic Church* (1993), and three documents of the Congregation for the Doctrine of the Faith (CDF): the *Declaration on Certain Questions of Sexual*

Ethics, Persona humana (1975); the letter on *The Pastoral Care of the Homosexual Person* (1986); and *Considerations regarding Proposals to Give Legal Recognition to Unions between Homosexual Persons* (2003).

The Catechism of the Catholic Church

Number 2357 declares: "homosexuality refers to relations between men or between women who experience an exclusive or predominant sexual attraction toward persons of the same sex."[2] After noting that "its psychological genesis remains largely unexplained" it goes on to affirm that Sacred Scripture "presents homosexual acts as acts of grave depravity" (see Gn 19:1–29, Rom 1 :24–27, 1 Cor 6: 10, and 1 Tim 1:10): and that therefore "tradition has always declared that 'homosexual acts are intrinsically disordered'"[3] and "contrary to the natural law" insofar as "they close the sexual act to the gift of life" and "do not proceed from a genuine affective and sexual complementarity." Thus "under no circumstances can they be approved." Here the *Catechism* indicates reasons why homosexual acts are immoral; it does not develop these reasons or attempt to show their truth.

Number 2358 states that "the number of men and women who have deep-seated homosexual tendencies is not negligible" and that "for most of them it is a trial." Homosexual men and women "must be accepted with respect, compassion, and sensitivity. Every sign of unjust discrimination in their regard should be avoided. These persons are called to fulfill God's will in their lives and, if they are Christians, to unite to the sacrifice of the Lord's Cross the difficulties they may encounter from their condition."

Persona Humana (December 27, 1975)

This document distinguishes between persons whose homosexual inclination is "transitory" and homosexuals "who are definitively such because of some kind of innate instinct or a pathological condition judged to be incurable." Referring to persons in the second category, it notes that some claim that since the tendency is "natural," this "justifies...homosexual relations within a sincere communion of life and love analogous to marriage, insofar as such homosexuals feel incapable of enduring a solitary life." While maintaining that "homosexuals must certainly be treated with understanding and sustained in the hope of overcoming their personal difficulties," it affirms that "no pastoral method can be employed which would give moral justification to these acts...for according to the objective moral order, homosexual relations are acts which lack an essential and indispensable finality. In Sacred Scripture they are condemned as a serious depravity."[4]

This *Declaration* clearly distinguishes the homosexual orientation or inclination from homosexual acts, deeming the later absolutely immoral, but it made no effort to give arguments based on reason to show why such acts are intrinsically immoral.

The Pastoral Care of the Homosexual Person (October 1, 1986)

This document provides a rather comprehensive examination of the issue. I will focus attention on the following topics considered in it: 1) mistaken interpretations of the *Declaration on Certain Questions of Sexual Ethics, Persona humana*; 2) erroneous interpretations of Scripture and their correction; 3) further bases for the Church's teaching; 4) a critique of one argument to justify homosexual acts; and 5) the homosexual's vocation.

MISTAKEN INTERPRETATIONS OF PERSONA HUMANA

Persona humana had distinguished between the homosexual condition and homosexual acts. But *Pastoral Care* notes that in the years following "an overly benign interpretation was given to the homosexual condition itself, some going so far as to call it neutral, or even good."[5] To correct this, *Pastoral Care* affirms that the homosexual inclination. while not a sin, "is a more or less strong tendency ordered toward an intrinsic moral evil; and thus the inclination itself *must be seen as an objective disorder*" (n. 3. emphasis added). This assertion elicited very strong opposition and charges of homophobia. I suggest that we might consider the inclination as a specific manifestation of the concupiscence that comes from sin (original sin) and leads to sin but is itself not sin,[6] just as are inclinations to be violent or to drink to excess.[7]

ERRONEOUS INTERPRETATIONS OF SCRIPTURE AND THEIR CORRECTION

Pastoral Care identifies as one of the major causes of current confusion "a new exegesis of Sacred Scripture which claims variously that Scripture has nothing to say on the subject of homosexuality, or that it somehow tacitly approves of it, or that all of its moral injunctions are so culture-bound that they are no longer applicable to contemporary life."[8] *Pastoral Care* declares that "these views are gravely erroneous" (n. 4). In correcting these views, *Pastoral Care* notes that, although many things have changed since the time the Scriptures were written,

> there is nonetheless a clear consistency within the Scriptures themselves on the moral issue of homosexual behavior. The Church's doctrine regarding this issue is thus based not on isolated phrases for facile theological argument, but on the solid foundation of a constant biblical testimony.

Moreover, it is "essential to recognize that the Scriptures are not properly understood when they are interpreted in a way which contradicts the Church's living Tradition. To be correct, the interpretation of Scripture must be in substantial accord with that Tradition" (n. 5). *Pastoral Care* then cites an important passage of Vatican II's *Dogmatic Constitution on Divine Revelation, Dei Verbum*, number 10, affirming that "sacred Tradition, Sacred Scripture, and the magisterium of the Church are so connected and associated that one of them cannot stand without the others" (n. 5). *This is a key hermeneutical principle in Catholic theology.* The Bible is the Church's book: thus the Church has the competence to give an authoritative interpretation of Scripture, and in doing so the Church takes seriously into account the way that Scripture has been understood throughout the Catholic tradition.

Pastoral Care then indicates the solid bases, within Scripture, for the Church's teaching: a) the creation of man as male and female, meant to cooperate with God in giving life to new human persons (Gn 1); b) the fall and resulting concupiscence (Gn 3); c) the judgments on homosexual behavior found in the Sodom and Gomorrah story (Gn 19), Leviticus 18:22, and Leviticus 20:13, the teaching of Paul in 1 Corinthians 6:9 and Romans 1:18–32, and finally the significance of 1 Timothy 1:10.[9] It seems to me that *Pastoral Care* offers a good presentation of the condemnation of homosexual behavior in Scripture, but obviously arguments based on Scripture are not very persuasive to persons who do not accept its authority. Consequently, *Pastoral Care* also offers other bases for the Church's teaching.

FURTHER BASES FOR THE CHURCH'S TEACHING

Pastoral Care affirms that the Church's teaching on homosexual acts is rooted in God's plan regarding the life-giving and loving union of man and woman in marriage. This entails that "only in the marital relationship [is] the use of the sexual faculty...morally good" (n. 7). From this it follows that

> to choose someone of the same sex for one's sexual activity
> is to annul the rich symbolism and meaning, not to mention
> the goals, of the Creator's sexual design. Homosexual activ-
> ity is not a complementary union, able to transmit life; and so
> it thwarts the call to a life of that form of self-giving which
> the Gospel says is the essence of Christian living.

Moreover, like every moral disorder, "homosexual activity prevents one's own fulfillment and happiness by acting contrary to the creative wisdom of God" (n. 7). This section of *Pastoral Care* sketches the rational grounds that can be used to show why homosexual acts are not morally good; I hope to develop these grounds below.

CRITIQUE OF AN ARGUMENT
JUSTIFYING HOMOSEXUAL ACTS

Pastoral Care notes that one common argument given to justify homosexual acts is that homosexually oriented persons have no other choice than to act in a homosexual way because of their lack of freedom

(n. 11). *Pastoral Care* rejects this position because it is rooted in "the unfounded and demeaning assumption that the sexual behavior of homosexual persons is always and totally compulsive and therefore inculpable" (n. 11). It insists that homosexual persons have the freedom to choose whether or not to engage in homosexual acts; this pertains to the dignity of the homosexual person.[10]

THE VOCATION OF THE HOMOSEXUAL

Pastoral Care maintains that homosexual persons "are called to enact the will of God in their life by joining whatever sufferings and difficulties they experience by virtue of their condition to the sacrifice of the Lord's cross." Self-denial is not pointless; "the cross is denial of self, but in service to the will of God Himself, who makes life come from death and empowers those who trust in Him to practice virtue in place of vice" (n. 12). Homosexual persons, like all of us, are called to chastity.[11]

Considerations regarding Proposals to Give Legal Recognition to Unions between Homosexual Persons (June 3, 2003)

These considerations, the Congregation states, "do not contain new doctrinal elements" but

> seek rather to reiterate the essential points on this question and provide arguments from reason which could be used by bishops in preparing more specific interventions....The present considerations are also intended to give direction to Catholic politicians by indicating the approaches to proposed legislation in this area which would be consistent with Christian conscience.[12]

Part I (nn. 2–4) summarizes the nature of marriage and its inalienable characteristics as a lifelong union of one man and one woman open to the gift of children, a union elevated by Christ to the dignity of a sacrament. The CDF declares: "there are absolutely no grounds for considering homosexual unions to be in any way similar or even remotely analogous to God's plan for marriage and family. Marriage is holy, while homosexual acts go against the natural moral law...[and] 'close the sexual act to the gift of life. They do not proceed from a genuine affective and sexual complementarity'" (n. 4, citing *Catechism of the Catholic Church*, n. 2357).

Part II (n. 5) considers positions on the problem of homosexual union—toleration, advocating legal recognition, giving such unions legal equivalence to marriage along with the legal possibility of adopting children. If the government's policy is *de facto* tolerance with no explicit recognition of homosexual unions, moral conscience "requires that...Christians give witness to the whole moral truth, which is contradicted both by approval of homosexual acts and unjust discrimination against homosexual persons." Prudent actions that can be effective include

> unmasking the way in which such tolerance might be exploited or used in the service of ideology; stating clearly the immoral nature of these unions, reminding the government of the need to contain the phenomenon within certain limits so as to safeguard public morality and, above all, to avoid exposing young people to erroneous ideas about sexuality and marriage.

If such unions have been given legal recognition or the rights and status of marriage, "clear and emphatic opposition is a duty."

Part III (nn. 6–9) sets forth arguments from reason against legal recognition of homosexual unions. First, in an argument *from the order of right reason*, the CDF answers those who ask how a law can be contrary to the common good if it simply gives legal recognition to a *de facto* reality which does not seem to cause injustice to anyone. Its reply:

> One needs first to reflect on the difference between homosexual behavior as a private phenomenon and the same behavior as a relationship in society, foreseen and approved by law, to the point where it becomes one of the institutions in the legal structure. The second phenomenon is not only more serious, but also assumes a more wide-reaching and profound influence, and would result in changes to the entire organization of

society, contrary to the common good....Legal recognition of homosexual unions would obscure certain basic moral values and cause a devaluation of the institution of marriage. (n. 6)

Considering the matter *from the biological and anthropological order* the CDF says that homosexual unions are

totally lacking in the biological and anthropological elements of marriage and family which would be the basis, on the level of reason, for granting them legal recognition. Such unions are not able to contribute in a proper way to the procreation and survival of the human race....

Homosexual unions are also totally lacking in the conjugal dimension, which represents the human and ordered form of sexuality. Sexual relations are human when and insofar as they express and promote the mutual assistance of the sexes in marriage and are open to the transmission of new life....The absence of sexual complementarity in these unions creates obstacles in the normal development of children who would be placed in care of such persons. They would be deprived of the experience of either fatherhood or motherhood. Allowing children to be adopted by persons living in such unions would actually mean doing violence to these children, in the sense that their condition of dependency would be used to place them in an environment that is not conducive to their full human development. (n. 7)

Here the CDF has clearly indicated *reasons* why homosexual acts are immoral and why homosexual unions ought not to be equated with marriage. The reasons given, however, need to be explained more thoroughly.

Considering the issue *from the social order*, the CDF holds that society owes its continued survival to the family founded on marriage, and that the inevitable consequence of legalizing "homosexual unions would be the redefinition of marriage, which would become...an institution devoid of essential reference to factors linked to heterosexuality; for example, procreation and raising children....The concept of marriage would undergo a radical transformation, with grave detriment to the common good" (n. 8).

Considering the issue *from the legal order* the CDF argues that married couples, because they ensure the succession of generations, are "eminently within the public interest [and therefore] civil law grants their marriages institutional recognition. Homosexual unions, on the other hand, do not need specific attention from the legal standpoint since they do not exercise this function for the common good" (n. 9). It seems to me that this is a very important argument against regarding homosexual unions as marriages; however, it needs to be more fully explained and developed.

Then, in a very important passage, the CDF declares:

> Nor is the argument valid according to which legal recognition of homosexual unions is necessary to avoid situations in which cohabiting homosexual persons, simply because they live together, might be deprived of real recognition of their rights as persons and citizens. *In reality, they can always make use of the provisions of law...to protect their rights in matters of common interest.* It would be gravely unjust to sacrifice the common good and just laws on the family *in order to protect personal goods that can and must be guaranteed in ways that do not harm the body of society.* (n. 9, emphasis added)

This passage is most important. It recognizes that it is morally permissible to concede to households formed by individuals who are indeed of the same sex (male or female) various civil rights *not* because of any *sexual relationship* but rather on the basis that they form a valid kind of economic/social household built on friendship, e.g., two widows or widowers, a son and his elderly widowed father, a daughter and her elderly widowed mother, etc., who choose to live together for purposes of friendship and of economy. It is worth noting that the archdiocese of San Francisco and the city of San Francisco made an arrangement of this kind to meet the *just* demands of nontraditional, i.e., nonfamilial, households, in 1997, when some sought to coerce the archdiocese of San Francisco to grant full spousal benefits to same-sex domestic partners of diocesan employees whose households were based on the *sexual orientation and sexual relationship* of its members. This effort was successfully thwarted by recognizing the just civil demands of households formed by persons of the same sex for purposes of economic stability and common friendship and not for the purpose of engaging in non-marital sexual acts.[13]

Part IV (n. 10) takes up the positions of Catholic politicians regarding legislation in favor of homosexual unions. I omit this part because it does not substantively relate to the morality of homosexual acts.

WHY ARE HOMOSEXUAL ACTS ALWAYS GRAVELY IMMORAL?[14]

Centuries ago, St. Thomas declared: "We offend God only by acting contrary to our own good,"[15] and Pope John Paul II instructs us that "the commandments of which Jesus reminds the young man are meant to safeguard the good of the person, the image of God, by protecting his *goods*."[16] From this it follows that if homosexual acts are gravely immoral they are so because they harm the *good*(s) of human persons. But what good or goods? As I noted in the introduction to this chapter, the goods harmed by such acts are the goods of marriage and of the body's capacity for the marital act as an act of self-giving which constitutes a communion of bodily persons—what Pope John Paul II calls the "nuptial meaning of the body." First, however, it is necessary to show that the marriage of a man and a woman is intrinsically, not instrumentally, good and that the marital act, whereby they give themselves to one another, honors this good and the "nuptial meaning of the body."

Marriage, an Intrinsic, Fundamental Human Good, and the Marital Act

St. Augustine explicitly held that marriage is only an *instrumental* good, in the service of the procreation and education of children so that the intrinsic, noninstrumental good of friendship of fathers with their sons will be realized by the propagation of the race and the intrinsic good of inner integration be realized by "remedying" the disordered desires of concupiscence. Had Augustine integrated the natural or companionship of the spouses into his understanding of marriage, he would, as John Finnis has noted, have recognized that in both sterile and fertile marriages "the communion, companionship, *societas* and *amicitia* of the spouses—their being married—is the very good of marriage and is an intrinsic, basic human good, not merely instrumental to any other good."[17] Vatican Council II clearly indicated this great truth, for it teaches that "God did not create the human person as a solitary," and after citing "male and female he created them" (Gn 1.27), explains that the two sexes' "companionship produces the primary form of interpersonal communion. For, by their innermost nature human beings are social, and unless they relate themselves to one another they can neither live nor develop their gifts."[18] As Germain Grisez says, in commenting on this passage, "This gloss on Genesis 1.27 implies that marriage is not merely an instrumental good: the companionship of man and woman belongs to humankind as image of God and is the primary form of one of the essential, intrinsic aspects of human fulfillment."[19] That marriage is a basic good is central to the teaching of Pope John Paul II. In *Familiaris consortio*, number 11, he identifies marriage as one way of realizing the human vocation to love and in *Mulieris dignitatem*, number 7, declares that the *communio personarum* of husband and wife is an image of the Trinitarian *communio personarum* of Father, Son, and Holy Spirit. In *Veritatis splendor*, he explicitly refers to "the communion of persons in marriage" as a fundamental human good in number 13, and it is evident that he includes this basic good among the other goods of the human person that must be respected and honored in every choice (nn. 48, 50, and 67). Moreover, as Finnis points out,

> The Church often speaks of the goods of marriage: 1) loving friendship between wife and husband; and 2) procreating and educating any children who may be conceived from the spouses' marital intercourse [see e.g., *Catechism of the Catholic Church*, nn. 2201, 2249]. They are interdependent goods....Being interdependent, these goods can also be properly described as two aspects of a single, basic human good, the good of marriage itself. In the Church's most explicit teaching on foundations of its moral doctrine [*Veritatis splendor*] in which Pope John Paul II points to the basic

> human goods as the first principles of the natural moral law,
> this single though basic good is called: "the communion of
> persons in marriage" [n. 13].[20]

Marriage is consummated by the marital act, which is far more than a *genital* act between a man and a woman who *happen* to be married. Men and women are capable of having *genital* sex because they have genitals, and thus fornicators and adulterers are able to have genital sex. But fornicators and adulterers are not capable of engaging in a conjugal or marital act precisely because they are not married, and it is marriage that capacitates spouses to engage in the marital act, i.e., to do what spouses are supposed to do, to become literally one flesh in an act whereby the man personally *gives* himself to his wife by entering into her body person, and in doing so *receives* her and whereby the woman personally *receives* her husband into her body person and by doing so gives herself to him. The husband gives himself to his wife in a receiving way, while she receives him in a giving way. The conjugal or marital act actually *unites* two persons who have made each other irreplaceable, nonsubstitutable, and nondisposable in their lives by giving themselves to one another and receiving one another in marriage. The marital act, consequently, is the kind or type of act intrinsically fit or apt both for communicating conjugal love and for receiving the gift of life if the couple is fertile.[21]

In short, marriage, considered as a two-in-one-flesh communion of persons consummated and actualized by the marital act, which is an act open to the *blessings* or *goods* of marriage—faithful conjugal love and the gift of children—is an intrinsic or basic human good and as such provides a noninstrumental reason for spouses to engage in the marital act.[22]

This act is and remains a *procreative* or *reproductive* kind of act even if the spouses, because of nonbehavioral factors over which they have no control, for example, the temporary or permanent sterility of one of the spouses, are not able to generate human life in a freely chosen marital act. Their act remains the kind of bodily act that alone is "apt" for generating human life. As Robert George and Gerard V. Bradley note in answer to a homosexual apologist's question regarding the point of sex in an infertile marriage:

the intrinsic point of sex in any marriage, fertile or not, is…the basic good of marriage itself, considered as a two-in-one-flesh communion of persons that is consummated and actualized by acts of the reproductive type. Such acts alone among sexual acts can be truly unitive, and thus marital; and marital acts, thus understood, have their intelligibility and value intrinsically, and not merely by virtue of their capacity to facilitate the realization of other goods.[23]

Pope John Paul II has written perceptively of the "language of the body" and the way in which the marital act speaks this language. His thought on this matter is nicely summarized in the following passage from *Donum vitae*, the 1987 Vatican *Instruction On Respect for Human Life in Its Origins and on the Dignity of Human Procreation*:

Spouses mutually express their personal love in the "language of the body," which clearly involves both "spousal meanings" and parental ones. The conjugal act by which the couple mutually expresses their self-gift at the same time expresses openness to the gift of life. It is an act that is inseparably corporal and spiritual. It is in their bodies and through their bodies that the spouses consummate their marriage and are able to become father and mother.[24]

The following passage from Finnis can serve to bring this section to a close:

The union of the reproductive organs of husband and wife really unites them biologically (and their biological reality is part of, not merely an instrument of, their *personal* reality); reproduction is one function and so, in respect of that function, the spouses are indeed one reality, and their sexual union can *actualize* and allow them to *experience* their *real common good—their marriage* with the two goods, parenthood and friendship, which (leaving aside the order of grace) are the parts of its wholeness as an intelligible common good even if, independently of what the spouses will, their capacity for biological parenthood will not be fulfilled by that act of genital union.[25]

Homosexual Acts Damage the Nuptial Meaning of the Body

Homosexual couples can surely live in a committed relationship with mutual affection and express this affection in ways appropriate for any friendship. Moreover, as we saw in reviewing the Church's teaching, such couples, as forming an economic unit, have a just claim to benefits that can be granted to other same-sex couples living together, for instance, widows or widowers. Such couples might claim that they cannot satisfy their sexual urges and natural inclination toward intimate union in any more adequate way than by establishing a more or less permanent relationship that includes sexual intimacy, and that one *appropriate* way *for them* to express their affection and friendship is to engage in homosexual acts.[26] Homosexual acts in the strict sense are anal or oral intercourse willingly engaged in by two males, with the intention that at least one of them achieve satisfaction by ejaculating within the other's body. Such acts are acts of sodomy or homosexual intercourse. A lesbian couple can, without engaging in intercourse, stimulate each other to orgasm, and such intentional acts can also be regarded as homosexual in a broader sense. And both male and female homosexuals may choose to masturbate each other as ways of expressing their affection. But are such acts the right means to choose to do so? Are they truly "appropriate"? To settle whether they are requires us to examine these acts and what they do to the persons choosing them.

Before giving a moral analysis of these acts it seems to me helpful to describe in some detail the physiology of one specific homosexual act, namely, anal intercourse, the sine qua non for many male homosexuals.[27] However, human physiology, as John R. Diggs, Jr., M.D., points out,

> makes it clear that the body was not designed to accommodate this activity. The rectum is significantly different from the vagina with regard to suitability for penetration by a penis. The vagina has lubricants and is supported by a net-

work of muscles. It is composed of a mucus membrane with a multi-layer stratified squamous epithelium that allows it to endure friction without damage and to resist the immunological actions caused by semen and sperm. In comparison, the anus is a delicate mechanism of small muscles that comprise an "exit-only" passage. With repeated trauma, friction, and stretching, the sphincter loses its tone and its ability to maintain a tight seal. Consequently, anal intercourse leads to leakage of fecal material that can easily become chronic. The potential for injury is exacerbated by the fact that the intestine has only a single layer of cells separating it from highly vascular tissue, that is, blood. Therefore, any organisms that are introduced into the rectum have a much easier time establishing a foothold for infection than they would in a vagina....Furthermore, ejaculate has components that are immunosuppressive. In the course of ordinary reproductive physiology, this allows the sperm to evade the immune defenses of the female....The end result is that the fragility of the anus and rectum, along with the immunosuppressive effect of ejaculate, make anal-genital intercourse a most efficient manner of transmitting HIV and other infections. The list of diseases found with extraordinary frequency among male homosexual practitioners as a result of anal intercourse is alarming: anal cancer, chlamydia trachomatis, cryptosporidium, giardia lamblia, herpes simplex virus, human immunodeficiency virus, human papilloma virus, isospora belli, microsporidia, gonorrhea, viral hepatitis types B and C, syphilis.[28]

I thought it relevant to cite this long passage because it gives reasons to show that anal sex is hardly an appropriate way to express friendship. However, it does not get to the heart of the reason why the choice to engage in homosexual acts damages the nuptial meaning of the body and the good of marriage. I will now offer an argument to show this.

Patrick Lee and Robert George articulate a claim central to this argument:

if one chooses to actualize one's bodily, sexual power as an extrinsic means of producing an effect in one's consciousness, then one separates in one's choice oneself as bodily from oneself as an intentional agent. The content of such a choice includes the disintegration attendant upon a reduction of one's bodily self to the level of an extrinsic instrument.[29]

When one treats one's body as *intrinsic* to one's self, there is a unitary activity, and various bodily actions share in this activity since they are not directed to an extrinsic purpose. In activity of this kind one is freely choosing to instantiate real goods, e.g., the good of play in basketball or the good of health in exercising or the good of friendship in writing a letter or in conversing, and one's efforts to realize those goods involve, where appropriate, one's bodily activity so that, as Finnis says, "that activity is as much the constitutive subject of what one does as one's act of choice is."[30] Thus in the *marital act*, spouses freely choose to instantiate their communion of persons in one flesh open to the gift of life in and through an act in which their *bodily activity* is as much the constitutive subject of what they are doing as is their act of choice.

However, in sodomitical and other kinds of homosexual behavior, the joining of the bodies of the persons of the same sex is not such that they become one complete organism. The bodies of persons engaging in homosexual acts do not contribute to a *communio personarum*. Although they may choose such acts as *means* of experiencing personal intimacy, the resulting experience cannot be the experience of any real unity between them. Rather, as Grisez has put it so accurately,

each one's experience of intimacy is private and incommunicable, and is no more a common good than is the mere experience of sexual arousal and orgasm. Therefore, the choice to engage in sodomy for the sake of that experience of intimacy in no way contributes to the partners' real common good as committed friends.[31]

Thus persons choosing homosexual acts choose to use their own and each other's bodies to provide subjective satisfactions, states of consciousness. Thus the body becomes an instrument used, and the conscious subject the user. The conscious self is alienated from the body, resulting in an existential dualism between the body and the conscious subject, i.e., "a division between the two insofar as they are coprinciples of oneself considered as an integrated, acting, sexual person."[32] Therefore, to choose to engage in homosexual acts is to choose a specific kind of self-disintegrity. The self-integration damaged in this way is the unity of the acting person as conscious subject and sexually functioning body. But, as Grisez continues, "this specific aspect of self-integration...is precisely the aspect necessary so that the bodily union of sexual intercourse will be a communion of persons, as marital intercourse is." Therefore, homosexual acts damage the body's capacity for the marital act as an act of self-giving which constitutes a communion of bodily persons, or in other words, the "nuptial meaning of the body."[33]

Homosexual acts, consequently, damage the good of the body's capacity for self-gift, its nuptial meaning. Such acts, moreover, are ones in which those engaging in them do not even encounter each other face-to-face, a uniquely *human* way of copulating, but rather in a way characteristic of subhuman animals. Because homosexual acts damage the nuptial meaning of the body, they also damage the good of marriage itself. They do so because the great good of marriage requires that spouses recognize that their bodies are integral to their being as persons and that it is precisely their sexual complementarity, revealed in their bodily differences, that makes it possible for the man to "give himself in a receiving way" to his wife in the marital act and for his wife "to receive him in a giving way" in this same act, an act having two common subjects.

AN ARGUMENT AGAINST SAME-SEX MARRIAGE

Persons of the same sex cannot marry because they cannot do what married couples can do, i.e., to consummate their union by a bodily act in which they become the common subjects of an act that, precisely as human behavior, is eminently fit both for the communication of spousal love and for the generation of new human life.

The spousal union goes beyond biological union, but biology is an essential component. By their marital acts, husband and wife express in a profound way their whole married life together: two-in-one-flesh. When those acts bear the fruit of children, the latter literally *issue from* the marital union: they embody this union and extend it in space and time.

Genital coition is the *only* bodily act intrinsically capable of generating new human life. Kissing, holding hands, fondling, and anal-oral sex cannot generate children. They can be generated through acts of fornication and adultery, but it is not good for children to be begotten in this way. For millennia every human culture has recognized the bond of linking sex, marriage, and the generation of human life, and frowned on begetting children out of wedlock. Although many today think it fitting to generate children outside of marriage, the tragic situations accompanying such phenomena, such as fatherless children, undisciplined youth, and abandoned women show the shallowness of such thinking.

Our society, as any society, can survive only if new human persons are generated. The marital union of a man and a woman who have given themselves unreservedly in marriage and who can consummate their union in a beautiful bodily act of conjugal intercourse is the best place to serve as a "home" for new human life, as the "place" where this life can take root and grow in love and service to others. A marriage of this kind contributes uniquely to the common good. It merits legal protection. Same-sex unions are not the same and sadly merely mimic the real thing. They can in no way be regarded as marriages in the true sense.

Notes

1. On the nuptial meaning of the body see Pope John Paul II, *The Theology of the Body: Human Love in the Divine Plan* (Boston: Pauline Books & Media, 1997), "The Nuptial Meaning of the Body" (January 9, 1980), 60–63.

2. *Catechism of the Catholic Church*, trans. United States Conference of Bishops (Vatican City: Libreria Editrice Vaticana, 1994).

3. See CDF, *Persona humana*, n. 8.

4. *L'Osservatore Romano* (English), January 22, 1976, n. 8.

5. *L'Osservatore Romano* (English), November 10, 1986, n. 3.

6. See H. Denzinger and A. Schönmetzer, eds., *Enchiridion Symbolorum*, 32nd ed. (Barcelona: Herder, 1963), Council of Trent, n. 1515.

7. On this see John Finnis, "'An Intrinsically Disordered Inclination,'" in *Same-Sex Attraction: A Parents' Guide*, eds. John F. Harvey, O.S.F.S., and Gerard V. Bradley (South Bend, IN: St. Augustine's Press, 2003), 89–99.

8. N. 4. The following works illustrate these views: *Human Sexuality: New Directions in American Catholic Thought*, eds. Anthony Kosnik et al. (New York: Paulist Press, 1977), 186–196; Daniel Maguire, "The Morality of Homosexual Marriage," in *Challenge to Love: Gay and Lesbian Catholics in the Church*, ed. Robert Nugent (New York: Crossroads, 1983); John J. McNeill, *The Church and the Homosexual* (Kansas City: Sheed, Andrews, and McMeel, 1976), 37–66.

9. N. 6. Sound studies of the biblical teaching on the immorality of homosexual acts are the following: Silverio Zedda, S.J., *Relativo e assoluto nella morale di San Paolo* (Brescia: Paideia Editrice, 1984), ch. 5, on the teaching of St. Paul; Manuel Miguens, O.F.M., "Biblical Thoughts on 'Human Sexuality,'" in *Human Sexuality in Our Time*, ed. George A. Kelly (Boston: Daughters of St. Paul, 1979), 102–119; Joseph Jensen, O.S.B., "The Relevance of the Old Testament," in *Dimensions of Human Sexuality*, ed. Denis Doherty (New York: Doubleday, 1979), ch. 1; Kevin E. Miller, "Scripture and Homosexuality," in *Same-Sex Attraction*, 53–74.

10. N. 6. The argument repudiated is in essence the one used frequently by Charles E. Curran to justify homosexual acts under certain conditions. See his "Dialogue with the Homophile Movement: The Morality of Homosexuality," in his *Catholic Moral Theology in Dialogue* (Notre Dame, IN: Fides, 1972), 184–219.

11. N. 12. John F. Harvey, O.S.F.S., has done wonderful work in developing a program, modeled in some ways on Alcoholics Anonymous, to help homosexually oriented persons live chaste lives. He founded the spiritual support group Courage to achieve this goal. He describes Courage and its work in his books *The Homosexual Person* (San Francisco: Ignatius Press, 1987), 137–161, and *The Truth about Homosexuality: The Cry of the Faithful* (San Francisco: Ignatius Press, 1996), 19–30.

12. *L'Osservatore Romano* (English), August 6, 2003, n. 1.

13. For this, see "Archdiocese, City of San Francisco Reach Accord on Employee Benefits," February 10, 1997, http://www.cwnews.com/news/viewstory.cfm?recnum=4248.

14. I acknowledge here my indebtedness to the work of Gemain Grisez, John Finnis, Robert George, Gerard V. Bradley, and Patrick Lee on this matter. See Grisez's *The Way of the Lord Jesus*, vol. 2, *Living a Christian Life* (Quincy, IL: Franciscan Press, 1993), 648–656; John Finnis, "Personal Integrity, Sexual Morality, and Responsible Parenthood," *Anthropos: Rivista sulla Persona e la Famiglia* 1.1 (1985): 43–55: idem, "Law, Morality, and 'Sexual Orientation,'" *Notre Dame Law Review* 69 (1994): 1049–1076; idem, "The Good of Marriage and the Morality of Sexual Relations: Some Philosophical and Historical Observations," *American Journal of Jurisprudence* 42 (1997): 97–134: Robert George and Gerard V. Bradley, "Marriage and the Liberal Imagination," *Georgetown Law Journal* 84 (1995): 301–320: Robert George and Patrick Lee, "What

Sex Can Be: Self-Alienation, Illusion, or One-Flesh Union," *American Journal of Jurisprudence* 42 (1997): 135–150.

15. St. Thomas Aquinas, *Summa contra gentiles*, bk. 3, ch. 122: "Non enim Deus a nobis offenditur nisi ex eo quod contra nostrum bonum agimus."

16. *Veritatis splendor* (Boston: Pauline Books & Media, 1993), n. 13, original emphasis.

17. Finnis, "Law, Morality, and 'Sexual Orientation,'" 1064–1065.

18. Vatican Council II, *Pastoral Constitution on the Church in the Modern World, Gaudium et spes*, n. 12. My translation.

19. See Grisez, *Living a Christian Life*, 557 note 5. Moreover, *Gaudium et spes* speaks of marriage as "a community of love" (n. 48) and indeed as an "intimate community of conjugal life and love" (n. 49). On marriage as a fundamental or basic good see ibid., 553–569.

20. Finnis, "'An Intrinsically Disordered Inclination,'" 93. In a note to this passage, 99 note 20, Finnis adds: "St. Thomas Aquinas long ago identified this as a single though complex primary (basic) human good": see John Finnis, *Aquinas: Moral, Political, and Legal Theory* (Oxford: Oxford University Presss, 1998), 82, 143.

21. On this see my essays, "La '*communio personarum*' e l'atto coniugale," in *Morale coniugale e sacramento della Penitenza: Riflessioni sul "Vademecum per i confessori"* (Città del Vaticano: Libreria Editrice Vaticana, 1998), 135–150; and "Marriage and the Complementarity of Male and Female," in my *Marriage: The Rock on Which the Family Is Built* (San Francisco: Ignatius Press, 1995), 48–49. See also Robert Joyce, *Human Sexual Ecology: A Philosophy of Man and Woman* (Washington, D.C.: University Press of America, 1980), 63–85. It is precisely because the conjugal or marital act is, *qua* marital, open to the blessings of marriage that Vatican Council II declared: "Married love is uniquely expressed and perfected by the exercise of the acts proper to marriage. Hence the acts in marriage by which the intimate and chaste union of the spouses takes place are noble and honorable; the truly human performance of these acts fosters the self-giving they signify and enriches the spouses in joy and gratitude." *Gaudium et spes*, n. 49.

22. See George and Bradley, "Marriage and the Liberal Imagination," 301–302.

23. Ibid., 305. They are answering an objection posed by Stephen Macedo, "Homosexuality and the Conservative Mind," *Georgetown Law Journal* 84 (1995): 278.

24. CDF, *Donum vitae*, II, B, n. 4.

25. Finnis, "Law, Morality, and 'Sexual Orientation,'" 1066.

26. See, for instance, Steven Macedo, "Sexuality and Liberty: Making Room for Nature and Tradition," in *Sex, Preference, and Family: Essays on Law*

and Nature, eds. David M. Estlund and Martha Nussbaum (New York: Oxford University Press, 1977), 90–97.

27. Gabriel Rotello, *Sexual Ecology: AIDS and the Destiny of Gay Men* (New York: Penguin, 1998), 92. Note that Rotello is himself an active homosexual.

28. John R. Diggs, Jr., M.D., "The Health Risks of Gay Sex" (working paper, Corporate Resource Council, 2002), 3. On page 12, in note 29, Diggs provides the scientific sources for the list of diseases associated with anal intercourse: Anne Rompalo, "Sexually Transmitted Causes of Gastrointestinal Symptoms in Homosexual Men," *Medical Clinics of North America* 74.6 (November 1990): 1633–1645; *LGBTHealthChannel*, "Anal Health for Men and Women," http://www.gayhealthchannel.com/analhealth/; *LGBTHealthChannel*, "Safer Sex (MSM) for Men Who Have Sex with Men," http://www.gayhealthchannel. com/stdmsm/.

29. Lee and George, "What Sex Can Be," 139.

30. Finnis, "Personal Integrity, Sexual Morality, and Responsible Parenthood," 46.

31. Grisez, *Living a Christian Life*, 653.

32. Ibid., 650.

33. Ibid. and 650 note 190. In the pages of his text referred to in notes 31–32 above, Grisez is specifically concerned with *masturbatory* sex, but the analysis he provides applies to homosexual acts as well.

17. The Magisterium's Arguments against "Same-Sex Marriage": An Ethical Analysis and Critique

Stephen J. Pope

This chapter first appeared in *Theological Studies* 65 (2004).

The most outspoken and consistently negative response to proposals that the state recognize same-sex marriage has come from the Catholic Church.[1] "Marriage" in this context concerns the state-sanctioned exclusive, consensual union of spouses that is terminated only with a legal divorce; "civil marriage" needs to be distinguished from "sacramental marriage," "common law marriage," or other uses of the term. Rather than taking a constructive position on the question of civil marriage, this chapter confines itself to examining the moral logic of the Church's opposition to same-sex marriage as expressed in documents issued by the papal and episcopal magisterium. It argues that the Church's strong suit is its recognition that marriage needs to be strengthened and has strong ties to particular cultural contexts, but that to do so it is not necessary to speak of gay people in a derogatory manner, to demean the value of committed gay partnerships, and to ignore the demands of social justice and the rights of gay people and their families.

The magisterium offers a variety of arguments supporting its rejection of same-sex marriage. It joins four basic themes: (1) the immorality of "homosexual acts," (2) the dignity of every person, including every gay person, (3) resistance to unjust discrimination, and specifically to unjust discrimination against gay people, and (4) the special good of marriage as a social institution. The second affirmation requires the third. The magisterium holds that all four themes, taken together, entail an obligation to reject proposals to grant legal recognition to same-sex marriage. The magisterium regards these positions as consistent with one another; their critics judge them to be mutually exclusive.

I now proceed to discuss each of the four major considerations involved in the magisterium's argument prohibiting support for same-sex marriage: the impermissibility of "homosexual acts"; human dignity; discrimination; and the value of marriage, and then examine its conclusion that same-sex marriage should not be recognized.

The Prohibition of "Homosexual Activity"

The magisterium frequently argues that same-sex marriage is impermissible because "homosexual activity" is always wrong. This principle is the center of its general argument against same-sex marriage. All the components of its argument are anchored in it the way that spokes are anchored in the hub of a wheel. Sexual activity should be restricted to the context of two people of the opposite sex who have undertaken a permanent commitment to live in an indissoluble marriage. Every person is called to live chastely—to integrate his or her sexuality into a virtuous personal life. Sexual activity must embody both sexual (male-female) complementarity and procreative fruitfulness and sexual practices that fail to do so are morally wrong (the same reason that all forms of artificial birth control are deemed "intrinsically evil"). Every sexual act within marriage must be both loving and open to procreation, and every sexual act failing to fulfill both conditions is objectively immoral even in cases where subjective conditions mitigate culpability. "Homosexual acts," like all sexual activity outside heterosexual, monogamous, and indissoluble marriage, are always wrong not only because they fail to fulfill the latter condition but also because, the magisterium teaches, they are intrinsically incapable of fulfilling the former condition. They are in all places and at all times, by definition, "intrinsically disordered."[2]

This moral teaching provides a ground for the magisterium's rejection of same-sex marriage. Indeed, it might even be taken to justify the revival of anti-sodomy laws that have been recently repealed in the United States. The Church, however, has long been able to tolerate a "lesser evil" in some circumstances, and seems to be willing to extend this category to de facto "homosexual unions." This presumably pertains to countries where "anti-sodomy" legislation would be detrimental to the common good, for example, where it would be unenforceable. At the same time, the document's extreme alarm about the social evils of all "homosexual unions," interpreted in light of the responsibility of the state to protect public morality, might suggest to some observers that the magisterium would lobby for a legal ban on these unions if doing so were politically feasible. This implication seems akin to the old preconciliar "thesis-hypothesis" theory of religious freedom: the proper "thesis" is the Catholic confessional state, but one can, under less than ideal circumstances, tolerate the "hypothesis" of the religiously-neutral state as a "lesser evil" in cases where the ideal is not attainable.[3] Applied to "homosexual unions," the Congregation would seem to be inclined to argue, the "thesis" is an entirely heterosexual society with "zero toleration" of gay partnerships, but the "hypothesis" can grant moral legitimacy to toleration as a "lesser evil" when the policy of repression entails prohibitively high costs.

The key question here concerns how to move from general moral principles to their practical application in concrete social settings....Bishops from different parts of the world differ to some extent on the public policy implications of their common moral principles. There is no one entirely consistent magisterial teaching on the issue of whether gay and lesbian individuals in committed relationships ought to be given some kinds of legal protection. The bishops of Switzerland and New Zealand support forms of civil registration, and the American bishops administrative committee seems to be open to conferring some (yet unspecified) legal rights and benefits on cohabiting gay couples.

This diversity of views is due not to overt magisterial disagreement over the morality of homosexual sexual activity per se but rather to (1) varying perceptions about what is needed in different cultures and political communities (e.g., what is appropriate for New Zealand might not be appropriate to Switzerland, and vice versa), (2) different interpretations of the social consequences of current practices (are current partnerships harming the common good? If so, how? If how, according to what evidence?), and (3) different predictions about the potential social consequences of various public policy options (will they contribute to the deterioration of marriage and the family as social institutions? Again, as indicated by what evidence?).

Catholic reflection on how to move from principles to policies and laws proceeds from a well-known set of moral categories. First, there are natural law obligations and virtues that pertain to all human beings everywhere whether they are Catholic or not, e.g., not to lie, steal, or kill. Second, there are obligations and virtues binding on Catholics in particular, e.g., to provide religious education for one's children, to attend Mass regularly, etc. Applied to public policy and civil law, this distinction issues in two critically important principles. First, the state is not allowed to enforce the *distinctive* requirements of any *particular* religious morality. In American civil law, this immunity is protected by the Constitutional separation of Church and state. The Church itself adopted this same protection in the Second Vatican Council's *Dignitatis humanae*: "The right to freedom in matters of religion is exercised in human society."[4] Civil society has a duty to protect itself against abuses committed in the name of religion, and civil authority must allow as much freedom as possible except when doing so is detrimental to public order. The notion of "public order," the Council Fathers taught, includes three components: the rights of citizens, public peace, and public morality.[5] Freedom should not be restrained except for the sake of public order.

Second, the state is required to enforce some aspects of the natural moral law. It is illegal, for example, unjustly to take another person's property, to lie under oath, or to take innocent life. The central concern of the natural moral law as it pertains to the civil law is, of course, justice and related notions of human rights, fairness, equity, and the common good. The state does in fact "legislate morality" in some sense, but, as St. Thomas Aquinas held, the civil law cannot and should not enforce the entire natural moral law.[6] The range of morality that the civil law enforces cannot embrace in its entirety even all the provisions of the natural moral law; it cannot, in other words, make all immoral acts also illegal acts.[7] This distinction is central to legislation regarding "homosexual activity."

John Courtney Murray provided the most lucid criteria for addressing this issue. He argued cogently that natural law ethics implements in the civil law only those moral standards necessary for public order. Murray's use of "public order" is a smaller subset of the more encom-

passing "common good," the phrase most often used by the magisterium. The problems with the "maximalist" view of the state as responsible
for the entire common good have been amply demonstrated in the cases of
the former Soviet Union and, on a different scale, by the policies of some
Islamic theocracies today. When the state is viewed as responsible for the
entire common good, it takes on more duties than it can or ought to assume.
It also thereby undermines the ability of other subsidiary bodies that have
their own obligations for the common good. There is much more to the common good than public order, and the reach of the law is restricted to the latter. On this basis, Murray argued, "the moral aspirations of the law are
minimal. Law seeks to establish and maintain only that minimum of actualized morality that is necessary for the healthy functioning of the social
order....It enforces only what is minimally acceptable, and in this sense
socially necessary."[8] Murray's public philosophy offers good reasons for not
banning "homosexual activity." His distinction between public order and
religious ethics encourages us to recognize that ethics in pluralistic societies
cannot always be a matter of directly applying moral norms to civil law,
especially when these norms are widely contested.

The magisterium would presumably agree that a ban on "homosexual activity" does pertain to public morality, but there is certainly no
broad public consensus on this matter. The magisterium is of course free
to preach this norm both inside and outside the Church. It should, however, cease employing it as a major component of its case against same-
sex marriage if it wants to build its public argument on the basis of
widely shared premises.

There are a variety of ways of interpreting the natural law within
Catholic theology, but the "new natural law" theory presents the most visible school of Catholic ethics engaged in the public debate over same-sex
marriage. The "new natural law theory" works from a key premise: "In voluntary acting for human goods and avoiding what is opposed to them, one
ought to choose and will those and only those possibilities whose willing is
compatible with integral human fulfillment."[9] Individuals may never legitimately attack a "basic good," including the "marital good."[10] According to
"new natural lawyers" Gerard Bradley and Robert George, "Marriage, considered not as a mere legal convention, but, rather as a two-in-one-flesh
communion of persons that is consummated and actualized by sexual acts
of the reproductive type, is an intrinsic (or, in our parlance, 'basic') human

good; as such, marriage provides a noninstrumental reason for spouses, whether or not they are capable of conceiving children in their acts of genital union, to perform such acts."[11] "Homosexual acts" are thus not ethically permitted because they are incapable of attaining this "one flesh unity"; in fact, "homosexual acts" merely create the "appearance" of true sexual intimacy.[12] The "new natural lawyers" in effect maintain that the "good of union" cannot be pursued unless the couple is also "open to procreation."

The "new natural lawyers" recognize that the law should neither simply legislate the entirety of the moral law nor outlaw all sexual acts such as contraception or fornication that violate the "marital good." The purpose of civil law is to secure the conditions that "favor, facilitate and foster the realization by each individual of his or her personal development."[13] Finnis argues that the state has a "compelling interest in denying that homosexual conduct—a 'gay lifestyle'—is a valid, humanly acceptable choice and form of life," and that it ought to do "what it *properly* can…to discourage such conduct."[14] Since the government is a teacher and the law has a pedagogical function, neither government nor law can remain "morally neutral" with regard to social institutions as important as marriage and the family. Thus in some settings a government could be perfectly justified in imposing legal restrictions on "the advertising and marketing of homosexual services, the maintenance of places of resort for homosexual activity, or the promotion of homosexualist 'lifestyles' via public education and public media of communication,"[15] and so forth.

The state should refuse to grant legal recognition to same-sex marriages because, Finnis argues, they threaten the well-being, and specifically the stability and integrity, of the family.[16] Those who defend same-sex marriages are committed, he argues, to the view that (a) sexual activity for the sake of self-gratification is ethically legitimate, and (b) anyone who accepts this premise supports a view of sexuality that is "an active threat to the stability of existing and future marriages."[17] Provision (a) provides a reason for disallowing any "homosexual activity," not to mention that protecting same-sex marriage.

The "new natural law" theory is vulnerable to two objections. First, it fails to build a logical case for the claim that acceptance of the ethical legitimacy of any and all "homosexual acts" necessarily implies that one regards sexual activity as nothing more than the pursuit of individual self-gratification.[18] Its sweeping ethical condemnation of all intentionally nonprocreative sex is excessively monolithic and undifferentiated. As legal scholar Stephen Macedo points out, it is "strikingly simplistic and implausible to portray the essential nature of *every form* of nonprocreative sexuality as no better than the least *valuable* form."[19] The same habit of gross overgeneralization is exhibited in its claims about gay people. It is a reductionistic exaggeration to epitomize the behavior of every gay person as driven by a "promiscuous, liberationist 'gay lifestyle,' which rejects all sexual restraints and value judgments."[20] If this were universally the case, there would in fact be few gay activists lobbying for same-sex marriage. Gay people are more diverse, and in morally relevant ways, than is recognized by the "new natural law theory."

Second, the "new natural law" argument does not take into account the concrete experience of gay people. Here it replicates the magisterium's oversight. It attempts to justify its position on the basis of a deductive argument and abstract philosophical analysis, but it cannot avoid making claims of a predictive nature about the real world, how people will act in it, and the probable consequences of their actions on their communities. This empirical dimension is especially important when considering moral arguments against same-sex marriage. The claim that the state has a compelling interest in promoting heterosexual marriage only yields a negative judgment on same-sex marriages if there are good reasons for thinking that the latter would, in fact, undermine the former. The exercise of practical reason, in other words, requires evidence and it is not sufficient to reason from a priori ethical principles alone.

THE DIGNITY OF THE PERSON

A second major component of the magisterium's case against same-sex marriage concerns human dignity and the distinction between engaging in "homosexual acts" and having a "homosexual orientation." The fundamental principle of the moral law is that each person has inherent dignity simply in virtue of being created in the image of God. This dignity includes sexual identity. As the American bishops once put it, "God does not love someone any less simply because he or she is homosexual."[21] The *Catechism of the Catholic Church* teaches that "Everyone, man and woman, should acknowledge his [or her] sexual identity"[22]—it does not hold that heterosexuals, and only heterosexuals, must accept their sexual identity. People with a "homosexual orientation" must thus be treated with "respect, compassion, and sensitivity" and their rights should be defended.[23] The American bishops call on all Christians and citizens of good will to "confront their own fears about homosexuality and to curb the humor and discrimination that offend homosexual persons."[24] They acknowledge, "that having a homosexual orientation brings with it enough anxiety, pain and issues related to self-acceptance without society bringing additional prejudicial treatment."[25]

The affirmation of the inherent dignity of gay people, however, is compromised by a fundamental ambiguity rooted in the somewhat recently drawn distinction between sexual act and sexual *orientation*. This distinction is employed so that the magisterium can prohibit a class of sexual acts without at the same time condemning their agents as such. The axiom, "love the sinner, hate the sin,"[26] recognized that concern for the agent can be joined with disapproval of his or her act. As a constituent feature of the person, orientation locates a condition for the sinful act more deeply in the person than did the old language of either temptation or "disordered concupiscence," since the latter was assumed to be susceptible to the healing, correcting, and reordering power of grace. If one is to "hate the sin," critics might wonder, how could one not also hate the inbuilt orientation that expresses it? And if the orientation is central to personal identity, then "hating the sin" that expresses this orientation seems to lead one to "hating the sinner" as well.

Clearly the magisterium believes that any act expressing a same-sex sexual orientation is inherently wrong. It teaches not only that same-sex sexual relations are "self-indulgent"—a description that could equally be applied to a considerable proportion of heterosexual sexual relations—but also that gays are inherently ordered to a kind of sexual love that will always be closed in on itself, psychologically sterile, and morally bankrupt. Any relationship expressing this form of love will be irredeemably dysfunctional.

The act-orientation distinction provides a few advantages. It attempts to keep up with the general modern acknowledgement that a variety of factors—genetic, hormonal, psychological, social, and cultural—interact with one another in complex ways to influence sexual orientation. Since orientation is regarded as prevoluntary, the language allows the Church to denounce acts of injustice perpetrated against gays on the ground that they cannot be assumed to carry responsibility or moral guilt for their orientation since it is prevoluntary. The distinction also helps to avoid the reductionism that identifies an entire person with his or her sexual identity. A person is much more than a "type" of sexual being.

Generalizations about act and orientation, however, need to acknowledge the complexity, diversity, and subtlety involved in the formation of sexual identity. The old moralistic language did not adequately capture this complexity. Moral theologians traditionally understood an internal orientation to a class of forbidden acts to be a "vice," e.g., lust, avarice, or dishonesty. Yet the "orientation" to same-sex sexual relations is not exactly the same as these vices because it is not simply the product of bad choices shaping habituation. Nor is it the result of bad choices expressing the "fallen" nature of concupiscence and habituating the sinner to vice. Choices are always part of human behavior, but the language of orientation registers the fact that being gay is not like deciding to take up golf rather than tennis. Many gay people who experience a natural attraction to members of their own sex, in other words, are inclined to do so by bio-psychological conditions that they experience as having been "given" to them by nature, a "deep-seated and relatively stable" dimension of personality.[27]

At the same time, the word "orientation" can be misleading if taken to suggest that all people have a definite and singular sexual identity that is genetically or biologically fixed throughout their lifetimes from the moment of birth. The language of orientation can also misleadingly suggest that every person has a sexual identity that is either entirely homosexual or entirely heterosexual. Some studies indicate that three or four percent of those who identify themselves as heterosexual find themselves from time to time somewhat attracted to members of their own sex.[28] Even many adults are neither completely straight nor completely gay in their orientation. This attentiveness to the fluidity of sexual identity usually comes from people who are not allies of the magisterium, but it actually lends some support to the policy of distinguishing the moral qualities of "homosexual acts" from the basic humanity of their agents.

The language sometimes suggests that all people are born with a fixed sexual orientation the way they are born with eye color or blood type. The development of sexual identity is influenced in complex ways by post-natal physical, psychological and social factors. Moreover, if personal identity in general is not a matter over which individuals are entirely passive, then the same is true, at least to some extent, of sexual identity. Legal scholar Janet Halley argues that some gay people view their sexual orientation as the product of their own decisions.[29] This is not to say that a mature adult's basic proclivity of sexual attraction can be reversed by a simple act of the will, only that this proclivity does not come into existence without some choices on the part of the person whose desire it is. Different individuals can exercise varying degrees of choice over the shape of their particular sexual identities and experience different degrees of "givenness" in their sexual identity.

Young people in particular can experience significant changes in sexual self-understanding over the course of their psychosexual development. Some young people who experience their sexual orientation as somewhat fluid make choices to act in ways that begin to give a direction to what becomes their sexual orientation. This is especially the case in Western societies, where sexual restraints have been loosened and popular culture encourages experimentation. Some teenagers and young adults go through a period in which they struggle with their sexual identity, seeing themselves, say, as straight for a while, then as gay, and then as bisexual, and then again as straight.

The bishops worry that same-sex marriage would lessen the social pressures that channel sexually immature young people into heterosexual identities. Some observers take the bishops to be afraid that some heterosexuals will "convert" to homosexuality if the traditional cultural discouragement of homosexuality continues to be relaxed. Yet as Judge Richard Posner points out: "Given the personal and social disadvantages to which homosexuality subjects a person in our society, the idea that millions of young men and women have chosen it in the same fashion that they might choose a career or place to live or a political party or even a religious faith seems preposterous."[30] The bishops are probably not concerned with defection, since the issue concerns people who have not yet formed a stable sense of sexual identity, but they want law to help individuals form their sexual identities in a heterosexual pattern by encouraging certain kinds of behavior and social roles. Unfortunately, the bishops have failed to appreciate the extent to which this channeling strategy employs negative images of gay people.

The assessment of same-sex orientation as "intrinsically disordered" can be especially misleading. Technically, the disorder in question lies precisely in the wrongful object of the "homosexual act," but this wrongful object is the end of intentions motivated by a disordered orientation that is rooted in the agent. The language of "intrinsically disordered" sexuality, in other words, can easily slide into the message that all gays are "intrinsically disordered" people.[31] This mistaken inference is understandable given our increased appreciation for the role of sexuality as a fundamental component of personal identity. Because sexuality pervades one's identity, having an "intrinsically disordered sexual orientation" is more profound than having a detached retina or bad kidney. As moral theologian Kevin Kelly puts it, "our sexuality is an essential dimension of our being human persons and so affects our whole approach to life and all our relationships."[32] This appreciation for the significance of sexuality is also registered by the magisterium. The Pontifical Council for the Family, for example, teaches that sexuality "concerns the intimate nucleus of the person."[33] The *Catechism of the Catholic Church* similarly recognizes that: "Sexuality affects all aspects of the human person in the unity of his body and soul. It especially concerns affectivity, the capacity to love, and to procreate, and in a more general way the aptitude for forming bonds of communion with others."[34] If one suffers from a fundamental disorder in sexual orientation, and orientation is essential to identity, then it would be hard to avoid the conclusion that a disordered sexual orientation involves a disordering of one's ability to engage in interpersonal relations and to form "bonds of communion" with others.

As it has been presented lately, the magisterium's message about gay sexual orientation is powerfully stigmatizing and dehumanizing. It is also at least tacitly, if not explicitly, liable to be used to support exactly the kinds of unjust discrimination that the Church has repeatedly condemned. Describing someone's sexual identity as "gravely disordered" would seem to arouse suspicion, mistrust and alienation. This conclusion is reinforced by the painful direct psychological experience of many gay people.[35] One can understand why observers conclude that the magisterium's teaching about homosexuality stands in tension with its affirmation that each gay person is created in the *imago Dei*. To avoid this problem, magisterium ought to cease employing the act-orientation distinction.

DISCRIMINATION

The main secular argument supporting same-sex marriages is that any other policy entails unjust discrimination against gay people.[36] In American legal terms, this is expressed as a violation of equal protection under the law as established by the Fourteenth Amendment to the U.S. Constitution.

The magisterium responds to this position by making two claims. One concedes that all forms of unjust discrimination, including those against gay people, are wrong and unacceptable. The second argues more controversially that excluding gay people from civil marriage is not a form of unjust discrimination because gay people have no right to marry. The first claim is tautologous and hardly worth mentioning, except for the fact that many people and their communities routinely ignore its truth. The second claim is also tautologous, at least in a sense, but unless it is explicated in some detail its advocates will be accused of begging the question. Claiming that "act x is not unjust" on the grounds that a "person does not have a right to do act x" is not an argument, it is the conclusion of an argument.

First, the magisterium insists on drawing a somewhat awkward distinction between justified and unjustified discrimination. The *Catechism of the Catholic Church* insists that, "every sign of unjust discrimination in their regard should be avoided."[37] The phrase "justified discrimination" sounds oxymoronic, something like "justified murder" or "justified theft," but in fact, the magisterium rightly holds that one can draw a distinction between two forms of differential treatment: one that is just because required by the common good and another that is unjust because it detracts from the common good. In the past, of course, many acts of injustice to minority individuals or groups have been legitimated by spurious appeals to the common good. Laws forbidding interracial marriage were thought by their advocates to protect the good of the community, but they were repealed when it was recognized that they violate the right of individuals to marry whom they choose. At the present time, advocates of same-sex marriage regard marriage to members of the same sex as an individual right that should not be overridden in pursuit of the broader collective good. The magisterium, however, argues that this analogy is flawed. Race has nothing to do with the sexual composition of married couple, they argue, since as male and female they participate fully in the meaning of marriage as sexual, unitive, and procreative.

The fundamental ethical principle here is that "every sign of unjust discrimination should be avoided."[38] By "unjust" discrimination the magisterium means arbitrary differential treatment in virtue of membership in a particular group. The relevant governing moral principle is that one ought to treat similar cases similarly, and dissimilar cases dissimilarly. Simply being a gay person does not in and of itself warrant differential treatment, either pro or con.

The Congregation does allow differential treatment of gays for the sake of the common good. I have already mentioned the argument that if error has no rights, neither does immorality. For this reason one cannot decry as unjust discrimination restrictive policies necessary for the common good. The common good can only be pursued within the framework of the rights proper to the human person, but since there is no right to engage in "homosexual activity," the argument runs, there can be no right of gays to have access to civil marriage. In the eyes of the magisterium, sexual orientation is, at least in this regard, not analogous to race, religion, or ethnicity because these associations do not in and of themselves incline people to engage in "intrinsically evil acts." Thus the Congregation explicitly declared in 1992 that "Sexual tendency is not a quality comparable to race, ethnic origin, etc., with respect to non-discrimination. Unlike these, homosexuality is an objective disorder and calls for moral concern."[39] At this point, the argument regarding discrimination overlaps with the argument from the immorality of "homosexual activity" that was examined above.

The Congregation's ability to offer a public moral argument breaks down precisely at this point, since there is no widely shared agreement about this norm or the evidence adduced to support it. In addition, the magisterium makes a significant rhetorical mistake when it engages the issue of discrimination. Given the pain and suffering heaped on gay people for millennia, it would seem most reasonable for the Congregation to begin with a criticism of these evils and a confession of guilt for its own failure to protect gay people. After having clearly established the Church's repudiation of unjustified discrimination as well as the bigotry, ignorance, and hatred that has often generated it, the Congregation would have been in a better position to argue that refusing to support same-sex marriage does not amount to a case of unjustified discrimination. Instead of making a kind of "preferential option" with gays—as with all people who are vulnerable to abuse—the magisterium suggests that since the "homosexual tendency" is an "objective disorder," it cannot—and, in principle, never can be—considered an object of immoral discrimination.[40] This conclusion, of course contradicts the moral logic, both implicit and explicit, of other magisterial statements that defend the dignity of gay persons.

The magisterium's treatment of the issue of discrimination replicates the confusions and ambiguities of its treatment of the dignity of gay people. The magisterium, and especially the Congregation for the Doctrine of the Faith, presents an important substantive principle that disallows unjust discrimination but then undercuts its own credibility by failing to register its understanding of the full extent to which discrimination against gays persists as a social evil. As such it prevents gays from participating in institutions within civil society that build up the common good, and it also fails to provide a moral vision that offers a sufficiently powerful challenge to those who would engage in violence against gays.

MARRIAGE AS A SOCIAL INSTITUTION

The fourth component of the magisterium's argument concerns the value of marriage as a social institution. Marriage is socially and interpersonally beneficial in many ways. Married men live longer, generate higher incomes, and have lower rates of suicide, homicide, and mental illness than unmarried men, and they are less likely to have serious accidents or engage in violent crime.[41] Marriage orders, stabilizes, and elevates male sexual desire and encourages men to assume their share of financial responsibility for their children. Children are more likely to flourish when they have a chance to be nurtured in stable, two-parent homes. Recent studies have highlighted the negative effects of divorce on women and especially their children.[42] Children from divorced homes do not do as well on average as children from "intact" families; girls from broken homes, for example, are much more likely to become the victims of sexual abuse.[43] Personal and interpersonal benefits also redound to the benefit of extended families, neighborhoods, and communities. The state has a responsibility to favor marriage and family and to create conditions in which couples can obtain the resources needed to make them viable.

The magisterium is appropriately alarmed at the weakness of marriage in contemporary society. A number of indicators suggest that marriage and family are indeed in a process of deterioration.[44] Roughly 43 percent of marriages end in divorce,[45] more than 33 percent of children are born to unmarried women,[46] and between 1990 and 2000 the rate of cohabitation increased 72 percent.[47] At the present time, nuclear families made up of married couples with children constitute only about 26 percent of all households in the United States. Households are marked by adoption, multiple generations, single-parenthood, cohabitation, and blended families constituted after divorces and remarriages. Roughly half of divorced couples have children, and many experience profoundly negative consequences from the breakup.[48] At the present time, around 25 million children in the United States live without their fathers.[49]

The Church has some way to go to overcome its patriarchal legacy and to develop a more egalitarian understanding of sex and gender.[50] Nevertheless, the magisterium has a powerful and socially significant moral vision of marriage, sex, and family to offer contemporary society. The sexual ethic generated by this vision contrasts sharply with the popular individualistic reduction of sexual ethics to the private choices of consenting adults. It understands marriage as an essential part of the social order rather than as a mere private contract, offers a powerful alternative to the trivialization of sex that has become so much a part of popular culture, and supports the full interpersonal context for child-bearing and child-rearing. The Church recognizes that marriage involves a social as well as an interpersonal ethic. Its sacramental doctrine infuses marriage with a religious meaning that radically transcends its function in civil society.

The magisterium argues that support for marriage, and especially for children, requires opposition to the legal recognition of same-sex marriage. There is, however, no convincing evidence showing that currently functioning gay households are causally related to the deterioration of marriage in the wider society.[51] The biggest threat to marriage comes from the high incidence of divorce that has followed the development of "no fault" divorce laws of the 1970s.[52]

The conservative gay position concurs with the Church's concern for the institution of marriage, but it argues that same-sex marriage would increase respect for the institution by enlisting more participants and extending its relevance to more sectors of society.[53] It maintains that gays themselves would benefit from ordering their lives to this institution, and that same-sex marriage would encourage fidelity, increase monogamy and reward loyalty, self-discipline, stability, and reciprocal emotional investment. It would extend rather than diminish respect for the institution. As Andrew Sullivan puts it:

> Society has good reason to extend legal advantages to hetero-sexuals who choose the formal sanction of marriage over simply living together. They make a deeper commitment to one another and to society; in exchange, society extends certain benefits to them. Marriage provides an anchor, if an arbitrary and weak one, in the chaos of sex and relationships to which we are all prone. It provides a mechanism for emotional stability, economic security, and the healthy rearing of the next generation. We rig the law in its favor not because we disparage all forms of relationship other than the nuclear family, but because we recognize that not to promote marriage would be to ask too much of human virtue.[54]

Same-sex marriage also provides a context for familial responsibility [for] those who adopt children or use reproductive technology. It would facilitate adults' taking mutual responsibility for children and reward the emotional attachment and personal self-sacrifice that is entailed in child-rearing. Put in the language of Catholic moral doctrine, gay-headed families can be said to fulfill the "procreative" function of marriage to the extent that they are engaged in the education of children. "Procreative" includes child-rearing as well as child-bearing (see *Gaudium et spes* no. 50; *Humanae vitae* no. 9; *Summa theologiae* Suppl. q. 41, a.1).

The magisterium, of course, does not accept these arguments. In its perspective, all of these purported benefits would be illusory because virtues cannot be generated from "intrinsically evil acts." Monogamy among gays is like honor among thieves, a virtue in other contexts but one that here is co-opted to facilitate wrongdoing. Here, too, the argument from marriage as a social institution is connected to the argument from the immorality of "homosexual acts."

In one of its least inspired judgments, the Congregation for the Doctrine of the Faith denies that families headed by gay adults are beneficial for either children or their communities. It insists that same-sex unions make no "significant or positive contribution to the development of the human person in society,"[55] and even asserts, without citing any evidence or proving any explanation, that gay parents actually do "violence" to the children that they raise.[56] The magisterium needs to address recent social scientific studies that maintain that gay partnerships are not, as a general rule, harmful either to children or to others.[57] A study conducted by the American Academy of Pediatrics, for example, found that, "there is no systematic difference between gay and non-gay parents in emotional health, parenting skills, and attitudes toward parenting. No data have pointed to any risk to children as a result of growing up in a family with one or more gay parents."[58]

Most magisterial statements have not been as aggressively negative toward gays as "Considerations." They have more consistently focused on the long-term effects of granting *legal* recognition to gay households or the institution of marriage. This argument need not rely on any negative stereotypes about gay people or their families. It maintains that the legal acceptance of same-sex marriage would involve a radical change in the definition of marriage, and in particular that it would detach marriage from procreation and its attending responsibilities. The Church's message is that marriage establishes stable bonds between men and women so that children will have mothers and fathers; if marriage is significantly diminished, so will the well-being of children. The Church also teaches that marriage is a relationship in which the local community, the wider civil society, and the state have a legitimate interest.

This argument over the meaning of marriage has also been at the center of attention in recent debates in family law in Canada and the United States. Catholicism, along with the Western tradition generally, has typically regarded marriage as a divinely and socially sanctioned institution that exists for the protection and rearing of children. In this view marriage is essentially conjugal and social, and derives its meaning from its function as the foundation of the family. It joins husband and wife in a lifelong bond that is ordered essentially, if not in every instance (e.g., as in the case of sterile couples), to their roles as father and mother and that assigns them responsibilities related to procreation and generational care-giving. Twentieth-century moral teachings, and Catholic moral theology generally, brought a new level of appreciation for the companionate values of marriage, its "unitive" purpose, but not in such a way that the "procreative" dimension would be eliminated.[59]

A radical alternative has been proposed by some legal scholars in Canada and the United States who argue that marriage ought to be regarded as nothing more than a contract between people who love each other. Cornell University law professor Martha Fineman argues that marriage ought to be completely eliminated as a legal category. Adult interpersonal relationships would be arranged according to contracts, whether monogamous or involving some form of "plural sexual grouping." Fineman regards the mother-child twosome as the key procreative relation. Fathers have no particular obligation to care for their children unless they voluntarily enter into a contract with their mates to do so. The state has no right to prevent gays from doing what heterosexual couples can do. No form of sexual relationship—permanent or temporary, gay or straight, monogamous or promiscuous, polygamous or polygynous—should be preferred to any other, subsidized, or prohibited by the state. For this school of thought, the extension of marriage to gays is but an intermediate step on the way to opening marriage to plural partners or the "full range" of family types. To pursue total equality in all choices and social relations, Fineman argues, requires that, "*we destroy the marital model altogether* and collapse all sexual relationships into the same category—private—not sanctioned, privileged, or preferred by law."[60]

This anti-marriage agenda is not the sole inspiration of a few law professors. It is promoted, among places, in the proposals for legal reform enunciated in the Law Commission of Canada's 1997 report entitled "Beyond Conjugality."[61] "Beyond Conjugality" made three recommendations: that judges presiding over dissolutions treat as identical the cases of similarly situated married couples and cohabiting couples, that laws be drafted to allow for officially registered partnerships, and that same-sex marriage be legalized. The radical "beyond marriage" legal theorists are cited in this study, and conservatives fear that the adoption of their convictions by this influential document signals not only the acceptance of same-sex marriage but also, and more ominously, the eventual destruction of marriage as an institution. A similar stream of thought has been seen in the United States, where the "Principles of the Law of Family Dissolution" issued by the influential American Law Institute recommends that judges effectively ignore the difference between domestic partners and married couples.[62]

This scenario is exactly what worries the magisterium and makes it easy to understand why the American bishops support the Federal Marriage Amendment to the Constitution. In contrast to the contractualists, the Church offers a much more realistic acknowledgement of human needs and a deeper awareness of mutual interdependence. It offers a more profoundly social understanding of human relations than is allowed in the egoistic self-concern often assumed by contractualists. The Church has known for some time what has recently been stressed by social scientists, namely, that marriages only work if couples develop the ability to act for the good of one another, the children, the marriage itself, and the family as a whole rather than only for their own individual benefit.[63] This point is especially important as an expanding "expressive individualism" increasingly inclines people to view marriage as a private "lifestyle" choice regarding only "close relationships."[64]

The magisterium fears that a purely non-procreative, contractualized notion of marriage might lead to the elimination of the family and to anarchy in child-rearing practices. They believe that even conservative gays who want to have their monogamous commitments receive the social support that comes from legal validation are, unwittingly or not, pursuing a Trojan horse policy in which entry into the institution will eventually lead to its demise. Instead of helping mothers, contractualism would leave them on their own and make it easier for fathers routinely to abandon their children.[65]

This argument is not necessarily rebutted by the fact that some states allow a gay person or couple to adopt children or by the fact that children can be born to a gay person or couple by the use of reproductive technology. These ways in which gay people can form families should not be confused with the intrinsically procreative relationship constituted by husband and wife. The state allows individuals and couples to adopt, the magisterium might argue, but it ought to give special support and encouragement to heterosexual couples because they generally provide the optimal setting for child rearing.

Concern with the health of marriage offers a more credible context for thinking about same-sex marriage than do their other arguments. It presents the most publicly compelling consideration because its moral logic does not rest on a moral condemnation of all "homosexual activity." One can hold that marriage between a man and woman is the best general context for the raising of children, and therefore receive legal recognition, without claiming that all gay partnerships are corrupt or all gay-headed families destructive. This presents the strongest aspect of the magisterium's argument in its best possible light. It also involves a significant re-casting of its argument, since the "hub" of the spokes is now marriage as an institution rather than the wrongness of "homosexual activity."

One aspect of this argument can be phrased in terms of the classical notion of the "pedagogical function" of the law. Legal scholar and ethicist M. Cathleen Kaveny contrasts the negative or restraining function of law in liberal legal philosophy with Thomas Aquinas's understanding of law as teacher of virtue. "Law is always and inevitably a teacher," she writes, and "sorely needed is critical self-reflection about what it teaches."[66] Murray's concern with minimal public morality pertains to the criminal law, and provides a helpful context for understanding why "anti-sodomy" statutes were properly overturned. Yet civil law, Kaveny emphasizes, has a much broader purpose in the way it gives positive social approbation to certain goods, functions, practices, and institutions. Though she writes about the ethics of life rather than sexual ethics, Kaveny's point is relevant to this debate. It is one thing not to *punish* same-sex relations through the criminal law and another actively to *encourage* same-sex commitments through putting the full force of the civil law behind them.

Magisterial statements about same-sex marriage are concerned that civil laws would teach that marriage is morally neutral with regard to procreation. The magisterium holds that, according to the natural law, love, sexual intercourse, and reproduction constitute three essential components of marriage that cannot be detached from one another and treated as independent goods. It also runs against the social and procreative understanding of marriage that has been not only promoted by the Catholic Church but held by the Western tradition for millennia.[67]

This line of argument was employed in a speech on October 2, 2003, by Archbishop Sean O'Malley of Boston,[68] who argued that the Massachusetts *Goodridge* decision attacked the common good. He claimed that redefining marriage in this way will undermine the well-being of marriage as a social institution and, in addition, will indirectly contribute to the incidence of poverty, child abuse, and drug addiction. Since divorce and cohabitation have contributed to these problems, the archbishop reasoned, giving any further impetus to the instability of marriage would exacerbate them even more.

This concern with marriage is not the sole preserve of Thomists and the magisterium. The recent development of the theory of "critical familialism" by Don Browning and his collaborators has united a wide variety of scholars who support an egalitarian marriage structure but who also want to recover a sense of marriage as the most appropriate context for childrearing and care-giving.[69] "Critical familialism" regards marriage as both the setting of companionate, romantic interpersonal bonds and a valuable social institution that channels male sexual desire and corrects the distinctively "male problematic" that militates against long-term commitments. Whatever their sexual orientation and marital status, men overall are more prone to engage in extra-partner sex than women who are similarly situated.[70] The health of marriage requires that the "unitive" and "procreative" purposes of marriage not be completely severed from one another.

The magisterium's most plausible argument against same-sex marriage concerns the long-term consequences that it might have on marriage. There seems no reason to think that gay households today are having deleterious consequences on their members or communities; on the contrary, they seem, as least to common sense observation, to be as healthy, or unhealthy, as their straight counterparts. Yet the magisterium is not unreasonable to raise a question about the long-term social effects of a proposed social change that would give the support of the state to same-sex partnerships and regard them as equal in worth to marriage between a man and a woman. It is hard to have confidence in predictions—pro or con—about the long-term effects that would follow from enacting same-sex marriage. In the absence of knowledge regarding matters of this magnitude, and involving courses of events that would be irreversible, the magisterium is not unreasonable to call for caution and even to resist the new social experiment proposed by advocates of same-sex marriage. It is possible for people of good faith to differ on this issue. At the very least, further discussion, investigation, and deliberation are in order.

Those attentive to the pedagogical function of the law insist, at the very least, that proposed legal changes that might have a major impact on the moral substance of marriage ought to be subjected to extensive discussion, debated thoroughly, and resolved through the legislative process.[71] Thus the American bishops object not only to the contents of *Goodridge* but also to the way in which such a radical change in social policy was set by a thin 4-3 decision of the court. If the law should ordinarily be supported by broad consensus based on shared communal values, as Murray, Finnis, and Kaveny all hold, then the judiciary is not the best means for bringing about such significant legal change. If this position is correct, the burden of proof for serious changes in the law shifts squarely onto the shoulders of the innovators.

CONCLUSION

The magisterium's recent statements regarding same-sex marriage have been flawed and need to be reformulated. The major flaw involves a persistent tendency to communicate a mixed message about the worth of gay people and their place in the life of the civil community.

The Church stands as the most visibly identifiable moral voice in the Western world. It offers a profound core of moral wisdom regarding sex, marriage, and the family that is badly needed by societies in which people feel increasingly isolated, objectified and bereft of moral substance.[72] The Church also offers a powerful basis for denouncing injustice against gay people. The Christian virtue of *agape* affirms not only that all classes and groups of human beings are worthwhile, but that they are *equally* worthwhile before God. As the bishops put it in "Always Our Children," "God does not love someone any less simply because he or she is homosexual."[73] If the magisterium wishes to be more persuasive regarding the topic of same-sex marriage, then Church authorities must embody this love in what they say about, and how they act toward, gay people.

Unfortunately, the ineffective, self-contradictory, and counterproductive manner in which the magisterium has tried to promote its case against same-sex marriage has made it seem more irrelevant than ever to the public debate on this topic. To be fair, even without a mixed message, the Church's best insights need to be carefully formulated when expressed in a society that usually allows individual rights, tolerance, and the duties of non-discrimination to trump the common good, moral tradition, and institutional authority. But the content and tone of its own statements have exacerbated matters by reinforcing the view of some observers that its sexual ethics is simply out of touch with contemporary experience. The magisterium's credibility was not helped by the fact that this debate was joined in the wake of the crisis of clerical sexual abuse and the episcopal abuse of power. A special source of consternation, and another indication of anti-gay bias, was caused by Church officials who blamed the crisis of sexual abuse on gay priests, despite the fact that most priests who are gay have not been guilty of these crimes.[74]

The magisterium is ethically entitled to work against same-sex marriage on the grounds that it might contribute to the disassociation of marriage and procreation. Yet the magisterium is not ethically entitled to connect this case about the social institution to anti-gay bias. The magisterium claims to appreciate the talents of gay people but questions whether there is a place in ordained ministry for them; it asks every person to accept his or her sexuality as a gift from God but then makes an implicit exception of the gay person; it praises Christian generosity but then condemns gay people who adopt orphans. It has no justification for continuing to issue documents that perpetuate stereotypes about gay people, stigmatize them, tacitly approve of unjust discrimination against them, discount their generosity, refuse to acknowledge their contribution to the common good, or suggest that they are in any way inferior human beings or less trustworthy members of the Body of Christ.

If the magisterium wants to work against same-sex marriage without confirming suspicions that it is homophobic, it needs, in addition to refraining from injustice, to take additional proactive steps on behalf of gay people. It ought to undertake a serious commitment to work against every form of prejudice against gays and to advocate for recognition of the rights of gay people wherever they are denied. It is incumbent on the Church to work for measures that would promote social justice for gay people as individuals and that would effectively enhance the well-being of the children and partners of gay households. If it fails to do this, the Church will rightly be judged negatively as an institution that labors to prevent gay parents from visiting their children in the hospital, attend teacher conferences, or receive the Social Security checks that would have been granted to a surviving spouse.

Finally, if it wants to communicate genuine love of neighbor, the magisterium must find a way to honor the experience of gay people, including gay Catholics who are sincerely trying to live in accord with the gospel and the best wisdom of Catholic morality. Murray believed that practical intelligence is rescued from ideology by maintaining a "close relation to concrete experience."[75] The documents of the Congregation for the Doctrine of the Faith suffer from a major defect in this regard because they have not taken into account the experiences of gay people. The magisterium has yet to show any interest in engaging in dialogue with gay people or in listening to what they have to say about what it means to be gay and Catholic at the present time.[76]

Many Catholic gay people do not always experience the magisterium as regarding them with respect, trust, and love. "Considerations" in fact communicates no sense of love for those involved in "homosexual unions," and indeed none for gays generally. One can infer from its language that this document was not crafted after a process of serious consultation and conversation with gay people. Ironically, the magisterium has engaged in extensive official dialogues with Protestants, Jews, and Muslims, but it has yet to do so with gay Catholics. Its tone and contents exemplifies in a particularly graphic way the result of speaking *about* gays but not *with* them. One can only hope that, at some point, the magisterium will learn that affirmation of the value of marriage need not be connected to questioning the worth of gay people.[77]

Notes

1. For the sake of economy this chapter will refer in a generic way to "same-sex marriage" as an umbrella term for partnerships between gay and lesbian people that are recognized by the civil law. Proposals for legal recognition of "civil union" will be considered under the one umbrella of "same-sex marriage," but there are significant differences between the two. This term "civil unions" is used in Vermont to describe the legal recognition of same-sex commitments. It should be taken here to include civil unions, though same-sex marriage grants more rights and benefits than do civil unions. "Civil union" is often the compromise option for those who want to maintain the traditional meaning of marriage, but it is rejected by some gay advocates as repeating the failed "separate but equal" logic long since rejected by the courts in the matter of racially segregated schools. Since the mag-

isterium rejects both same-sex marriage and anything it considers "tantamount" to it, including civil unions, they will be treated as one category here.

2. See *Economic Justice for All*, #2396 and #2357, respectively. For an elaboration of the meaning of "intrinsically disordered," see Livio Melina, "Homosexual Inclination as an 'Objective Disorder': Reflections of Theological Anthropology," *Communio* 25 (Spring 1998) 57–68. For a more extensive discussion of the Church's moral doctrine, see James P. Hanigan, *Homosexuality: The Test Case for Christian Sexual Ethics* (New York: Paulist, 1988) and Edward A. Malloy, *Homosexuality and the Christian Way of Life* (Washington: University Press of America, 1981).

3. See Joseph Pohle, "Tolerance, Religious," *Catholic Encyclopedia*, vol. 4 (New York: Encyclopedia, 1913).

4. *Declaration on Religious Liberty, Vatican Council II: The Conciliar and Post Conciliar Documents*, ed. Austin Flannery (Northport, N.Y.: Costello, 1996, rev. ed.) no. 7.

5. Ibid.

6. *Summa theologiae* 1–2, q. 96, a. 2, ad 3.

7. Ibid.

8. John Courtney Murray, SJ, *We Hold These Truths: Catholic Reflections on the American Proposition* (New York: Sheed and Ward, 1960) 166.

9. John Finnis, "Law, Morality, and 'Sexual Orientation,'" *Notre Dame Law Review* 69 (1994) 1075, n. 63.

10. See Germain Grisez, *The Way of the Lord Jesus*, vol. 2: *Living a Christian Life* (Quincy, Ill.: Franciscan, 1993) 651; and Finnis, "Law, Morality, and 'Sexual Orientation,'" 1049.

11. Gerard V. Bradley and Robert P. George, "Marriage and the Liberal Imagination," *Georgetown Law Journal* 84 (1995) 301–20, at 301–2.

12. Grisez, *The Way of the Lord Jesus* 2.653. Finnis argues that sexual intimacy between two members of the same sex can by their very nature accomplish no more than what is expressed in casual sex, sex contracted with a prostitute, or solitary masturbation. (See Finnis, "Law, Morality, and 'Sexual Orientation,'" 1049, 1067.) Some critics of course object strenuously to this description of gay and lesbian sexual activity, but this debate need not be entered here. See Paul J. Weithman, "Natural Law, Morality, and Sexual Complementarity," in David M. Estlund and Martha C. Nussbaum, eds., *Sex, Preference, and Family: Essays on Law and Nature* (New York: Oxford University, 1997) especially 239–41.

13. John Finnis, *Natural Law and Natural Rights* (Oxford: Clarendon, 1980) 147.

14. Finnis, "Law, Morality, and 'Sexual Orientation,'" 1070, emphasis in original text. See also Robert P. George, "'Same-Sex Marriage' and 'Moral Neutrality,'" in Christopher Wolfe, ed., *Homosexuality and American Public Life* (Dallas: Spence Publishing Company, 1999) 141–53.

15. Finnis, ibid.

16. Ibid, 1076.

17. Ibid, 1070.

18. Weithman, "Natural Law, Morality, and Sexual Complementarity" 242–43.

19. Stephen Macedo, "Homosexuality and the Conservative Mind," *Georgetown Law Journal* 84 (December 1995) 261–300, at 282; emphasis in the original text.

20. Ibid.

21. Committee on Marriage and Family, United States Conference of Catholic Bishops, "Always Our Children," revised in 1998, reprinted in John F. Harvey, OSFS, and Gerard V. Bradley, eds., *Same-Sex Attraction: A Parents' Guide* (South Bend, Ind.: St. Augustine's, 2003) 215.

22. *Catechism of the Catholic Church* no. 2333.

23. Ibid. 2358.

24. National Conference of Catholic Bishops, *Human Sexuality: A Catholic Perspective for Education and Lifelong Learning* (Washington: United States Catholic Conference, 1990) 55.

25. Ibid. Unfortunately, the magisterium omits discrimination on the basis of sexual orientation from its usual list of injustices.

26. This axiom is sometimes inaccurately attributed to St. Augustine.

27. "Always Our Children" 214.

28. See Edward O. Laumann, G. H. Gagnon, R. T. Michael, and S. Michaels, *The Social Organization of Sexuality: Sexual Practices in the United States* (Chicago: University of Chicago, 1994).

29. Janet Halley, "Sexual Orientation and the Politics of Biology: A Critique of the Argument from Immutability," *Stanford Law Review* 46 (1994) 503–68, at 517–21.

30. Richard Posner, *Sex and Reason* (Cambridge, Mass.: Harvard University, 1992) 296–97.

31. Some of what follows was first argued in Stephen J. Pope, "The Vatican's Blunt Instrument," *The Tablet*, 9 August 2003: 4–5.

32. Kelly, *New Directions in Sexual Ethics* 137.

33. Pontifical Council for the Family, "The Truth and Meaning of Human Sexuality: Guidelines for Education within the Family" no. 3.

34. *Catechism of the Catholic Church* no. 2332.

35. See, for example, the moving account provided in an Op-Ed essay by Andrew Sullivan, "Losing a Church, Keeping the Faith," *New York Times*, November 17, 2003, and Daria Donnelly, "A Gay Parent Looks at His Church: An Interview with Novelist Gregory Maguire," *Commonwealth* (October 24, 2003) 20–22.

36. See Robert Wintemute, *Sexual Orientation and Human Rights: The United States Constitution, the European Convention, and the Canadian Charter* (New York: Oxford University, 1997); William N. Eskridge, *Equality Practice: Civil Unions and the Future of Gay Rights* (New York: Routledge, 2002); Jonathan Goldberg-Hiller, *The Limits to Union: Same-Sex Marriage and the Politics of Civil Rights* (Ann Arbor: University of Michigan, 2002); Kevin Nourassa and Joe Varnell, *Just Married: Same Sex Marriage and the Expansion of Human Rights* (Madison: University of Wisconsin, 2002).

37. *Catechism of the Catholic Church* no. 2358.

38. Ibid.

39. "Considerations," no. 10, 181.

40. On something like this basis Michael Pakaluk argues for the revival of anti-sodomy laws in "Homosexuality and the Principle of Nondiscrimination," in Christopher Wolfe, ed., *Same-Sex Matters: The Challenge of Homosexuality* (Dallas: Spence Publishing Co., 2000) 67–85.

41. See James Q. Wilson, *The Moral Sense* (New York: Free, 1993) and Linda J. Waite and Maggie Gallagher, *The Case for Marriage: Why Married People Are Happier, Healthier, and Better-Off Financially* (New York: Doubleday, 2001).

42. See Judith Wallerstein, Julia Lewis, and Sandra Blakeslee, *The Unexpected Legacy of Divorce: A 25 Year Landmark Study* (New York: Hyperion, 2000) xxiii.

43. See Robin Fretwell Wilson, "Children at Risk: The Sexual Exploitation of Female Children after Divorce," *Cornell Law Review* 86 (2001) 251–327.

44. See Don S. Browning, *Marriage and Modernization: How Globalization Threatens Marriage and What to Do about It* (Grand Rapids: Eerdmans, 2003).

45. Centers for Disease Control and Prevention, Nat'l Ctr. for Health Statistics, Births, Marriages, Divorces and Deaths: Provisional Data for September 2001, National Vital Statistics Reports, Vol. 50, No. 8, (May 24, 2002) available at http://www.cdc.gov/nchs/data/nvsr/ nvsr50/nvsr50_08.pdf (last visited Oct. 21, 2003).

46. See Joyce A. Martin, et al., "Birth: Final Data for 2000," *National Vital Statistics Reports* 50, no. 5 (Hyattsville, Md.: National Center for Health Statistics, February 12, 2002). The rate of out-of-wedlock children rose dramatically between 1940 and 1990, some 1,300 percent between 1940 and 1994, and the birth rate for single women rose 600 percent. See Stephanie J. Ventura and Christine A. Bachrach, Centers for Disease Control and Prevention, Nat'l Ctr. for Health Statistics, Nat'l Vital Statistics Report, Nonmarital Childbearing in the United States, 1940–1999, National Vital Statistics Report, Vol. 48, No. 16. (Oct. 2000) available at http://www.cdc.gov/nchs/data/nvsv/nsvr48/nvs48_16.pdf (last visited May 2, 2004).

47. See Genaro C. Armas, "Cohabitation on the Rise: Unmarried-Partner Households Increase by 72%," Associated Press (May 21, 2001); Hilda Rodriguez,

"Cohabitation: A Snapshot," Center for Law and Social Policy, at http://www. clasp.org/DMS/Documents/1011885243.62/cohabation_snapshot.pdf (accessed May 2, 2004).

48. See J. S. Wallerstein and S. Blakeslee, *Second Chances: Men, Women, and Children a Decade after Divorce* (New York: Ticknor and Fields, 1989).

49. See Gallagher and Waite, *The Case for Marriage*, 75.

50. See Lisa Sowle Cahill, *Sex, Gender and Christian Ethics*, and also her *Women and Sexuality* (New York: Paulist, 1992).

51. Accounts of the state of contemporary marriage rarely attribute a significant negative causal influence to the increased tolerance of gay and lesbian sexual activity. See, for example, the major historical study by John Witte, Jr., *From Sacrament to Contract: Marriage, Religion, and Law in the Western Tradition* (Louisville: Westminster/John Knox, 1998).

52. Divorce prior to this time was granted in cases where one spouse could show that the other had been guilty of a grave offense such as adultery, cruelty, persistent neglect, desertion or the like. "No fault" divorce laws emerged in the 1970s to allow a spouse to sue for divorce without demonstrating the other's wrongdoing. Their enactment was followed by a dramatic rise in divorce rates. Included among the extensive literature on this topic is Leora Friedberg, "Did Unilateral Divorce Raise Divorce Rates? Evidence from Panel Data," *American Economic Review* 88 (1998) 608–27; J. Herbie DiFonzo, *Beneath the Fault Line: The Popular and Legal Culture of Divorce in Twentieth Century America* (Charlottesville: University of Virginia, 1997); Allen M. Parkman, *Good Intentions Gone Awry: No-Fault Divorce and the American Family* (Lanham, Md.: Rowman and Littlefield, 2000).

53. See Sullivan, *Virtually Normal*.

54. Andrew Sullivan, "Here Comes the Groom," *New Republic*, August 28, 1989, 20.

55. "Considerations," no. 8, 181.

56. Ibid. no. 7, 181.

57. Some empirical studies argue to the contrary. See Bridget Fitzgerald, "Children of Lesbian and Gay Parents: A Review of the Literature," *Marriage and Family Review* 29 (1999) 57–75; Charlotte Peterson, "Children of Lesbian and Gay Parents," *Child Development* 62 (1992) 1025–42; David K. Flaks et al., "Lesbians Choosing Motherhood: A Comparative Study of Lesbian and Heterosexual Parents and Their Children," *American Psychological Association* 31 (January 1995) 105–14.

58. See n. 9: Ellen C. Perrin, MD, and the Committee on Psychosocial Aspects of Child and Family Health, "Technical Report," 344. See Charlotte J. Patterson, "Family Relationships of Lesbians and Gay Men," *Journal of Marriage and the Family* 62 (2000) 1052–64; *Lesbian, Gay, and Bisexual Identities in Families: Psychological Perspectives*, ed. Charlotte J. Patterson and Anthony R. D'Augelli (New York: Oxford University, 1998). These kinds of studies are controversial. For a critical review of this literature and a summary of counter-arguments, see Timothy J. Daily, "Homosexual Parenting: Placing Children at Risk," Family Research Council, available at http://www.frc.org (accessed May 11, 2004).

59. See Lisa Sowle Cahill, "Marriage: Developments in Catholic Theology and Ethics," *Theological Studies* 64 (2003) 78–105.

60. Fineman, *Neutered Mother*, 5; emphasis added. See Martha Fineman, *The Neutered Mother, the Sexual Family and Other Twentieth Century Fantasies* (New York: Routledge, 1995) and Fineman, *The Illusion of Equality* (Chicago: University of Chicago, 1991).

61. Law Commission of Canada, *Recognizing and Supporting Close Personal Relationships Between Adults*, available at http://www.lcc.gc.ca/en/themes/pr/cpra/paper.asp (last visited May 2, 2004).

62. See American Law Institute [ALI], *Principles of the Law of Family Dissolution: Analysis and Recommendations* (New York: Matthew Bender, 2002). See Robert Pear, "Legal Group Urges States to Update Their Family Law," *New York Times*, November 30, 2002. Lynne Marie Kohm argues that ALI's domestic partnership proposal would diminish marriage, see "How Will the Proliferation and Recognition of Domestic Partnerships Affect Marriage?" *Journal of Law and Family Studies* 4 (2002) 105 f.

63. See, for example, Judith S. Wallerstein and Sandra Blakeslee, *The Good Marriage: How and Why Love Lasts* (Boston and New York: Houghton Mifflin, 1995).

64. On "expressive individualism," see Robert Bellah et al., *Habits of the Heart: Individualism and Commitment in American Life* (San Francisco: Harper and Row, 1985).

65. See Wilson, "Children at Risk."

66. M. Cathleen Kaveny, "Toward a Thomistic Perspective on Abortion and the Law in Contemporary America," *The Thomist* 55 (July 1991) 371. See also her "The Limits of Ordinary Virtue: The Limits of the Criminal Law in Implementing *Evangelium Vitae*," in *Choosing Life: A Dialogue on Evangelium Vitae*, ed. Kevin Wm. Wildes, SJ, and Alan C. Mitchell (Washington: Georgetown University, 1997) 132–49, and "Autonomy, Solidarity and Law's Pedagogy," *Louvain Studies* 27 (Winter 2002) 339–58.

67. Witte, Jr., *From Sacrament to Contract*, and Don S. Browning et al., *From Culture Wars to Common Ground: Religion and the American Family Debate* (Louisville: Westminster/John Knox, 2000).

68. See http://www.rcab.org/News/statement031002.html (accessed December 1, 2003).

69. On "critical familialism" in relation to civil law, see Don Browning, "Critical Familialism, Civil Society, and the Law," *Hofstra Law Review* 32 (2003); on "critical familialism" generally, see Browning et al., *From Culture Wars to Common Ground*; Don S. Browning and Gloria Rodriguez, *Reweaving the Social Tapestry: Toward a Public Philosophy and Policy for Families* (New York: W. W. Norton, 2001) and Don S. Browning, *Marriage and Modernization: How Globalization Threatens Marriage and What Should Be Done about It* (Grand Rapids: Eerdmans, 2003).

70. See P. Blumstein and P. Schwartz, "Intimate Relationships and the Creation of Sexuality," in D. McWhirter, S. Sanders, and J. Reinisch, eds., *Homosexuality/Heterosexuality: Concepts of Sexual Orientation* (New York: Oxford University, 1990) 96–109.

71. This case is stated clearly in Mary Ann Glendon, *Abortion and Divorce in Western Law* (Cambridge, Mass.: Harvard University, 1987).

72. The ecumenical nature of this common core is discussed in John Witte, Jr., "The Goods and Goals of Marriage," *Notre Dame Law Review* 76 (April 2001) 1019–71, and Browning et al., *From Culture Wars to Common Ground.*

73. Committee on Marriage and Family, United States Conference of Catholic Bishops, "Always Our Children," revised in 1998, reprinted in John F. Harvey, OSFS, and Gerard V. Bradley, eds., *Same-Sex Attraction: A Parents' Guide* (South Bend, Ind.: St. Augustine's, 2003) 215.

74. On the crisis, see United States Conference of Catholic Bishops, "Report on the Implementation of the 'Charter for the Protection of Children and Young People,'" *Origins* 33 (January 15, 2004) 521–40; National Review Board, "Report: Causes and Contents of the Sexual Abuse Crisis," *Origins* 33 (March 11, 2004) 633–88; John Jay College of Criminal Justice, *The Nature and Scope of the Problem of Sexual Abuse of Minors by Catholic Priests and Deacons in the United States* (Washington: United States Conference of Catholic Bishops, 2004).

75. *We Hold These Truths* 106 (see n. 40 above).

76. For a clear analysis of this weakness in Catholic sexual ethics generally, see Patrick T. McCormick, "Catholicism and Sexuality: The Sounds of Silence," *Horizons* 30 (Fall, 2003) 191–207.

77. Earlier drafts of this chapter received helpful criticism from James F. Keenan, SJ, John Paris, SJ, Lisa Cahill, Don S. Browning, and an anonymous referee for *TS* [*Theological Studies*].

Cohabitation

18. The Myth of Cohabitation

Willard F. Jabusch

This chapter first appeared in *America* 183 (October 7, 2000).

Every parish priest and university chaplain knows the story. The young couple visits their pastor to make arrangements for their wedding. The pastor begins to ask the questions on the prenuptial questionnaire. The young man gives his address and later the young woman. It appears they live at the same address and in the same apartment. Like so many others, they have been living together, perhaps for some time. There is, however, no embarrassment or apology, not the slightest hint of shame. Cohabitation has become so common that it seems it is the rare couple, at least in the big cities, who have not been living together before marriage. In fact, the common wisdom is that this is helpful for a future wedded life, since both man and woman will certainly get to know each other's follies and foibles, virtues and vices as they have breakfast and supper together every day; share a bathroom, take out the garbage and vacuum the rug. It is, supposedly, a sort of dress rehearsal for married life.

But is it true that you can improve your chances of having a successful marriage by living together to see what it's like? Not according to two recent studies, one by a sociology professor, Linda Waite of the University of Chicago, and another by the National Opinion Research Center [N.O.R.C.], a University of Chicago research facility. According to Professor Waite, cohabiting couples lack both specialization and commitment in their relationships. And although these couples are abundant in today's society, they are also more prone to make less money and are more likely to abuse one another physically than are married couples.

"Cohabitation isn't marriage," says Professor Waite, "and cohabitation people don't act the same way as married people. They don't have the same characteristics; they don't get the same benefits; and they don't get to pay the same costs."

Unlike Scandinavian countries, where cohabiting relationships tend to be long-term, Waite has observed that in the United States they are usually short-term and lead to a lack of committed marriages. Thomas W. Smith, director of the National Opinion Research Center survey, also notes that cohabitation remains in the United States a short-term phenomenon, but that it is, both before the first marriage and between marriages, the general rule. He remarks that the average duration of cohabitation is a little over a year, and these temporary relationships usually end in break-ups or marriage.

Statistics show that almost two-thirds of Americans choose to cohabit before getting married. According to Census Bureau figures, four million heterosexual couples are currently involved in these relationships, eight times more than in 1970.

"One of the things people get out of marriage is insurance," Waite remarks. "If you think of the Christian marriage vow—in sickness and in health—it seems that people will stay together even if one gets M.S. or cancer or gets disabled. It's insurance, and insurance is expensive. Emotionally, it's important in that if you get sick, there's someone who will take care of you."

When cohabitation is short-term, as in the United States, there is a lack of what might be called specialization. Waite points out that in marriage "you can say, I like to cook and you like to clean, and I'll get to be a terrific cook because I'll never have to clean. Two people together produce more. They can have a high quality life because they have two specialists, whereas people who live alone don't specialize." Also, according to Professor Waite, cohabiting couples do not pool their money, and those with separate incomes must pay separate taxes. They lack the shared financial resources upon which married couples rely.

In her article "The Negative Effects of Cohabitation," written for *The Responsive Community*, an academic journal, she writes that partners in the typical cohabitation relationship are also less likely to connect with their mate's family and to take care of their mate's children. "The parenting role of a cohabiting partner toward the child(ren) of the other person is extremely vaguely defined. The non-parent partner—the man, in the substantial majority of cases—has no explicit legal, financial, supervisory, or custodial rights or responsibilities regarding the child of his partner." Since many religions disapprove of cohabitation, it is not surprising that cohabiting couples are frequently not involved with any church.

The cohabiting man and woman are also more likely to lead separate lives and are less likely to have a monogamous sexual relationship than those who are married. Waite observes: "Four percent of married women had a secondary sex partner, compared to 20 percent of cohabiting women and 18 percent of dating women." Her study indicates that "to preserve their exit option, they are not really working in a partnership. They are being two separate people—it is trading off freedom and low levels of commitment for fewer benefits than you get from commitment." It also seems that many unmarried mothers remain in cohabiting relationships because they fear the domestic violence of marriage. Yet the study reports that married women are half as likely as women in cohabiting relationships to acknowledge physical abuse. "When it comes to 'hitting, shoving, and throwing things,' cohabiting couples are more than three times more likely than the married to say things that get far out of hand; people who live together are 1.8 times more likely to report violent arguments than married people."

Research at N.O.R.C. has shown, according to Smith, "the surprising result that people who cohabit before marriage are more likely to divorce. A trial marriage that would allow people to pick a lifetime partner and therefore lead to a better marriage doesn't work." Professor Waite attributes this to the non-committal attitude created during cohabitation. She says, "There is sort of a myth that you can improve your chances of having a successful marriage by living together to see what it's like, and there is no evidence at all that that helps people make a better decision; so it's not a good reason for living with somebody." She points out that her findings do not apply to couples living together who are engaged. "They are not planning an easy exit; they are planning to get married, they just have not done it yet." Since engaged couples are truly planning on spending the rest of their lives together, they are able to specialize and have fewer reasons for friction and distrust.

Social scientists have studied the cohabiting relationship for some time, ever since they began to wonder if it is just "marriage without the paper, or something else."

"I think," says Linda Waite, "we are pretty convinced that it is something else."

19. Cohabitation: Living in Sin or Occasion of Grace?

Kevin T. Kelly

This chapter first appeared in *The Furrow* 56 (2005).

What I am about as both parish priest and moral theologian is "trying to make faith-sense of experience and experience-sense of faith." (See Jack Mahoney, *Bioethics and Belief*, London, Sheed & Ward, 1984, p. 112.) That is why, when couples who have been living together for some time, many with children of their own, come to me to arrange their wedding, I cannot bring myself to tell them that they are "living in sin." I do not believe they are! They are coming to me because they want to make a more formal commitment before God to a living and growing relationship which they have already experienced as a grace from God. I was nearly going to insert the phrase "despite its rough patches" after the word relationship above. However, that would not reflect what these couples are saying to me. Many are encouraged and inspired by the fact that their love for each other has grown through their being able to overcome the difficult problems they have faced together, including problems in relating to each other. They have caught a glimpse of God in the midst of the storms and struggles they have been through. To describe their experience as "living in sin" would scandalize them and would be a denigration of something they had experienced as sacred and from God. Such language would almost be tantamount to blasphemy. In my experience, most of these couples seem blissfully ignorant that the church disapproves of the way they have been living. In fact, they are simply grateful that they can come to the church to celebrate the gift of their love for each other and to give it a new permanence through the solemn commitment of their marriage vows to each other and to God.

To make "faith-sense" of this new phenomenon of living together before marriage, we need to listen to how such living together affects the lives of those involved. Is it a good thing for them? Does it help them to grow together in love and mutual support? Could it be compared to a kind of novitiate in the religious life, gradually preparing them to make a full and unconditional commitment to each other? If, in fact, it seems to be a "good" experience in terms of human growth and fulfilment, does the church need to find a more positive and appropriate way of describing it?

In his book, *Living Together and Christian Ethics* (Cambridge University Press, 2002), the Anglican theologian, Adrian Thatcher lists twenty-five "probably true" propositions about cohabitation. Some carry a kind of health warning. For instance:

- "trial marriages" are unlikely to work;
- men are less committed to their female partners and much less committed to children;
- cohabitors with no plans to marry report poorer relationship quality than married people;
- cohabitors with children are very likely to split up;
- their children are more likely to be poorer and victims of abuse;
- cohabitation leads to an increase in the number of single-parent children.

That paints a rather bleak picture, especially if the increase in cohabitation is interpreted as one of the signs of creeping individualism and weakening religious belief.

However, Thatcher also offers some "good news":

- people who live together with their partner before they marry value fidelity almost as much as married people do;
- the stability of cohabitation and marriage may be measured by the beliefs and attitudes partners bring to each;

- cohabitors with plans to marry report no significant difference in relationship quality to married people.

Another Anglican theologian, Duncan Dormor, has written an equally interesting book on cohabitation, *Just Cohabiting? The Church, Sex and Getting Married* (London, Darton Longman & Todd, 2004). The way he presents some of the data is more hopeful than Thatcher's. For instance, he is able to report:

> More recent research, conducted when a majority of those marrying have cohabited first, has shown that it is no longer the case that those who cohabit in preparation for marriage are more likely to get divorced after the event. (p. 10)

Hence, to maintain that "the experience of pre-marital cohabitation has a destabilising effect on subsequent marriage" is simply "incorrect," even though it is "the simplest and most popular interpretation." (p. 10) However, Dormor does accept that "whilst it is clear that marital stability *per se* is not affected by premarital cohabitation, children born to cohabiting parents are twice as likely to experience parental separation as those born within marriage" (p. 88).

A post–Vatican II understanding of marriage recognises that it involves a growth process which neither begins nor ends with the marriage promises. At the heart of this process is the couple's growing together into a communion of life and love. The sexual expression of their love in intercourse is such an intimate part of this growth process that the consummation of their marriage lies in the achievement of an integrity between their making love and their living together rather than in any single post-wedding act of intercourse. Even their consent, which the church has always put center stage, is subject to the demands of growth. Time is needed for them gradually to grow in an appreciation of what they are undertaking together and in their mutual capacity for and commitment to this life-long creative task. All of this cannot be contained in a specific moment on their "wedding day."

Both Thatcher and Dormor agree that prenuptial cohabitation, that is, cohabiting prior to getting married, is a totally different reality to cohabiting without any intention of getting married. In prenuptial cohabitation the couple accept the values of marriage as their norm and have every hope and intention at some future date to make a solemn commitment to their relationship through the exchange of their nuptial vows in some kind of public wedding ceremony. Whereas couples who cohabit without any intention of getting married are simply living together for as long as suits them. The thought of life-long commitment is not on their agenda. Their relationship is a kind of consumer commodity, to be discarded when no longer needed by one or other partner. It is this form of cohabitation to which Thatcher's health-warnings mentioned above apply.

Dormor reports that less than 1% of couples getting married today actively adhere to the church's teaching on the undesirability of sexual intercourse before marriage. Certainly, for most couples today, at least in Britain, cohabitation is part of the process of getting married. They do not seem to be rejecting marriage nor seeing cohabitation as a desirable alternative. Rather they seem so aware that the health of a marriage is dependent on the potentiality for growth in their relationship that they are keen to get that growth process established on a solid foundation. Not until that foundation is laid, will they have the confidence to commit themselves for the rest of their lives. They do not see this as denying that marriage is for life. In fact, they would claim that this is their way of trying to ensure that their marriage actually will be for life. In their minds, to commit themselves before experiencing this initial part of the growth process and discovering whether as a couple they are up to it, would be foolhardy and irresponsible. It would be like teaching a person to swim by throwing them into the deep end rather than helping them gradually to feel confident in the water before risking themselves out of their depth. For many years Jack Dominian has argued that trial marriages are a recipe for disaster. Commitment cannot be experimental. Nevertheless, according to Dormor (p. 10), many young people today do not see cohabitation as a kind of "trial marriage." Rather, they see it as "a 'trailer' for the absolute commitment which marriage entails." Is this just a clever use of words or is there something more substantial to it?

Of course, making faith-sense of experience cannot ignore the negative aspects of cohabitation, however sensitively it is handled in pastoral practice. After all, it contains no built-in expression of commitment or binding framework of rights and responsibilities. Although in theory that can sound liberating and in keeping with the modern emphasis on individual freedom and internalised commitments, in practice when things do not work out, the partner in the weaker economic, social or legal position can be left in a desperate situation. Remember Thatcher's second health warning, "men are less committed to their female partners and much less committed to children." It is not by accident that many young mothers are left literally "holding the baby"! Moreover, if, as Christians and most people believe, marriage has a social dimension to it, with or without children, it is hardly doing justice to it to leave it as a purely private arrangement between consenting adults. Perhaps the warning note sounded in this paragraph applies less to prenuptial cohabitation than to cohabitation with no intention of marrying.

Thinking back over the weddings I have been involved with in recent years, I get the impression that the main reasons why many couples live together before their marriage are economic and social. They see the public celebration of their marriage as demanding a "big do." It is all part of a key "rite of passage" for them. If they are Christians, the wedding in church is an essential part of this—but only a part, not the whole. If they had only the church wedding, they would probably feel something lacking—shades of the wedding feast at Cana! But weddings are expensive—though the church celebration is probably the least expensive item! In our contemporary culture of self-sufficiency and independence, many couples feel that they should pay for their own wedding.

Nevertheless, in terms of their embarking on the process of their life-long sharing of life and love together, it is not the wedding which is first on their list of priorities. Before that, they want to set up home together—ideally in their own house, though, tragically, this is becoming more and more an impossibility for many young couples. Some are keen to start a family before they marry—though they would do well to heed Thatcher's second health warning. I sometimes wonder whether, at least for some cohabiting couples, the baptism of their first child is an important public statement about their growing into marriage together. That would explain the increasing trend to invite family and numerous friends to the baptism and the celebration afterwards. It would also put their cohabitation firmly in the pre-nuptial category!

A very important document, *On the Way to Life*, written principally by James Hanvey of the Heythrop Institute for Religion, Ethics and Public Life, has been published very recently by the Catholic Education Service. It was commissioned by the Department for Education and Formation of the Bishops' Conference of England and Wales. Hence, at least implicitly it has the support of the Bishops' Conference. It tries to analyse the present-day culture which is in the air we breathe and which, inevitably, has an influence on the way we live and the decisions we make. It also offers an interpretation of our own post–Vatican II Catholic culture and tries to discern how we can translate and interpret our Christian vision into language (not just words, but also life and action) which is enriched by the deepest and truest insights of contemporary culture, while refraining from being colonised and taken over by its less desirable elements. *On the Way to Life* sees freedom as one of the dominant values in present-day culture. (cf. pp. 13–14) It points out that freedom and its associated values "are not just static concepts but are subtly embedded in our ways of understanding both ourselves and the cultural dynamics in which we are engaged." In struggling to see if it is possible to make faith-sense of cohabitation, perhaps one important question that needs to be faced is this. Is today's social trend of cohabitation no more than an expression of the kind of freedom which claims that we humans are the sole arbiters of the truth of our actions and that the only criterion to follow is self-authentication, "Be true to yourself—do your own thing"? In terms of giving meaning to marriage, Dormor would interpret such an approach as equivalent to Anthony Giddens' notion of "pure relationship." (cf. Dormor, pp. 91–104) In other words, all that matters is the relationship between consenting adults, to last only as long as their consent lasts (and presumably that means, as long as they find each other attractive or their relationship satisfying their needs), with children having no say in it, since it is an "adults only" relationship.

I must confess that the cohabiting couples who come to me to be married would be horrified by the Giddens approach. It might be in tune with some of what they see on television but it is certainly not how they would interpret their own relationship. They would see the Giddens scenario as failing to do justice to how they see themselves as human persons and to the kind of relationship they have struggled to build up as a couple. Love, tenderness and stability are the values they seem to believe in and which they would want to be hallmarks of their own marriage. They would also see these values as offering the right environment for the upbringing of their children, whether already born or hoped for in the future. They believe in freedom, certainly. Perhaps unthinkingly it is their freedom of spirit which has empowered them to leave home and cohabit together. I have even met couples who have seen their cohabitation was a very deliberate way of entering into the marriage process on their own terms and under their own free volition. For them, to start the marriage process with their wedding would be to let their parents and family take over this important stage in their life together.

One of the key insights of *On the Way to Life* is its focus on "the ordinary" as the realm of God's grace:

> The "ordinary" is only a problem in a desacralised world in which the secular refuses to be graced. The theology of grace that informs Vatican II recovers "the ordinary" as the realm of grace, God's "better beauty"; hence the aesthetic of holiness is something exceptional but something that is shaped in the realm of the domestic, giving it the weight of glory; the Alchemist's stone is Christ.

In making faith-sense of cohabitation, I am left wondering whether some cohabiting couples might, at least implicitly and maybe even unconsciously, be laying claim to the holiness of "the ordinary" of their relationship. They are holding back from celebrating that in the solemnity of their marriage until they have sufficient appreciation of the wonder and beauty ("the weight of glory") of this "ordinary" reality of which they are the co-creators.

In recent years I have also noticed that some couples—admittedly, very few at present—are wanting to mark much earlier wedding anniversaries than their Silver or Golden with a religious blessing or renewal of vows, either in church or as an intimate family celebration. Could this be an indication that they are becoming more conscious of the power of symbols both to consolidate and celebrate key moments in the growth of their marriage and to reveal the sacredness of their "ordinary" life together?

In this little chapter I have tried to make some kind of "faith-sense" of the fact that many couples living together before marriage find this a "good" experience and want to thank God for its goodness when they eventually celebrate their wedding. If there is any truth in what I have written—and I believe there is—maybe it is also a challenge to those of us who are theologians. Does our Christian theology of sexuality need to develop imaginatively and creatively so that what it says about cohabitation actually makes "experience-sense" for the many Christians who are actually living this reality? If our theology can move in that direction, perhaps such a move could be reflected in some imaginative and innovative moves in the fields of liturgy—and even canon law. After all, the best liturgy emerges out of life—and custom often gives rise to the best laws.

Indissolubility and Divorce

20. Propositions on the Doctrine of Christian Marriage

International Theological Commission with Commentary by Philippe Delhaye

This chapter first appeared in *Contemporary Perspectives on Christian Marriage*, ed. Richard Malone and John R. Connery (Chicago: Loyola University Press, 1984).

INDISSOLUBILITY OF MARRIAGE

4.1 The Principle

The early Church's tradition, based on the teaching of Christ and the apostles, affirms the indissolubility of marriage, even in cases of adultery. This principle applies despite certain texts which are hard to interpret and despite examples of indulgence—the extension and frequency of which is difficult to judge—toward persons in very difficult situations.

4.2 The Church's Doctrine

The Council of Trent declared that the Church has not erred when it has taught and teaches in accordance with the doctrine of the gospel and the apostles that the marriage bond cannot be broken through adultery. Nevertheless, because of historical doubts (opinions of Ambrosiaster, Catharinus, and Cajetan) and for some more or less ecumenical reasons, the council limited itself to pronouncing an anathema against those who deny the Church's authority on this issue.

It cannot be said then that the council had the intention of solemnly defining marriage's indissolubility as a truth of faith. Still, account must be taken of what Pius XI said in *Casti Connubii*, referring to this canon: "If therefore the church has not erred and does not err in teaching this, and consequently it is certain that the bond of marriage cannot be dissolved even on account of the sin of adultery, it is evident that the other causes of divorce, which are usually brought forward, have even less value and cannot be taken into consideration" (DS 1807).

4.3 Intrinsic Indissolubility

The intrinsic indissolubility of marriage can be considered under various aspects and be grounded in various ways:

- From the point of view of the spouses: their intimate conjugal union as a mutual self-giving of two persons, just like their very marital love itself and the welfare of the offspring, demands indissoluble unity. From this is derived the spouses' moral duty to protect, maintain and develop the marital covenant.
- From God's vantage point: from the human act by which the spouses give and accept each other there rises a bond which is based on the will of God and inscribed in nature, independent of human authority and removed from the sphere of power of the spouses, and therefore intrinsically indissoluble.
- From a Christological perspective: the final and deepest basis for the indissolubility of Christian matrimony lies in the fact that it is the image, sacrament, and witness of the indissoluble union between Christ and the Church that has been called the *bonum sacramenti*. In this sense indissolubility becomes a reality of grace.
- The social perspective: indissolubility is demanded by the institution of marriage itself. The spouses' personal decision comes to be accepted, protected, and reinforced by society itself, espe-

cially by the ecclesial community, for the good by the offspring and for the common good. This is the juridico-ecclesial dimension of matrimony.

These various aspects are intimately tied together: the fidelity to which the spouses are bound and which ought to be protected by society, especially by the ecclesial community, is demanded by God the creator and by Christ who makes it possible through his grace.

4.4 Extrinsic Indissolubility and the Power of the Church over Marriages

Hand in hand with practice, the Church has elaborated a doctrine concerning its powers over marriages, clearly indicating the scope and limits of that power. The Church acknowledges that it does not have any power to invalidate a sacramental marriage which is contracted and consummated (*ratum et consummatum*).

For very grave reason and out of concern for the good of the faith and the salvation of souls, all other marriages can be invalidated by competent Church authority or—according to another interpretation—can be declared dissolved. This teaching is only a particular application of the theory explaining the evolution of doctrine in the church. Today it is generally accepted by Catholic theologians.

Neither is it to be excluded that the Church can further define the concepts of sacramentality and consummation by explaining them even better, so that she can present the whole doctrine on the indissolubility of marriage in a deeper and more precise way.

COMMENTARY

Proposition (4.1–4.4)

The indissolubility of marriage is bound up in a very special way with the sacramentality of marriage (Proposition 2.2). It is made possible by the fact that human love is inserted into the agape that binds Christ to his church (Propositions 3.1; 3.2; 3.3, etc.), in spite of any stubbornness of the heart. We now need examine indissolubility in its own terms and attend to the problems it raises in our time.

When we submit to a close scrutiny the fourth set of propositions, prepared under the direction of Fr. E. Hamel,[1] we notice that we are indeed dealing with the traditional church doctrine which has recently been reaffirmed by Vatican II. However, there is a large difference between *Gaudium et Spes* in 1965 and these 1977 propositions. This is the difference that separates what used to be called a doctrine "in tranquil possession"[2] from a doctrine exposed to challenges that call for response.

The 1965 text does not even mention the "Zoghby affair,"[3] which called in question the meaning of the statements of the Council of Trent on the basis of the hesitations we note in the early centuries of the Church and of the doubts expressed by some theologians. Since 1965 many studies, books, and articles have appeared. Some theologians believe that these supply overwhelming evidence in support of the historical dissolution of some marital bonds. Others refuse to grant that, with one or two exceptions, there has been any hesitation. The ITC [International Theological Commission] could not undertake to resolve these historical questions. It wisely acknowledged that the questions are difficult. It has expressed the hesitations of the fathers of Trent better than Vatican II did. It is not possible to speak of indissolubility as a dogma of faith in the strict sense of the phrase, but neither can it be denied that we are dealing here with Catholic doctrine[4] endowed with all the solidity implied in that theological note. In taking this position, the ITC finds support both in the teaching of Pius XI and in the tridentine clause which mentions the "fidelity to evangelical and apostolic doctrine" (Proposition 4.2).

The postconciliar discussion has also induced the ITC to use the distinction between extrinsic and intrinsic indissolubility, a distinction unknown to Vatican II. Extrinsic indissolubility is involved when an authority intervenes and annuls a marriage or declares with authority that a particular union is null and void (Proposition 4.4).

Consonant with the general phenomenon of "the development of doctrine" (Proposition 4.4), the Church has claimed certain powers over the nonsacramental marriages of pagans (Proposition 4.4), in line with what is known as the "Pauline Privilege" or the "Privilege of the Faith."[5] But the Church does not claim any power to dissolve consummated sacramental marriages. We can avoid being scandalized by any apparent contradiction if we perceive that in the former case we are dealing with a human covenant and in the latter with a union grounded in Christ. This does not mean, of course, that progress cannot be made (Proposition 4.4, at the end). As we learn more about the way in which the conjugal bond comes to be constituted, the consummation theory of medieval canonists may well turn out to be too inadequate to be tenable any longer. According to this theory, marriage is consummated by one act of sexual intercourse, no more, no less. However, no one has yet elaborated another acceptable theory. The theory which has been some times suggested, that consummation ought to be equated with a long process of psychological maturation, contains the problem of seeming to promote trial marriage.

The intrinsic indissolubility of marriage concerns not the level of authority bearing on marriage from outside but the level of the very realities involved. The bond which unites in Christ a man and a woman who have given themselves to each other, or accepted each other, is inherently indestructible. It escapes the reach of every authority. "Let no man separate what God has joined!" (Mt 19:6). Read Proposition 4.3 over and over again, and note how it insists upon the arguments which, convincingly and forcefully, lead to the conclusion that Christian marriage is indissoluble. We are a long way from the serenity displayed by Vatican II in 1965. There, the position was taken for granted; here, we notice an anxious concern with defending church doctrine against criticism leveled at it from all directions. Yet this indissolubility emerges from exigencies intrinsic to the conjugal union itself, from the will of God the creator, from the love of the redeemer, as well as from considerations relative to the good of society and the well-being of the offspring.

Instead of summarizing these clear and powerful texts, let us follow the example of Proposition 4.4 and coordinate all the arguments into a dynamic dialectic. The wish that marriage should be permanent and faithful resides above all in the will, the affectivity, and the desire of the spouses who give themselves to each other in the totality of their own selves—what they are and what they are going to be. Each spouse expects to be able to count on the other for better or for worse. They both build their lives and activities on the basis of this expectation, so much so that when one is away the other feels lost.

Alas! Just as much as any other human value, this beautiful ideal is threatened by weakness, boredom, egoism, and aggressiveness. The other may be in danger of being made into an object or an instrument for the attainment of self-centered pleasure, or even a scapegoat. This is the reason why, even before a crisis occurs, the grace of Christ undertakes to heal conjugal love from its faults, to transform desire into gift, to elevate eros to the level of agape, which does not seek its own good but cares above all for the good of the other.[6] Love shifts from the key of desire to that of gift. These are the graces which Christ gives his faithful by means of a permanent sacrament.

This sacrament is constituted by a communion which is ontological as well as psychological and moral and includes its own *mysterion* of love. If the spouses suffer in their fidelity, or for the sake of it, they must remember that Christ has already traveled that road. If he asks much of them, he himself has given them much more. The indissolubility precept could not have made sense—the sense which, in the Old Testament, sinful nature failed to perceive because of stubbornness of heart—if Christ had not brought grace and light. Here, too, we may repeat what is said in John 1:17: "…though the law was given through Moses, grace and truth have come through Jesus Christ" (JB). Perhaps those scholastic theologians were not so far wrong who maintained that the fidelity and the indissolubility of marriage hinge on the precept that prescribes forgiveness and appeals to the example of the universal forgiveness which has come to us in and through Christ.

THE DIVORCED WHO HAVE REMARRIED

5.1 Gospel Radicalism

Faithful to the radicalism of the gospel, the Church cannot refrain from stating with St. Paul the Apostle, "To those now married, however, I give this command (though it is not mine; it is the Lord's): a wife must not separate from her husband. If she does separate, she must either remain single or become reconciled again. Similarly, a husband must not divorce his wife" (1 Cor 7:10–11). It follows from this that new unions following divorce under civil law cannot be considered regular or legitimate.

5.2 Prophetic Witness

This severity does not derive from a merely disciplinary law or from a type of legalism. It is rather a judgment pronounced by Jesus himself (Mk 10:6 ff.). Understood in this way, this harsh norm is a prophetic witness to the irreversible fidelity of love which binds Christ to his Church. It shows also that the spouses' love is incorporated into the very love of Christ (Eph 5:23–32).

5.3 Nonsacramentalization

The incompatibility of the state of remarried divorced persons with the precept and mystery of the paschal love of the Lord makes it impossible for these people to receive the sign of unity with Christ in the Eucharist. Access to Eucharistic communion can only come through penance, which implies detestation of the sin committed and the firm purpose of not sinning again (see DS 1676).

Let all Christians, therefore, remember the words of the apostle: "Whoever eats the bread or drinks the cup of the Lord unworthily, sins against the Body and Blood of the Lord. A man should examine himself first; only then should he eat of the bread and drink of the cup. He who eats and drinks without recognizing the Body eats and drinks a judgment on himself" (1 Cor 11:27–29).

5.4 Pastoral Care of the Divorced Who Have Remarried

While this illegitimate situation does not permit a life of full communion with the Church, Christians who find themselves in this state yet are not excluded from the action of divine grace and from a link with the Church. Therefore they must not be deprived of pastoral assistance (see the address of Pope Paul VI, Nov 4, 1977).

They are not dispensed from the numerous obligations stemming from baptism, especially the duty of providing for the Christian education of their children. The paths of Christian prayer, both public and private, penance, and certain apostolic activities remain open to them. They must not be ignored, but rather helped like all Christians who are trying with the help of Christ's grace, to free themselves from the bonds of sin.

5.5 Combating the Causes of Divorce

The need for pastoral action to avoid the multiplication of divorces and of new civil marriages of the divorced seems ever more urgent. It is recommended that future spouses be given a vivid awareness of all their responsibilities as spouses and parents. The real meaning of matrimony must be ever more adequately presented as a covenant contracted "in the Lord" (1 Cor 7:39). Thus Christians will be better disposed to observe the command of God and to witness to the union of Christ and the Church. That will redound to the greater personal advantage of the spouses, of their children, and of society itself.

COMMENTARY

(Propositions 5.1–5.5)

When we deal with the indissolubility of Christian marriage, we inevitably raise the urgent and distressing problem of Catholics who are divorced and remarried. When we deal with this problem in turn, our concern is both doctrinal and pastoral in nature, for we should never separate the two domains of doctrine and pastoral practice.[7] We also examine the effect upon the faith of the church and her fidelity to the Lord Jesus of practices which call in question the impact of his teaching and his will to deliver humankind from sin. It is not possible to do justice to the precept and the demands of the Lord by announcing, "A sacramental Christian marriage contracted and consummated is indissoluble," and then going on to accept remarriage as normal and legitimate. To admit remarried divorcees to the Eucharist amounts to abandoning the apostolic rule which declares that we should not partake of the Body and Blood of the Lord Jesus unless we have relinquished a situation which, objectively considered, implies sin, and unless we are determined not to dwell within the situation any longer. Of course, this determination is a human one, and so it is fragile. All the same, it must be genuine.

Having said this much, note how the text of the propositions makes it clear that the ITC had no trouble parting company with a rigoristic pastoral practice which, even if it did not go as far as advocating formal excommunications (as was the case until very recently in some countries), did all the same ostracize divorced and remarried Catholics and left them pretty much to their own devices as sheep without a shepherd. Throughout the preparatory phase, the ITC greatly appreciated a document issued by the Pontifical Committee on the Family under the title "Pastoral Care of Divorced and Remarried Catholics" and written by His Excellency Bishop Gagnon, the Committee's President, with the assistance of Fr. Diarmuid Martin.[8] Between the time this document was issued and the time the ITC held its meeting, the Holy Father Paul VI had also gone on record in favor of a pastoral practice that stresses benevolence and charity.

In light of what has just been said, it is easier to understand the meaning of the propositions in this fifth set, especially those which relate to the civil remarriage of divorcees, as well as the impossibility of admitting these individuals to Eucharistic communion. The members of the ITC were aware that exegetes have been debating—even very recently—the clause "lewd conduct is a separate case—*nisi fornicationis causa*" in Matthew 19:9. This is why they chose to anchor their position on Mark 10:6–12 (Proposition 5.2), which is clear cut and justifies the last words in proposition 5.1. They were aware that specialists in biblical moral theology wonder whether Jesus' interdiction of divorce is a law, or a norm, or only an ideal to which we are being summoned. They refer to 1 Corinthians 7:10–11, where Paul, on the basis of his authority and charism as an apostle, certifies that a command is at stake (*paraggello*). At a lower level no doubt, and yet ineluctably, the theologian is here what St. Paul was: a witness who is not entitled to evade the radicalism of Jesus (Proposition 5.1). The Lord has issued a verdict (Proposition 5.2) which has nothing to do with legalism or with a will to repress and oppress. That verdict is a prophetic sign of the extent of the agape of Christ and its all-encompassing demand.

The rigor of this demand led Christ to surrender his life for us. In the Eucharist, we relive this mystery. If Christians do not follow Christ to the end, what could possibly entitle them to partake of the sacrificial meal which the Lord has renewed? How could they participate in the offering which the faithful make through the mediation of the priest acting in the person of Christ (*in persona Christi*)? When conjugal love assumed into agape is ruptured, a break with the sacrament of agape follows as a consequence. St. Paul mentions this (Proposition 5.3) in relation to all sinners to be sure, but certainly without excluding divorced and remarried persons who were numerous in the Greek and Roman society of his time. Doesn't Paul prescribe, as the Church does, that in sexual matters Christians should conduct themselves in a manner totally different from the pagans (Proposition 1.3)?

Objections will no doubt be raised. Some could object that Paul recommends that the faithful should examine their consciences and ascertain whether they are worthy to eat the Body of Christ. Paul speaks about conscience, not about the Church. This objection forgets that, while conscience passes judgment, this judgment is ruled by the judgment of the Lord himself. Conscience is not a valid guide unless it be an echo of God's own voice. The Apostle to the Gentiles says this often. Suffice it to quote here another passage of that same epistle: "Mind you, I have nothing on my conscience. But that does not mean that I am declaring myself innocent. The Lord is to judge me" (1 Cor 4:4).

Another possible difficulty: why exclude from the Eucharist those who commit serious sins in the area of sexuality and not those who commit serious sins in the area of justice? True, the collective conscience of Christians has now grown more sensitive to sins against justice, solidarity, and charity. This is genuine progress. But can this be a good reason to throw overboard all the demands of Christian morality in matters of family life and sexuality, as if they were long dead taboos? The objection reveals the need for greater severity towards public sinners in matters of justice, not for permissiveness in matters of sexual morality. However, two remarks are in order. It is not easy to ascertain whether a charge of injustice is justified. There is the risk of being swayed by one's own interests. In the second place, the situation of divorced and remarried persons has an element of tragedy, insofar as divorce creates a perduring situation difficult to escape. Since it is grounded on juridical acts, it is verifiable and public.

This is precisely why, although objectively we must accept the impossibility of admitting such persons to Eucharistic communion, we should strive for a pastoral practice which will make a return home possible. Contempt, rejection, and insults neither are called for by the gospel, nor are effective. There is room here for a new kind of pastoral ministry that would follow the directives of Pope Paul VI in his allocution of November 6, 1977 (Proposition 5.4).[9] Is not this valid for many other areas as well? In a Christian environment, the moral life of the large majority of Christians can be assumed not to fall below that minimum degree of adherence to Christ which is indispensable for Eucharistic life. When needed, the sacrament of penance sets things right. But in our secularized world which everywhere projects a vision of man and of the world in which God no longer has a place, one is not a disciple of Christ unless one knows and wills oneself to be. This does not mean that we are succumbing to the temptation of elitism. Can there really be an elite in the ordinary sense of the word if every Christian value is a gift of grace? Yet we must accept the fact that not all of those who believe in Christ respond equally to this grace, as we well know from the parable of the sower. Thus forbearance toward the weak is in order, but vigilance also. We must help them so that the deeds they do as Christians be more mature and more deliberate (Propositions 2.3; 2.4).

It is in this sense that Proposition 5.5 advocates preventive action. If there are so many divorced persons, is it not because so many hurry into marriage? Some marriages are, in fact, null and void for lack of commitment and maturity. But in many other cases, young people have freely, and hence validly, engaged in a venture which turns sour. Here there is room for a new form of family apostolate. The successes already achieved give hope that we are not merely expressing here a pious wish.

It is time to bring to a close this commentary, already too long and yet still too short. The members of the ITC dare to hope that readers of this commentary will display, in reading it, as much good will, as much concern for theological methods, and as much commitment to Christ as the members themselves have tried to use in preparing the propositions here commented upon.

Notes

1. E. Hamel, "The Indissolubility of Completed Marriage," in *Contemporary Perspectives on Christian Marriage*, ed. Richard Malone and John R. Connery (Chicago: Loyola University Press, 1984), 181–203.

2. I am alluding to a procedure once used in many textbooks, a procedure whose legitimacy I do not intend to endorse. When writing the history of a doctrine, one would run into an empty period. At this point it was customary to say that this doctrine was so well known and accepted that people would not speak of it. Of this argument from silence I keep only this fact: when a doctrine is resisted and controverted, the arguments for it grow more plentiful than they are during times when the doctrine is taken for granted and admitted by everyone.

3. See the learned and serious study of Fr. Wenger in *Vatican II: chronique de la quatrième session*, 6, 200–246. The Patriarchal Vicar for Egypt and Sudan took the position that the economy as practiced in the Oriental Churches not in communion with Rome should be extended. The spouse who has been deserted should be allowed to contract a second marriage which would not be sacramental yet would be recognized by the ecclesiastical authority.

4. The expressions *catholic truth* and *catholic doctrines* are used interchangeably, as noted by J. Beumer, in "Katholisch Wahrheiten," *Lexikon für Theologie und Kirche* 6 (1961): 88. The exegesis of this technical term is to be found in A. Michel, "Verité," *Dictionnaire de Théologie Catholique* 15 (1950): 2681. See the valuable observations of L. Ott, *Fundamentals of Catholic Dogma* (6th ed.; St. Louis, MO, 1964), 8: "Corresponding to the purpose of the teaching authority of the Church of preserving unfalsified and of infallibly interpreting the truths of revelation (D 1800) the primary object (*obiectum primarium*) of the teaching office of the church is the body of immediately revealed truths and facts. The infallible doctrinal power of the Church extends, however, secondarily to all those truths and facts which are a consequence of the teaching of revelation or a presupposition of it (*objectum secundarium*). Those doctrines and truths defined by the Church not as immediately revealed but as intrinsically connected with the truths of revelation so that their denial would undermine the revealed truths are called *catholic truths* (*veritates catholicae*) or ecclesiastical teachings (*doctrinae ecclesiasticae*) to distinguish them from the *divine truths* or divine doctrines of revelation (*veritates vel doctrinae divinae*). These are proposed for belief in virtue of the infallibility of the Church in teaching doctrines of faith or morals (*fides ecclesiastica*)."

5. His Excellency Mgr. Ch. Lefebvre, Dean of the Rota, has been kind enough to assist the ITC in the exploration of this question. We want to express here our respectful gratitude.

6. God's love is never "self-seeking" (1 Cor 13:5). There also comes to mind this scholastic description of love: [to love is] to take pleasure in the good of the other (*delectari in bono alterius*).

7. This is certainly the import of note 1 in *Gaudium et Spes*.

8. E. Gagnon, "Problèmes pastoraux relatifs aux catholiques divorcés et civilement remariés," *Esprit et Vie* 88 (1978): 241–45.

9. Specific directives to be found in the Pope's allocution and in the article of Bishop Gagnon. Experience of another sort has evoked a rectification by Msgr. Le Bourgeois which some seem to ignore. See *La Documentation Catholique*, n. 1723 (July 3, 1977): 645–47.

21. Caring for Committed Love in Good Times and Bad

Elsie P. Radtke

This chapter first appeared in *Chicago Studies* 45 (2006).

---

*Weddings are a family affair. Everyone gathered to launch
Emily and David into their life as a married couple. The day
was beautiful, the ceremony was meaningful, the party was
fun and after two and a half years, they were divorced. What
happened?*

When a couple marries, they rarely, if ever, expect the marriage to
end in divorce. This was not in the plan for their lives. Their families, their
Church, and they themselves hold marriage in high regard. Marriage is a
sacrament. It is holy and it is forever. It is their dream and they want to
succeed at it.

Then what does a couple do when they hit bumpy times and trouble
begins? When they find out that marriage isn't all the things they thought
it would be? When they don't have any idea how to fix their relationship?
What happens when they turn to their Church for help?

*David expected Emily to keep house and cook meals as his
mother had done for his father. Emily thought she had made it
clear to him that she loved her career and independence and
felt if he wanted to cook and clean he could go right ahead
and do that for himself. Even though David knew she was like*

*this before the marriage, he thought she would change once
they were married and living together.*

Church teaching is very specific on marriage. For a marriage to be valid it must have four qualities: permanence, fidelity, openness to children, and consent. On the surface, these are simple enough concepts, yet in our culture the couple getting married may not really understand them. They may have experienced the divorce of their parents, aunts, uncles, siblings, and friends, and have never seen permanence. They see celebrities stay in their marriages for "as long as we both shall love" rather than "as long as we both shall live." Fidelity is a flexible term for many people. Casual sex on business trips may be seen as a recreational activity that is not emotionally binding, and not as a violation of commitment. Openness to children requires generosity and understanding of the sacramental nature of matrimony, a lot to ask of a couple in a "me" centered culture. Consent with understanding and acceptance may not be possible if they are unaware of the shallow nature of their relationship, and so they consent without an adequate understanding of themselves or their prospective spouse.

SOME THINGS WE KNOW ABOUT RISKS FOR FAILURE

We have more information about marriage available to us than ever before. Social scientists have conducted rigorous and thorough research and studies for decades. Researchers have found predictors that can make a couple more likely to divorce. Dr. John Gottman, from his Seattle "Love Lab," is able to predict with more than 90 percent accuracy, after studying the interactions of couples, which couples are likely to see their marriages fail, based on studying their interactions. While the fact that a couple argues does not have to lead to divorce, since all married couples have disagreements and argue, he has found that it is *the way* they argue, and *the damage* they inflict on each other that causes their marriages to break down. He calls these indicators of marital problems the four horsemen—contempt, criticism, defensiveness, and withdrawal or stonewalling. A marriage suffers under the onslaught of this kind of warfare.

Studies also show a higher rate of divorce for couples that have cohabited before marriage, which couples today do with great frequency. Many

couples today slide from cohabitation right into marriage without any understanding of the differences in the two living conditions. Dr. Scott Stanley,
from the Center for Family Life and the University of Denver, advises young
couples to avoid the "slippery slope" of going from cohabitation into marriage without some serious soul searching and marriage preparation.

Some of what we know about failed marriages comes from what we
have learned through the annulment process. It is not unusual to hear a
petitioner or respondent in the declaration of nullity process question how
they could have made the decision they did to marry the person they married. It is not unusual to hear that as the bride was walking down the aisle
she knew she was making a mistake but was too embarrassed to back out
at that point. A woman may have discounted or diminished the negative or
abusive behaviors of the man she intends to marry because she hopes once
they are married things will get better. Others marry to escape a dull or
abusive life at home.

> *David and Emily had not considered what their careers meant
> to their personal lives as a husband and wife. They each
> wanted what they wanted and were unwilling to be flexible, or
> to give up anything of their expectations for the sake of each
> other and for the marriage. They never attempted to move
> from a "me" centered world to a "we" centered life together.*

On occasion a priest, deacon, or marriage minister may be able to
influence a couple to postpone or cancel their wedding plans to let time
and maturity better influence their decision. In most cases, however, we
reach the couples too late; weddings are performed even with doubts
present. It is presumed that the marriage is valid and will endure. The
Church is trying to respond to this situation by more thorough programs
for marriage preparation, also realizing that preparation for marriage
needs to start at a very young age.

APPROACHING THE CHURCH TO MARRY

When a couple approaches the Church to be married, they do so
for a variety of reasons. They may choose a particular church because it

will provide a great background for the wedding pictures. They may marry in the Church because their parents and grandparents expect it, whether they practice their faith or not. Whatever the reason, when they come to a Catholic parish to marry, it is a chance for us to welcome the couple warmly to our faith community. If they are not regular churchgoers, we have the opportunity to build a relationship with them. We can reach out to them, have a caring conversation, let them know how happy we are that they have decided to marry in the Church, and then start the education process to instruct them in what that means. Attendance at good marriage preparation programs, and continuing education after marriage, has been shown to be helpful in building a strong foundation for the first years of marriage.

In order to promote the most thorough marriage ministry possible, the Archdiocese of Chicago has prepared the newly revised *Marriage Ministry Guidelines*, which give pastoral ministers a structure to follow. Research shows that couples benefit more in their marriage if they have between nine and 12 contacts with a marriage minister. The first contact is the welcome and introduction to the wedding process. The second contact takes place when the couple takes the FOCCUS, or a similar premarital inventory, a process often facilitated by a lay or deacon couple. The third contact is a good discussion about the outcomes from the inventory. In this meeting, couples identify their strengths and challenges in their future life together. It is this meeting that helps them understand that marriage requires real work and effort, and that the upcoming marriage preparation program will be a good source of further education and support for them.

A marriage preparation program, such as the Pre-Cana or Discovery Weekend, is the fourth contact, whether it is held at the local parish or is one of the archdiocesan programs. The fifth contact is a choice of a Christian Sexuality workshop, or an introductory Natural Family Planning (NFP) class. Many couples learn things about Church teaching at this session that they had no idea of before. They also learn a method for achieving or avoiding a pregnancy that is in concert with Church teaching. It is also worth noting that studies show that couples who practice NFP in marriage have a considerably lower divorce rate.

The sixth meeting is with the pastor or deacon to complete the final papers, review the FOCCUS and Pre-Cana, and take care of any last-minute concerns the couple may have. Meetings seven and eight are the rehearsal and the wedding day itself.

The critical last pieces outlined in the *Marriage Ministry Guidelines* extend beyond the preparation process into the first years of marriage. Couples may attend two continuing education workshops in the first year after the wedding. These workshops are concerned with time, sex, and money, the areas research has shown to be the main "deal-breakers" in the first three years of marriage. Expectations, adjustments, and the role of faith in marriage are also explored.

> *If David and Emily had taken the time to attend such a session, they would have met other couples just like themselves, couples struggling with similar issues in their new life together. They missed an opportunity to be part of a community of newly married couples who might have reminded them of the commitment they had made to each other.*

Couples in marriages where there are children from a previous relationship, whether marital or not, have another set of challenges different from first-time marriages. While they follow the same steps to marry, the conversations will be different. The focus will be more on the family and not just the couple. The challenges they face will be former spouses or the ghost of a former spouse, the children, and money. Time and sex are also issues, though they may not be quite as immediate. The annual Successful Stepfamily Conference hosted by the Archdiocese of Chicago, www. familyministries.org., is a great learning experience for those considering creating a step-family or for those who are already in a stepfamily.

HEALING TROUBLED RELATIONSHIPS

Providing couples with strong marriage ministry is a great alternative to divorce. Yet even with that, problems occur. What is a pastoral minister to do when asked to deal with a couple or individual who is hurting in their marriage? Michele Weiner Davis, the *Divorce Buster* from Woodstock, Illinois, notes that couples are generally in trouble for six years before they ask for help in the marriage. By the time they reach out for help, it is often very hard to repair the damage that has been done.

There are a few things every pastoral minister and clergy person needs to know when dealing with couples in distress. They must not take sides. They can help screen for abuse, identify addictions, and provide assistance if that is needed. Marriage ministers need know whom to refer people to when they come to them for help. A counseling or resource referral list is important to have at the parish.

One major help to the couple is referral to a "marriage friendly" therapist or counselor. Unfortunately, our court system is full of people who went for marriage counseling only to find that the therapist encouraged each spouse to think of themselves first—what they wanted, and not of the other spouse or family. The idea of sacrifice or working things through for the sake of the children is rarely heard today from secular therapists, some of whom see religion as an oppressive force in a marriage. That there may be a difference between becoming the kind of person we want to be, and the kind of person God wants us to be—or that the community has a stake in the success of our marriage—is truly a countercultural message that the couple needs to hear. There is now a website to locate good therapists who support marriage (www.marriagefriendlytherapists.com).

Just as couples living together may find that they inevitably slide into marriage, couples separating must find ways to avoid sliding into divorce. Married couples in trouble need other options. Marriage Encounter can be a fine option if the couple is not in too much trouble. There is Retrouvaille (www.retrouvaille.org.), a nationally recognized Catholic program for couples in trouble led by lay people who have experienced difficulties yet saved their marriages. Couples can be referred to a marriage skills seminar (for example, find information at www.chicagolandmarriage.org); or attend a good marriage enrichment program. Books and tapes that are marriage-supportive and contain skill-building exercises can be suggested or kept in a parish library. There are many marriage enrichment programs that can be run at the parish level to build awareness and knowledge about marriage. Married couples today are used to a marketplace of choices for all of their needs. They are more likely to commit their "couple time" and their own resources into something that is of interest to them.

Couples contemplating a separation or divorce can be offered a "Couple's Time Out," which uses a process of controlled separation (www.

controlledseparation.com). Giving them a time out relieves some of the pressure to make a decision. A "time-out" can give the couple some space and thinking time to reorganize their thoughts, defuse some contentious living situations, restore order to the chaos of their daily life, and give them a chance to breathe and recover from the tensions that have developed in the marriage. If they must divorce, and some couples do need to divorce, they can be helped to do that responsibly and thoughtfully, with the welfare of the children as the most important consideration, reminding them that while a marriage may end, parenting never does.

Helpful interventions have helped many couples reclaim the marriage they wanted from the beginning. For some, marital discord can be a time to recommit and grow up into the marriage. With proper assistance—skill building in communication, fighting fair, and growth in attentiveness to each other—the couple can develop a fulfilling marriage.

WHEN MARRIAGE FAILS: MINISTRY TO DIVORCED COUPLES

The sad truth is that some couples do not want to save their marriage. We've seen this, for example, in the popular film, *The War of the Roses*. A couple may be unwilling to trudge through the mundane and the frequently challenging aspects of marriage and family life. They may buy into societal images of sex with only one person as boring and unfulfilling and exit the marriage. Barbara Dafoe Whitehead, a professor at Rutgers University, says that 80 percent of divorces do not need to happen; and that with proper intervention and better outreach to couples, more families would not be disrupted and torn apart by divorce.

The other side of this statistic is that about 20 percent of marriages may be better off ending. In cases of abuse, whether it is physical, emotional, or spiritual abuse, when real harm of body or spirit is occurring, Canon 1153 provides for these couples to separate. For legal protection, they may need to divorce to provide housing, child support, and maintenance for the family.

For more than 30 years, the Catholic Church has provided for and supported divorce ministry. The rationale for this was developed by the Pontifical Council for the Family. Church leaders are asked to "make a special effort towards those who are suffering the hurtful consequences of divorce" using three objectives: to support fidelity in marriage; support families in difficulty; and provide spiritual guidance.

A successful and effective ministry to the divorced provides a safe place for people to gather and talk. Small groups can meet in church basements and meeting rooms to cry and share and heal from the loss of the most important commitment they have ever made. A time-limited program of study and prayer that educates and offers solace to those who attend can be offered. A popular program that challenges people no longer to be victims, but to mirror the resurrection and the hope of our faith, is found in *Divorce and Beyond* (ACTA Publications, Chicago). Masses can be, and currently are, offered in dioceses throughout the country to increase awareness and understanding about the loss of marriage in the family and community. Every year a national conference is held at the University of Notre Dame in South Bend to educate and enrich leaders for divorce ministry (www.nacsdc.org).

Once a couple is divorced, they may no longer feel welcome in their parish. Other parishioners may assume divorced people should not come to Mass, that they cannot go to communion, that they are not allowed to be Extraordinary Ministers of Holy Communion or help in church, and think they are excommunicated simply by being divorced. Clergy and parish leaders can refute these myths, educate parishioners, let them know that the divorced are welcome in the Church, that they can be Extraordinary Ministers of Holy Communion, that they may receive Eucharist as long as they have not remarried without an annulment.

After divorce, the Catholic Church provides an inquiry process to aid the healing of the divorced couple. Familiarly called annulment, it is an investigation of the marriage to see if it was valid in the eyes of the Church. The Church recognizes that with a license from the state and property legally owned by both, in the civil sense, there was a marriage. During the annulment process there may be the finding that some essential element was missing from the consent that was exchanged. If that is so, the marriage may not actually be sacramentally valid and a declaration of nullity is granted.

> *Harriet has been trying for three years to get her annulment.*
> *Her story may not be typical, but it is true. Her divorce had*
> *been expensive and mean. Her children were confused and*

> torn apart by the divorce. Her family told her the children
> would be illegitimate if she got an annulment. Her grand-
> mother told her she was excommunicated because of the
> divorce. A girlfriend told her it would take over $10,000 to
> get the annulment and only then if she paid in full. She heard
> from a co-worker that it might take as long as fifteen years
> before a decision was reached and the case would be looked
> at by the Pope.

While none of this information was true, Harriet was still upset. To add to her misery, her annulment application got lost in the mail, and she had to redo it. Her story was painful to write and she felt no support from her family, friends or parish. It was the hardest thing she ever had to do. She felt alone and unsure of herself. Yet through the process, she came to understand why she married the man she did. She also came to understand how the marriage unraveled. She decided that even if she did not get the annulment, she felt better and somewhat healed after completing the papers. She finally felt she had the closure she needed to understand why her marriage ended.

Many Catholics are upset about the perceived injustice of the annulment process. After an acrimonious and often brutal civil divorce process over property and children, feelings are raw, people are hurting, and they resent having to respond again to another authority about the loss they have been through. They see their marriage as private and of no concern to others. Lay people and ordained alike oppose scrutiny of the marriage and question the right of the Church to engage in this process. Many people who divorce do not enter into the annulment process until they meet someone and decide to marry again and are angry at the length of the process. And, of the divorced people who choose to remarry, the vast majority of them do not get married in the Catholic Church, often because of the difficulty, perceived or real, with the annulment process. The likelihood of these families ever again practicing their Catholic faith is remote.

Unless the laws of the Church are changed, annulment is part of the procedure that people are asked to undergo before attempting another marriage. If taught properly to the individuals who undertake the process, it will give them answers and resolution to a great loss that they had not wanted nor anticipated. It teaches them about themselves and better prepares them for their next marriage. People testify to the great healing that occurs during and after the annulment process. It does the work that many people accomplish in therapy. It gives the petitioner and the respondent the insight to what went wrong in the relationship. It helps each party own his or her part in the relationship. Good divorce ministry can help the divorced person heal by supporting their journey through the annulment process.

Perhaps if David and Emily had reached out to their parish, had attended a Retrouvaille weekend, gone to marriage enrichment workshops, found a marriage friendly therapist, and fought for and saved their marriage, they would have been able to join with the 500 couples a year who gather at Holy Name Cathedral to celebrate their Golden Wedding Anniversaries. They could celebrate, with their peers, their lives together, how they persevered through the struggles, and share the sense of accomplishment and joy in their life together. In a world of uncertainty, they would be a marvelous testament to marriage, faith, and healing.

22. American Annulment Mills

Robert J. Kendra

This chapter first appeared in *Homiletic and Pastoral Review* 106 (December 2005).

"Take no part in the unfruitful works of darkness, but instead
expose them."   (Eph 5:11)

An important characteristic of American history has been its innovative application of mass production. A paradigm would be the famous
industrialist Henry Ford, who perfected the assembly-line to produce the
Model T Ford around 1915 at an affordable price for many Americans.
Fifty years later, American marriage tribunals seem to have caught on
and began applying similar methods of streamlining the annulment process, with liberal interpretations of Vatican II and even disregard of *The
Code of Canon Law* to accommodate a mushrooming divorce ethos.

The result has been an increase from 338 annulments in 1968, to
5,403 in 1970, to a peak 61,945 in 1991. Since then, the explosion has sta-
bilized at around 40,000 U.S. annulments per year. However, these commonly quoted statistics implying a recent decline are deceiving. Tribunals
are not getting tougher on granting annulments. They are getting fewer
petitions for annulments, probably due to divorced Catholics cohabitating
and not bothering with annulments. Since 1964 the tribunals have consistently ruled for annulment in about 97 percent of the cases they accept.
Seventy percent of annulments worldwide are accounted for by American
marriage tribunals though the U.S. has a mere six percent of the world's

Catholic population. So prevalent has been the granting of annulments that they are often referred to as Catholic divorces.

Nearly every recent book on annulment has been an apologetic for America's preeminence in the production of annulments, or a rosy explanation of annulment friendly tribunals. The only book to critically study the entire tribunal system is Robert H. Vasoli's *What God Has Joined Together*, a godsend for opponents of wholesale annulments.

THE PROBLEM OF DIVORCE

Modernists, bent on melding Catholicism with late-20th century acceptance of divorce, have a problem—how to permit civil divorce, without simultaneously admitting to a Catholic divorce. The "solution" is semantic deception. Instead of allowing a Catholic divorce, they deny that the couple was ever married.

Church tribunalists pretentiously assert that they are not annulling a marriage, but simply acknowledging that the marriage never existed. They further assure that despite the couple never having been married their children are not illegitimate, "because the marriage was entered into in good faith and thought to be a valid marriage." However, this fiction causes another problem since the state insists that the couple were in fact married, and requires a divorce to dissolve the marriage. So tribunals insist that a divorce precede the annulment process. Then the canonical magicians on the tribunal can make the sacramental marriage disappear without any civil ramifications.

But Jesus Christ sternly forbade divorce. "…[W]hoever divorces his wife and marries another commits adultery against her" (Mk. 10:1–12; Lk. 16:18; 1 Cor. 7:10–11). Reinforcing the New Testament condemnations of divorce, Popes Leo XIII and Pius XI elaborated on the evils of divorce in their encyclicals "Arcanum," and "Casti Connubii," respectively. Vatican II continues by condemning the plague and profanation of divorce in "Gaudium et Spes," and the *Catechism of the Catholic Church* calls divorce "a grave offense against the natural law," and "immoral." *Canon Law* even requires ecclesiastical approval for the separation of spouses. Rather than confront the dilemma, the American Church just sweeps 2,000 years of teachings under the rug. When was the last time you heard a bishop or priest condemn divorce?

A worse problem for the Church is complicity in promoting divorce. A conscientious petitioner (the party seeking the annulment) would first seek an annulment to be assured that no valid sacramental marriage existed, prior to seeking a civil divorce. However, faced with this request, tribunal officials respond that a divorce is required prior to accepting an application for annulment, allegedly to assure that the marriage is irreconcilable. But Jesus clearly condemned divorce even without remarriage, "Therefore, what God has joined together let no man put asunder" (Mk. 10:9), and canon 1060 stipulates, "in a case of doubt the validity of a marriage must be upheld until the contrary is proven." Therefore, a tribunal must prejudge the marriage to be invalid prior to judging its validity, in order to justify a divorce preceding an annulment. Assurances of obtaining an easy annulment, given by the pro-annulment pastoral tribunals to perplexed petitioners (little or no effort is made toward reconciling the couple), actually precipitates the divorce. Once divorce is granted, which is a given with no-fault divorce laws, the tribunal is programmed to grant an annulment.

Realistically, in my opinion, tribunals might be reversing the prudent order of annulment then divorce to avoid ramifications in civil court and embarrassing publicity. Since extremely few Americans are severely deranged, tribunals exaggerate the gravity of disorders to justify most annulments. Divorce lawyers could have tribunal files subpoenaed to use the exaggerated, and even fictitious evaluations to attack the sanity of their client's spouse to reap a more favorable court decision affecting custody of children, child support, alimony and distribution of the couple's financial assets. An aggressive lawyer could argue that his client had to bear the burden of a deranged spouse when symptoms of hidden incapacity for marriage manifested themselves not only to the detriment of the marriage, but to the well-being of his client who was subjected to mental and/or physical abuse. The civil court proceedings could turn into a circus; one lawyer disingenuously arguing for validity of tribunal assertions, and the other making a laughingstock out of flimsy tribunal opinions and judgments based on junk science and counterfeit psychology. The entire annulment process would be subjected to public ridicule. No, it would be much safer to have the civil divorce settled before writing the fiction necessary to justify nullity of a marriage.

Whether or not the tribunal judges theorize that a sacramental marriage exists, the fact remains that a civil marriage existed. With rare exception, divorce from that marriage is wrong, has been condemned by the Church since the time of Christ, and has undeniably harmful consequences, particularly to children of the marriage, and should not be facilitated by compliant tribunals.

CANON LAW

The ecclesiastical term for annulment is declaration of nullity. Tribunals never use the term annulment, since there is no such thing as the annulment of a consummated sacramental marriage. *The Code of Canon Law* describes 101 canons for trials in general, 170 canons for contentious trials, and another 37 canons for certain matrimonial processes. The most important canon for a contentious respondent (the party opposing an annulment) is probably canon 1598-1, which requires that parties be permitted to inspect the acts (evidence) of the case to guarantee their rights of defense, and which can be easily disregarded to avoid cumbersome delays and conceal biased opinions. Of equal importance for the bewildered respondent upon discovery that he or she was never married are canons 1417 and 1444, which permit an appeal of a decision by a U.S. tribunal to the more conscientious, canonically firm and unbiased Roman Rota, and which is routinely ignored to expedite a speedy conforming decision in the second instance. Other important canons are canons 1554, 1555 and 1576, requiring that parties be notified of witnesses and experts and given the opportunity to request their exclusion; canons 1534 and 1564, prohibiting the judge from asking the parties or witnesses leading questions; canon 1608 requiring moral certainty in the judgment; canon 1614 requiring a judgment to indicate the ways in which it can be challenged (including appealing to the Roman Rota); canon 1616 requiring a judgment to be corrected if there is material error in presentation of the evidence (including false testimony); canon 1620 enabling the Rota to nullify a decision by a U.S. tribunal; and canon 1634 giving the respondent the right to obtain a copy of the judgment.

However, American tribunals circumvent many of these canons to expedite production of annulments. Only when an appeal is made to the

Roman Rota, which nullifies some ninety percent of U.S. annulments, is the mischief of American tribunals redressed. Unfortunately, the Rota only reviews about 10 to 20 U.S. cases per year. This is less than a miniscule 0.04 percent, or one case per 2,500 decisions.

The Rota recently irremediably nullified a U.S. tribunal sentence nullifying a marriage and remanded it back to the U.S. tribunal for retrial, based primarily on violations of canon 1598. Brief excerpts from that Rotal decree, stressing the importance of a respondent's right of defense, are as follows:

- Rotal jurisprudence has enjoined and established a hundred times that canonical judgment cannot be conceived without a validly constituted opportunity for rebuttal between the parties and that is required for the exercise of the right of defense.
- The Supreme Pontiff also warned…"One cannot conceive of a just judgment without the 'contradictory,' that is to say, without the concrete possibility granted to each party in the case to be heard to be able to know and contradict the requests, proofs and deductions adopted by the opposing parties…."
- Therefore, it is logically established in canon 1620-7 that a sentence is vitiated by irremediable nullity if the right of defense was denied to one or the other party…the essence of the right of defense consists of two elements: the right to cross-argument and the right to a hearing….
- So that the respondent party can use this faculty to contradict and object in the matrimonial process it is necessary that the proofs brought forth during the course of the process be published at a suitable time or before the sentence is given, again so that he can bring forth his arguments immediately or in the discussory phase.
- …[T]he principal intention (of canon 1598) is to establish, and indeed under pain of invalidity, the right of the *parties* to inspect the acts.…[T]he parties are the true protagonists in a process, and certainly the essential ones.
- …To prohibit one or another party from the inspection of the acts, by restricting either all or an indeterminate number of documents under secrecy, entails a nullity of the process.

Most tribunals carefully secure the confidentiality of cases largely to mask their own loose adherence to *Canon Law* and questionable judgments, and take short cuts to expedite annulments. The most blatant examples of ecclesiastical injustice are the erroneous interpretation of canon 1095, which U.S. tribunals interpret to permit an amorphous lack of discretion to declare a party incapable of contracting marriage, but which is contrary to Rotal requirements for extreme psychopathology; failure to initially appoint resolute advocates to guide and assist the parties (especially contentious respondents), who have no experience with the process; failure to honor a contentious respondent's right of defense of the marriage; and failure to inform the parties that an appeal can be made to the Roman Rota which will probably overturn or remand a U.S. annulment, instead of an appeal being automatically sent to another U.S. tribunal for a conforming decision in the second instance and an inevitable rubber stamp of the annulment. U.S. tribunals dislike having appeals sent to Rome, not only because of the likely overturn or remand, but also due to the Rota's backlog and a wait that could take years.

About two-thirds of American annulments are based on canon 1095, which involves psychological opinions—hardly an exact science and subject to facile adulteration. The boiler plate of one decree, which is probably typical, devotes some 2,000 words of ecclesial mumbo jumbo to interpreting this canon. It would take a separate article to properly criticize its substance, which is contrary to Rotal jurisprudence. Suffice it to say that this logorrhea includes many dubious rationalizations for determining the mental capacity for marital consent at the time of the wedding, such as the following: "the court may be faced with the seemingly impossible task of reconstructing the consenting capacity of a person after a decade or two. When such a case comes to trial, the history of the party's contractual performance will be the primary evidence concerning contractual capacity."

In other words, the tribunal admits that there really is no way to assess the condition of the bride's and groom's minds when they exchanged vows (consent), but that the behavior of the couple ten or twenty years hence can reveal, with moral certitude, that they suffered from a grave lack of discretionary judgment concerning essential matrimonial rights and obligations of permanence, fidelity and openness to children at the time of their wedding. Yet these same couples, despite allegedly incriminating evidence of contractual incapacity for ten or twenty years, can suddenly transmogrify into having adequate capacity for a second marriage!

Realistically, the very few people incapable of contracting marriage as specified in canon 1095, are so deranged that they simply don't get married.

A CASE STUDY

The writer was victim to two decrees of nullity by a U.S. Tribunal, both decrees of which were nullified by the Roman Rota. In my case, which is probably similar to other U.S. cases, the judges claimed that both of us were handicapped by "a very defective understanding of the nature and purpose of marriage and of the rights and obligations to be mutually given and accepted." However, if anyone in this case misconstrued the nature and purpose of marriage, it was the U.S. Tribunal. Canon 1095-3 states that parties who, due to causes of a psychological nature, are unable to assume the essential obligations of marriage are incapable of contracting marriage. But what are the essential obligations? The Church has long taught that they are permanence, fidelity, and openness to children, a teaching that goes back to St. Augustine. Conspicuously absent from the Tribunal's decree of nullity was any effort to examine how these fundamental components figured in our exchange of consent and in the marriage itself. Like most couples, we entered marriage with some uncertainty and reservation. Nevertheless, when we consented to marry both of us were fully aware of the essential elements and sincerely committed to them. Whatever problems beset our marriage, it undeniably remained intact for twenty years, and, in my opinion, could have endured until my wife or I died. Moreover, we were faithful to each other throughout the marriage, and the four daughters we conceived and raised attested to our openness to children. But the Tribunal simply avoided the Magisterial essential elements of marriage to circumvent this vital Church teaching.

In his 1987 and 1988 allocutions to the Roman Rota, Pope John Paul II provided important clarification to canons 1095-2 and 3. As tests for marital validity, both canons require that one of the parties, or both, suffered from a serious psychopathology (anomaly) when marriage was contracted. Incapacity as a basis for nullity must derive from grave psy-

chological disorders and it must be nearly total in magnitude. Some incapacity does not warrant nullity, if only because human capabilities are by
nature and original sin short of perfection. Moreover, it must be shown
that the disorder rendering them incapable was present and operative
when consent was exchanged. It should be further noted that a judgment
of incapacity requires compelling clinical evidence. Without it, little cre-
dence can be given to assumptions that psychological disorders and problems surfacing well after the marriage was contracted were present from
the outset. The Tribunal seemed oblivious to these considerations.

The sole semblance of serious psychopathology in the case consisted
of alleged alcoholism of both parties derived almost exclusively from the
petitioner's testimony, subsequently repeated in the testimony of the tribunal expert, counselors, and her sister. I flatly denied that alcoholism was a
problem and the court failed to establish the claim. The counselors scarcely
qualified to pontificate on the presence, absence, or dynamics of serious
mental disorders. The court appointed expert's views, at least those cited by
the Tribunal, were not sufficiently discriminating to apply to the question
of marital validity. That both parties were credited with "certain traits of
immaturity" did not differentiate them from most of the human race, much
less those who marry.

What in my view was little more than social drinking was elevated
to the level of a crippling disorder. Yet the record did not show any
drunken brawls, chronic alcoholism, or evidence that drinking influenced
my long and successful career as an engineer or my wife's work as a
Catholic school teacher and devoted mother of four children. Despite
lacking hard evidence other than my wife's claims, the tribunal leaped to
the extraordinary and rash conclusion that "It is clear that alcohol seems
to have been the primary bond between them." Summarily dismissed or
relegated to secondary status were ties engendered by both of us being
practicing Catholics, our conception and rearing of four children, and our
living together for nearly two decades.

Unable to establish that my wife and I were incapable of fulfilling the
obligations of permanence, fidelity, and openness to children, the Tribunal
found that we were incapable of giving ourselves "to each [other] in the
communion of the whole of their lives." Several popes (Pius XI, Paul VI,
John Paul II) and the *Catechism* refer to marriage in similar terms—as a
communion of life and love. Manifestly, such expressions represent what

marriage should be, a noble ideal toward which all married couples should aspire. But there are compelling and obvious reasons why it cannot be an acceptable test for validity. Neither papal pronouncements, the *Catechism*, nor Rotal jurisprudence have designated the communion of life and love as a determinant of validity. To do so would be tantamount to conferring Church approval on divorce and remarriage inasmuch as most marriages fall short of that ideal. What can be more destructive of the communion of life and love than divorce? American Catholics now divorce at much the same rate as non-Catholics. Can tribunals rightly and routinely assume that such unions—now numbering in the millions—are ipso facto invalid?

Most parties to marriages that remain intact until death must constantly struggle to even approximate a communion of life and love. For them, more often than not it is a marital state that comes and goes, much akin to the personal journey toward sanctification. Making valid marriage stand or fall on whether a communion of life and love is achieved is analogous to requiring sainthood for membership in the Church. Finally, while hardly a Catholic alive does not know that marriage entails permanence, fidelity, and openness to children, very few realize it must be a "communion of life and love," and still fewer can articulate what a "communion of life and love" consists of. As inspirational a goal as it may be, it has yet to be authoritatively provided with clear-cut juridic and doctrinal content. If popes, canonists, and theologians have not yet given it such content, how can those entering marriage be held to such nebulous measure of validity?

There was no clear-cut showing—nothing close to the moral certitude requisite—that either of us was in the throes of a serious mental disorder when we exchanged consent, and therefore gravely lacking due discretion or incapacity with respect to the essential rights and obligations of marriage. What the Tribunal did was to confuse incapacity with unhappiness. Put another way, the Tribunal equated "unhappy" marriage with invalid marriage. It would have been a sad—nay, tragic day for Church teaching on the permanence and indissolubility of marriage had the Tribunal's decision been ratified by the Sacred Roman Rota.

A contentious respondent, faced with the near impossible task of arguing for validity of a marriage on substantive grounds, is no match for the Jesuitical wizards controlling American tribunals and set on annulling the marriage. Only with guidance from an expert in matrimonial canon law can substantive arguments be effective, and then almost only before the Roman Rota, or threat of appealing to the Rota. Lacking this expertise, a better strategy to combat the stacked deck might be to utilize procedural tactics and demand strict adherence to *Canon Law*, especially canon 1598's right of defense, and plan on appealing a likely tortuous decree of nullity in the first instance, to the Roman Rota in the second instance. This would likely stall a definite sentence and maintain technical validity of the marriage indefinitely. It has even happened that one of the parties died after a fourteen (14) years wait—a pathetic way to obtain theological justice. Then, a definite sentence is never issued in any tribunal regarding the question of nullity, and the case is consigned to the archives. The delay would also put a cog, albeit small, in the connived American mechanism cranking out annulments wholesale.

Unfortunately, when neither party contests an annulment, there is no effective check on the decision, and annulments can be granted en masse with impunity. It is anybody's guess how many valid sacramental marriages are nullified by phony annulments ("invalid" decrees of nullity), followed by remarriage by one or both parties that result in effective tribunal approved adultery. Why hasn't a scrupulous and courageous tribunal insider exposed the misfeasance of tribunals in granting phony annulments? Modernism, "the synthesis of all heresies" resulting from subjectivist thinking and condemned by Pope St. Pius X in 1907, survived underground until resurfacing in the mid-1960s. Has it now metastasized throughout the entire Church bureaucracy? Why must it take a determined respondent to experience the travesty of tribunal dishonesty to expose, after feeling morally obligated, the insidious undermining of the sacrament of Matrimony by American annulment mills?

St. Joan of Arc, victim of earlier tribunal injustice, pray for us.

23. Pastoral Ministry: The Divorced and Remarried

Oskar Saier, Karl Lehmann, and Walter Kasper

This chapter first appeared in *Origins* 23 (1994).

The three bishops of the German ecclesiastical province of the Upper Rhine urged greater pastoral ministry to divorced and to divorced-and-remarried persons in a joint pastoral letter widely reported for its call for a pastoral dialogue with individuals who are divorced and remarried regarding their participation in the sacraments. The letter was dated July 10, 1993. It was issued by Bishop Karl Lehmann of Mainz, president of the German bishops' conference; Archbishop Oskar Saier of Freiburg, conference vice president; and Bishop Walter Kasper of Ruttenburg-Stuttgart.

Most people seek their personal happiness in marriage and family. Marriage and the family are the basic cell of human society. It is part of the dramatic change of our times, however, that many marriages break down and that divorces have increased enormously.

The difficult human situation of divorced people and of those who have entered into a civil marriage after a divorce is a serious question facing the church. For the joy and hope, the grief and anguish of the people of today are also the joy and hope, the grief and anguish of the followers of Christ.[1]

Therefore synods, diocesan forums, bishops' conferences and pastoral and priests' councils have repeatedly concerned themselves with this question over the last two decades. As this problem exceeds the area of responsibility of an individual bishop, the three bishops of the ecclesiastical province of the Upper Rhine have decided to direct a joint pastoral letter to their faithful and to give common pastoral guidelines for those responsible for pastoral care.

SITUATION OF DIVORCED AND REMARRIED CHRISTIANS

First we would like to comment on the present situation. It appears to be of a dual nature. If one asks younger people especially how they envision their future happiness, most will wish for a marital partnership based on mutual love that will last a lifetime. These expectations stand in clear contrast to the fact that in our society very many marriages break down. Christian and ecclesiastically solemnized marriages are here no exception. Many divorced people find a new partner and join in a civil marriage or else they live together without benefit of marriage. There are more and more stepfamilies with children from different families. The number of single parents, both mothers and fathers, is also increasing.

The causes that have led to this situation are extremely diverse. To a not inconsiderable degree, they lie with social changes: The separation today between the family and the world of work and the resulting tension between family and profession, new understandings of the roles of men and women, the increased length of a marriage, the dissolution of the traditional extended family and isolation of the nuclear family, and the insufficient support given marriage and family in this social climate all play a role. Alongside these there are diverse personal reasons: unreasonable expectations of happiness that will necessarily be disappointed, human immaturity and personal failure in daily life, mutual misunderstanding and insufficient dedication to the point of infidelity and culpable destruction of the marital community or even physical abuse in the marriage.

The consequences of a divorce are usually disappointment, sadness, personal injury, self-doubt and feelings of guilt. A divorce affects relationships with society, the family and with friends; not infrequently, it leads to isolation. Added to that are fear and uncertainty about the future. Those who bear the principal burden are the children. They are torn between the parents; they lose their home and their emotional shelter.

Divorced people and those who have divorced and remarried feel that the church and society lack understanding and that they are left alone with their problems. Many feel discriminated against, cast out, even condemned. They can accept the church's rules and regulations only with great difficulty or not at all; they find them incomprehensibly hard and merciless.

This situation is a serious question for the church. We must ask ourselves how we can be credible witnesses to the closeness of God to the divorced and to the divorced and remarried in their difficult human situation. How can we stand by them and help them, how can we give them new perspectives, courage for life and reconciliation? For many people today the church's credibility rests on the answer to this question.

THE GOSPEL STANDARD

In its pastoral care of the divorced and of divorced-and-remarried people the church is not simply free. It cannot proceed based on the approval of individuals or even of majority opinions. The standard for the church is the word, will and example of Jesus. The practice of the church must be measured against them.

The word of Jesus is clear. As the question of the divorce practice of his time was laid before him, he made it clear that, once entered, a marriage was no longer subject to human desires and powers: "But from the beginning of creation, 'God made them male and female. For this reason a man shall leave his father and mother [and be joined to his wife], and the two shall become one flesh.' Therefore what God has joined together, no human being must separate" (Mk.10:6–9).

Thus by his response Jesus refers to the original order of creation according to which God made man and woman completely equally in his image (Gn. 1:27). At the same time he made them for each other and gave them to each other. They were to become one flesh, i.e., a concrete community (ibid., 2:24); and they should also be fruitful in their children (ibid., 1:28). Such mutual love demands lasting fidelity. Only fidelity opens up the space in which a man and woman can realize their marital partnership and responsibly bring children into the world.

Through sin, a person refuses love, shutting himself up in himself. That makes him—as Jesus said—hardhearted. Thus the original order of

God and the original happiness in marriage are disturbed. Already in the Old Testament law detailed regulations for divorce were necessary.

Jesus did not permit himself to become entangled in the dispute at this level. He answered neither by increasing the severity of the law nor by adding exceptions to it. He placed his answer concerning marriage and divorce within the framework of his message regarding the coming of the kingdom of God. This last will overcome the inimical power of hate, of selfishness and of force. Jesus' word is therefore no crushing law, but rather an offer, an invitation, an exhortation and a gift, which is to realize the original sense of marriage in lifelong fidelity. For where God gives himself completely, there too can man and woman fully and finally give themselves and unite themselves in love and fidelity.

Therefore, Christian marriage, entered into according to the norms of the church, makes God's covenant present to people. That is why the church calls Christian marriage a sacrament. That means that the love of God embraces, strengthens, heals and sanctifies the love and fidelity of the couple.[2] God's love and fidelity were proven finally in the cross and resurrection of Jesus. The cross and suffering therefore belong to a Christian marriage but so do also an ever new forgiveness and an ever new beginning.

Clearly the church's experience from earliest times shows that despite the radically new beginning in Jesus Christ the power of sin continued to be effective within its own ranks and that even marriages among Christians could fail. The church cannot assume the right to disregard the word of Jesus regarding the indissolubility of marriage; but equally it cannot shut its eyes to the failure of many marriages. For wherever people fall short of the reality of redemption, Jesus meets them in mercy with understanding for their situation. Even in failure and guilt he opens to them the path of conversion and new life. Thus it has been necessary for the church throughout its history to distinguish among the most varied circumstances and to ask itself how it can remain unreservedly true to the word and example of Jesus while still helping concretely those whose marriages have failed. It must ask itself how it can stand by them in solidarity and be a helpful companion along the way.

RESPONSIBILITY OF THE CHRISTIAN COMMUNITY

Faithful to the word and example of Jesus, Christians should be in the forefront of the struggle for successful marriages of lifelong fidelity. In a Christian community an atmosphere should reign in which it should not even come to a situation in which divorce appears to be the only way out. We must therefore with united energy work against the trend that would regard divorce and remarriage as something normal. This mission will best be served by proper preparation for marriage, by support for marriage and by counseling where marriages have broken up.

As part of the same attitude, we should greet with respect and sympathy fellow Christians whose marriages have broken up yet who out of inner conviction do not intend to enter into a new relationship but rather to give witness as single people to the indissolubility of their validly contracted marriages. The person who does not undertake a civil marriage following a divorce suffers no restriction with regard to his or her rights or position in the church. If the church does not want to betray the message of Jesus, it cannot set up a legal order in which divorce followed by remarriage can be made a normal event or even a right. Precisely by respecting and protecting the indissolubility of marriage, the church renders an indispensable service to humankind.

However, the church must offer solidarity to those who have failed in marriage and who have decided upon a second, civil marriage. Despite some mistaken opinions and information, it must be said that all divorced people and divorced-and-remarried people belong to the church and thus to the parish community in which they live. Even though their membership rights are somewhat reduced, they are neither excommunicated nor excluded from the church; they are and remain members of the church. The church must, in fact, give them special care because of the difficult situation in which they find themselves.

In his apostolic exhortation *Familiaris Consortio* (1981), Pope John Paul II pointed out in direction-giving fashion the enduring membership in the church of those whose marriages have failed but who have not remarried. "The ecclesial community must support such people more than ever. It must give them much respect, solidarity, understanding and practical help." The pope says specifically that there is not "any obstacle to admission to the sacrament."[3]

As for the divorced who have remarried civilly, one must, according to the pope, "exercise careful discernment of situations." There is a difference whether one has been abandoned unjustly or whether one has destroyed an ecclesiastically valid marriage through one's own grievous fault. One should help divorced-and-remarried people, too, "with solicitous care to make sure that they do not consider themselves as separated from the church." They can—indeed they must as baptized Christians—share in the life of the church, listen to the word of God, attend Mass, pray regularly and contribute to works of charity and community efforts to promote justice. The church should pray for them and encourage them. They should be confident that they "will be able to obtain from God the grace of conversion and salvation."[4] Divorced-and-remarried people should realize that they remain part and should feel a part of the community and are welcome at all church services and activities. Unfortunately, in our congregations there is much hardness and intransigence side by side with a willingness for healing relationships. Divorced-and-remarried people should feel that they are accepted by the congregation and that the congregation understands their difficult situation. They should experience the church as a healing and helping community. The congregation should help them to rebuild their lives and their faith, to recognize guilt but also to experience forgiveness. That presupposes discussion and advice, because a new orientation of one's life is only possible when the shadows of the past have been overcome in intensive discussion.

This goal is served by support groups of family members and friends such as already exist in many congregations as well as by church marital and family counseling services and pastoral discussion with a priest or expert laypersons. In the final analysis, the responsibility of the entire congregation is demanded.

Participation in the Sacraments?

Leading divorced-and-remarried people to active participation in the life of the congregation will usually proceed step by step, during which there are many different grades and possible forms of participation depending on the individual's situation in life and in the faith. One must not take an all-or-nothing stance here. In the end, there is of course the question of participation by the individual divorced-and-remarried person in the sacraments of reconciliation and the eucharist.

The more recent ecclesiastical pronouncements declare, in adherence to the instructions of Jesus, that divorced-and-remarried people generally cannot be admitted to the eucharistic feast as they find themselves in life situations that are in objective contradiction to the essence of Christian marriage.[5] Anyone who acts otherwise does so contrary to the order of the church.

Canon law, however, can "set up only a valid general order; it cannot regulate all of the often very complex individual cases."[6] Therefore it ought to be clarified through pastoral dialogue whether that which is generally valid applies also in a given situation. This cannot be generally presumed, especially when those involved have, based on good grounds, satisfied their consciences of the nullity of their first marriage but no legal proofs exist to obtain a declaration of nullity from an ecclesiastical tribunal. In these and similar cases a pastoral dialogue can help those involved to reach a personal and responsible decision according to the judgment of their own consciences that must be respected by the church and the congregation. To accompany others on their way to such a mature decision of conscience is the service and mission of pastoral care, especially by priests, who are officially commissioned with the service of reconciliation and unification.

In guidelines specifically prepared for those responsible for pastoral care we have formulated some basic tenets for the pastoral accompaniment of people whose marriages have broken up. We must of course be clear that there cannot be a simple, smooth solution to the complex situations of divorced-and-remarried people. The grace of reconciliation is always postulated on personal conversion. We must not make it "cheap grace." Neither an exaggerated strictness nor a weak flexibility will help. The model for our speech and action must be only Jesus Christ. It is a matter of continually entering a relationship with him and of giving his Spirit room to work. Such continual conversion is not only the duty of divorced people and those who are divorced and remarried, but of all Christians and the entire church.

Finally, we would like to thank all who labor in the pastoral care of divorced people and of the divorced and remarried. We intend to expand such efforts in the future and must make clear that God's fidelity and mercy await each person in that situation, each person who is prepared to repent and open his or her heart anew to God. We beg you all, brothers and sisters, for your prayers for all young people who are preparing for marriage, for married people and their families, and for those whose marriages have failed. It is true for all: God is faithful; he will strengthen you (cf. 1 Cor. 1:9; 10:13; 2 Thes. 3:3).

Special Concerns regarding Divorced-and-Remarried People

All that has previously been said applies in large part also to those who after divorce have entered into a civil marriage. The church can do a great deal precisely for this group, even though the second marital partnership is not recognized as ecclesiastically valid and there can be no general admission to the sacraments. It is necessary in this regard to discard widespread misinformation and prejudices. Divorced-and-remarried people are not excluded from the church nor are they excommunicated, i.e., completely and thoroughly shut out of the community of divine worship and the sacraments.[7] Since these people, however, according to the conviction of the church, stand in objective contradiction to the word of the Lord, they cannot be admitted indiscriminately to the sacraments, especially to the eucharist. That sounds, and certainly for many is, disappointing. Nevertheless, one thing is clear: Divorced-and-remarried people are at home in the church and are inside the community of the church even though they are to some extent restricted with regard to some of the rights of all church members. They belong to us. Under no circumstances may one simply deny these people the real possibility of salvation.

1. Divorced-and-Remarried People in the Eyes of Church and Community

In this area too the apostolic exhortation *Familiaris Consortio* gives some substantial instructions that up to now have been too little regarded: Divorced-and-remarried people must not simply be left to themselves; the church will always invite them to participate as much as possible in its community. The pope says:

> Together with the synod, I earnestly call upon pastors and the whole community of the faithful to help the divorced and with solicitous care to make sure that they do not consider themselves as separated from the church, for as baptized persons they can and indeed must share in her life. They should be encouraged to listen to the word of God, to attend the sacrifice of the Mass, to persevere in prayer, to contribute to works of charity and to community efforts in favor of justice, to bring up their children in the Christian faith, to cultivate the spirit and practice of penance and thus implore, day by day, God's grace (No. 84).

We are concerned here in the first place with the active witness of everyday Christian life. This is also required of the divorced and remarried. Anyone who neglects or omits this dimension of active Christian life or remains in fatal isolation insisting only on "admission to the sacraments" would be on the wrong path. Divorced-and-remarried people, as members of the church, can give an important witness when, despite the limitation regarding admission to the sacraments, they continue to work in the community. For example, they can share the experiences of their unsuccessful first and not infrequently more successful second marriages in discussions about marriage and family. Consider, for example, inviting them to collaborate in family circles, in retreats, etc.

Those who are divorced and remarried should find help in coming to terms with their difficulties. The shadows of the past must be overcome in candid discussions. The church should include precisely these people in its intercessions. It "should pray for them, encourage them and show herself a merciful mother and thus sustain them in faith and hope" (*Familiaris Consortio*, 84). This should be manifest strongly in public liturgical services.

2. *"Admission" to the Sacraments*

The more recent official pronouncements explain clearly that divorced-and-remarried people cannot be admitted to the eucharist because "their state and position in life objectively contradict that union of love between Christ and the church that is signified and effected by the eucharist" (ibid.). This is a general statement that precludes any general admission of those who are divorced and remarried to the sacraments. Anyone who acts otherwise does so against ecclesiastical regulation.

The church has long granted admission to the sacraments to those divorced and remarried who form a close partnership of life, but live as brother and sister with regard to their personal relationship to one another, i.e., in complete continence (cf. ibid., and Congregation for Bishops, letter to bishops of April 11, 1973). This is also called the "tried-and-true practice of the church" (*probata praxis ecclesiae*). Many consider such a position unnatural and unbelievable. Any judgment here calls not only for realism and sobriety, but also for discretion and tact. Not just a few divorced-and-remarried people have indeed chosen this extraordinary, even occasionally heroic path with bravery and self-sacrifice. They deserve respect and recognition. Clearly, in the long run such a way of life cannot be achieved by all people who are divorced and remarried and only seldom by younger couples.

3. *Need for a Discriminating View of the Individual Situation*

Bishops as well as priests understand the plight of many such divorced-and-remarried people and sympathize with them. It would be of considerable help if, in keeping with the previously shown possibilities, this were more generally known and appreciated. *Familiaris Consortio*, however, leads us one step further. The exhortation states, namely, that the pastors of the churches are duty bound "to exercise careful discernment of situations. There is in fact a difference between those who have sincerely tried to save their first marriage and have been unjustly abandoned and those who through their own grave fault have destroyed a canonically valid marriage. Finally, there are those who have entered into a second union for the sake of the children's upbringing and who are sometimes subjectively certain in conscience that their previous and irreparably destroyed marriage had never been valid" (No. 84).

The apostolic exhortation *Familiaris Consortio* points out these differences in situation, but clearly leaves concrete consequences up to the wise pastoral judgment of the individual spiritual adviser. This must not be considered carte blanche for arbitrary caprice. The evaluation of various situations, however, cannot and should not be left merely to individual opinions.

After long effort on many levels (theologians, advisory boards, synods, forums, etc.), more and more common criteria are recognizable today. They are of assistance in that discernment and judgment of the various situations called for also by Pope John Paul II.

Only an honest accounting can lead to a responsible decision of conscience. An examination of the following criteria is therefore indispensable:

- When there is serious failure involved in the collapse of the first marriage, responsibility for it must be acknowledged and repented.
- It must be convincingly established that a return to the first partner is really impossible and that with the best will the first marriage cannot be restored.
- Restitution must be made for wrongs committed and injuries done insofar as this is possible.
- In the first place this restitution includes fulfillment of obligations to the wife and children of the first marriage (cf. Code of Canon Law, Canon 1071, 1.3).
- Whether or not a partner broke his or her first marriage under great public attention and possibly even scandal should be taken into consideration.
- The second marital partnership must have proved itself over a long period of time to represent a decisive and also publicly recognizable will to live permanently together and also according to the demands of marriage as a moral reality.
- Whether or not fidelity to the second relationship has become a moral obligation with regard to the spouse and children should be examined.

- It ought to be sufficiently clear—though certainly not to any greater extent than with other Christians—that the partners seek truly to live according to the Christian faith and with true motives, i.e., moved by genuinely religious desires to participate in the sacramental life of the church. The same holds true in the children's upbringing.

Divorced-and-remarried people must seek to clarify and evaluate these various situations and circumstances in candid discussion with a wise and experienced priest. Such a discussion is necessary in any case for basic clarification of the facts. For this, criteria have just been stated. The pastors should also point out to those concerned the ways and means given within the church for a legal resolution of their situation.

4. The Possibility of an Individual Decision of Conscience to Participate in the Eucharist

In conjunction with all this falls the decision regarding participation in the celebration of the sacraments. As already stated, there can be no general, formal, official admission because the church's position on the indissolubility of marriage would thereby be obscured. Nor can there be any unilateral admission in individual cases, admission, that is, for which an official of the church alone would be responsible. But through clarifying pastoral dialogue between the partners of a second marriage and a priest, in which the situation is thoroughly, candidly and objectively brought to light, it can happen in individual cases that the marriage partners (or else just one of the partners) see their (or his/her) conscience clear to approach the table of the Lord (cf. Canon 843.1). This is especially the case when the conscience is convinced that the earlier, irreparably destroyed marriage was never valid (*Familiaris Consortio*, 84). The situation would be similar when those concerned already have come a long way in reflection and penance. Moreover, there could also be the presence of an insoluble conflict of duty, where leaving the new family would be the cause of grievous injustice.

Such a decision can only be made by the individual in a personal review of his or her conscience and by no one else. However, he or she will be in need of the clarifying assistance and the unbiased accompaniment of a church officeholder; such assistance will sharpen the conscience and see to it that the basic order of the church is not violated. Those concerned must therefore submit to advice and accompaniment. Each individual case must be examined: There should be no indiscriminate admission or indiscriminate exclusion. Without such a basic spiritual and pastoral dialogue, which should include elements of repentance and conversion, there can be no participation in the eucharist. The participation of a priest in this clarifying process is necessary because participation in the eucharist is a public and ecclesiastically significant act. Nevertheless, the priest does not pronounce any official admission in a formal sense.

The priest will respect the judgment of the individual's conscience, which that person has reached after examining his own conscience and becoming convinced his approaching the holy eucharist can be justified before God. Certainly this respect has different degrees. The divorced-and-remarried person may be in a certain borderline situation that is extremely complex, where the priest cannot in the end forbid his approach to the Lord's table and must therefore tolerate it. It is also possible that an individual, despite the presence of objective indications of guilt, may not have incurred any grievous guilt subjectively. In this case the priest could, after diligent examination of all circumstances, strongly encourage an examination of conscience.

The priest will defend such a decision of conscience against prejudice and suspicion, but he must also take care that the parish does not thereby take offense. If after an examination of conscience receiving communion is not an option, that still does not mean—as was already explained—that one simply has been excluded from the community of the church or that his salvation has even been denied. Such people are not excluded from appealing for grace and for faith, hope and charity, and they especially are not excluded from intercession on the part of others (cf. *Familiaris Consortio*, 84). There are still other ways open to them for committed participation in the church's life.

5. The Place of Divorced People Who Have Remarried in the Whole Community

There remains the question whether divorced-and-remarried people are subject to still other aspects of a reduced position as members of the church. For baptismal and confirmation sponsors, a way of life is required that corresponds to the doctrine of the faith and to the duties to be assumed (cf. Canons 872, 874, 893.1). For work in the pastoral area, good morals are required, for example (cf. Canon 512.3). Divorced-and-remarried people are not automatically excluded thereby. Of course the parish priest must ask himself, together with those concerned, whether the qualification demanded for specific duties can be fulfilled as a general rule. Here again it depends upon the already-presented discernment of individual situations.

Divorced-and-remarried people are not, as a matter of course, excluded from participating in church activities and from membership in advisory councils. Details for the various diocesan committees are explained in the respective diocesan statutes. More appropriate is participation in various volunteer services that have no representative character, although not in public leadership positions. For similar reasons, helping to prepare children and young people for the sacraments is inappropriate.

For the rest, the parish priest is not only responsible for the administration of the sacraments and thus has competency over participation in their celebration, but he must also take into consideration the position of divorced-and-remarried people in the church as a whole and within the specific context of a particular congregation. The responsibility of divorced-and-remarried people is not limited to their own lives but also includes the common welfare of the church. This is especially important in the possibility of assuming representative services. The parish priest must consider discomfort and scandal in the congregation. In any case it always comes back to the actual extent divorced-and-remarried people become rooted and are at home in their parish. In particular, external motives such as recognition and improvement of status, for example, or even an increase in prestige should be prevented from playing a decisive role.

Unreasonable demands regarding reception of the sacraments especially must be avoided with respect to the sick and the dying, as has always been the practice of the church. Refusal of Christian burial can usually be avoided today in most cases, although there still must have been "some indication before death of repentance" (cf. Canon 1184.1.3).

6. Prayers and Church Services for Divorced-and-Remarried People

The church should pray for divorced-and-remarried people. This is especially true for the pastor. It is, however, strictly forbidden for "any pastor for whatever reason or pretext even of a pastoral nature to perform ceremonies of any kind for divorced people who remarry" (*Familiaris Consortio*, 84). An official liturgical ceremony would not only lead to serious misunderstandings among many of the faithful regarding the indissolubility of a validly contracted Christian marriage, but would also introduce official liturgical acts that create the impression of a new, sacramentally valid marriage. Communal prayer with the marriage partners concerned fulfills a discerning pastoral care of people from broken marriages. This can take many forms. One could consider, for example, personal prayers or an invitation to the parish worship services and specific intercessions. Ritual and formal prayers that approach an official liturgical act are inappropriate. Misinterpretations in such situations are almost unavoidable. This is especially true of special Masses celebrated at specific times, namely in conjunction with the civil marriage. In the interests of a specific pastoral care, the pastor can and must avoid public appearances of this kind. Divorced-and-remarried people must not ask this of him. One can express support in other ways such as through visits, discussions, letters and the like.

7. Concrete Responsibility for Pastoral Care

Everyone engaged full time in pastoral care can lead those concerned back closer to the congregation within the given principles. The clarifying dialogue must be led by an experienced priest, who must in any case inform the parish priest of an approach to the eucharist. This is demanded by the parish priest's responsibility for the order of the celebrations and for the reception of the eucharist in the congregation, but also for all forms of reconciliation with the church (cf. 2 Cor. 5:11–21).

The question whether in the future there ought to be an experienced priest available in each deanery for especially difficult situations can for the time being remain open, but it should at least be brought up here. Certainly the ecclesiastical authorities can be consulted.

These last considerations show in particular how much sensitivity and a sense of responsibility are required on the part of all pastoral workers, especially pastors and other priests. This is also valid regarding the regular proclamation of the word and for instruction in the faith from Sunday homilies to religious instruction. This goal cannot be reached without intensive attention to these basic principles in training and in continuing education.

PROSPECTS: GOSPEL STRENGTH AND BORDERLINE SITUATIONS

The pastoral care of people from broken marriages and for divorced people who have remarried must not become narrow or isolated. It should be integrated into the overall care for marriage and the family as a whole. It should be aware of the vulnerability of human relationships and of their need for support. It should help in the formation of conscience and know that conscience is irreplaceable. It should be aware of the need for discriminating pastoral dialogue. Only within such an all-embracing approach can the special care of these people be successful. Long and patient processes of theological, spiritual and pastoral education are also needed here.

These principles need corresponding application in other areas such as church employment policies and labor law. The German bishops' conference is giving attention to such clarification.

Furthermore, judgments regarding those living together before marriage or of those living together in long-standing nonmarital relationships as well as of Christians who contract merely a civil marriage also require discernment. Blanket condemnations or indulgences regarding the question of admission to the sacraments are as inappropriate here as with divorced-and-remarried people.

Many of the problems treated here represent general duties of contemporary pastoral care as well. Strict demands need not be addressed

solely to divorced-and-remarried people, for example regarding requirements for reception of communion; discussion of the pastoral care of
people from broken marriages also covers deficits in other areas that
concern everyone such as the required correct disposition for participation at the Lord's table. One might also recall in this connection the
rediscovery and revival of "spiritual communion."

With that we are brought back to a basic requirement. Only when
the theory and practice of marriage are fundamentally strengthened in the
Christian community can the church intervene on behalf of those from
broken marriages and most especially for divorced-and-remarried people
without creating misunderstandings. In the end, everything depends on
the living witness of Christian married people. This is irreplaceable. The
lived strength of the Gospel yields the wisdom to treat borderline cases
correctly. This is especially true at a time when these cases are on the
increase and even beginning to gain the upper hand. A well-considered
basic attitude is therefore all the more necessary and of course requires
continual renewal. The great church father St. Gregory of Nazianzus
gives this measure: "Do not oppress by strictness, do not destroy by weak
indulgence."

Notes

1. Vatican Council II, *Pastoral Constitution on the Church in the
Modern World*, 1.
2. Ibid., 48–49.
3. Pope John Paul II, *Familiaris Consortio*, 83.
4. Ibid., 84.
5. Ibid.
6. German bishops' conference, *Catechism for Adults*, "The Creed of the
Church," p. 395 (German edition).
7. Discussion of Canon 915 of the Code of Canon Law has indeed shown
that a universal application of these norms to divorced-and-remarried people as a
group is not possible and that to this extent Canon 915 does not preclude discussion
such as in the present paper of a discriminating "admission" to the sacraments.

24. Indissolubility, Divorce, and Holy Communion: An Open Letter to Archbishop Saier, Bishop Lehmann, and Bishop Kasper

Germain Grisez, John Finnis, and William E. May

This chapter first appeared in *New Blackfriars* 75 (1994).

Your joint pastoral letter regarding ministry to the divorced and "remarried" (hereinafter *PL*), dated July 10, 1993, and part IV of the accompanying principles of pastoral care (*PPC*) have been translated and published by *Origins: CNS Documentary Service* (March 10, 1994), pp. 670–76. Our letter is addressed to you personally, but is being sent also to certain other prelates and published, not only because this matter concerns the entire Church but also because of the publicity it already has received.

We focus on only one of the things you treat: a divorced and "remarried" person's possible decision of conscience that he or she may receive Communion. While we respect your desire to help the divorced and remarried, we believe your handling of this matter cannot be genuinely helpful, but is injurious not only to those whom you wish to help but to the whole Catholic Church.

I

Your pastoral initiative is not concerned with "remarried" individuals who unilaterally decide, whether in good or bad faith, to receive Communion. Rather, you are establishing a way in which "remarried" individuals can obtain an *admission* to the sacraments which they and others will be able to regard as legitimate.

With respect to divorced and "remarried" individuals, you make it clear that "there can be no general, formal, official admission because the church's position on the indissolubility of marriage would thereby be obscured" and that "There should be no indiscriminate admission or indiscriminate exclusion" (*PPC*, IV, 4).

But you also specify and authorize a way in which "remarried" individuals can gain admission to the sacraments: they are to decide for themselves, "in a personal review of...conscience [Gewissensentscheidung]" (*PPC*, IV, 4), whether or not they may receive Communion. You *require* that in this review and decision they apply eight criteria ("An examination of the following criteria is therefore indispensable" [*PPC*, IV, 3]) and engage in dialogue with a priest ("The participation of a priest in this clarifying process [Klärung] is necessary" [*PPC*, IV, 4]).

You also indicate that the admission to the sacraments gained in this way has ecclesial significance and will be recognized in the Church as legitimate: "pastoral dialogue can help those involved to reach a personal and responsible decision according to the judgment of their consciences [Gewissensentscheidung] that must be respected by the Church and the congregation" (*PL*, IV). "The priest will respect the judgment of the individual's conscience, which that person has reached after examining his own conscience and becoming convinced his approaching the holy eucharist can be justified before God" (*PPC*, IV, 4). "The priest will defend such a decision of conscience against prejudice and suspicion..." (ibid.)

Our response to your initiative focuses on that decision of conscience and the beliefs on which it can depend. Those who suppose that conscience can determine good and evil autonomously or that it merely registers moral feelings would say the decision need not be either correct or erroneous. But Catholic teaching, recently reaffirmed in *Veritatis Splendor* (62–63), always has been that in every instance conscience either is correct or in error. We shall examine, however, not the thoughts and good or bad faith of those making the decision, but what you yourselves can think about the decision's correctness, and about your responsibility in authorizing individuals to make it and in directing that they then be granted admission to Communion.

Since, as you say, "The standard for the church is the word, will and example of Jesus" (*PL*, II), our examination will proceed in the light of Jesus' word: "Whoever divorces his wife and marries another commits adultery against her; and if she divorces her husband and marries another, she commits adultery" (Mk 10.11–12).

That word of Jesus is recognized as decisive not only by the divorced who have resolved not to remarry but also by the "remarried" who reach their decision of conscience thus: *Sexual acts with my present partner would be adulterous, and adultery is always wrong. But if I abstain from such acts and am not guilty of some other mortal sin, I may receive Communion.* When the "remarried" promise to live as brother and sister (see *PPC*, IV, 2), you obviously can suppose that their decision of conscience is reached in that way and think it correct; as pastors, you also obviously can responsibly inform "remarried" persons that it is fitting for them so to judge and act, and can responsibly inform "remarried" persons that it is fitting for them so to judge and act, and can responsibly give effect to that decision by directing that such persons be admitted to the sacraments (ibid.), even if their receiving them could occasion mistaken and uncharitable judgments by others.

II

As you say, however, "remarried" individuals who engage in sexual acts also sometimes will reach a decision of conscience that they may receive Communion. You specify diverse situations, beginning: "This is especially the case when the conscience is convinced that the earlier, irreparably destroyed marriage was never valid" (*PPC*, IV, 4). Such individuals could reach their decision of conscience thus: *Since my irreparably destroyed "marriage" never was a real marriage, I am free to be married to my present partner. And, while I did not obtain an annulment from a Church tribunal and did not marry my present partner in the Church, this partnership is a valid marriage. So, I am not committing adultery and, provided I am not guilty of some other mortal sin, I may receive Communion.*

Though we believe there are very serious problems in your authorizing the making of that decision and giving ecclesial effect to it, we will not examine those problems. Instead, we shall focus on the problems raised by cases in which the "remarried" individual's decision of conscience concedes that the first relationship was a valid marriage.

You do make provision for such cases. For, while you say that individuals, having met the requirements you set regarding criteria and process, may have a clear conscience about receiving Communion *especially* if they are convinced that their earlier partnership was not a valid marriage, you at once add: "The situation would be similar when those concerned already have come a long way in reflection and penance. Moreover, there could also be the presence of an insoluble conflict of duty, where leaving the new family would be the cause of grievous injustice" (*PPC*, IV, 4). Plainly, if the first relationship were thought to have been invalid as a marriage, staying in the second relationship would not seem to generate a conflict of duty.

We set aside your questionable assumption that an insoluble conflict of duty can exist in some cases and, in regard to all the cases in which "those concerned already have come a long way in reflection and penance," consider only the possible grounds on which you could believe the decision of conscience to be correct.

If this decision of conscience is to be correct, the individual making it must not ground it on a false belief. But consider a person who previously contracted a sacramental marriage whose validity is not in question, consummated it, obtained a divorce, and "remarried"; and who currently lives in sexual intimacy with a second partner. On what belief can such an individual attempt to ground a decision of conscience that he or she may receive Communion? There are only three possibilities.

First: *In accord with the Lord's word, I admit I am committing adultery, and agree that adultery is a mortal sin. However, even persisting in mortal sin is not inconsistent with receiving Communion. So, I may receive Communion.* Is it open to bishops to think that the decision of conscience thus reached can be correct? No. Insofar as the decision depends on the belief that persisting in mortal sin is consistent with receiving Communion, it cannot be correct, and it would be wrong for a bishop to teach the belief on which it depends. For that belief contradicts St. Paul's warning to examine oneself before receiving Communion (1 Cor 11.27–29), as that warning has been understood in the teaching of the Catholic Church (see, e.g., DS 1646–47, 1661).

Second: *According to the Lord's word, I am committing adultery. However, I need not be committing a mortal sin, since extramarital intercourse is not always grave matter. Therefore, provided I am not guilty of some other mortal sin, I may receive Communion.* Is it open to bishops to think that the decision of conscience thus reached can be correct? No. Insofar as the decision depends on the belief that extramarital intercourse is not always grave matter, it cannot be correct, and it would be wrong for a bishop to teach the belief on which it depends. For that belief contradicts scriptural teaching about the various forms of extramarital intercourse (see, e.g., 1 Cor 6.9–10), as those judgments have been understood in the teaching of the Catholic Church (see, e.g., DS 1544; *Veritatis Splendor*, 49–81).

Third: *After my first marriage failed or was destroyed, I was divorced and, at some point, that marriage dissolved. While my present relationship does not meet the Church's official, canonical requirements, it has come to have the moral reality (sittliche Realität) of marriage, and so is valid. Therefore, I am not committing adultery, and provided I have followed the three German bishops' directions in carrying out my personal review of conscience and am not guilty of some other mortal sin, I may receive Communion.* Again we ask: Is it open to bishops to think that the decision of conscience thus reached can be correct?

You do seem to think so, for you regularly speak of remarriage and second marriage, and even suggest as an appropriate example of "witness of everyday Christian life" that such individuals "share the experiences of their unsuccessful first and not infrequently more successful [menschlich besser] second marriages in discussions [das Gespräch der Kirche] about marriage and family" (*PPC*, IV, int.). Considered together, these expressions suggest that you think the second relationship can be a valid marriage, though not officially recognized as such by the Church.

However, insofar as the decision depends on the belief that the first marriage dissolved and the second relationship is valid as a marriage, it cannot be correct, and it would be wrong for a bishop to teach the belief on which it depends. Taken in reference to a valid, consummated, sacramental marriage, that belief contradicts Jesus' word about

marriage, divorce, and adultery, as that word has been understood by the
Catholic Church.

III

Very likely you will object at this point: The preceding paragraph
begs the question by uncritically assuming the dogmatic foundation of
the former pastoral practice, which we have found to be unhelpful and so
are replacing on the basis of a different dogmatic foundation. This foundation's acceptability is supported by critical historical research, which
shows that indissolubility does not exclude the possibility of remarriage
in exceptional situations.

But as you say: "The church cannot assume the right to disregard the
word of Jesus regarding the indissolubility of marriage" (*PL*, II). Jesus'
word, *whoever divorces and "remarries" commits adultery*, is exception-
less: "whoever" indicates that the proposition is universal. Moreover, that
word is not a mere unconditional prohibition of divorce ("bedingungsloses
Scheidungsverbot" [*PPC*, II, 1]). Rather, it is an assertion that obtaining a
divorce cannot succeed in dissolving one's marriage. For, if Jesus' word
merely forbade divorce, the "remarriage" could be a marriage, and the sexual relations pertaining to it could be marital, not adulterous. So, Jesus'
word is that marriage is indissoluble without exception. Consequently, to
vindicate your pastoral initiative, you must teach, at one and the same time,
both that valid, sacramental, consummated marriages sometimes dissolve
and that marriage is indissoluble without exception. Since those propositions are contradictory, that position is untenable, and your pastoral initiative is indefensible.

To this you might reply: Very clear and logical! But the clarity is
specious and the logic manifests ignorance of history. To begin with,
Jesus' word about indissolubility refers to marriage "in the beginning," not
just to sacramental marriage. Yet St. Paul, while understanding Jesus' prohibition to be unconditional, authorized exceptions in one kind of case
(see 1 Cor 7.10–16). Subsequent history reveals many additional instances
of the same sort of thing: various leaders of the church, including some
popes, admitted the real possibility of divorce and remarriage in particular cases, and assumed that their doing so was compatible with Jesus'

word. There also are the *porneia* clauses (see Mt 5.32, 19.9). Whatever they mean, they were taken in some times and places to allow for divorce. Even the Council of Trent apparently took care to avoid condemning that view and practice, for, rather than condemning anyone who teaches that marriage can be dissolved because of adultery, Trent condemns anyone who says the Church errs in having taught and in teaching that the bond of marriage cannot be dissolved on that ground (see DS 1807). So, you can conclude, the historical data require an account of Jesus' word about indissolubility which leaves room in particular cases for exceptions which should not exist but, unfortunately, do, including the exceptions for which your pastoral initiative makes arrangements, insofar as possible.

Not only do we recognize the force of that historical argument, but as persons having divorced and "remarried" friends, relatives, and even family members, we feel its appeal. On this view, as you say: "Jesus' word is therefore no crushing law, but rather an offer, an invitation, an exhortation and a gift, which is to realize the original sense of marriage in lifelong fidelity" (*PL*, II). In forming their marriage covenant, a Christian couple undertake to remain faithful, despite everything, until death, and Jesus is present in their covenantal relationship so that they can keep their commitment. Nevertheless, even Christian marriages fail, and parties to that failure even go so far as to attempt remarriage. Therein, you might say, lies the adultery of which Jesus speaks.

At this point your initiative departs from past pastoral practice: holding that conversion remains possible, you offer the divorced individual—though now living in a new, ongoing, and sexually intimate relationship—a possibility of obtaining an admission to the sacraments which he or she, and others too, will regard as legitimate. To obtain it, the individual must put behind himself or herself what you call the "shadows of the past" or what one might call the "adultery," literal or figurative, which definitively sealed his or her marriage's failure. Thought of in this way, the exceptions for which you make room appear compatible with Jesus' word on indissolubility.

Still, the dogmatic foundation of the pastoral practice which your initiative is meant to improve upon provides its own account of the historical data. Admittedly, this account, like any other, must strain to cover them all, and must characterize as abuses and mistakes some practices during the first half of the Church's history. By this account, nevertheless,

Jesus' word is neither a "crushing law" nor merely "an offer, an invitation, an exhortation and a gift." Jesus' word is, indeed, those good things but, besides, it is a mysterious truth: marriage simply cannot fail, nor can the partners themselves or anyone else on earth destroy it, for marriage is without exception indissoluble in earthly society, just as sand is without exception indissoluble in water. Still, in covering the data, this account limits indissolubility thus understood to marriage of a specific kind: valid, sacramental, and consummated marriage.

This account's characteristic conception of indissolubility, together with the pastoral practice implementing it, has prevailed, as you well know, throughout the Roman Catholic Church since well before the Reformation. Therefore, the notion of indissolubility-with-room-for-exceptions, which you require, is incompatible with the notion of indissolubility-excluding-the-very-possibility-of-exceptions, used by the whole Catholic Church in her teaching and pastoral practice since before the Reformation.

You might deny the incompatibility of the two notions and say that the one you require holds true only of particular cases, while that used by the whole Catholic Church holds true of marriage in itself. We reply: An indissolubility which holds true only of marriage in itself holds true of nothing, since marriage and its properties are realized only in particular marriages.

Still, you might rejoin: While marriage in itself always and necessarily remains indissoluble, the apparent logical implication of indissolubility for particular cases need not follow. After all, reality is not always logical: for instance, human persons by nature are two-legged, but some people are born without, or lose, their legs. This rejoinder, however, will not work. Unlike lacking and having legs, dissolubility and indissolubility are properties which cannot be observed directly; they are known to belong to things of a certain kind only because all behave consistently under specified conditions; and so they can be used to determine whether or not an individual belongs to a certain kind. For instance, salt is soluble in water, while sand is not, and so one can distinguish between salt and sand by testing a sample in water. Thus, if this or that particular marriage is dissolved, any marriage is dissoluble, not indissoluble.

Your pastoral initiative therefore requires a notion of indissolubility incompatible with the notion used by the Roman Catholic Church since before the Reformation. If you persist in this initiative, you cannot consistently affirm what the Church has believed for centuries about the indissolubility of marriage *in the same sense in which the Church has believed it.*

Instead, you must hold that the belief of the whole Church, from the bishops down to the last of the laity, has been in error on this matter of faith and morals—a position excluded by Vatican II (see *LG* 12). Neither can you consistently affirm *in the same sense in which Trent taught it* what that Council straightforwardly taught, in a canon which you neglect to mention, about the indissolubility of marriage: "If anyone says that the marriage bond can be dissolved by reason of heresy, domestic incompatibility, or wilful desertion by one of the parties: let him be anathema" (DS 1805). Indeed, to be consistent you must even deny the canon of Trent which you do mention (DS 1807; *PPC*, II, 2), and say the Catholic Church has erred and errs in teaching *in Trent's sense* that marriage cannot be dissolved on the ground of adultery.

IV

In the two preceding sections, we have argued that there is no true belief that could ground the decision of conscience which your pastoral initiative authorizes people to make and to which it gives ecclesial effect. Still, could not your initiative be a pastorally responsible way of tolerating and responding to "remarried" individuals' objectively *incorrect* decisions of conscience assumed to be made in good faith? There are three reasons for answering no.

First, since the decision is objectively incorrect, you hardly can assume responsibly that it is made in good faith; for all the beliefs that might be thought to ground it are excluded by well-known Catholic teachings.

Second, while pastors sometimes can rightly tolerate an error of conscience made in good faith, to authorize the making of a decision is to cooperate formally in making it, not to tolerate it. You surely will agree that pastors, especially in a published document, cannot responsibly cooperate formally in the making of decisions they know to be erroneous, since doing so would violate their pastoral duty to teach and preach the truth and to correct error.

Third, since anyone erring in good faith believes his or her decision of conscience to be well-grounded, those authorized to make an erroneous decision by their pastors would be likely to draw the logical conclusion that at least one of the beliefs that could ground it must be true; other faithful who think the decision could be correct will draw the same conclusion. You would be unable, however, to explain publicly that the decision of conscience must be in error, since doing so would greatly impede individuals' making it in good faith. Thus, authorizing individuals to make the decision in question inevitably would dispose all the faithful to assent to one or more of the false beliefs that could ground the decision. If you tried to correct one or more of those false beliefs, you would more strongly dispose the faithful to assent to the other or others. But if you tried to correct all the false beliefs without admitting that the decision of conscience whose making you authorize must be incorrect, you would dispose the faithful to suppose as they already are far too likely to suppose—that conscience can determine good and evil autonomously and without regard to faith's teachings, or that conscience, merely registering moral feelings, need not be true or false, but only peaceful and self-satisfied.

V

Your Excellencies, Esteemed Colleagues, and dear Brothers in Jesus:

We realize that you are capable and learned men who have devoted many years and much work to the theology of marriage, as have we. We realize, too, that you love the Church, as we do, and are circumspect, so that you would never have taken your pastoral initiative were you not persuaded of its soundness. We are conscious that you and we use quite different theological methodologies, and we expect that you will be far less impressed by our sort of argumentation than you might be if you shared our methodology. Therefore, much as we hope and pray for such an outcome, we hardly expect you to read this letter, agree that you have made a mistake, withdraw your pastoral initiative, and replace it with teaching and pastoral guidance which we would regard as sound.

Why, then, have we taken the trouble to write? In the hope that you and other concerned leaders and members of the Church will think through the implications of what you have done. The methodology we use is helpful in distinguishing confused ideas and drawing out implications that the confusions had obscured. Our analysis also makes clear the significance of the fact that you are bishops speaking and acting officially and publicly, no longer only theologians or pastors quietly handling particular cases. Then too, even if you find little that impresses you in our analysis, it should show you how Catholics who do not share your methodology (including most of the faithful) will draw from your pastoral initiative conclusions that you, we are confident, did not intend.

Even if you think the indissolubility-with-room-for-exceptions, which your pastoral initiative requires, somehow is compatible with indissolubility-excluding-the-very possibility-of-exceptions, we hope you will agree that very few other Catholics will see their compatibility. So, your pastoral initiative will be pastorally injurious, even to very many Catholics who welcome it, because your documents do not clearly tell the faithful which belief, notwithstanding the Church's well-known relevant teachings, can ground the decision of conscience made with your authorization and given effect by you. Therefore, even on the hypothesis that there is some such true belief, your pastoral initiative leaves the faithful in much the same position as if there were none: it disposes them to assent to one or more of the relevant false beliefs, and/or to conclude that all the relevant Catholic teachings are questionable, and/or to infer that truth is irrelevant to conscience, which need only be at ease with itself.

What, then, is to be done? You may be tempted to try to smooth over the tension between your pastoral initiative and what most Catholics, even those who reject the Church's teaching about divorce and "remarriage," believe that teaching to be. Far from helping, however, any such attempt will cause greater injury. When the leaders of a church try to solve problems by embracing contradictory propositions, ordinary people regard their effort as sham.

It should, instead, be openly admitted that there is a conflict between two notions of indissolubility. It should be openly admitted, too, that, while you see that conflict as paradox, there are capable and learned people who see it as contradiction. Please consider the importance of the issue and the urgency of resolving it. In our opinion, nothing short of a definitive judgment, collegially arrived at, will serve the purpose. We beg you to consider that possibility prayerfully, and if you find merit in it, to recommend it to the Holy Father.

Editors' Note

On October 14, 1994, the Congregation for the Doctrine of the Faith sent a letter "Concerning the Reception of Holy Communion by Divorced-and-Remarried Faithful" to the bishops of the world. The letter stated that divorced-and-remarried faithful may not receive communion. Since marriage is a public reality, one cannot appeal to conscience in this case. For the full text, see *Origins* 24 (1994): 337–41. For the response of the three German bishops to this letter, see Archbishop Oskar Saier and Bishops Karl Lehmann and Walter Kasper, "Response to the Doctrinal Congregation's Letter," *Origins* 24 (1994): 341–44.

25. Of Spouses, the Real World, and the "Where" of Christian Marriage

David S. Crawford

This chapter first appeared in *Communio* 33 (Spring 2006).

INTRODUCTION

The Church's teaching concerning the indissolubility of sacramental marriage has been a source of controversy for a long time. But the liberalization of divorce in modern western societies has dramatically increased pastoral challenges for the Church. A number of authors have recently addressed the issue by interpreting the indissoluble bond in terms of moral obligation.[1] Others have argued that the indissoluble bond is something to be accomplished as the spouses' love matures over a lifetime.[2] Indissolubility does not therefore occur in a single moment of sexual consummation, which in any case is said to be "outside sacrament."[3] Certainly, it is argued, the couple in entering a Christian marriage is entering into a sacrament, and surely there is a moral obligation of love, care, and fidelity.

However, in a sinful and fallen world we often fail to live up to our obligations or to achieve the ideal. Sometimes, the argument continues, the relationship itself dies. This is a reality that must be taken into account by the Church. Once a given marriage has in fact dissolved, the response of the Church should be to offer the mercy and reconciliation of Christ and of all the faithful. Thus, while it is true that marriage is "indissoluble" in terms of its moral commitment or as an ideal to be achieved, it is not true that it is absolutely indissoluble in the sense that no power on earth can cause the dissolution of a marriage *ratum et consummatum*, at least as this last phrase has been understood by the Church. "Therefore it is not helpful for the Church to speak of indissolubility as being the effect of the sacrament independent of the wills of the spouses. Instead the sacrament's effect is to assist the couple in their efforts to build a consortium of intimate love so that the destruction of their love becomes virtually unthinkable."[4]

Several authors have used the scholastic tradition to buttress these arguments. What is the bond, it is asked, but a relation? This relation does not exist, somehow, somewhere, above and beyond the couple.[5] Therefore it must be "in" the couple themselves. Marriage is not a character sacrament, so the content of this "in" cannot be an indelible sacramental character such as that of Baptism or Holy Orders. So what type of relation is the bond? From a scholastic point of view, a relation is an accident. Thus the marital relation cannot have some kind of separate or autonomous existence. While, as an accident, the bond is "ontological,"[6] this does not mean that it escapes human freedom. It is "a relationship of obligation," "sealed by God's grace and commitment to the spouses."[7] The bond is therefore essentially moral.[8] As a relation, it therefore has no necessary or essential indissolubility.

Of course, the question of sacramental marriage's indissolubility raises many important issues, including its ecumenical implications, historical background, and doctrinal status—not to mention the best interpretation or even the theological sufficiency of scholastic understandings of "relation."[9] However, this essay can only address one basic question. As we can see, an important starting point for the issue of indissolubility is in fact the question of "where" this bond is to be located. Does the bond lie solely within the spouses? If so, is it to be located in the order of being, of freedom? Is it rooted in something above and beyond the spouses, however much it might also arise from and shape their freedom? So, the question returns, "where" is this bond and what does it have to do with the real-world marriages of men and women, of flesh and blood?

PAN-SACRAMENTALITY

In order to address our question, we must begin with a counterintuitive claim: an adequate understanding of the sacrament of matrimony emerges only in a consideration of that which is apparently opposed to it, viz. the renunciation of marital and family life in Christian virginity. My warrant for making this claim is the fact that it is precisely through the advent of Christian virginity in Christ's and Mary's *fiats* that the possibility for marriage as a modality of belonging to the Church (that is to say, as a sacrament and as an ecclesial status[10]) is possible at all. As with so many questions in Christianity, then, the question of sacramental marriage begins in paradox.

Crucial to elaborating the meaning of this paradox is Hans Urs von Balthasar's claim that, while Christian virginity is not a sacrament, neither is it simply non-sacramental, let alone "anti-sacramental." It is also not simply outside of or parallel to the sacramental order. Rather, it is "pan-sacramental."[11] To say that Christian virginity is "pan-sacramental" means not only that it stands above the sacramental order, but that it in fact gives birth to it. Certainly the Church and "all the individual sacraments…have their root in the universal sacramentality of the flesh of Jesus Christ (as a historical, Eucharistic, and Mystical Body)." Indeed, "the formation of the hypostatic union," beginning as it does in Mary's consent, "is already a nuptial, ecclesial mystery." It is from within this consent and the Son's consent to become man that God descends "into the flesh of the Virgin and into his own flesh."[12]

This starting point helps us to discover the meaning of our specific question by placing it in its proper framework: viz. the wider question of "the 'where' of the Christian" and his sacramental life in general.[13] Let us consider this broader and foundational point in greater detail before turning back specifically to marriage.

Christ

Clearly, the "where" of the Christian is in Christ. The Incarnation is the actualization of God's covenant with his people, described in both the Old and New Testaments in nuptial terms.[14] It is the content of the Son's "taking responsibility" for the risk of creation,[15] as the one "in," "through," and "for" whom all was created (Col 1:15–16). The formula of Chalcedon ("in two natures without confusion, change, division, or separation"—"*in duabus naturis inconfuse, immutabiliter, indivise, inseparabiliter*"[16]) serves to define the radically encompassing meaning of God's commitment in the person of the Son to the world as a whole. It therefore effects and articulates the real relationship between God and the world. In the Incarnation, God joins himself indissolubly to all of humanity and, in an extended sense, to all of the cosmos—to "all flesh."[17] As is reflected in the passages quoted above from Balthasar, this bond has often been thought of by the tradition in nuptial terms. The nuptial analogy is apt because it brings out the unity of the divine and human natures of the "one flesh" of the Incarnation. Like the unity of man and woman in marriage, the unity (*indivise, inseparabiliter*) in the hypostatic union also holds in place the irreducible difference (*inconfuse, immutabiliter*) between the divine and human natures.[18] Hence, in his classic formulation, St. Thomas is able to base the indissolubility brought about by sexual consummation on the analogy with the indissoluble union of the two natures in the person of Christ.[19]

The Incarnation is likewise the condition for the possibility of the nuptial relationship between Christ and the Church. Like Eve, taken from the fruitful wound opened in Adam's side during his paradisal sleep, the Church springs from the lance-wound opened in Christ's side while hanging in the "sleep" of the Cross. The nuptial couple of paradise prefigures the nuptial couple of the New Covenant in the Father's eternal plan and, in fact, is given its fullest meaning only in view of this "second" couple. As Balthasar puts it, "[t]he root from which the Church unfolds is the Incarnation of the Son of God, the Word of the Father, in whom already everything was created and given an orientation toward his coming in the fullness of time."[20] As in Eve's relationship to Adam, the Church is both "body" and "bride" of Christ. Christ, like Adam, recognizes in this Bride, presented to him by the Father, his own body. The "members" of the Church are not members in the sense that any community has its members. Rather, they are members in the sense that a body has its members (1 Cor 12:12-17). Christ is the "head" (*kephale*) of the Church, not only in the sense of being the highest and first "member" of the body, but also in the sense that he is its "source," the body from whom the bride/body is generated.

As Balthasar often emphasizes, underlying the Incarnation and Christ's nuptial relationship with the Church is the Son's eternal "yes" to the Father. Unlike the first Adam, he did not "grasp at" equality with God but "humbled himself and became obedient," even to death on the Cross (Phil 2:5–8). Christ is the Son who lives solely in the truth of his eternal generation from the Father and, in so doing, takes on the "flesh" of the world. But in this taking on flesh, the Son in Christ expresses the inner life of God and the relations of the Persons of the Trinity. As Benedict XVI's first encyclical puts it, God in Christ "turns against himself," in the sense that his mercy turns aside his anger at sin, but also in the sense that the Son now stands before the Father as man.[21] He offers himself to all of humanity and on behalf of all of humanity to the Father precisely in the flesh of his Incarnation. Indeed, as we have just seen his Incarnation—which is not dissolved by his death—is the enactment of the indissoluble bond sought by God with the world and made personal with every member of the Church in Christ's ecclesial body and bride.

Nothing in Christ's life is insignificant or unrelated to the hypostatic union and its implications for the Church. Most especially, however, Christ's manner of bodily self-bestowal is crucial for understanding his identity and what it reveals to us about human destiny. This bodily self-bestowal begins in his accepting to take on human flesh and to live among men and women in all of the complexity and ambiguity of their concrete situation in the world and in culture. The fact that Christ's own mission entailed the renunciation of marriage—that he remained a virgin—is therefore deeply significant. Of course, his mission could not have centered on a particular set of children or a wife. Rather, his mission, which as we have seen, is nevertheless carried out in the nuptial unity of his divine and human natures and in his relationship with the Church, is for the salvation of all of humanity. His virginity therefore represents an open-ended love that pours forth in universal fruitfulness.

This last point indicates that Christ's virginity cannot be merely juxtaposed to his mission or his taking on flesh and dwelling among us. Rather, it is interior to, and expresses the inner meaning of, his Incarnation. In this sense, then, Christ's virginity is inscribed in the very structure of his Incarnation, as universal mission, for the salvation of the world, and indeed is the crucial foundation of the embodied and humanly lived-out "yes" he gives to the Father.

Mary

Likewise, according to Balthasar's provocative claim, Mary's virginity is "pan-sacramental." Mary cannot be separated from either her Son's Cross or his Incarnation without a distortion of both. Her *fiat* is necessary for both because God awaits the "yes" of the world. Mary is the Theotokos, the God-bearer and mother of Jesus. But as the figure of the Church, and as spouse of the Holy Spirit, Mary is the one who prefigures the bride of Christ. It is in both of these capacities that she is found at the foot of the Cross in John's Gospel.

As St. Thomas tells us, Mary's consent, as virgin, is the consent for—stands in the place of—the whole of human nature (*"consensus virginis loco totius humanae naturae"*).[22] All human yeses are, in the final analysis, enabled by the yeses of Christ and Mary. They are the ones who give consent on behalf of all creation. Mary gives birth to the God-man Jesus, who is the nuptial consummation of the God-world relation, made absolutely concrete in Christ's Incarnation.

But what is the place and significance of Mary's virginity? Like her Son's, Mary's *fiat* is *itself* virginal. This does not mean that her *fiat* is simply externally enabled by her virginity, as though we could understand it as an apt moral excellence or one necessary for the magnitude of her yes. The difference between Mary's yes and that of everyday believers is not simply one of degree. Mary's yes offers the prototypical form of consent; her virginity *is* in a significant sense this consent. Mary's aptness and virtue can only be understood in view of the simple fact that Mary's yes is that of her whole being, rooted even in her body; it is the concrete ground in which the Word can take on flesh.

It is true, of course, that Mary is both married and virgin. In this sense, she is herself paradoxical. But the tradition has not only stressed her unique role, but has also always given a priority to her virginity. Her title as Theotokos, a reality rooted in her virginity, indicates this. And while the tradition has insisted on the validity of her marriage to Joseph, the emphasis in Mariology is decidedly on *Maria-Ecclesia*, that is to say, on Mary as prefiguring the Church, which is itself the virginal bride of Christ. This is why it is sometimes pointed out that Mary is not mother despite being a virgin but *because* she is a virgin.[23] In fact, the truth of this statement goes in both directions: she is also a virgin because she is

Theotokos, since her Immaculate Conception is a proleptic participation in the graces of the Cross. She is the one who bears in her womb her own salvation and that of the world.

The virginity of Christ and Mary, therefore, is not additional or marginal to their yeses, or even simply ingredient in their yeses, but at the heart of (indeed the very form of) their "let it be done unto me according to your word" (Lk 1:38) and "according to your will and not mine" (Mt 26:39; Mk 14:37: Lk 22:42). Because the relationships between God and the world and God and every individual can only be mediated through the life of Christ and its universalization in time and space through the Holy Spirit and the Church, Christ and Mary's consent forms the axis around which all of history and the universe turn. It is in and through their consent that the nuptial "bond" between humanity and God is forged in the hypostatic union of divine and human natures in the person of Christ. Thus, their virginity is, in a significant sense, at the center of the God-world relationship.

Consecrated Virginity

Central to Balthasar's argument is the role of consecrated virginity as a state of life within the Church. As he tells us, "[t]here exist in the Christian life—mediated by the sacraments and the ministry but not identical with these—particularly close and central forms of participation in the…pansacramental mystery, viz. those forms of life that explicitly made the Marian-ecclesiological law of life their own…."[24]

Every Christian state of life represents and unfolds the consents of Christ and Mary. However this is especially the case with consecrated virginity. Of the three evangelical counsels the tradition has gathered from Sacred Scripture, obedience is typically (and for good reasons) given priority. However, from another perspective, a primacy may be given to virginity. This priority can be seen in the teaching of John Paul II, when he tells us in *Vita consecrata* (1996), for example, that chastity is "the first and essential…sacred bond" among the three counsels (14; cf. also 26, 32). Similarly, in *Redemptionis donum* (1984) he argues that the key to an adequate understanding of the consecrated life is to see that it makes Christ one's "only spouse" and that its meaning lies in bringing about an "exclusive" nuptial belonging (cf. 3, 5. 8, 11). Virginity "is addressed in a particular way to the love of the human heart. It places greater emphasis [as compared to the other two counsels] on the spousal character of this love, while poverty and still more obedience seem to emphasize primarily the aspect of redemptive love contained in religious consecration" (11). Notice that according to John Paul the priority of virginity is based on its representing the complete nuptial-bodily gift of self entailed in the Christian life. The fullness of love is the very vocation of human nature itself precisely because God, as a Trinity of Persons, is love. For human beings, this vocation can only be specified and actualized in the body.[25] The vow of virginity then is a bodily actualization of this vocation precisely according to the pattern established by Christ and his mother. It brings into the time and space of history and culture the visible and explicit form of their consent. It manifests in history and culture the offering made on behalf of all creation.[26]

Directly participating in the pan-sacramental character of Christ and Mary's virginal consent, consecrated virginity is not a sacrament, although its universal fecundity is also directed toward the salvation of "all flesh." As such, the common claim that virginity is a rejection of the goods of the body is not only wrong but misses the point entirely. In fact, virginity is a radical affirmation of the foundational character and importance of those goods in relation to God and through God to the world. It is the giving over of oneself—unmediated by the sacrament of matrimony—precisely as *corpore et anima unus* to God. And as such, it shows us that human love and self-giving are always mediated through the body.

Christ and Mary's virginity constitutes the ground which offers itself to all of humanity and in which every response must be rooted. Consecration's direct participation so thoroughly embeds itself *ex opere operantis* in that ground that it becomes an explicit and outward participation in Christ and Mary's consent on behalf of the world. In this sense, then, the "pan-sacramental" character of consecration's "direct" participation in the *consensus virginis loco totius humanae naturae* stands "within" the foundational source of marriage's sacramental bond.

THE INDISSOLUBLE BOND

What can be drawn from the discussion up to now with respect to the particular sacramentality of marriage and its indissolubility? A common difficulty today in understanding the theological foundation of the sacramental bond of marriage is the tendency to see the bond as extrinsic to, rather than as a "real symbol" of, foundational Christian mysteries such as the Incarnation and the Christ-Church relation. At the root of this problem is the tendency to treat the relationship of the Christian to these mysteries in exclusively moral and juridical terms. A weakness of the arguments reviewed at the beginning of this essay is to presuppose precisely this extrinsicism. But the very nature of a sacrament is to be a symbol that contains (or is contained within) the reality which it signifies.

Certainly it is true that the marital bond cannot be located "somewhere above and beyond the couple." On the other hand, the bond cannot be understood as a merely juridical entity or "contractual" obligation existing "in" the couple understood as an essentially autonomous pair of individuals. As we have seen, the "where" of the Christian is in Christ himself. This "where" is not a spatio-temporal one, nor the mere prefiguration of an ideal or life program, nor the external assumption of a task or dignity as would be the case if one were installed in a political or civil office. It is rather a radically real "where." It entails a new orientation of the whole existence into which all else in life is assumed and thereby given a new significance. But this is not only an ethereal and "spiritual" reality; it is a bodily one, as the Eucharist and the meaning of the Church and the Incarnation testify. Our first conclusion, therefore, must be that the marital bond exists "in" the spouses who are themselves "in" Christ. Like the situation of the Christian in general, the couple *as such* now has a new form of existence in the Incarnation and the nuptials of Christ and the Church. Our question, then, is what this implies for our understanding of the marital bond.

As we have seen, the condition for the possibility of Christian marriage (as well as the other sacraments) is the virginal consent of Christ and his mother on behalf of the world. But their consent is not only consent given on behalf of the world without the active involvement of the world. Rather, human freedom is drawn into their consent on behalf of all of humanity and is invited to share in its outward form, as the state of consecrated virginity shows. Thus, Christ's and Mary's consent is the central axis and ground not only of the world's consent, but of every individual consent.

Like consecrated virginity, sacramental marriage is a fundamental response to the human vocation to love,[27] a "fundamental choice"[28] in love and faith. This can be seen when we consider marriage's anthropological significance. It is true, of course, that the consent of marriage does not result in an "indelible character," as in the character sacraments. Likewise, virginity does not entail such an indelible character. Neither state requires a sacramental character because each in its own way is a further articulation of the interior meaning of Baptism. Thus, marital consent engages the full depth of freedom shown explicitly in the consent of virginity, since each state precludes in absolute terms the possibility of consenting to the other. Once the spouses have given themselves in marriage, the possibility of self-gift in virginity, is no longer available. Neither state leaves some remainder portion of one's life to be bestowed according to the other mode of consent. Rather, in both, the whole of a given life is taken up and given its form. In a profound sense, all else in life either leads up to or flows out of this definitive moment of consent.[29]

Once we realize this fact, it becomes apparent that the difference between marital consent and other types of moral obligation is not one of degree. Rather, it is a difference in kind at the most fundamental level. Marital consent does not simply flow from an agreement between the spouses, which could potentially "not work out." Rather, spousal "consent" (*consensus matrimonialis*) takes up the freedom and capacity of the human person for God. It tracks the very ordination of human nature itself as *capax Dei*. It therefore necessarily arises within—is enabled and made real by—the consents of Christ and Mary on behalf of all of humanity. Indeed, because the consents of Christ and Mary are not only on our behalf but enable and take up our consent, marital consent is part of the content of what they offer to the Father. Thus, the consent of marriage is a fundamental form of giving oneself—albeit in and through sacramental mediation—to God.

In a way that is analogous to the assumption of human nature in the Incarnation, the Council Fathers tell us, "[a]uthentic conjugal love is assumed into divine love...and enriched by the redemptive action of Christ."[30] Without this "assumption," there could be no sacrament of marriage. But with it, marriage possesses the character of a kind of (*quasi*) "consecration." That is to say, Christian marriage entails the orientation of the couple's life together for an ecclesial task—mostly fundamentally, the service of life. Sacramental marriage, and the family to which it normally gives rise, constitute an indwelling of the sacred in the time and space of secular life, precisely in the task of marriage to raise members of the Church, society, and, ultimately, the kingdom of God.[31]

The "where" of marriage's bond, then, is in the virginal and nuptial mystery of the Incarnation and its mission, but not simply in terms of external symbolism. Again, the virginal consent of Christ and Mary is not simply their consent on our behalf "without us." Marital consent is taken up within the indissoluble bond between God and the world in the flesh of Christ and Mary precisely as part of what they offer "in" their own virginal consent to the Father. But as part of the content of their "vicarious" yeses, marital consent must necessarily take on the irrevocable form of their consent. Because marital consent is taken up in the consents of Christ and Mary, the bond to which it gives rise is located in the concrete form those consents take—the Incarnation and the nuptial relation between Christ and the Church that flows out of it.

THE PARADOX OF SACRAMENTAL MARRIAGE

And what of the role of sexual consummation? Recall that, while the consent of baptized spouses makes a sacramental marriage, it is only the consummation of that marriage (when it becomes *ratum et consummatum*) that renders the bond indissoluble "by any human power or by any cause other than death."[32] Thus, while consent gives rise to sacramental marriage, only consummation places the bond beyond any human power. As the *Catechism* puts it, the "consent that binds the spouses to each other finds its fulfillment in the two 'becoming one flesh.'"[33] Sexual consummation, while not necessary for sacramental marriage, nevertheless cannot therefore be reduced to something extrinsic to the sacrament—as if it were only significant as a kind of juridical addition.[34] This fact only deepens the paradox with which we began this chapter: while the radical ground for marriage's indissolubility is the "pan-sacramental" virginity of Christ and Mary, the "fulfillment" or "perfection" of this indissolubility is realized in sexual consummation.

Our question then is why sexual consummation would bring about the "perfection" of the marital bond's indissolubility. As we saw, the consents of Christ and Mary are made concrete in the bodily realities of their virginity. The fact that their consent culminates in a concrete bodily gift suggests the nature of human giving. Their consent does not suggest that the response to God can entail a "bodiless" or "angelic" "yes." Rather, it indicates precisely the opposite. It discloses the centrality of the body in the human response to God and, in God, to others. Indeed, the body, precisely in its masculinity and femininity, manifests the human vocation to love. It is, as John Paul II said, a "sacrament" of the person.[35] By this he means that it expresses the interior reality of the human person's ordination to love and enables the free actualization of that love. There is, therefore, a "language of the body" expressed in both virginity and marital union.[36]

This is not a question of sexualizing the virginity of Christ or Mary. Nor is it to collapse marriage and virginity into each other as states of life. Rather, it is simply to point to what Angelo Scola calls the "sacramental logic" of the Incarnation.[37] For the Catholic faith, authentic human love always includes and even becomes concrete in the body. The Incarnation, Crucifixion, and Resurrection of Christ are central testaments to this fact. The Eucharistic sharing of his life with the faithful is another, as are the rest of the sacraments. But with respect to what John Paul II called the "nuptial body," virginity itself is a radical verification of the necessary bodiliness of human love. As an expression of nuptial love, virginity is certainly not a choice for a purely spiritual love from which the body is excluded or irrelevant. If the body were unimportant to love, then virginity would make no sense. Rather, virginity expresses the fact that the body plays a crucial role in the vocation of human nature itself to love. In virginity, the body is given in love directly—that is to say, by way of direct participation in the pansacramental yes of Christ and Mary—to God. "As an incarnate spirit, that is a soul which expresses itself in a body and a body informed by an immortal spirit, man is called to love in his unified totality. Love includes the human body, and the body is made a sharer in spiritual love."[38]

Indeed, love necessarily requires openness to its characteristic fruitfulness if it is to be fully actualized. Virginity allows the consecrated person to possess a "spiritual" paternity or maternity that is universal in its scope, tracking the fruitfulness of Christ's and Mary's love. The virgin is free to give to anyone and to everyone. His or her concern is not centered on a particular family, a spouse, or particular children. Rather, virginal love is free to give to anyone God places in its path.

What is said about virginity is also true *mutatis mutandis* of marriage. Marital consummation is a "fulfillment" of the conjugal love of the spouses because it expresses in the flesh the fullness of the implications and meaning of conjugal love: its full actualization in becoming "one flesh" and its commitment and openness to the characteristic fruit of that love. Because love is by its very nature fruitful, it is not until the bodily commitment and expression of openness to that fruitfulness is realized that the sacramental bond is entirely "fulfilled" or "consummated." The characteristic fruitfulness of conjugal love is the child. Certainly, the spouses can also give more broadly. But they have a particular and sacred duty, which is characteristic of their vocation to marriage and family, to take into account first of all the welfare of the children and each other. Thus, marriage's consummation stands for the openness of the spouses to love's fruitfulness. The sexual consummation of marriage is the fulfillment of conjugal love's consent in and through the body. It is a way of fulfilling in the flesh the spouses' consent to the indissoluble consent of Christ and Mary. In this sense, the body "perfects" marital consent.

Sin aggravates the paradox for us. The reality of concupiscence makes it difficult to associate sexuality with the absolute giving away in love implied by indissolubility. The sin of the first couple shattered marital relations, dividing marriage in this world from its primordial oneness with virginity.[39] The physical union of man and woman was reduced to the merely sexual and not yet—or no longer—fully nuptial. Yet, the medieval resolution of the so-called *consensus-copula* debate did, in fact, affirm not only the centrality of consent in making marriage, but also the role of consummation in bringing the perfection of indissolubility to the resulting bond. This development in the Church's understanding of marriage is only possible given the fact that the virginal consent of Christ and Mary wins back the possibility for the absoluteness of the bond of conjugal love—its existence beyond human authority and power but, nevertheless, "in" the spouses.

What then, does sexual consummation have to do with the bond that arises in the consent of the spouses? What can it add to this consent? The suggestion that sexual consummation is merely extrinsic to the sacrament implies an angelic anthropology. As virginity shows us, the fullness of human giving is mediated through the body; human love is never fully manifested in a bodiless consent. Human love in its fullness is always a giving away of everything that one is, as *corpore et anima unus*. Sexual consummation therefore carries the mutual belonging begun in consent to its fulfillment. It carries forward what is already implicit in verbal consent and brings it to its culmination and fulfillment in the flesh. It is on this basis that the tradition understands the role of sexual consummation as signifying Christ's union with the Church or the unity of the divine and human natures in the Incarnation. In short, sacramental marriage's bond is indissoluble because the union of divine and human nature in the Incarnation and through Mary's motherhood is indissoluble.

At stake in marital indissolubility is the possibility of freedom in its most important and radical depths. Under the well-intentioned guise of promoting human freedom and autonomy, and to deal with pressing pastoral issues, the tendency to moralize the sacramental bond evacuates human freedom of its central role in bringing man to his destiny in Christ. What is not possible under such an understanding of the sacramental bond of marriage is precisely the freedom to give oneself away, which in the end is rather meaningless if it cannot be done irrevocably. But this irrevocability is precisely the inner character of the Christian freedom inaugurated by Christ and Mary. The effect of moralizing the bond is to abstract the consent of the spouses from the central axis of man's consent to God. As such, it is radically to de-Christianize sacramental marriage. In the effort to render the teaching on marriage relevant to the world as we "see" it, it thereby alienates the bond from the world as it really is.

Notes

1. See, for example, Kenneth Himes and James Coriden, "The Indissolubility of Marriage: Reasons to Reconsider," *Theological Studies* 65, no. 3 (September 2004): 453–499, where we are told that "[v]ows of marriage are vastly more important than promises to make a dinner engagement. But the pattern of making a commitment through free consent and then breaking it is similar" (489). See also Ladislas Örsy, *Marriage in Canon Law: Texts and Comments, Reflections and Questions* (Wilmington, Del.: Glazier, 1986), 272, n. 10.

2. See, for example, Michael Lawler, "Blessed Are the Spouses Who Love, for Their Marriages Will Be Permanent: A Theology of the Bonds of Marriage," *The Jurist* 55 (1995): 218–242. According to Lawler, the point at which marriage is consummated, and therefore "indissoluble," occurs when conjugal love has become perfected (241), a point which he grants lacks precision (236A). The effect is to place

emphasis on the spouses' own moral development within the obligations of marriage, rather than on the character or nature of marriage as such. See also, Edward Schillebeeckx, "Christian Marriage and the Reality of Complete Marital Breakdown," in *Catholic Divorce: The Deception of Annulments*, ed. Pierre Hegy and Joseph Martos (New York: Continuum, 2000), 82–107.

3. Lawler, "Blessed Are the Spouses Who Love," 219.

4. Himes and Coriden, "The Indissolubility of Marriage," 496.

5. Örsy, *Marriage in Canon Law*, 271; Lawler, "Blessed Are the Spouses Who Love," 221; Himes and Coriden, "The Indissolubility of Marriage," 486. Cf. also Walter Kasper, *Theology of Christian Marriage* (New York: Crossroad, 1981), 49.

6. Lawler, "Blessed Are the Spouses Who Love," 221: Örsy, *Marriage in Canon Law*, 204f, n. 3.

7. Örsy, *Marriage in Canon Law*, 204f, n. 3.

8. Himes and Coriden, "The Indissolubility of Marriage," 486.

9. For criticism of this view of "relation," see David L. Schindler, *Heart of the World, Center of the Church: Communio Ecclesiology, Liberalism, and Liberation* (Grand Rapids: Eerdmans Press, 1996), 275f; Joseph Ratzinger, "Concerning the Notion of Person in Theology," *Communio: International Catholic Review* 17 (Fall 1990): 439–454; Hans Urs von Balthasar, "On the Concept of Person," *Communio: International Catholic Review* 13 (Spring 1986): 18–26; and John D. Zizioulas, *Being as Communion: Studies in Personhood and the Church* (Crestwood, N.Y.: St. Vladimir's Seminary Press, 1985).

10. Cf. *Lumen gentium*, 11.

11. Hans Urs von Balthasar, "The Layman and the Church," trans. Brian McNeil, in *Explorations in Theology*, vol. 2: *Spouse of the Word* (San Francisco: Ignatius Press, 1991), 315–331; 330.

12. Balthasar, "The Layman and the Church," 15.

13. Balthasar, *The Christian State of Life* (San Francisco: Ignatius Press, 1983), 212.

14. Consider the entire legacy of the prophets' use of the analogy of marriage for Yahweh's stormy relationship with Israel (see, e.g., Hos 1–3; Is 54:1–17; Is 62:1–5; Jer 3; Ez 16), culminating in the repeated New Testament use of the image of "the Bridegroom" for Christ (see, e.g., Mt 9:15; Mk 2:19–20; Lk 5:34–35; Jn 3:29; 2 Cor 11:2; Eph 5:27; Rev 19:7–8; 21:2 and 9). For a discussion of the relation of nuptiality to the Old and New Covenants, see Ratzinger, "The New Covenant: A Theology of Covenant in the New Testament," trans. Maria Shrady, *Communio: International Catholic Review* 22 (Winter 1995): 635–651.

15. Cf. Juan Martinez Camino, "'Through Whom All Things Were Made': Creation in Christ," *Communio* 28 (Summer 2001): 214–229; 226.

16. Denzinger-Schönmetzer, *Enchiridion Symbolorum: Definitionum et Declarationum de Rebus Fidei et Morum*, 302.

17. *Dominum et vivificantem*, 50 (1986).

18. Angelo Scola, *The Nuptial Mystery*, trans. Michelle K. Borras (Grand Rapids: Eerdmans, 2005), 100.

19. St. Thomas Aquinas, *Suppl.* q. 61, a. 2, ad 1.

20. Balthasar, "The Layman and the Church," 316–317.

21. Cf. *Deus caritas est* (= *DCE*), 10, 12 (2005). Benedict tells us that God's "heart recoils" from abandoning sinful man; his "compassion grows warm and tender" (*DCE*, 10, quoting Hos 11:8). Man's situation draws out God's mercy, which in turn elicits a decisive "turn ...against himself" (*DCE*, 10: "*contra se ipsum vertat Deus*"; *DCE*, 12: "*contra se vertit Deus*"), "his love against his justice" (*DCE*, 10).

22. *Summa theologiae* III, q. 30, a. 1, cited in Balthasar, "The Layman and the Church," 315.

23. Balthasar, "The Layman and the Church," 330 (emphasis original); id., *The Christian State of Life*, 205. Cf. also Joseph Ratzinger, *Introduction to Christianity* (San Francisco: Ignatius Press, 1990), 208–212; Alexander Schmemann, *For the Life of the World* (Crestwood, N.Y.: St. Vladimir's Seminary Press, 2000), 83.

24. Balthasar, "The Layman and the Church," 319.

25. *Familiaris consortio*, 11 (1981).

26. Cf. Balthasar, *The Laity and the Life of the Counsels: The Church's Mission in the World*, trans. Brian McNeil, with D. C. Schindler (San Francisco: Ignatius Press, 2003), 13–35.

27. Cf. *Familiaris consortio*, 11.

28. Cf. *Veritatis splendor*, 65–68 (1993).

29. As the burden of this chapter's argument already suggests, this fact can in no way be taken to suggest a leveling of the two states into a sterile parallelism, as though they were merely "alternative choices" canceling the irreducible and "objective" superiority of the virginal state (cf. John Paul II, *Vita consecrata*, 32 [25 March 1996]; cf. Ecumenical Council of Trent, Session XXIV [11 November 1563], Canon 10 [*DS*, 1810]). Rather, marriage depends on virginity's pan-sacramentality for its sacramentality. Nevertheless, it remains true that they occupy the same "space" from an anthropological point of view, in the sense I have indicated.

30. *Gaudium et spes*, 48.

31. E.g., *Code of Canon Law Annotated*, ed. E. Caparros, et al. (Montreal: Wilson & Lafleur, 1993), 1134 ("in a Christian marriage the spouses are by a special sacrament strengthened and, as it were, consecrated for the duties and the dignity of their state"); this passage is also quoted in the *Catechism of the Catholic Church*, 1638. However, marital "consecration" is consistently qualified by the

Church with phrases such as "in a manner" or "as it were." See for example, *Casti connubii*, 41: *AAS* 22 (1930), 555 ("By [the] sacrament [of matrimony, spouses] will be strengthened, sanctified and in a manner consecrated") and *Gaudium et spes*, 48 ("Spouses...are fortified and, as it were, consecrated for the duties and dignity of their state by a special sacrament"). These qualifications point to the fact that marital consecration exists in a different modality and order than that of virginity. If consecrated virginity, the fullest sense of consecration, is a consecration directly to God in the modality of Christ and Mary, the analogous sense of consecration found in sacramental marriage is a consecration of the spouses *to each other* in God, and only through their mutual mediation, *to* God.

32. *Code of Canon Law*, 1141.

33. *Catechism of the Catholic Church*, 1627. See also, *Casti connubii* 36: *AAS* 22 (1930), p. 552 (spousal self-giving is "fully perfected [*plene perficitur*]" in marital consummation); *Gaudium et spes*, 49 ("*Haec dilectio proprio matrimonii opere singulariter exprimitur et perficitur*").

34. Thus, when Michael Lawler (see note 3, supra) argues that the first act of sexual intercourse cannot consummate a marriage because it is "outside" of the sacrament, he is begging the question.

35. E.g., John Paul II, *The Theology of the Body: Human Love in the Divine Plan* (Boston: Daughters of St. Paul, 1997), 76. See also Scola, T*he Nuptial Mystery*, 41, 129, 135.

36. E.g., John Paul II, *Theology of the Body*, 357–360. Cf. also *Familiaris consortio*, 11, and *Veritatis splendor*, 48.

37. Cf. *The Nuptial Mystery*, 98–99.

38. *Familiaris consortio*, 11.

39. Cf. Balthasar, *The Christian State of Life*, 95–103, for an overview of patristic and medieval thought on the unity of marriage and virginity in paradise.

26. Divorce, Remarriage, and Pastoral Practice

Margaret A. Farley

This chapter first appeared in *Moral Theology: Challenges for the Future: Essays in Honor of Richard A. McCormick,* ed. Charles E. Curran (New York: Paulist, 1990).

The last twenty-five years have seen significant changes in Roman Catholic belief and practice regarding divorce and second marriages. These changes are sharply visible in the writings of moral theologians, in the activities of marriage tribunals, and in the general perceptions and judgments of growing numbers of persons who consider themselves faithful members of the Roman Catholic community. Sympathy with the changes is not unanimous among theologians, but it is widespread enough to be characterized fairly as a clear majority response.

Major changes so cautiously but relentlessly forged in theological circles are often not reflected in the pronouncements and teachings of church officials, however. They are generally not to be found, for example, in the positions articulated by Pope John Paul II or in documents promulgated by Vatican congregations and commissions or in the 1983 Code of Canon Law. Indeed, the polarization between opinions of many theologians and canonists on the one hand, and traditional positions taken by Vatican officials on the other, now seems extreme. This is true despite the fact that the impetus for change (here as in so many other ethical questions) is traceable at least in part to the Second Vatican Council and to national episcopal conferences as well as individual bishops who have pressed for just the sort of changes that theologians are formulating. The perception of a need for change is fueled by western culture's massive contemporary experience of the breakdown of marital relationships and by the gradual recognition of legitimate differences in cross-cultural interpretations of marriage and family.

DEVELOPMENT AND IMPASSE

Changes in theological opinion and pastoral practice regarding divorce and second marriages lean strongly in the direction of allowing first efforts at marital union (first marriages) to end and second efforts (in new marriages) to be sustained by full participation in the sacramental life of the church. Key changes have to do, therefore, with new understandings of the requirement of permanence in Christian marriage. No one proposes eliminating this requirement, but ways are sought to interpret it which appear more adequate to human and Christian experience and less likely to place unjust and tragic burdens on individual persons and partnerships. The ultimate goal of such changes can be described in terms of nurturing lifelong marriages, but the proximate concern is with the irretrievable loss of (or failure to achieve) union in some marriages and the possibilities for subsequent new marriages in a Christian context.

More specifically, the issue for Roman Catholics has become the meaning and application of the notion of "indissolubility": Insofar as indissolubility characterizes a first marriage, can a second marriage ever be justified (so long as the spouse of the first marriage remains alive)? This question often translates into: May persons in a second marriage ever be allowed to share fully in the life of the church, even to the point of receiving the eucharist? The last quarter century of theological and pastoral responses to these questions may be understood best against the background of the tradition that stretches directly and most identifiably from the twelfth century to the 1983 Code of Canon Law and that continues to be strongly represented in the teachings of Pope John Paul II. As a tradition it has had its own developments, primarily legal but also theological, and it has not been without some pluralism in its interpretation.[1] It found its focus in the mediating decisions of Pope Alexander III, received further articulation at the Council of Trent in opposition to the

Protestant reformers, became incorporated into the first Code of Canon Law in 1917, and remains relatively intact in the revised Code of 1983.

The Tradition

According to this tradition (with its evolved specifications), some marriages are absolutely indissoluble, and some are not. Those marriages which may never be dissolved (short of the death of one of the spouses) are marriages between two baptized persons who have validly consented to and sexually consummated their marriage. These are considered sacramental marriages, and the absoluteness of their bond is sealed by sexual intercourse. While the partners in such marriages may be "separated" (according to church law as well as by civil separation or divorce), they may never marry another—precisely because their first marriage is considered in an important sense still to exist. If they do remarry (civilly), the church does not recognize their second marriage; and as long as they continue to live with this new partner (unless they do so not only for serious reasons but with sexual abstinence), church discipline requires that they be excluded from receiving the sacraments. The only way they may be declared free to enter or remain in a second marriage (again, short of the death of their original spouse) is if it can be determined that something was so deficient, so invalidating, in their first "marrying" that in fact no marriage took place. If it can be determined, for example, that there was not full and free mutual consent, or that some invalidating impediment prevented a marriage from being effected, or that the required form for valid marrying was absent, then it may be concluded that the first marriage does not continue to exist because, in fact, it never existed. The "annulment" of such a marriage must be pronounced officially by an ecclesiastical marriage tribunal.

But, also according to this tradition, some marriages do indeed exist whose indissolubility is not absolute (the marriage is vulnerable to being dissolved on some conditions). If a marriage, for example, has never been sexually consummated, it may in certain circumstances be dissolved by papal authority. Or if either or both of the partners were not baptized at the time of their marriage, the marriage can be dissolved for a variety of serious reasons that are determined to constitute a "privilege of faith" for the spouse who did or comes to believe. In these cases, it is possible to justify a second marriage and to admit spouses in second marriages (who either were or later became baptized Catholics) to the full sacramental life of the church. Determination of such cases must also be made officially—sometimes by a marriage tribunal, sometimes by papal authority.

Loosened by Vatican II, a veritable avalanche of literature in moral theology has poured forth since the mid-1960s, struggling with both the logic of this tradition and the logic of contemporary human experience regarding marriage and divorce. Richard McCormick's "Notes on Moral Theology" in the volumes of *Theological Studies* from 1965 to 1989 provide a remarkable view not only of the avalanche of literature but of what can happen to a thinker who tries to be faithful to both of these logics. In these years McCormick directly addressed the problem of divorce and remarriage nine times, and indirectly addressed it several more times (in relation to, for example, questions of moral reasoning or general problems in sexual ethics). The changes in moral theology that characterize this period of thinking about divorce and remarriage are clear in McCormick's chronicles, and the key issues and sub-issues emerge in his analyses. What comes into view, too, is the rather dramatic collision course or stand-off of much of moral theology on the one hand and Vatican leadership on the other in a struggle for the evolution of the tradition.

Theological Development

In 1966 McCormick reported on four articles that discussed the situation of persons divorced (from sacramental, consummated marriages) and remarried. Of these articles, two accepted the present formulation of the church's traditional position, and two attempted to move beyond it.[2] Of the first two, one simply reinforced the view that persons in second marriages must either separate or, if this is not possible, continue to live together but only insofar as they resolve to avoid sexual activity. In no other way can they return to the sacraments of the church. The second article acknowledged that persons who remain sexually active in second marriages cannot be admitted to the sacraments—in particular, the eucharist—but it probed the reasons for this. Because of the "adulterous situation" of a second marriage, the partners' life together is at odds with the faith of the church. Hence, they are in basic conflict with the sign-dimension of the eucharist (insofar as it is a sacrament of the unity of individuals in the church with one another and with God). Nonetheless, persons in second marriages must not be rejected by the church, and they should even be encouraged to participate in the life of the church to the extent that it can be open to them—to come to mass, to avail themselves of devotional practices, etc.

A third article in these 1966 "Notes," however, disputed the necessary exclusion of persons in second marriages from the sacraments, arguing that reception of the eucharist does not require perfect holiness and that, moreover, if it is justified at all for two persons to continue to live together in a marital relationship, their engagement in sexual activity is not necessarily a moral evil. Theirs need not be, in other words, an "adulterous situation." A fourth article goes beyond discussion of pastoral policy to raise theological questions about the nature of Christian sacramental marriage—to ask, therefore, about the status of the first marriage of these divorced persons. If, for example, the concepts of "consent" and of "consummation" are expanded to include elements of process and development, might it be the case that what looked like an absolutely indissoluble marriage was not yet that (and hence, implicitly, persons who had been in such marriages might after all be free to live legitimately as full Christians in their present second marriages)?

While these articles seem hardly revolutionary, their details are important because they signal some of the key issues which will preoccupy moral theologians for the decade to follow: the moral status of the conjugal lives of persons living in stable second marriages; the possibility of their returning to the sacraments; the meaning of both the sacrament of marriage and of the church's other sacraments (especially the eucharist); the minimal and maximal requirements for absolutely indissoluble marriages.

McCormick's own response to the articles and issues in these early "Notes" is also important. In 1966 he saw little reason for any serious change in the traditional formulations to which as a moral theologian he was heir. "There are legitimate questions," he agreed, but "one only hopes that this continuing theological task can be acquitted quietly and unsensationally without offering the cruel comfort born of false hope."[3] He left open the possibility of a pastoral solution to the problem of reception of the sacraments by those in second marriages whose first marriage was invalid. But when a first marriage was genuinely sacramental (that is, validly consented to by two baptized persons) and sexually consummated, its indissolubility cannot be ignored no matter how important the relationship may be in a second marriage. Someone in this situation still belongs to another. To ask whether she or he can nonetheless approach the eucharist may be a legitimate question, but, McCormick concluded, "...it is not clear to me how anything but a negative answer to this question is possible."[4] In 1966 McCormick's position probably represented a majority opinion among moral theologians.

In 1971 Richard McCormick returned to the question of divorce and remarriage.[5] It was obvious by then that doctrinal winds were blowing, and they had already turned McCormick himself around in some significant respects. In place by now were at least three important contributions from Vatican II: a description of the nature of marriage as a "community of love"[6]; a history of council interventions such as Melchite Archbishop Elias Zoghbi's proposal to allow acceptance of divorce and remarriage on the model of the eastern churches;[7] conciliar openness to sharing the eucharist with persons not fully in union with the Roman church (as articulated in the *Decree on Ecumenism* and the *Decree on the Eastern Churches*).[8] Also in place were initial groundbreaking biblical and historical studies that served to relativize for many moral theologians what had been previously perceived as absolutes in the tradition regarding divorce and remarriage.[9]

McCormick's primary focus in the 1971 "Notes" was on the issue of admission of persons in second marriages to the eucharist. Treatment of this issue in the literature, of course, necessarily included treatment of the status of both first and second marriages. McCormick identified four positions advanced by writers in the immediately preceding years. The first was the traditional position that Roman Catholics in second marriages are living in a "state of sin" and hence cannot be admitted to full participation in the sacraments (a problem, of course, ameliorated only if the couple agrees to forgo sexual relations). A second position suggested that individuals in second marriages might be accepted by the church under a "sign of forgiveness." When a first marriage is both valid and absolutely indissoluble a second marriage begins marked by the sin of the divorce which makes it possible. But this is not an unforgivable sin, and though the second marriage can never have the full sacramental status of the first, it can (through repentance and fidelity) be incorporated into the life of the church. This solution approximates the practice of the eastern churches.

The third position was the one that by 1971 had achieved growing support from many theologians and canonists, including Richard McCormick. It was the "good faith" or internal-forum solution. It provided for reception of the eucharist by individuals in second marriages who believe that their first marriage was not a valid Christian marriage even though this fact cannot be verified on canonically acceptable grounds (even though, that is, they cannot obtain an official "annulment"). It also applied to those individuals in second marriages who, despite the fact that their first marriage might have been valid, are nonetheless convinced in conscience that their second marriage is their only true marriage. McCormick himself saw no difficulty with these applications of an internal-forum solution. However, in order to justify an overall pastoral policy which refuses to unite canonical marital status with sacramental practice,[10] he was concerned with what it would mean for situations in which persons' consciences are unclear and conflicted—situations in which persons believe their first marriages to have been genuine Christian marriages and who therefore do not experience complete "good faith" about their second ones. Rather than approach such cases by bringing them under a "sign of forgiveness" (as in position 2), McCormick (and others) offered a way in which they, too, might be included in an internal-forum solution. If traditional categories of "consent" and "consummation" were enlarged to include such factors as capacity for a shared life, maturity for choice and human relationship, spiritual as well as physical consummation, etc., there was a good possibility that many first marriages may not have been genuine Christian sacramental marriages at all. This possibility now seemed strong enough to McCormick to justify a broadened internal-forum approach. He favored this approach because it did not imply approval in principle of second marriages. Nonetheless, as a practical solution to the situation of many persons in stable second marriages he recognized that it moved him beyond where he had been in 1966.

> Several years ago in these Notes I stated: "It is not clear to me how anything but a negative answer to this...question [of admitting to the eucharist remarried persons whose first marriage was apparently canonically valid] is possible." Recent

literature is a chastening reminder that the matter is certainly more difficult and debatable than that sentence would indicate. Indeed, as will be clear, I would substantially modify that opinion.[11]

There was a fourth position, however, that went farther than McCormick at the time thought justifiable. Proposed as theoretically probable by Bernard Häring.[12] It held that it is possible for marriages—even Christian sacramental consummated marriages—to die (truly to end). If a first marriage has been thoroughly destroyed, it cannot any longer be considered an existing marriage. In such a case a second marriage may be not only acceptable to the Christian community; it may be itself a sacramental marriage in the full sense of the term. McCormick recognized that "probably a fair number of theologians would agree that Haring has accurately sniffed the direction of the winds of doctrinal development or, more accurately, pastoral practice."[13] But for McCormick in 1971, "The notion of the 'dead' marriage, especially if it means the Church's ability to tolerate a second 'living' marriage, needs a great deal more study."[14]

One year later McCormick turned again to these questions, noting that "there has been no letup in the flow of literature during the past year."[15] The issues this year were extensions of the year before. The problem of marital failures was addressed by arguments for the power of the church to dissolve marriages ("let no human put asunder" need not rule out a power of divine origin dissolving marriages) and by proposals to institutionalize the developmental aspects of marriage by distinguishing forms and levels of marriage. That is, the church might recognize an initial form of marriage, constituted by mutual consent and aimed at growing union ("consummation" in a personal, integral sense) and an advanced form of marriage, tested by time, faithful, and finally fully consecrated. Only the latter would be sacramental and absolutely indissoluble.

Consideration of the internal-forum solution continued, with growing emphasis on its usefulness and potential expansion as a pastoral policy. This was the pastoral approach which McCormick himself still seemed to prefer to other forms of institutional accommodation of marital failures. For McCormick this solution provided a way to hold the line against what he feared would be complete separation of the moral from the juridical (if indissolubility were to be seen as purely regulatory);

against expanding the use of church power to dissolve marriages (though not against calling the church to accept those who fail in their marriages); and against legitimizing a notion of a marriage's "death." The internal-forum solution, as McCormick saw it in 1972, was still to be directed primarily toward discerning the original invalidity of a first marriage, not its validity and eventual demise.

By 1975 a consensus seemed clear on some issues, particularly the issue of the admission of persons in stable second marriages to the sacraments.[16] Here theological opinion had moved strongly in a positive direction. The reasons varied, but the conclusions were strikingly similar. Key arguments and clarifications had evolved to ease some of the remaining troubling questions. Among the most important of these resolving insights were: (1) Persons otherwise welcomed to participate in the life of the church are not reasonably to be judged as living in a serious "state of sin" (that is, since everyone agreed that persons living in stable second marriages should be encouraged to participate as far as possible in the life of the church, it seemed contradictory to continue to assert that they are nonetheless in a lethal state of sin). (2) Individual consciences are to be respected especially in situations of recognized limitations of juridical structures and processes. (3) Pastoral accommodations can be made without denying a doctrine of indissolubility. (4) Dangers of scandal are now minimized by changes in culture and in religious insight. (5) The eucharist has two finalities—not only as a sign of unity but also as a means of grace (so that it is appropriate for it to be shared by persons not yet in complete unity with the church). Expressions of consensus came in documents from national associations of theologians and canon lawyers and in leading religious publications.[17]

Resolution of the question of admission of persons in stable second marriages to the sacraments led inevitably, however, to the more difficult question of the entrance of divorced persons into a second marriage. In a common struggle with this question some significant disagreements became clear among moral theologians who shared the consensus on the earlier question. Positions turned on analyses of the content and form of the requirement of indissolubility. Conflict also centered on whether church doctrine or only pastoral practice regarding indissolubility should be changed. A good example of these disagreements is visible in the joining of issues between Richard McCormick and Charles Curran.

McCormick and Curran shared the majority opinion on readmission of persons in second marriages to the sacraments. They also shared to some extent the view that first marriages, even if they had been sacramental and consummated, could die—could cease to exist. For by 1975 McCormick's reluctance to accept this construal of the ending of a Christian marriage was largely gone. Influenced by writers like Charles M. Whelan, Joseph MacAvoy, and Charles Curran, McCormick was cautious but moving. He was still saying that "the very concept of a 'dead marriage' is somewhat problematical to the Christian,"[18] yet it was clear that this notion was one of the examples of his own "deepening understanding and consequent modification of opinion over the past seven or eight years."[19]

Though offering proposals "very much in the category of a thought-experiment,"[20] McCormick proceeded to reject the traditional view of indissolubility as based on a bond, a *vinculum*, of ontological or juridical proportions. He suggested, rather, that indissolubility is a "moral ought," an "absolute moral precept" grounded in the union of spouses and their responsibilities to children. It is a "most serious obligation" to permanence in marriage, one that implies a couple's (1) obligation to strengthen and support their union and not allow it to die, and (2) if it does fall apart, their obligation to resuscitate it.[21] When a marriage dies, McCormick thought that it does so through the moral fault of at least one of the partners, through some failure on the part of one or both to keep the obligation to the union. Nonetheless, "a marriage, like a human body, can die without any hope of resuscitation."[22] And once a marriage has been utterly and irretrievably lost, the precept of indissolubility becomes moot. The judgment that an ending so definitive has been reached must be made by the partners themselves; it can only be (but presumably should be) notarized by the legal representatives of the church.

Curran had for some time been convinced that a marriage, however genuine in the first place, might nonetheless cease to exist. He recognized (as did McCormick and others) that this view presupposed an interpretation of marriage as an interpersonal relationship (which is also, but not solely or even primarily, a social institution). Within the relationship of every Christian marriage lies an essential requirement of permanence; marriage is under the obligation of indissolubility. Curran argued, however, that indissolubility was not an absolute rule or precept (as it was for

McCormick) but a moral ideal. It exists, as the church had long taught, under the call and the command that it participate in and bear witness to the love of God for human persons and of Jesus for the church. This, however, must be understood in an eschatological perspective: Its call is to a goal, to a fullness it will not achieve in this life. Its obligation is limited by the capabilities of individuals and the possibilities of situations. In Curran's view (unlike McCormick's), not every failure to achieve the goal, or every failure to sustain an effort toward it, can be attributed to the moral fault of one of the spouses; for sometimes human limitation and the "not yet" aspects of grace make it impossible to succeed.[23]

Once a marriage does die, Curran and McCormick differed on how we are to think about the freedom to remarry. For McCormick, there can be no general freedom to marry again. In fact, there remains in place a general prohibition against second marriages. The reasons for the prohibition are twofold: (1) a second marriage "continues and memorializes" the failure of the first because it cuts off all hope of reconciliation, and (2) marriage is a social as well as a personal reality. In other words, it is an interpersonal relationship but also a social institution; what happens to any individual marriage has social consequences for other marriages. Remarriage threatens the stability of other persons' marriages, for it blunts the radical imperative of indissolubility. Yet, according to McCormick, the prohibition against remarriage is not absolute. "Proportionate reasons" in favor of other values may override it. These reasons will be particular to each individual (for they relate to special needs, responsibilities, concrete circumstances), so they (just like the reasons for divorce) must be weighed not by juridical institutions or officers but by the individuals concerned.

Curran, on the other hand, argued that when a first marriage has died, there remains no obligation not to remarry. There is no general prohibition against second marriages. It is not remarriage, but divorce, that is against the requirement of indissolubility. If a divorce was justified, so is remarriage. If the divorce was not justified (if the first marriage failed because of sin), repentance is needed; but the sin is not unforgivable, and its repentance does not include a requirement not to remarry.[24]

The differences in McCormick's and Curran's views on indissolubility and on the freedom to remarry coincided with differences in their positions on doctrinal change. McCormick preferred change only in pastoral practice, not in the doctrine of indissolubility. His construal of the obligation of indissolubility did not, he believed, attack the original doctrine itself. An absolute obligation was still in place. Moreover, he argued that invoking a principle of "proportionate reason" to determine the justification of remarriage would simply be an extension of the traditional category of "privileges of the faith."[25] Finally, he thought that if judgments about the demise of marriages and about proportionate reasons for remarriage are left in the hands of individuals it will not be necessary to "institutionalize" exceptions (either to the precept of indissolubility or to the prohibition against remarriage). Hence, no change in doctrine is needed, and pastoral accommodations can be made for individuals without threatening the overall stability of the institution of marriage.

Curran, on the other hand, argued in 1975 that a change only in pastoral practice would not go far enough in assisting persons who struggle with these issues in their personal lives; nor would it be as faithful to the changing insights in moral theology. A minimalist move to change only pastoral practice might be justified pedagogically and politically, but it can only be a "temporary move which logically must go further."[26] One of the logical pressure points will be recognized by individuals contemplating second marriages: "From a theoretical viewpoint it seems very difficult to say that sometime during the second marriage a couple can be reconciled with the sacraments of the Church, but it is wrong for them to enter the second marriage."[27]

The debate over indissolubility as precept versus indissolubility as ideal has not been resolved in the 1980s, though both points of view continue to be represented. McCormick repeated much of his 1975 formulation in a 1979 article and again in an expansion of that article ten years later (though in his 1989 analysis McCormick's notion of an "absolute" precept of indissolubility modulates more clearly into a "serious" precept).[28] Curran, too, has remained convinced of his view of indissolubility as moral ideal, and has added to his argument a consideration of the role of culture.[29] There may be little motivation for others to take sides on this matter, perhaps because Curran's "imperative goal" sometimes looks strong enough to be a *prima facie* precept;[30] and McCormick's obligation not to remarry is clearly *prima facie* (even if indissolubility is "absolute").[31] Similarly, there may be little perceived need to draw further battle lines on the question of change in doctrine or in pastoral practice, perhaps because Curran allowed for a gradual movement from one to the other; and McCormick moved in 1979 to advocate change not only in pastoral practice but in pastoral policy, and in 1989 to propose theological as well as juridical "adjustments."[32]

Critical analysis by canonists in response to the revised Code, major new historical studies, and ongoing biblical research all provided the 1980s with rich resources on the problem of divorce and remarriage.[33] But the avalanche of literature in moral theology slackened considerably. Probably a number of reasons accounted for this. Theologians had resolved in their own minds the questions they had been pressed by contemporary experience to confront. Most of the interesting ideas seemed to be already on the table. The urgency for pastoral solutions to concrete situations of anguish and neglect had lessened, for the consensus regarding changes in pastoral practice (though not in doctrine) emerged not only in theory but in action— in the work of marriage tribunals, the pastoral approaches of the clergy, and new forms of ministry with the divorced and remarried. Annulments of first marriages between baptized persons, dissolutions of first marriages where at least one partner is unbaptized, readmission to the sacraments of persons in stable second marriages—all of these were more possible now than they were prior to 1965.[34]

But the complex story of a quarter of a century of change in theology and practice regarding divorce and remarriage has another part to its plot—the responses and initiatives of the official leadership of the church. Significant movement has taken place here, too, though its present results look very different from the consensus among most theologians.

Official Response to Development

Much of the history of the institutional church's thinking about divorce and remarriage is in the interpretation and application (and sometimes formulation) of law. To some extent the changes in moral theology have a parallel in juridical practices and decision. Broadening the base for annulments, expanding the use of the Pauline privilege, evolving the so-called Petrine privilege—all of these have been twentieth century innovations in the application of canon law. They have reflected, but also sometimes anticipated and influenced, moral theology.[35] As in theology, new ways of addressing the indissolubility of nonsacramental marriages and the nonvalidity of apparently sacramental marriages posed less than radical problems for the courts once they had been introduced. The issue of the indissolubility of truly sacramental, consummated marriages was another matter altogether. Here there is little parallel with the struggles of moral theology, for the institutional question has at least for now been closed.

Gaudium et Spes had in 1965 provided a new conciliar description of marriage as an "intimate partnership" of life and love, "rooted in the conjugal covenant of irrevocable personal consent," and constituting essentially "a whole manner and communion of life."[36] This description raised the standards of personal capability for undertaking a marriage commitment; from then on considerations of psychological health, emotional maturity, and moral character were pertinent in granting annulments of first marriages. The description might also have allowed consideration of the possible "death" of some marriages (for if marriage is essentially a whole way of sharing life and love, clearly this may in some cases cease to exist). But here Vatican officials drew a sharp line.

Overturning the Dutch lower courts' decisions in the Utrecht-Haarlem Case, the Congregation of the Signatura asserted in 1975 that "It is false to say that the council changed the doctrine about marital consent, as if it had substituted for the traditional notion a certain so-called existential consent, so that when this ceases the matrimonial bond automatically ceases to exist."[37] In this same vein, Paul VI reminded the Roman Rota in 1976 that *Gaudium et Spes* actually spoke of marital consent as effecting a "sacred bond [that] no longer depends on human decisions alone."[38] From this he argued that marriage continues to exist as a "juridical reality" no matter what subjective elements in it may die. As an institutional reality, marriage "in no way depends on love for its existence."[39]

The absolute indissolubility of consummated sacramental marriages was affirmed with traditional force also by the International Theological Commission (appointed by the Congregation for the Doctrine of the Faith) in 1978. It allowed no room whatever for such a marriage to end short of the death of one of the spouses. Every consummated sacramental marriage is indissoluble, the commissioners argued, because it comes into being through the total self-gift of each spouse to the other (a "gift of self which…transcends any change of mind"[40]); it is established not only by the will of the spouses but by God's will; it not only images the relationship of Christ to the Church but is incorporated into it in a way that empowers the spouses to fidelity and makes their union utterly indestructible; and it is "a demand of the marital institution itself [so that] even when love has ceased to exist, the marriage has not."[41] Here is a theology of indissolubility whose center is a notion of sacramental union which ultimately founds and incorporates a decision for union and a law of fidelity; the absoluteness of the indissolubility lies not only in a juridical demand but in a mystical foundation of the marital union itself.

Following the 1980 Synod on the Family, Pope John Paul II issued his *Apostolic Exhortation on the Family*. Like the Theological Commission he grounded the absolute indissolubility of consummated sacramental marriage ultimately in its reality as a sacrament. His explication of this reality focused on the "total self-giving" of the spouses to each other and the signification of this through sexual intercourse. The bond between them becomes a sign of and a participation in the saving love of Jesus Christ, which is a nuptial love for the church.[42] Should spouses be unfaithful—should they let their love die—they are nonetheless bound to one another irrevocably, and their infidelity becomes a sign of the infidelity of a people who still belong to God.[43] Absolute indissolubility lies in the very being of a relationship that can be violated but not destroyed. In 1983 the revised Code of Canon Law combined the interpersonal covenantal emphasis of *Gaudium et Spes* (and the theology of John Paul II) with the traditional juridical requirement of indissolubility.[44]

The issue of readmission of divorced persons in stable second marriages to the sacraments has not been as effectively closed by church leadership as the issue of the possible ending of a consummated sacramental marriage. The sympathy of large numbers of bishops for this latter issue has been marked. Numerous pastoral letters have addressed it, and many interventions at both the 1980 and 1985 Synods called for better solutions to the problem. But the responses of John Paul II and of the International Theological Commission were clearly opposed to any changes in pastoral policy in this regard. The Commission wrote simply: "From the incompatibility of the state of the divorced-remarried with the command and mystery of the risen Lord, there follows the impossibility for these Christians of receiving in the eucharist the sign of unity with Christ."[45] Citing reasons of disunity with the church and the dangers of scandal, John Paul II also reiterated: "The church reaffirms its practice, which is based upon sacred scripture, of not admitting to eucharistic communion divorced persons who have remarried …[unless] they take on themselves the duty to live in complete continence…."[46] Theologians have taken solace in the fact that even in such positions there is included a concern for divorced and remarried persons and a recognition of their needs for special care. Still, the years of inquiry and interchange in moral theology on this question seem either to have been ignored by church leaders or simply and completely rejected.

A stand-off between moral theologians and church leaders cannot be beneficial for those whose lives are at stake in decisions of marriage and divorce. Hence, the work of moral discernment and communication must proceed. The question of readmission to the sacraments of persons in stable second marriages can perhaps be set aside for a time, since its theoretical and practical problems have largely been settled despite Vatican disagreement. But the question of indissolubility as it relates to the ending of first marriages and the right to remarry must be probed still further.

Marriage as "Commitment": Another Try at the Impasse?

There are three perspectives from which the absolute indissolubility of sacramental consummated marriages has been and is today understood—juridical, moral, and ontological. When the sacramental dimension of marriage is appealed to as the ultimate ground of indissolubility, it, too, is considered from these three perspectives. The categories here of "juridical," "moral," and "ontological" are not completely discrete, nor is their meaning univocal for everyone who uses them.[47] One way to take account of all three perspectives—avoiding in a sense, but perhaps shedding light on, disagreements among those who use them—is to consider the obligation of indissolubility in terms of marriage as a "commitment." Everyone, no matter where they are on the spectrum of positions regarding indissolubility, presupposes that marriage entails an initial and ongoing covenant (a concept and term now in favor over the traditional "contract") to which the parties come in freedom and in which they are bound because of the obligation they have themselves assumed.[48] Indissolubility as a requirement of

Christian marriage is part of the content of the marriage commitment, but it also specifies the way in which one is to be committed (that is, unconditionally or with very few conditions). The moral meaning of the marriage commitment bears examination first, and juridical considerations can be incorporated into it.[49]

Like any other explicit, expressed, interpersonal commitment, marriage involves the giving of one's word in a way that gives to another a claim over one's self. It is a promise which, like any other promise, includes an intention regarding future action and a placing of oneself under a moral claim regarding that action. In the case of marriage, the intended action includes interior actions (of respect, love, trust, etc.) and exterior actions (a way of sharing a life together). Marriage, of course, is a mutual commitment—two persons' words given one to the other, two persons yielding and receiving a claim, two persons establishing by their commitments a new form of relationship intended to move into the future.

There are good reasons why marriage involves commitment as such. Love can desire it; experience can show its need. All commitments in the human community imply a state of affairs in which there is doubt about our future actions; they imply the possibility of failure to do in the future what is intended in the present. Commitments are made (claims given, obligations undertaken, bonds embraced) precisely to assure others and to strengthen ourselves—to give assurance that our word will endure and to strengthen ourselves in keeping our word. This is especially true of profound commitments like marriage, where commitment is a way of safeguarding our desire to do what we deeply want to do not only now but in the future. By committing ourselves we give, as it were, a law to ourselves; we bind ourselves by the claim we give to another. A Christian commitment to marry involves a commitment to more than one person.[50] That is, in a marriage not only is a commitment made by each partner to the other, but both partners also commit themselves to God and to a community of persons (to the church and to society, however that is construed in terms of family, community, and wider society). In each of these directions a word is given, intentions and expectations are clarified, an obligation is undertaken, and a newly qualified relationship is formed.

A marriage commitment is made to persons, but its content includes a commitment to a certain framework of life in relation to persons. While those who marry commit themselves to love one another, they do so (precisely in marrying) by committing themselves to whatever is understood to be the institution, the framework of life, that is marriage—not for its own sake but as the form of their life together.[51] This "framework" can have different levels of specification. There is a kind of generic understanding of "marriage" as a social institution that crosses cultures and religions. But "marriage" will also always have a particular framework in particular societies and religious traditions. Finally, there is a level of framework which is the particular structure of the marriage of two individuals—informed by but not necessarily limited to the institutional frameworks of their own historical context. The commitment to marriage as a framework of life and a way of loving at all of these levels is not necessarily explicit in every marriage, but it is nonetheless there.

In our own culture, and certainly in the Roman Catholic tradition, an intention of permanence in the relationship of marriage is included in marital commitment. Given massive historical changes in social contexts, some of the reasons for incorporating the notion of permanence in the framework of marriage have changed, though many remain the same. The importance of interpersonal reasons has grown, and institutional reasons have receded. Yet there have always been reasons intrinsic to the marital relationship itself and reasons of social utility beyond the relationship. Love itself can want to give its whole future, to bind itself irrevocably to the one loved and to express itself in this way. Some interpreters of the possibilities of human sexuality have also argued that sex is best served by being activated in a context of commitment and of commitment that intends to be permanent.[52] Insofar as marriage is a social institution, permanence can serve the good of children (who need a stable context in which to survive and mature), the general good of society (which depends on the institutions within it for its own stability and growth), and the good of the church (in which marriage can function as a way of Christian life and a sign of God's presence to all).

If an intention of permanence is intrinsic to the meaning of marriage, and if marriage as a commitment is self-obligating, can it ever be justified to end a marriage short of the death of one's spouse? In other words, can the claim that is given to another in the commitment of marriage ever be released? This is the central moral question for both divorce and remarriage. It is the central moral question even when the context is a Christian sacramental and consummated marriage (though there are complexities here that we must still address).

We are used to acknowledging release from a marriage obligation when it can be determined that some basic flaw marked the original marrying—a flaw in the procedure, or a lack of capacity to commit to marital life on the part of either partner, or a situation of unfreedom. Strictly speaking, however, this kind of release from obligation is not a "release" but a recognition that no marriage obligation was ever truly undertaken; the marriage did not exist. The much more difficult question is whether or not a truly valid marriage (and even one that is genuinely sacramental and consummated) may no longer bind.

My own position is that a marriage commitment is subject to release on the same ultimate grounds that any extremely serious, nearly unconditional, permanent commitment may cease to bind.[53] That is, an obligation to sustain a marriage ceases when (1) it truly becomes impossible to sustain it; (2) the marriage no longer serves the purposes, or has the *raison d'etre*, it was meant to have; (3) another obligation comes into conflict with, and takes priority over, the marriage commitment. It is a difficult matter to discern when such conditions actually come to be, but that they do and that they can be identified seems to me to be without doubt. Some brief observations about each of these may help to make this clear.

First, then, when it truly becomes impossible to sustain a marriage relationship, the obligation to do so is released. Impossibility has long been accepted as a general justifying reason for release from the obligation of a promise. The kind of impossibility that is relevant for marriage commitments is not, of course, physical but psychological or moral impossibility. Hence, recognizing it is less like perceiving an incontrovertible fact than like making a judgment or even a decision. Still, examples can be given (of irremediable rupture in a relationship, or utter helplessness in the face of violence, or inability to go on in a relationship that threatens one's very identity as a person); and it seems true that a threshold of real impossibility does exist.

Interestingly, while McCormick and Curran do not construe marital obligation in just the way I have, they both appeal to a kind of impossibility as justification for releasing the requirement of indissolubility. The irretrievable death of a marriage relationship is that point at which, according to McCormick, resuscitation of it is no longer possible; it is at this point that the obligation of indissolubility is discontinued.[54] And Curran argues that precisely where it is impossible "for pilgrim Christians to live up to the fullness of love"—whether because of the limitation of creation, or sin, or the lack of the fullness of grace—there the obligation of indissolubility meets its limit.[55]

The second condition under which a marriage obligation may no longer bind is when it has lost its point, its *raison d'etre*, its own intrinsic meaning. It is meant to serve love for spouses, for family, for society, for God. In order to do this it includes a commitment to a "framework" for loving, providing love with a way of living. But if the framework becomes a threat to the very love it is to serve, if it weakens it or contradicts it or blocks it, then the very commitment to love may require that the commitment to marriage as a framework must come to an end. Marriage has multiple meanings and purposes, but all of them may be undermined by the marriage itself (or some of them so gravely as to jeopardize them all). If so, the obligation to the marriage commitment is released.

Closely related to this is the third condition under which a marriage obligation may end—that is, when another obligation conflicts with and takes priority over it. Given the seriousness of the commitment to marriage, there are not many other obligations that can supersede it, for it is made with the kind of unconditionality that is meant to override other claims almost without exception. Still, there are times when other fundamental obligations can take priority—fundamental obligations to God, to children, to society, even to one's spouse (when, for example, commitment to the *well being* of the spouse conflicts with continued commitment to relationship within the framework of marriage). It is also possible for a fundamental obligation to one's own self to justify ending a marriage (not because love of self takes priority over love of another, but because no relationship should be sustained that entails, for example, the complete physical or psychological destruction of a person—including oneself).[56]

When under certain conditions a marriage commitment ceases to bind, are there no obligations (human and Christian) that remain in relation to one's spouse? Clearly there are. Though commitment to a framework for loving (to a relationship as an ongoing marriage) is not completely unconditional or absolute, there are unconditional require-

ments within it. For example, there is never any justification to stop loving someone altogether—not a marriage partner any more than a
stranger or even an enemy. When it is no longer possible or morally
good to love someone within the framework of a married love, it is still
possible and called for that we love that individual at least with the love
that is universally due all persons. It may even be that an obligation continues to a particular love that is faithful to the relationship that once
existed. But here we come to the most difficult (for the Roman Catholic
tradition) question of all: When the commitment to marriage no longer
binds as such, when a true divorce is morally justified,[57] is it also justifiable to remarry? This question will ultimately take us to a consideration of the ontological perspective on divorce and remarriage.

The traditional Roman Catholic position has been and is, as we have
seen, that even if an end must come to a marriage in the sense of a separation from shared "bed and board," there remains nonetheless an obligation
not to remarry. The reason for this lies ultimately in a conviction that the
original marriage in some sense still does exist.[58] Against the position I
have just been outlining, the issues might be joined in the following ways:
(1) Christian sacramental marriage is unlike other commitments in that it is
under the command of God and the decree of Jesus Christ; hence, whatever
our reasoning about the release of commitments, the indissolubility of marriage remains an absolute obligation. (2) The "framework" or institution of
Christian marriage is regulated by the law of the church. Herein is a special stipulation whereby there will always be a juridical "remainder" of the
covenant of marriage—to the effect that even if every other aspect of a
marriage has become impossible (or without meaning or in conflict with
greater obligations), it is still possible not to marry anyone else. This much
of the marriage commitment still holds. (3) A commitment to marriage,
when it is consummated as a sacramental reality, changes the partners in
their very being. No longer is their union only a matter of moral or juridical bonding, but an ontological or mystical, indestructible, new reality.
However it is lived out—with or without an actually shared life and love—
it remains, and it makes impossible another commitment to marriage. All
of these arguments have in one form or another been sustained in the tradition, but it is the third that currently is key.

One should not, of course, dismiss the first two of these arguments
too quickly, though the limitations of this chapter prohibit more than a

brief response. Roman Catholic biblical scholars have effectively shown in recent years the exegetical difficulties of using New Testament texts as evidence of an absolute requirement of indissolubility. Indeed, if the various "sayings of Jesus" show us anything clearly it is that the Christian community from its beginnings believed it was responsible to modify these "sayings" in their application to different contexts.[59] But even if this were not the case—even if we could find in the biblical traditions a clear command in regard to divorce and remarriage—it is difficult to see how the logic of its application would not require the sort of analysis I have proposed. That is, for example, if something is in fact impossible, it cannot in the concrete be obligating.[60]

On the other hand, should the basis of a prohibition against remarriage be a purely juridical requirement, it can be questioned for its appropriateness to life, and it can also be changed. This is in part why the tradition has not appealed to a purely positive law as the basis for its ban on remarriage after divorce. Similarly, social utility arguments for the positive law are subject to empirical verification and to the challenge that the laws sanction the misuse of individuals for the sake of the common good.

The third argument—that indissolubility finally rests on an ontological union between spouses—is strongly entrenched in the Roman Catholic tradition. It has not gone away by the mere insistence on the part of moral theologians that (a) the bond of marriage is obviously not a reality independent of the relationship of spouses, and (b) insofar as the bond is in the "objective order" it is only a juridical or a moral reality. These theses serve as correctives to some popular misunderstandings and some unusual claims made here and there in the tradition. But they do not finally meet the position of those who, recognizing quite well that there is no ontological bond separate from the relationship of spouses, nonetheless find in this relationship an indestructible binding of being.

The most important spokesperson for an ontological perspective on the permanence of marriage today is John Paul II. The International Theological Commission serves as a careful supporter and explicator of the themes he has so painstakingly developed. The substance of the position, as we have already seen, is this: When two persons marry they yield themselves to one another in a kind of ultimate gift, a gift of self that changes them at the core of their being. By a mutual commitment they become so one with each other that they can no longer be separated.

They belong to each other, are joined with each other as "two in one flesh."[61] Indissolubility is a consequence as well as an obligation of their mutual exchange. "For the gift of self, which engages one at the core of the person, transcends any change of mind. It is final."[62]

Both anthropological and sacramental foundations are offered for this view. Human persons are essentially intersubjective and essentially complementary as male and female.[63] Even their bodies have a "nuptial meaning" which incarnates the complementarity of their gendered persons and mirrors the relationship between Christ and the church. When a man and a woman come together in the covenant of marriage they are sealed in the grace of Christ's covenant with the church—imaging it, empowered by it, one with it. So transformed are they that even though their union is in process, or even though they choose at some point to violate their own new reality, they are nonetheless absolutely joined. "There is no separation between them in spirit or flesh."[64] This now is the way of their salvation, since it is thus that their sexual union can be redeemed: In being "converted" to one another, they transcend the selfishness in their bodily love.[65] So important is their sexual union that "the sacramental sign is determined, in a sense, by 'the language of the body,'"[66] though it is the whole of two lives that become one.

Here is a position with great appeal. It takes account of persons (and not only laws), whole lives (and not only bodies or spirits), the transforming power of grace (and not only a theology of marriage as an image of the relationship between Christ and the church). Yet the picture it offers of marriage as a bond in being, settled once and for all by freedom and grace, is finally misleading and potentially harmful to individuals and to the church. There are at least three grave problems with the position which I can only point to here (though they deserve a much fuller response).

First, while this position depends on a description of Christian marriage as a covenant, it takes no account of the limits of human freedom in the making and keeping of commitments. Our power of choice, self-determining in profound ways as it is, is not a power that can finish our future before it comes. Commitment is indeed a way to influence our future; by it we are changed in the present so that a new relationship can have both a history and a future. But even with the power of grace, the bonds that we forge are simply not completely indestructible. And while it is true that freedom may fail only in the sense that we betray, rather than fulfill, our promises, nonetheless it is also true that we can thereby destroy the relationships our promises have made. Moreover, there is surely what philosophers call "moral luck," and situations beyond our control that also have the terrible power to undo the projects of our freedom. A view of marriage that borders on a new mysticism can burden marriage more than liberate it, crush it even while it aims to inspire.

Second, the theological anthropology assumed into this position is not benignly separable from its core; and it is an anthropology that has already harmed persons in its consequences for centuries. The complementarity asserted between women and men, structured on a problematic understanding of the relationship between Christ and the church, perpetuates a cultural "framework" for marriage that (for all its protests to the contrary) is essentially a union between unequals. Today this framework is more likely to contribute to divorce than to the sustaining of marriage.

Third, the ontological union that this position depicts is itself cause for question, if not alarm. Drawing on the traditional metaphor of "two in one flesh," it risks violating the human nature it wants to affirm. The unqualified emphasis on "total self-giving" yields a view of the fusion of selves that entails loss of autonomy in person and body. Nothing has been more dangerous in marriage, especially for women, than ideals of self-giving that mean loss of identity and self-agency. Efforts to explain the meaning of this in terms of mutuality of giving only make it more problematic, since they are joined still to a view of a husband as active and a wife as passive.[67]

All of this is not to say that there is no ontological union effected in and by marriage. I am not myself inclined to dismiss this possibility— nor even the consequence that some bond remains after the breakdown of a marriage and a justifiable divorce. In fact, when two persons commit themselves to one another in a profound sense, and when they share their lives together for whatever period of time, they are somehow changed in their beings. There are many ways in which this change continues—call it a bond or a residue or whatever. What remains after the radical rupture of a marriage may even include a "bodily" bonding (now experienced positively or negatively) as a result of the sexual relationship that once was a part of the marriage. It may also include a spiritual bonding (now experienced positively or negatively) as a result of months or years of a shared history together. If the marriage resulted in children, their lives will be held together for years in the ongoing project of parenting. In any case, the lives of two persons once married to one another are forever qualified by the experience of that marriage. The depth of what remains admits of degrees, but something remains.

The question becomes, then: Does a remaining bond from a first marriage disallow a second marriage? My own opinion is that it does not (or at least in some situations it does not). Whatever ongoing obligation a residual bond entails, it need not include a prohibition of remarriage. Indeed, it may be that only a view of marriage that sees it primarily within an economy of sexuality and purity can sustain an absolute prohibition of remarriage after a justifiable divorce. The formulations of a position heavily dependent on extrapolations from a metaphor like "two in one flesh" are at least likely to provide such an inadequate view.

These considerations remain incomplete. That is as it should be while we continue the task of moving beyond an impasse on the issues. Everyone shares a concern to reduce the misery in people's lives and to nurture the possibilities for well-being and love. How theology and law and social responsibility can converge to do these things is part of our question. We know ways in which we cannot go. We cannot solve the suffering of divorce by restoring patrilinear societies, by returning women to situations of economic dependence, by using law simply to coerce or condemn, by crushing expectations of worthwhile shared lives. In a culture where the earth quakes beneath us with the massive shifts in social institutions, discernment cannot be easy. What is certain is that the wisdom we need must come from a communal effort. That is why a serious impasse must be broken.

Notes

1. For ample evidence of this from a contemporary vantage point see the three-volume historical study of Theodore Mackin, *What Is Marriage?* (New York: Paulist, 1982), *Divorce and Remarriage* (New York: Paulist, 1984), *The Marital Sacrament* (New York: Paulist, 1989); John T. Noonan, *Power to Dissolve: Lawyers and Marriages in the Courts of the Roman Curia* (Cambridge: Harvard Univ., 1972); E. Schillebeeckx, *Marriage: Human Reality and Saving*

Mystery (New York: Sheed and Ward, 1965), originally *Het Huwelijk: aardse werkelijkheid en heilsmysterie* (Uitgeverij H. Nelissen, Bilthoven, 1963).

2. See Richard A. McCormick, *Notes on Moral Theology 1965 through 1980* (Washington, D.C.: Univ. Press of America, 1981) 82–86.

3. Ibid. 83.

4. Ibid. 86.

5. Ibid. 332–47.

6. See *Gaudium et Spes*, no. 47. in *The Documents of Vatican II*, ed. Walter M. Abbott (New York: America, 1966) 249.

7. *Civiltà cattolica* 4, 116 (1965) 603.

8. See *Unitatis Redintegratio*, nos. 8 and 15, in Abbott 352 and 359: and *Orientalium Ecclesiarum*, no. 26. in Abbott 383–84. These texts assume an understanding of the sacraments as means to grace, not only signs of grace (in this case, graced unity). Hence, the eucharist can under certain conditions be shared with persons not yet in complete unity with the Roman Catholic Church. By extension, this insight has been thought by many theologians to apply to divorced and remarried Roman Catholics.

9. E.g. Schillebeeckx, n. 1 above; W. J. O'Shea, "Marriage and Divorce: The Biblical Evidence," *Australasian Catholic Record* 167 (1970) 89–109. Of course, some of the most important work was yet to come in the late 1970s and 1980s, e.g. Joseph A. Fitzmyer, "Matthean Divorce Texts," *Theological Studies* 37 (1976) 197–226.

10. McCormick, *Notes on Moral Theology 1965 through 1980* 346.

11. Ibid. 338.

12. Bernard Häring, "Internal Forum Solutions to Insoluble Marriage Cases," *The Jurist* 30 (1970) 21–30. It should be noted that McCormick does not interpret Häring's position in this article as a fourth position (as I do).

13. McCormick, *Notes on Moral Theology 1965 through 1980* 341.

14. Ibid.

15. Ibid. 372–81 at 372.

16. Ibid. 544–61. See also Charles E. Curran, "Divorce: Catholic Theory and Practice in the United States," *American Ecclesiastical Review* 168 (1974) 3–34, 75–96.

17. See e.g. an early committee report from the Canon Law Society of America published in *The Jurist* 30 (1970) 12–13; a document from the professional organization of French theologians published as "Le problème pastoral des chrétiens divorcés et remarries," *Vie spirituelle: Supplement* 109 (1974) 125–54; a committee report from the Catholic Theological Society of America published in America 127 (1972) 258–60; an editorial in America 131 (1974) 362.

18.McCormick, *Notes on Moral Theology 1965 through 1980* 557.

19. Ibid. 556.

20. Ibid.

21. Ibid. 557.

22. Ibid. 558.

23. Charles E Curran, *Ongoing Revision: Studies in Moral Theology* (Notre Dame: Fides, 1975) 101–5.

24. Ibid. 84.

25. McCormick, *Notes on Moral Theology 1965 through 1980* 559. For a succinct description of current canonical meanings of "Privileges of the Faith" see Ladislas Örsy, *Marriage in Canon Law* (Wilmington: Michael Glazier, 1986) 215–33.

26. Curran, *Ongoing Revision* 105.

27. Ibid. 83–84.

28. McCormick, *Notes on Moral Theology 1965 through 1980* 826–41; *Notes on Moral Theology 1981 through 1984* (Washington, D.C.: Univ. Press of America, 1984) 99–104; "Indissolubility and the Right to the Eucharist: Separate Issues or One?" in *Ministering to the Divorced Catholic*, ed. James Young (New York: Paulist, 1979) 65–84; *The Critical Calling: Reflections on Moral Dilemmas Since Vatican II* (Washington, D.C.: Georgetown Univ., 1989) chap. 13. See also Lisa Sowle Cahill, "Notes on Moral Theology: Sexual Ethics, Marriage, and Divorce," *Theological Studies* 47 (1986) 102– 17.

29. Charles E. Curran, *Issues in Sexual and Medical Ethics* (Notre Dame: Univ. of Notre Dame, 1978) 3–29.

30. What I mean by this is that Curran's notion of an ideal seems to be only analogous to (not univocal with) ideals of virtue or to something like Reinhold Niebuhr's "impossible possibility." That is, it is not an ideal that is in principle impossible to achieve nor is it (as a final achievement of indissolubility) achievable in degrees; and it does hold a radical imperative. See Curran, *Ongoing Revision* 76.

31. What I mean by this is that McCormick's use of "absolute" here is tempered by his apparent willingness to have it go out of existence when one fails of it. He cites approvingly Schüller's term "presumptive precept" which seems to me more apt than "absolute" for what he wants to convey. See *Notes on Moral Theology 1965 through 1980* 556. It may also be that McCormick's "readjustment" of concepts and use of the term "serious precept" in the 1989 *Critical Calling* represents just such a move. An interpretation of this needs to take account also of McCormick's work on moral rules. See e.g. *Notes* 644.

32. McCormick, "Indissolubility and the Right to the Eucharist" 80; *Critical Calling* 26.

33. Örsy, n. 25 above; Mackin, n. 1 above. See also Jean Gaudemet, *Sociétés et Mariage* (Strasbourg: CERDIC, 1980); and the important work by Piet F. Fransen on the meaning of Trent, in *Hermeneutics of the Councils and Other Studies* (Leuven: Univ, 1985).

34. As a canon lawyer active currently in a marriage tribunal described it to me: "All of the outrageous cases have now pretty much been taken care of."

35. "The main decisions, especially in modern times, have been made at the Curia. Exercising their freedom to shape a central human institution, the makers of the system have been co-makers with the Lord of institutions." Noonan, *Power to Dissolve* xviii.

36. *Gaudium et Spes* nos. 48 and 50.

37. Quoted in Mackin, *Divorce and Remarriage* 511; see also *What Is Marriage?* 316.

38. *Gaudium et Spes* no. 48.

39. Paul VI, *Acta Apostolicae Sedis* 68 (1976) 204–08; quoted in Mackin, *Divorce and Remarriage* 513; see also *What Is Marriage?* 320–22.

40. International Theological Commission, Commentary on Proposition 4.3, as quoted in Theodore Mackin, "The International Theological Commission and Indissolubility," paper delivered at Univ. of Dayton, 1989,…in a volume ed. by William P. Roberts (Sheed and Ward, 1990).

41. Ibid.

42. John Paul II, "The Apostolic Exhortation on the Family," *Origins* 15 (1985) 172–75; "Homily on Family Life," *Origins* 18 (1988) 29–32.

43. Ibid. no. 12, p. 442. See also John Paul II, "The Family, Marriage and Sexuality," *Origins* 13 (1983) 316–18; "Building Family Life," *Origins* 15 (1985) 172–75; "Homily on Family Life," Origins 18 (1988) 29–32.

44. See Canons 1056–57 and 1134, 1983 Code of Canon Law.

45. International Theological Commission, "Christological Theses on the Sacrament of Marriage," *Origins* 8 (1978) 200–4.

46. John Paul II, "The Apostolic Exhortation on the Family," no. 84, p. 465.

47. E.g. Örsy interprets the marital "bond" as a legal relationship which gives rise to and is characterized by moral obligations, in *Marriage in Canon Law* 202–5, 270–72. McCormick argues against a juridical interpretation of the indissolubility requirement in favor of a moral interpretation, but he clearly does not rule out institutional considerations (at least as a safeguard for the social dimension of marriage). John Paul II offers an ontological perspective on marriage, but in the last analysis this is protected by law.

48. See e.g. *Gaudium et Spes* no. 48; 1983 Code of Canon Law, Canon 1055; McCormick, *Critical Calling*, chap. 13 (McCormick's theological "adjustments" are in the direction of viewing marriage as a commitment); John Paul II, "Apostolic Exhortation on the Family," no. 12; Curran, Ongoing Revision 106.

49. The general theory of commitment that follows is based on my analysis in *Personal Commitments: Beginning, Keeping, Changing* (San Francisco: Harper, 1986) esp. chaps 2 and 7.

50. What I say here would, I believe, apply to a great extent to so-called "natural" marriages as well as Christian marriages.

51. Even if the persons marrying wish to resist the cultural forms of marriage as an institution, their understanding of marriage will somehow be influenced by these.

52. See my treatment of this in "An Ethic for Same-Sex Relations," in *Challenge to Love*, ed. Robert Nugent (New York: Crossroad, 1983) 103–4. See also Paul Ricoeur, "Wonder, Eroticism, and Enigma," in *Sexuality and Identity*, ed. H. Ruitenbeck (New York: Delta, 1970) 13–24; and John Paul II, "Apostolic Exhortation on the Family," no. 11.

53. I do not mean to imply here that there can be no commitments that are absolutely binding (for example, commitments to love God and to love one's neighbor as one's self); but any that are absolutely binding are so because they are not vulnerable to the conditions I outline here. Also, it should be noted—though without opportunity to elaborate—that the unconditionality of the marriage commitment is sufficient to rule out simple release by the agreement of the partners—or, for that matter, by the advent of circumstances other than the ones I identify here.

54. McCormick, *Notes on Moral Theology 1965 through 1980* 558; "Indissolubility and the Right to the Eucharist" 82.

55. Curran, *Ongoing Revision* 105. My way of construing here the justifiable end of a valid marriage can be related to the debate in moral theology about the guilt or innocence of the spouses whose marriage ends. Surely there are instances where the death of a marriage comes through the fault of one or both of the partners (as McCormick insists and Curran allows). When this is the case (though I believe with Curran that it is not always so), it is accurate to say that the fault of the partners brings the marriage to the point of impossibility (the death of "capacity" in McCormick's terms); but once this has happened, then the marriage obligation as such no longer holds. The end of a marriage comes finally in a decision by the spouses (it does not, strictly speaking, as a marriage just "die"); and it is this decision that can be morally justified and necessary (however unjustified it may have been to reach the point where this decision must be made).

56. This does not mean we are not called to great and noble loves that are self-sacrificing in a radical sense. But to sacrifice oneself is morally unjustifiable if it means violating one's very nature as a person.

57. By "true divorce" here I mean as distinguished from an annulment or a separation.

58. There are, of course, other arguments in the theological tradition as well—as e.g. McCormick's argument that even though the first marriage does not continue to exist, considerations of social utility ground a *prima facie* duty not to remarry.

59. See Mary Rose D'Angelo, "Remarriage and the Divorce Sayings Attributed to Jesus,"...in a volume ed. by William Roberts (Sheed and Ward, 1990).

60. I am presupposing here the fact that the Roman Catholic tradition, unlike some Christian traditions, has never held that God asks the impossible of human persons.

61. John Paul II, *Original Unity of Man and Woman* (Boston: St. Paul, 1981) 75, 106, 110.

62. International Theological Commission, quoted in Mackin, "The International Theological Commission and Indissolubility."

63. John Paul II, ibid.

64. John Paul II, "The Apostolic Exhortation on the Family" no. 13. John Paul II here quotes Tertullian favorably.

65. John Paul II, *Love and Responsibility* (New York: Farrar, Straus & Giroux, 1981) 215.

66. John Paul II, Audience January 5, 1983, quoted from *Osservatore Romano* in *Moral Theology Today: Certitude and Doubts* (St. Louis: The Pope John Center, 1984) 277.

67. See John Paul II, *Love and Responsibility* 275.

List of Contributors

Florence Caffrey Bourg teaches theology at the Academy of the Sacred Heart in New Orleans.

Lisa Sowle Cahill is the J. Donald Monan Professor of Theology at Boston College.

Bernard Cooke taught theology and sacramentology for many years at different institutions, retiring from Holy Cross College.

David S. Crawford is associate professor of moral theology and family law at the John Paul II Institute for Studies on Marriage and Family, Washington, DC.

Charles E. Curran is the Elizabeth Scurlock University Professor of Human Values at Southern Methodist University.

The late Philippe Delhaye taught theology at the University of Louvain and was secretary of the International Theological Commission.

Margaret A. Farley is the Gilbert L. Stark Professor Emerita of Christian Ethics at Yale Divinity School and the Yale University Department of Religious Studies.

The late John C. Ford was a Jesuit priest. He taught moral theology and contributed to the "Notes on Moral Theology" in *Theological Studies*.

John Finnis is professor of law and legal philosophy at Oxford University, as well as the Biolchini Family Professor of Law at the University of Notre Dame.

John S. Grabowski is associate professor of moral theology/ethics at the Catholic University of America.

Germain Grisez is the Rev. Harry J. Flynn Professor of Christian Ethics at Mount St. Mary's University in Emmitsburg, Maryland.

Richard M. Hogan is a priest of the Archdiocese of St. Paul and Minneapolis and is associated with Natural Family Planning Outreach.

Willard F. Jabusch is a retired priest of the Archdiocese of Chicago, who has served as a seminary professor and chaplain at the University of Chicago; he's also a published musician.

Luke Timothy Johnson is the R. W. Woodruff Professor of New Testament and Christian Origins in the Candler School of Theology of Emory University.

Walter Kasper is a cardinal of the Roman Catholic Church, currently serving as president of the Pontifical Council for Promoting Christian Unity in the Roman curia.

The late Gerald Kelly, SJ, taught moral theology and contributed to the "Notes on Moral Theology" in *Theological Studies*.

Kevin T. Kelly is a retired professor of moral theology and pastoral minister in the Archdiocese of Liverpool, England.

Robert J. Kendra is a Catholic layman in Connecticut, who writes on contemporary church issues.

Michael G. Lawler is professor emeritus of theology and former director of the Center for Marriage and Family at Creighton University.

Karl Lehmann is a cardinal of the Roman Catholic Church, bishop of Mainz, and former chair of the Conference of German Bishops.

John M. LeVoir is the bishop of New Ulm, Minnesota.

The late Theodore Mackin taught theology and marriage at Santa Clara University for many years.

David Matzko McCarthy teaches moral theology at Mount St. Mary's University in Emmitsburg, Maryland.

William E. May is the Michael J. McGivney Professor of Moral Theology at the John Paul II Institute for Studies on Marriage and Family, Washington, DC.

Stephen J. Pope is a professor of theology at Boston College.

Elsie P. Radtke is a pastoral minister, working with married couples in the Archdiocese of Chicago.

William P. Roberts is a professor in the Department of Religious Studies at Dayton University.

Susan A. Ross is a professor of theology and director of the Ann Ida Gannon, BVM, Center for Women and Leadership at Loyola University in Chicago.

Julie Hanlon Rubio is associate professor of theology at St. Louis University.

Oskar Saier is the retired archbishop of Freiburg im Breisgau, Germany.

Angelo Scola is cardinal patriarch of the Archdiocese of Venice, Italy.